MINING AND SOCIAL CHANGE

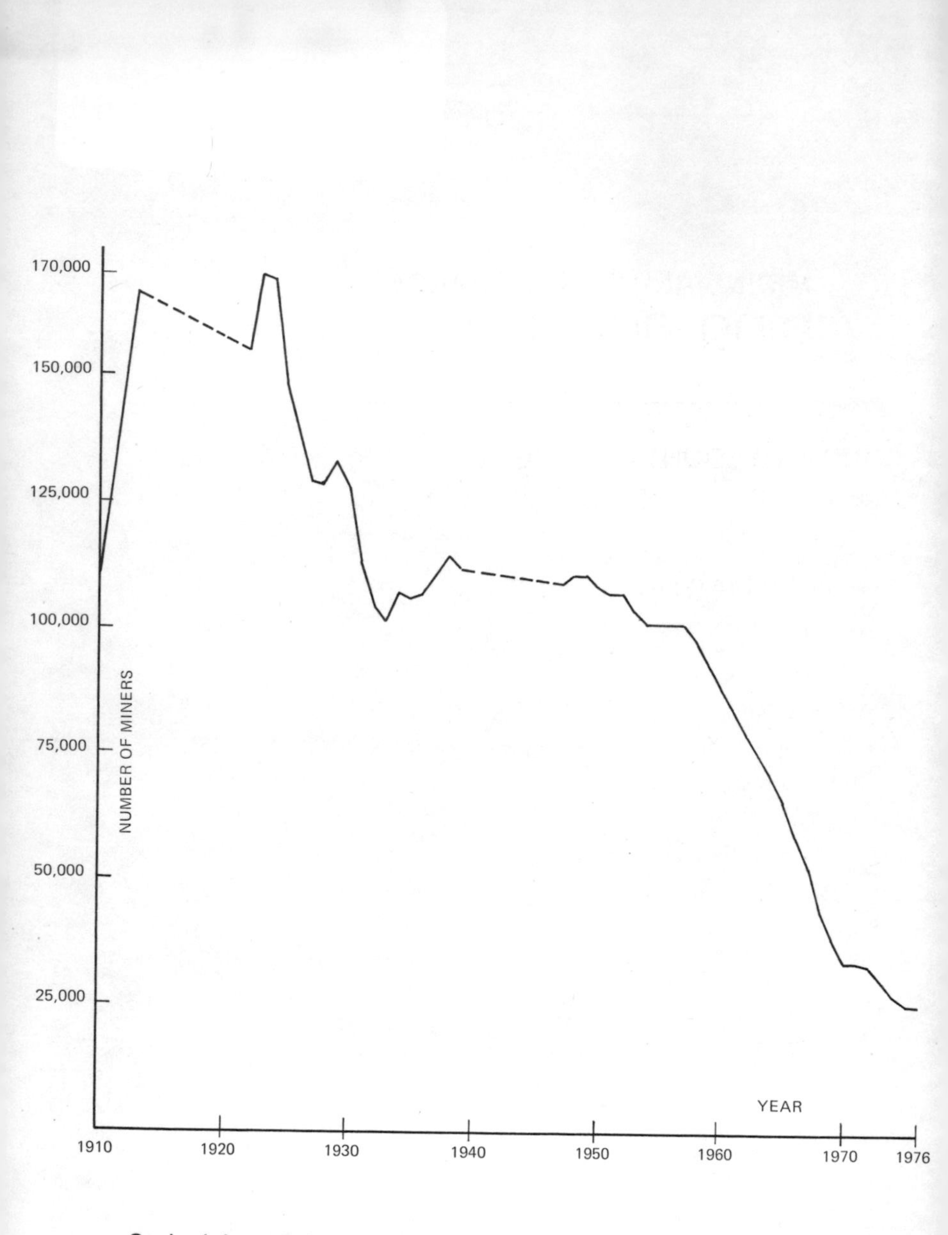

Coal-mining employment in County Durham 1910-1976

Source: Table 11.1

Mining and Social Change

DURHAM COUNTY IN THE TWENTIETH CENTURY

Edited by MARTIN BULMER

CROOM HELM LONDON

Croom Helm Ltd, 2-10 St John's Road, London SW11
ISBN 0-85664-509-5

British Library Cataloguing in Publication Data

Mining and social change.
1. Coal miners – England – Durham (County) – History 2. Durham (County) – Social life and customs
I. Bulmer, Martin
942.8'6 DA670.D9

ISBN 0-85664-509-5

Printed in Great Britain by Biddles Ltd, Guildford, Surrey

CONTENTS

CONTRIBUTORS

Mark Benney (1910-1973) is best known in Britain as a writer of books such as *The Big Wheel* (1940), *Over to Bombers* (1943) and *Goal Delivery* (1948). His life is told in two fascinating volumes of autobiography, *Low Company* (1936) and *Almost a Gentleman* (1966). As a social scientist he achieved distinction in both Britain and America. In addition to writing *Charity Main: a coalfield chronicle* (1946), he was on the staff of the London School of Economics (1949-51), where he wrote *How People Vote* (1954). At the University of Chicago in the 1950s he collaborated in a research project on the sociology of the interview with David Riesman.

Peter J. Bowden is Senior Economist with the Tariff Board, Federal Government of Canada. In 1953-4 he was Research Officer with the North-East Industrial and Development Association, publishing *Development Area Policy in the North-East of England* (with E. Allen and A.J. Odber) in 1957. From 1954 to 1957 he was Senior Planning Assistant with Durham County Council, responsible for industrial promotion. After teaching economic history at Sheffield University, he returned to Durham in 1963-4 as Rowntree Research Fellow. From 1964 to 1968, before moving to Canada, he was Senior Research Fellow in the Business Research Unit, Durham University, working on a report on *Economic Growth in North-East England* for the DEA (with A.A. Gibb, 1967), a study of industrial retraining, and a study of Newton Aycliffe supported by the Joseph Rowntree Memorial Trust.

Martin Bulmer, who was born at Newcastle-upon-Tyne, is Lecturer in Social Administration at the London School of Economics and Political Science. Previously he was at Durham University, from 1968-70 as Rowntree Research Fellow, and from 1970-74 as Lecturer in Sociology. He has also edited *Working Class Images of Society* (1975), and *Sociological Research Methods* (1977).

Sid Chaplin, who was born in Shildon in County Durham, is a well-known north-eastern writer and novelist who lives in Newcastle. His novels include *The Thin Seam* (1950), *The Big Room* (1960), *The Day of the Sardine* (1961), *The Watchers and the Watched* (1962), and *Sam in the Morning* (1965). He has also written, with A. Plater and A. Glasgow, the musical entertainment about the coal industry

Close the Coal House Door (1969), and two volumes of essays, *The Smell of Sunday Dinner* (1971) and *A Tree with Rosy Apples* (1972). He comes from a mining family in County Durham, and began life as a screen boy at the local pit, later becoming a blacksmith and underground maintenance mechanic.

G.H.J. Daysh, who lives in the Tyne valley, is Professor Emeritus of Geography at the University of Newcastle-upon-Tyne, where he taught for 36 years and became Deputy Vice-Chancellor. His publications include surveys of both the North-East and West Cumberland, initially when these areas were designated as Special Areas in the 1930s, and in conjunction with the Commissioners for the Special Areas. *West Durham* (1953) was a study made possible by a grant from the Nuffield Foundation at a time when Professor Daysh was Adviser to the Northern Industrial Group and the North-East Development Association. J.S. Symonds, co-author of *West Durham,* was the Research Officer for this investigation.

Jack Lawson (1881-1965) was born at Whitehaven in Cumberland, moved with his parents to County Durham in the 1880s, and went to work at Boldon Colliery in 1893 at the age of twelve. He was Labour Member of Parliament for the Chester-le-Street Division from 1919 to 1949, a junior minister in the Labour governments of 1924 and 1929-31, and Secretary of State for War from 1945 to 1946. Created Lord Lawson of Beamish in 1950, he was Lord Lieutenant of the County of Durham from 1949 to 1958. In addition to the biography of Peter Lee, he also wrote a volume of autobiography, *A Man's Life* (1932), which is a vivid personal document of Durham mining life in the early years of the twentieth century.

Ken Patton is a producer with the BBC, Open University, for whom he has produced television and radio programmes for courses including DE352 *People and Organisations,* DE351 *People and Work,* P881 *Industrial Relations,* and has shot film in County Durham on the subject of the relocation of villages. From 1966 to 1969 he was a member of the staff of the Rowntree Research Unit, University of Durham.

Ellis Thorpe is Lecturer in Sociology at the University of Aberdeen. Previously he was on the staff of Salford University (1967-8) and the University of Durham (1968-70), where he was Rowntree Research Fellow. While at Salford he completed original research for his thesis on 'Industrial Relations and Social Structure: a case-study of Bolton cotton mule-spinners 1884-1910'. His research for the Rowntree Trust in Durham is contained in two reports, *Coalport: an interpretation of community in a mining town* and *The Miner and the Locality,* referred to in Chapter 7. He has published articles in *Sociology, Social Work Today* and other social work, medical and educational journals, and is currently engaged on research into the sociology of Judaism. His main teaching interests are in the sociology of culture, language and community.

Graham Turner is a freelance journalist and writer who was formerly Economics Correspondent for the BBC. A Northerner by origin, he has written, in addition to *The North County* (1967), books on *The Car Makers* (1963), *The Persuasion Industry* (with John Pearson, 1965), *Business in Britain* (1969), *The Leyland Papers* (1971), *Towards a New Philosophy for Industry and Society* (1973), and *More Than Conquerors* (1976).

Bill Williamson, who was born at Throckley in Northumberland in a pit house, is Lecturer in Sociology at the University of Durham. He is the author, with D. Byrne and B. Fletcher, of *The Poverty of Education* (1975), and of other papers and articles on the inequality of educational provision with reference to north-east England. He has written and broadcast on different aspects of north-east culture, and is currently working on aspects of development and under-development in education, and on a study of the effects of the Second World War on the North-East.

To the memory of Edith Bulmer

1 INTRODUCTION

Martin Bulmer

Coal miners form one of the most important and distinctive occupational groups in British society. This book is about miners and the mining community in County Durham, where mining was long the dominant industry and where even today the National Coal Board remains one of the largest employers. The sixteen chapters cover both the contemporary scene and social history in the twentieth century. Durham County in the last quarter of the twentieth century is very different from what it was in 1900 or even 1918. This book attempts to explain how, and to some extent why, such social changes have occurred.

A series of themes is explored in the pages which follow, starting with the nature of the traditional mining community and the ways it may be changing. The distinctive local character of politics in County Durham is examined, as is the history of employment and unemployment in the mining industry. Town planning in the area is described, with chapters on the foundation of the new towns of Newton Aycliffe and Peterlee. The concluding chapters report research on the run-down of coal-mining and its replacement by factory industry.

A feature of the early chapters is the use made of personal documents to bring to life the local mining community and its past. Sid Chaplin, local novelist and writer, provides an evocative picture of social life in Durham mining villages in the early years of the century. Bill Williamson considers leek growing. Jack Lawson describes the political life of the area's most important twentieth-century political leader, Peter Lee.

These first-hand accounts are integrated with the results of social research carried out at the University of Durham over a number of years on social history, social structure and social policy in the county since the First World War. Four fields are singled out for detailed consideration, apart from the general characteristics of mining communities. Firstly, the unique character of local politics is emphasised. Then employment trends are outlined as background to a review of industrial development and town planning. Finally, detailed studies are presented of the problems of industrial change.

A guide to social science literature on County Durham is provided in

Appendix A, as a starting point for further reading and research. It may be helpful at the outset to emphasise that *Mining and Social Change* is only a selective study of certain aspects of coal-mining. There are many good books about mining in County Durham; this is not, for example, a study of mining trade-unionism, which is already available in Dr W.R. Garside's *The Durham Miners 1919-60.*[1] Nor is it a study of mining culture, such as provided by A.L. Lloyd's *Come All Ye Bold Miners,*[2] Robert Colls's *The Colliers Rant*[3] or William Moyes's evocative portrait of past Galas, *The Banner Book.*[4] A central theme of social science studies of coal-mining has been the nature of mining work, the social relations of work, and the wider social class structure within which mining is located. The classic study of this kind, *Coal is Our Life,*[5] was carried out in West Yorkshire. *Mining and Social Change* is not an attempt to replicate such a study in Durham, and is not a 'community study' in the traditional sense.

Nevertheless, the theme of *Mining and Social Change* is community, making an attempt to characterise the social features of a mining region rather than of a single locality. The 'community' characteristics of mining settlements have sometimes been neglected in studies of trade union history or class struggle; they are the central focus here, though seen within the broader class structure. Mining communities have more to them than physical surroundings and quality of housing, a fact which middle-class observers have frequently failed to perceive. Though it would be quite presumptuous to claim that what follows is an insider's view, it does attempt to take seriously people's own views of their community, the social meanings which folk attach to living in a particular place, and the web of social relationships which are built up. Mining communities were not, even at the height of the Great Depression, simply socially deprived areas. Men and women lived and died and children were born and lived in them. How did people experience the world in which they had to exist, often in a harsh employment market and severe material deprivation?

Answers to some of these questions are attempted, but their limitations should be borne in mind. The pages which follow are a broad-brush picture of some features of social life in the area, about which there can be disagreement. Existing sources have been used where possible, but this study lacks the detailed local research of, for example, Dr R.S. Moore's study of Methodism in west Durham mining villages, *Pitmen, Preachers and Politics.*[6] In parts, this study is necessarily impressionistic. Its justification lies in making social research about County Durham available to a wider audience, and in raising for discussion and further research certain key issues in the social history and sociology of this mining region. The comparative study of coal-mining is still in its infancy, despite the richness of (particularly) historical monographs upon specific localities, sub-regions or regions.[7] *Mining and Social Change* is intended to encourage comparison and generalisation.

A further reason for undertaking this work was the significance of long-term historical change. County Durham is the nineteenth-century was a melting-pot for immigrants from all parts of England, from Scotland and from Ireland. In the twentieth-century, in total contrast, its most striking characteristic is immobility – although there has been much emigration the very large majority of those who remain were born in the county. This twentieth-century continuity is evident in some of the political tendencies described in Chapters 8 and 9. The legacy of the past is evident in the existence of the new towns, the origins of two of which are traced in Chapters 13 and 14. Life in and policies for the North-East since the 1930s have been profoundly influenced by the social conditions briefly outlined in Chapters 10 and 11. Experience of common misfortune in the past has shaped the post-war picture, both in terms of public policy – as described in Chapter 12 – and in the personal experiences and existence of those who lived through the 1920s and 1930s. County Durham has changed and is changing; mining is in rapid decline; older settlements are decaying or being renewed; new towns have been established, roads and landscaping are changing the visual impact of the area. But in an age when the small, tightly-knit and socially homogeneous community is very much the exception, there may be some interest and some value in looking back to a society in which such a community was once dominant.

Notes

1. W.R. Garside, *The Durham Miners, 1919-60,* London, Allen & Unwin, 1971.
2. A.L. Lloyd (compiler), *Come All Ye Bold Miners: Ballads and Songs of the Coalfields,* London, 1952.
3. R. Colls, *The Collier's Rant: song and culture in the industrial village,* London, Croom Helm, 1977.
4. W.A. Moyes, *The Banner Book: a study of the banners of the Lodges of the Durham Miners' Association,* Newcastle, Frank Graham, 1974.
5. N. Dennis, F. Henriques and C. Slaughter, *Coal is Our Life,* London, Eyre & Spottiswoode, 1956.
6. R.S. Moore, *Pitmen, Preachers and Politics,* Cambridge University Press, 1974.
7. Cf. J.H.M. Laslett, 'Why some do and some don't: some determinants of radicalism among British and American coalminers 1872-1924', *Bulletin of the Society for the study of labour history,* 28, 1974, pp.6-9. For a more

theoretical discussion, see M.I.A. Bulmer, 'Sociological models of the mining community', *The Sociological Review,* 23, 1975, pp.61-92.

2 SOCIAL STRUCTURE AND SOCIAL CHANGE IN THE TWENTIETH-CENTURY

Martin Bulmer

The thread of 'community runs through this book. Settlements based on coal-mining are widely regarded as being strong in 'community feeling', 'community solidarity', 'community spirit', or in 'having a sense of community'. In the research reported in chapters 15 and 16, the writer asked miners and ex-miners interviewed in the south-west Durham area: 'Do you think the place you live in has a community spirit?' The interpretations put upon this question differed markedly. Some men answered in terms of everybody knowing everybody else, of the friendliness of local people, or of residents of long-standing moving out and strangers moving in:

> 'At one time everybody knew everybody else. Over the last four or five years, a lot of strangers have moved in and a lot of local people moved out. The new people don't seem to be so friendly, so easy to get on with.'
>
> 'Yes, everybody likes everybody else – very friendly towards each other'.
>
> 'It has now. More so than in the past'.
>
> 'If you walked into the Club, everyone would know you were a stranger. Within two or three minutes, somebody would speak to you. Don't just talk about the weather – personal matters, family life, etc. People from the south say how friendly people are up here'.
>
> 'Not now, since pits closed. But still a happy lot'.
>
> 'No, not like there was. Don't know half of them in this street'.
>
> 'At one time everybody knew everybody else. Over last four or five years a lot of strangers have moved in and a lot of local people moved out. Not what it used to be. Big change when they built a lot of houses for the GPO workers. Now people don't seem to be so friendly, not so easy to get on with'.

Others interpreted the question in terms of collective, organised, village activities:

> 'Yes, I think so. A few years ago, started to get a village hall built,

that seemed to knit people together'.

'Yes, proved that by Langley Moor Carnival and football team. Small place, hell of a lot of interest. If it's to do with Langley Moor, people are interested'.

'Yes, very good. Don't think its dying out. Community Centre, Carnival. Mostly found in villages, not so much in towns'.

'Lots of organisations for kiddies. Scouts, etc.'

'Should think so. Lot of organisations. Club life is booming'.

'No, don't think so. Dying out over the years. No organisation to bring the communities together. Only churches get communities together. Was talk of building a community centre years ago. People are better off now, have cars. Will go out of the place to seek enjoyment'.

'Couldn't tell you. Sometimes they have "do's" at the Community Centre. Church has dominoes, whist drive, etc. The Salvation Army is well-attended. We never have been a family that's gone in for that association business, apart from an uncle who was a Mason'.

A different interpretation was in terms of lack of social facilities for recreation (Community Spirit?)

'A dying one. There isn't any future here. Pits closing. A lot have left for the Midlands. There isn't any places for people to go to. Only pubs and clubs. For a cinema, you have to go to Newcastle or Sunderland or Durham'.

'Slowly on the decrease – still a lot. Taking mines away from local places where families were close-knit. Minds broadened – broader outlook. Everyone had a common cause in mining. Used to make own recreation in own community. Didn't have the money to go to places like Newcastle'.

'Not what there used to be. Take away bingo halls, just left with the club – nowhere to get together. May be pockets of it – perhaps amongst the women. It's tending to die out, changed over the years'.

'No, not now. Very bad in this place. Got to go to Sunderland or Darlington for anything at all. Not a cinema, not a dance. Right up till just after the war well taken care of – cinema, dances, all over'.

Yet another kind of response was in terms of neighbourliness and mutual aid:

'Would say there is in ——. Was only a small village years ago. Has

> grown and grown. More people interested in each other. Got to know everybody down the pits, got to know everyone just the same in the new factories. Can go right through every house in the estate and you know all the family and what they do. More concerned about other people'.
>
> 'Breaking up into different groups. Not enough friendliness and neighbourliness. When I lived in — Street, I knew everybody, went into their homes. Not here in —. People come and go, strangers come in, cosmopolitan. On the whole, compared to other places, there is community spirit'.
>
> 'Yes, very definitely, very sociable. Help you if you're in trouble'.
>
> 'Not as much as to be found in small villages. Seems to be fading. In pit villages your neighbour would come in and help you if you were in trouble. You lived closer together. In semi-detached houses it is lessened. Not as bad here as a place like Newton Aycliffe, which is cosmopolitan. On new estates, different outlook on life. Miner's comradeship is still there but it seems to have faded a bit. People seem to be able to fall out with each other more easily. In the pit you were working close together. Same in wartime'.

What is striking is not just the different evaluations of 'community spirit' in their own locality, but the different meanings attached to the word 'community'. What do we mean by 'community'?

An answer will be attempted by means of a discussion of what is sociologically most distinctive about County Durham. County Durham is distinguished, as an area of Britain with its own particular character, by the existence of a large number of mining or former mining settlements dispersed over the county, and by the predominance of the working class in the population. The pattern of mining is shown in Figure 2.1; the preponderance of the working class is markedly different both from the large conurbations such as Newcastle-upon-Tyne or Greater London, and from the county as a whole, as shown in Table 2.1. The proportion of the population in the right hand column, all manual workers, closely reflects the relative predominance of the working class in different areas. The comparison with Durham City is included because those who know or visit the city only may hold a wholly erroneous impression of the social composition of the county, if they use the city as as a stanard. Just as the University is in many respects isolated from its surrounding area (an 'educational Crewe'?[1], Durham Cathedral, Castle and Market Place are quite untypical of the surrounding area.

Table 2.1 Percentage of Economically Active Males in Certain Socio-economic Groups, 1961

	Profes-sional and managerial	Other non-manual	Skilled manual	Semi-and unskilled manual	All non-manual	All manual
County Durham	8.6	11.6	43.6	34.1	20.2	77.7
Durham City	19.6	21.6	30.6	26.3	41.2	56.9
Newcastle-upon-Tyne	11.4	18.3	41.2	26.1	29.7	67.3
Greater London	16.9	22.9	34.8	22.8	39.8	57.6
England and Wales	14.3	16.5	39.3	26.2	30.8	65.5

Source: Census of England and Wales, 1961. Armed Forces and unclassified are not included.

Within a short compass, and with only scattered empirical studies to draw on, it is not possible fully to do justice to the range of social structures in County Durham. Certain themes have been picked out which are highlighted in later chapters. These are the nature of the traditional mining community and the ways in which it may be changing; the distinctive local character of politics in County Durham; the history of unemployment in the area in the inter-war period; planning in the country including the setting up of new towns; and the course and effects of the run-down of mining and the growth of factory employment.

For many reasons, the richness and variety of documentary materials and field opportunities have been little exploited until recently by sociologists, and there is a comparative paucity of local material of a sociological kind. In part this reflects the slow development of sociology in Britain prior to the present decade. More particularly, it can be related to the absence of Sociology departments in the universities of Durham and Newcastle until the mid-1960s, and hence the lack of a local impetus to research. It undoubtedly reflects also a general scepticism among sociologists about the value of locality studies, and a tendency to pursue lines of inquiry in terms of problems and sub-disciplinary topics (like class, or industry, or politics) rather than to address attention and frame research plans in terms of the distinctive characteristics of one's local area.

Our main concern here is *locality* and its social structure, rather than on one specific aspect of social life. In this the focus differs from many conventional sociological studies and embodies on approach more characteristic of regional geography or anthropology. The study of particular places, areas and regions has at present a rather uncertain

Figure 2.1 Durham Coalfield Showing Collieries Operating in 1942

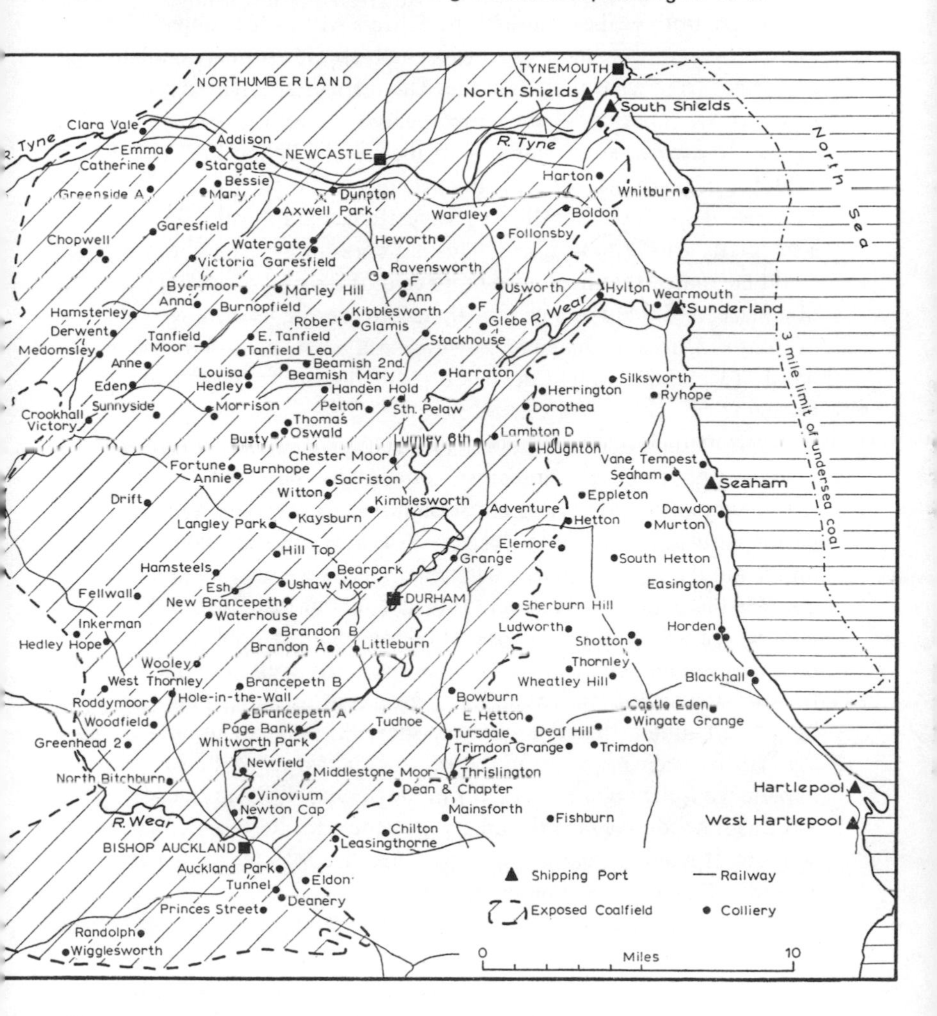

status in sociology. Although urban sociology and community studies are both well-established specialisms within the subject, there is increasing concern as to what such studies actually explain, as distinct from what they describe. The territorial origin of those whose behaviour is being investigated cannot be assumed *a priori* to provide an explanation of their social behaviour. As R.E. Pahl, for instance, has argued, 'any attempt to tie particular patterns of social relationships to a specific geographical milieu is a singularly fruitless exercise'.[2] This is a continuing debate, but it could be argued that in a sense there cannot ever be a sociology of a place, and that there cannot therefore ever be a sociology of County Durham. One may, however, ask what, from the point of view of a student of society, is distinctive about County Durham?

Some of the evidence included in this book is therefore not of a kind usually found in sociological monographs. The use of local autobiographies, novels, and impressionistic accounts by journalists and participants (particularly in chapters 3, 4, 5, 6 and 8) provides important data not otherwise available. The uses of such sources is discussed in detail in Appendix C at the end and fully justified there. However, a word of caution against taking such material entirely at its face value should be entered. Their authors may well have had grounds for special pleading (for example, Lawson writing about Peter Lee was himself a Labour MP and unlikely to show his party in an unfavourable light) or for seeing the past in the light of their own particular experience (growing up out of the mining community in the case of Sid Chaplin, coming into the area as outsiders in the case of Benney and Turner). It would be surprising if they had not selected their data accordingly, and it must be read sceptically.

Their inclusion is justified, however, because they enable something to be said about important aspects of local social life which would otherwise be left unsaid. Durham has a rich history and distinctive character which is worthy of being chronicled. Some aspects of it have been well-covered. Its geography, its economy, and the history of mining trade-unionism have been extensively and thoroughly examined by academic social scientists. This book is attempting to fill a gap by looking at local social structure, which has not been so thoroughly studied. Hence the use of sources beyond those conventional in academic social science.

This book tries to perform several tasks. Through a general survey, it attempts to locate certain key social structural features, and to provide a guide to the growing amount of social scientific research done in County Durham, both in the footnotes of chapters and the further reading in Appendix A at the end. It puts forward some bold and to an extent speculative hypotheses about change in mining communities, for critical examination and refutation. It attempts the near impossible task of characterising County Council politics over the last 50 years. It documents more carefully the history of planning and new town policy from a sociological point of view. It analyses two case studies of recent industrial change in south-west Durham. It provides a provisional introductory statement, more as a spur to further research than as a description of the existing state of knowledge. Unlike three standard geographical texts, A.E. Smailes's *North England,* J.W. House's *Industrial Britain: The North East,* and K. Warren's *North East England,*[3] it cannot aspire to be a rounded account, because the resources put into geographical research in the region in the last 30 years have not been matched by those put into social research.

The geographical focus of this volume is the old administrative county of Durham prior to reorganisation, that is the area between Tyne and Tees excluding the three conurbations of Tyneside, Wearside and Teesside. Its main geographical and industrial features are described in the books mentioned by Smailes, House and Warren. From a sociological point of view the study of social change in County Durham in the twentieth century is primarily the study of change in working-class institutions and culture in the small and medium-sized communities which are scattered over this area. Although no one settlement is particularly large, a high concentration of population is found within a radius of a few miles of any one centre. Durham County is not wholly urban, neither is it purely rural; rather it is a mixture of small urban centres, small industrial settlements originally associated with mining, and traditional rural villages. Although mining and former mining communities are most distinctive (and in the typical mining community of the past at least seven-tenths of the local adult male population would be miners) mining was not totally predominant. Table 2.2 shows that the proportion of occupied males in mining was never more than half the occupied male population of the county during the present century, because of the presence of Durham City as an administrative centre, a number of market towns and small settlements not wholly dependent on mining, as well as the rural agricultural population.

Mining communities are not by any means the only localities which have been studied in the area. An early classic of social science, Lady Bell's *At the Works,*[4] was a study of Middlesborough steel workers and their families. The first social survey in which random sampling was used (financed, most ironically, by an Indian philanthropist) by A.L. Bowley and A.R. Burnett-Hurst, included Stanley in north-west Durham as one of four towns where the incidents of poverty was determined.[5] Studies of inter-war unemployment are referred to in chapter 11, and of planning and new towns in chapters 12 to 14. Other studies of particular localities as well as statistical studies of the county or region as a whole, are described in detail in Appendix A.

Table 2.2 Proportion of Occupied Males in County Durham* Working in Coal-mining at Certain Dates.

Year	Total occupied male population	Total employed in coalmining	% of total occupied male population
1911	281,291	132,005	46.9
1921	284,827	140,950	49.5
1931	283,762	127,500	45.1
1951	269,721	86,632	32.1
1961	274,090	68,160	24.9
1966	265,720	43,800	16.5
1971	236,820	25,100	10.6

*County Durham is defined as the pre-1974 Administrative County (minus Stockton M.B. up to 1966) i.e. the County except for the large towns on its periphery.

Source: Censuses of England and Wales: Occupation Tables.

Nevertheless, two facts about mining in the county overshadow such other concerns. Firstly, the dominance of coal-mining in the past was greater than Table 2.2 may suggest, when one excluded Durham City and smaller market towns. In the typical mining settlement, more than two-thirds of the male working population were miners, and numerically miners formed the dominant occupation in the area. Secondly, Table 2.2 also shows the rapid decline in the predominance of mining in the middle years of the century.

The remarkable reduction in the proportion of the male labour-force working in mining is demonstrated more accurately in the frontispiece, which shows that over a sixty-year period, the number of miners in County Durham fell from about 165,000 to 25,000, or to one-sixth of its former size. In particular, with the reduction of the mining labour force in the county since 1957, discussed in chapter 11, the proportion of the population of any settlement who are miners is very greatly reduced (except in a few places in the east of the county), and less than one-seventh of the occupied male population of County Durham today are miners.

Small and medium-sized mining and former mining settlements, where formerly (if no longer) work and non-work ties were closely integrated, remain the most unusual feature of social structure in County Durham. In discussing Durham mining communities, the social structure of the traditional mining community will be briefly described, followed by a discussion of the directions in which such communities may be changing, and an indication of some of the sociological problems which require further investigation. Although coal-mining in County Durham is passing, there is considerable interest in documenting the social structures it brought into being, particular as they may persist long after mining itself ceases as an economic activity in a particular locality. Some research has been done,[6] a few personal documents and impressionistic data are available,[7] but the account which follows has to be qualified as a provisional and tentative one.

In the traditional mining village or small town, the physical appearance of the place – pit-head buildings, pit-heap, rows of terraced houses, tawdry commercial and public buildings – is immediately striking, and tends to fix an image in people's minds. And indeed for this reason the mining settlement has attracted widespread condemnation, morally by writers and practically by planners seeking to change or erase. Yet surely what is significant for the sociologist is not the surface appearance, the bricks and mortar, the sheerly physical – although these are the most obvious features – but the pattern of economic and social relationships which are developed, and which justify describing such settlements as mining 'communities'.

The economic system, for instance, has a far more pervasive influence upon the inhabitants than the environment of itself. Local novelist Sid Chaplin has made the point well in a description of such a community:

> The house is one of a street containing sixty exactly like it. There are twenty such streets which go to make up the mining seaport town in which they are situated. They have the appearance of barracks. Uniformity, lack of beauty, greyness – these are obvious points. The colliery yard, too, set bang in the middle of the street, providing a daily pall of dust and noise, takes the place of the barrack-room

> square. No bugle but instead the sound of the buzzer at regular intervals days and night, calling to parade with as peremptory a tone, not martial but rather the reverse, a grumbling stridency: shrieking 'Bread and Butter! Bread and Butter!' or as you like it, 'Beer and Baccy! Beer and Baccy!' During the night, for sleep conquers the command of the buzzer, there is the dull thud, thud of the knocker-up, walking the night streets, flashing his lamp upon the chalk slates at each door, these are the more obvious resemblances. The others, the more deadly, are difficult to describe. The atmosphere in homes dominated, indeed subordinated to, the hellish shift system. 3.00 a.m., 9.00 a.m., 3.30 p.m., 5.00 p.m., 9.00 p.m., 11.00 p.m. Not counting the intermediate shifts.
>
> An inhuman timetable, a devilish system of fatigues, making men into pit fodder, subordinating men, in the modern jargon, to the cycle of operations. Pre-occupation with the daily task.[8]

The working life of the miner is hard, dangerous and uncertain: 'Although old miners insist on the increasingly easier nature of the colliers' work today, it is invariably said by miners that pit work can never be other than an unpleasant, dirty, dangerous and difficult job' (*Coal is Our Life*). Miners work in conditions which are probably only worse in one other industry in Britain, deep-sea fishing,[9] and this is reflected in the high accident rate and the high incidence of disability. A recent study of disability among miners has shown that about one-tenth of Durham miners suffer from disability, 40 per cent of which was due to accidents and 31 per cent to industrial diseases such as pneumoconiosis and chronic bronchitis.[10]

Moreover, the miner's job, status, and earnings in the pit depend largely on his own skill and physical capacity. The pieceworkers at and near the coal face have the highest pay and status, but their work is the most physically exacting. Next in status come underground workers paid a day wage, and then the surface workers. Cutting across these functional divisions at the stages of the miner's life cycle. The boy out of school starts work on the surface, then graduates to day-wage work underground, and perhaps in his early twenties becomes a pieceworker. Among older men, those for whom piecework has become to arduous, and at all ages those suffering from disability, may go back on to day-wage work or surface work. Thus a miner may in the course of his life do many of the mining jobs in the pit, depending on his age and physical capacity, principally the latter. Parallel to the miners are the craftsmen grades – fitters, electricians, bricklayers – trained and qualified to work underground. At the supervisory level there are the various under-officials (shotfirer, deputy, overman, under-manager), most of whom will have worked their way up from being miners, and above them the specialist engineers and colliery manager.

Yet pit work, for all that it is hard and dangerous, is also a source of pride and satisfaction to those who work in the industry. As John Rex has observed:

> Those who merely pass through pit villages and occupationally homogeneous industrial towns see their squalor without seeing their grandeur. True the workers here suffer what industrial sociology, adapting Marx's term, nowadays calls alienation. They have little actual control of their work. But in one sense of the term 'alienation', they certainly do not suffer as the city worker does. They do not see their work as meaningless. They are not mere cogs in the machine whose ultimate purpose is beyond their ken. The pit is quite self-evident *there.*[11]

At work in the pit, groups of men working together tend to be closely knit and well integrated, and there is a good deal of evidence of a collective or group orientation to work among miners. (By group is meant the immediate work group engaged upon a particular operation.) For while the economic end in view is the weekly wage, work is experienced not simply as a means to that end but as a group activity. Thus economic returns from the job are likely to be foregone where going all out to earn as much as possible would offend group norms and threaten group solidarity. For instance, voluntary earnings might be limited in accordance with group output norms. Such an orientation does not only have an economic aspect. The continual presence of physical danger in mining leads both to a high level of involvement in the work, and a strong sense by the individual of his responsibility for, and dependence on, his workmates. Miners attach great importance to working as members of established groups of known and tried companions. A very vivid and moving picture of such a group in a Durham pit is given in Sid Chaplin's novel *The Thin Seam.* Studies of technical change in mining carried out some years ago in north-west Durham, have shown that new systems of production which enable integrated work groups to remain in existence give rise to greater job satisfaction and fewer conflicts than do systems which involve individuals working on their own, or frequent changes in the membership of work groups.[12]

Work, in the mining community, is dominant. The locality is centred on the pit, and the community is to a large degree occupationally homogeneous though there are a number of exceptions to this, where the pit is or was sited in or near a conurbation – for example, the Rising Sun Colliery in Wallsend, Monkwearmouth Colliery in Sunderland, and Westoe Colliery in South Shields. Moreover, the community's solidarity is strengthened by a shared history of living and working in one place, and often by the memory of bitter struggles with the coal-owners and of large-scale unemployment. Family continuity in the work has been usual. Like doctors, sons have tended to follow their fathers into the same occupation. An observer writing at the end of the last war noted: 'More than most men, too, the miners had a sense of the past. Their fathers and grandfathers had been miners, and had talked to them of their craft . . . and out of the long evenings of pit talk reaching back through generations had developed something like a tribal memory'.[13]

These tendencies are reinforced by the social and geographic isolation which turns the community in upon its own resources. Since the social relationships of work overlap with those of residence and leisure, pit work carries over into leisure time. The same observer wrote of the north-west Durham village that he knew during the war:

> The miners' work obsessed them. They loved and hated it, were proud and ashamed of it, fascinated and repelled by it . . . 'They's more cowels won in t'Club than they is in t'Pit', they would confess of their inability to leave work behind them at the end of the shift. And one man solemnly said that whenever he went to the local cinema he took good care to sit beside a woman – 'If Ah sits next a man, he'll start tahking pitwark an' spoil t'show!'

The mining community has had, in the main, to meet its needs from within. Benney's prose is somewhat hyperbolic, but he makes the fundamental point about the capacity of the community for collective action:

> Nothing had come easily to this village. When it had felt a need, it had tried to supply it for itself, and if anyone opposed the effort the village had fought. Every institution in the village, with the exception of the cinema, the post office and the church, the people had built themselves or struggled for through their union . . . Personal ambition was tamed to the Lodge office, the committee table, the pulpit and the craft of the pit. The customs of the community, both

> underground and on the surface, were old and honoured for their age; the double isolation of craft and geography had turned these people in upon themselves, so that they took their standards from their forbears instead of from the strangers in the city.[13]

Collective action of a political kind took two closely related forms, the long and bitter struggles against hostile employers through the local Lodges of the Durham Miners' Association; and the development of a working-class political movement in favour of social reform which found expression in the Labour Party. A notable history of the DMA since 1919 has been published by W.R. Garside;[14] it is the standard reference on the history of mining trade-unionism in County Durham in the twentieth-century. A different picture, more critical of the established union leadership, is provided by D. Douglass.[15] The overriding importance of collective strength through organisation cannot be over emphasised. The DMA provided not only a means of defending its members' economic interests against coal-owners, but also established through union subscriptions a system of financial benefits for members in time of adversity, a system which was sorely strained in the period between 1918 and 1939 by the economic difficulties of the industry and industrial conflict.

The story of the Labour Party in County Durham is more difficult to treat adequately. There are a number of political biographies and autobiographies of prominent local figures; an extract from Jack Lawson's biography of Peter Lee is included here as giving some impression of the political career of the most important Labour politician in the county between 1918 and the early 1930s. More recently an autobiography by Alderman Ned Cowen provides useful insights into the political career of a Durham miner which extended into the 1960s.[16]

There does not exist any sociological study of the structure and dynamics of grass-roots politics in County Durham. A description of past political life has recently been given by a local Member of Parliament:

> People lived in small tightly-knit communities and had little contact with people and places outside the immediate neighbourhood. A train journey was a major undertaking and transport was usually by horse and trap, bicycle, or Shank's pony. There were 'natural leaders' in every village who were the public representatives in the Miners' Lodge, the Co-operative Store committee and the local council.

> Everyone knew them intimately and they knew the people they represented and shared all the ups and downs of local village life . . . I have listened to conversations and arguments about cavils, being 'on the minnie', union dues, and so on. The pit loomed large over every activity. Lodge officials were known personally to every member.[17]

More detailed evidence is unfortunately lacking. What were local relations like between the DMA and the Labour Party, and did the former usually control the latter? What was the level of active participation in union and party activities? Was it higher because of the close-knit social ties within the community, or did a small minority run both organisations? What were the social backgrounds of local leaders? Did they tend to be miners, and among miners pieceworkers? Were the Labour Party and the DMA the principal means of upward social mobility? Did those who moved upward to union and party posts at County and national level retain their local connections? Why did several of those who achieved high office in the local union or party – most notably Peter Lee and Samuel Watson – prefer to remain in County Durham and refuse offers of a parliamentary seat and probable ministerial office when the Labour Party was in power nationally?

Both trade union and political movements came together and found powerful expression in the Annual Gala of the Durham Miners' Association, held every third Saturday in July annually almost without a break since 1871. The Gala is partly a demonstration of solidarity, symbolised by leading trade union and Labour Party speakers, partly a popular festival, with bands, banners and people from each pit, and a variety of entertainments provided on the race course. As Trotsky remarked in another context, 'only the participant is a profound observer'. Those who attend modern galas can have little idea of its former glory. Two, admittedly partial, testimonies follow; Sid Chaplin at the end of chapter 4 provides a third.

To Hugh Dalton, for many years Labour MP for Bishop Auckland

> The Durham miners' gala is the most moving event of its kind that I have ever seen, when more than a quarter of a million people converge, marching with their colliery bands and banners, upon the old city of Durham, in perfect order and with the minimum of traffic control. Out of this tremendous demonstration of democratic socialist comradeship and industrial power, I get my biggest political kick of the year. I never miss it.[18]

Jack Lawson was equally emphatic:

> The Annual Big Meeting of the Durham miners . . . is the great mining family on the march; the spontaneous expression of their communal life . . . As they arrive (in Durham City) the marchers fall into ranks, banners are raised, bands strike up, and for some hours such a sight can be seen as is seldom beheld in this or any other land. You may see 50 banners in one sweep with their many-coloured mottoes and pictures – portraits of old leaders who have passed on, portraits of present leaders, men known in local circles, the county, in national or international life . . . Under the banners walk the Lodge officials . . . Deep walls of people line the route along the twisting winding streets of the old city. There is no break in the procession for hours. Some men carry children on their shoulders, and some women have children in their arms, but it is the boast of many that their bairns have been to the Big Meeting since the year of their birth. It is a kind of social baptism . . .
>
> On the great green (race) course, edged by the curving river . . . two platforms are set up where great crowds collect. It is to gather round these platforms the vast mass is supposed to have come. The meetings play a great part, but to tens of thousands they are merely incidental, for it must be confessed the Big Meeting means much more than that. It is now more an institution than a meeting; more social than economic.[19]

Though the great days of the Gala have passed a visual reminder of its glories remain the banners of the DMA Lodges. J. Gorman has traced the history of banners nationally,[20] and W.A. Moyes for County Durham in two publications which provide a powerful visual impression of this great mining demonstration.[21]

Matters of particular concern to the trade union and political movements in the early part of the twentieth-century were public health and housing. These are discussed more fully in chapters 6 and 7, but it is important to emphasise the extent to which political power was used in mining areas simply as a means of improving social conditions of the working class, when employers or central government were reluctant or tardy in doing so. The incidence of poor sanitation, bad housing and ill-health in mining areas is further discussed at the end of this chapter and in chapter 11. Social conditions before 1914 and between the wars were of a shocking kind. The Medical Officer of Health for Durham reported in 1921 that in one colliery area he visited, liquid excreta ran from the doors of ash-closets into the back street. Outside one house was a miniature cess-pool, round which young people played. In 1922 Peter Lee reported to the Miners' Federation of Great Britain that Durham was one of the worst districts of Britain so far as housing was concerned.[22]

Political mobilisation in mining areas had as one of its aims the ending of such social evils and municipal action in the sewerage and housing areas. This, moreover, linked directly to the trade union struggle, since such a large proportion of local housing was built and owned by colliery companies and let free of charge to mineworkers. In 1925, for example, when there were 147,000 miners employed in the Durham coalfield, nearly 49,000 houses were provided free to miners by or on behalf of colliery owners.[23]

While the attractions of free housing of inadequate standard may have contributed to the widespread overcrowding, it also had political consequences. If colliery owners controlled both jobs and housing, was their power in such company towns not much greater than if they just controlled jobs? The building of council housing by Labour-controlled councils (as described in chapter 7) was to be both a way of improving housing standards, and of wresting control from coal owners.[24]

No account of the Durham mining community would be complete with reference to the importance and influence of Methodism, established in Durham in the early days of mining in the nineteenth century. As Jack Lawson wrote, 'The chapel gave [these communities] their first music, their first literature and philosophy to meet the harsh and cruel impact of the crude materialistic age. Here men first found the language and art to express their antagonism to grim conditions and injustice.' Certainly, Methodism must be reckoned as significant an influence as union affairs or politics in these communities, and the relations between religion and politics have until recently been neglected. Moral influences, too, have not been adequately considered; the teetotal miner, for instance, has usually been forgotten. To what extent did religion provide a source of moral dissent in mining communities? To what extent did it hold these communities together in times of adversity? To what extend did religious belief lead to social aspirations for upward mobility and to what extent were community leaders staunch Methodists? Considerable light on these problems is thrown by an important monograph by Dr Robert Moore, *Pitmen, Preachers and Politics,* an historical study of Methodism in four West Durham villages.[25]

If union, politics and chapel provided avenues for collective solidarity and organisation, so too did the Co-operative movement, as an economic organisation to try to maintain the autonomy of the working-class community from outside control. Again this is largely a blank in our knowledge of the history of the movement in County Durham, but an important unknown.

Co-operation, too, is an essential element in another central institution in the mining community, for leisure. As Dennis and his colleagues pointed out in *Coal is our Life,* the pattern of leisure in mining is dominated by insecurity, which stems in part from the dangers of death, disablement or injury in the work of a miner. As the local ballad has it:

> Oh, let's not think of tomorrow, lest we disappointed be,
> Our joys may turn to sorrow as we all may daily see,
> Today we may be strong and healthy, but soon there comes a change,
> As we may see from the explosion that has been at Trimdon Grange.[26]

In part, insecurity also derived from the nature of mining and fluctuations in a man's skill and pay according to physical capacity. The resulting pattern of leisure activity, Dennis and his colleagues found, was predominantly vigorous and concentrated on enjoying oneself in the present. Thus earnings tended to be spent on leisure pursuits rather than on the purchase of consumer goods.

The central leisure institution of the Durham mining community is the Working Men's Club. Although the Club's principal activity is to operate a co-operative society for the sale and consumption of beer, its significance is very much wider. In some respects it resembles a pub – as a place to go for a drink, meet people, engage in conversation, have a game of darts or dominoes – but in other respects it is somewhat different. In particular, Clubs are owned and controlled by their own members, and the facilities are exclusive to those who are members and their guests. Profits from the sale of alcohol are ploughed back in various forms – investment in new equipment or premises, free concerts for members, free drinks on certain days during festive seasons, free trips for older members and children of members. Clubs are usually affiliated to the parent body, the Working Men's Club and Institute Union, founded in 1862. For the first 20 years of its existence it was teetotal and controlled by aristocrats, until the latter were unseated by democratic vote. As the first working-class President said: 'Each Club shall be altogether free from all vexatious infantile restrictions on the consumption of intoxicating drinks and all similar matters'. So they have remained. The mere recital of what goes on in a Club does not convey its full social significance. It is a place for a drink, a chat, a game, a concert or dance at the weekends, a place for local groups to hold meetings, a place to read the newspaper. Above all, the Club (or Clubs – most communities except the smallest have more than one) lies at the centre of the community's inter-locking social networks; the Club is the meeting place for workmates, neighbours, kin, and friends, and is the centre of communal sociability.

The variety of local voluntary organisations is very considerable. They range from sporting associations – west Durham could boast of some of the finest amateur football clubs in the country – through leek-growing and pigeon-fancying to the British Legion and the St John Ambulance Brigade. There are others which are mainly the women's preserve. Indeed, the division between the sexes is striking. The Club is primarily a male preserve – in some, women cannot be members, only guests – and in most the attendance of wives would be limited to the weekend concert.

In considering family structure and the roles played by husband and wife, a pattern related to that of leisure appears. According to *Coal is Our Life,* the husband's centres of activity are predominantly outside the home, in work, the Club, and the overlapping social contacts of work and leisure. He comes home from work for a meal, and then goes out. The wife's activities, on the other hand, are centred on the home, on her husband and her children. Her task is to run the home; for instance, she must be at home to provide a warm meal for her husband when he comes out of the pit, regardless of the time.

It is unusual in such a community for the family to arrange a social event in the home, and jointly entertain friends. The adult men form a closed group which excludes the wives: 'There exists a series of groups and activities in Ashton confined to the mature males, and these groups are separate from and fundamentally *opposed* to the families of these men' *(Coal is Our Life).* In part this derives from the nature of work and in part from the traditional role of housewife and mother confined to the home.

For the miner's wife, the extended family takes on a greater significance. Born and brought up in this or a nearby community, she will often see a good deal of her kinsfolk, visiting between them being very well developed, and one of the main forms of social contact for the women. Beyond that, the custom of calling on neighbours is often the limit of the wife's social contacts.

What are the general sociological features of mining communities?

Time, a sense of a shared past, is of fundamental importance. The overlapping social ties of work, leisure, family and neighbourhood are reinforced through the sharing of a common past, and of family traditions of working in mining and often living in that community for two or more generations. Sons are destined to be miners, and daughters the wives of miners. This is reinforced by occupational homogeneity, and social and geographical isolation from the rest of society. The young lad grows up into a system of social relations centred on the pit and the community around it, and these mutually reinforcing ties, together with the prospect of relatively high earnings, point to his naturally going into the pit. It is in terms such as these that one must try to explain why mining families remain in mining communities.

The traditional mining community described above has a firm foundation in fact, but the use of the 'historic present' tense, in the above account, is deliberate. The ambiguity is intended to focus attention upon the central question: Do such traditional communities exist in County Durham today, or has their community structure changed in significant respects? If it has changed, to what extent and in what directions is change taking place? Such a very compressed and over-simplified characterisation as that above should not be taken to imply that mining communities are static, or were in the past. The static impression is conveyed because, in order to characterise the social structure, a skeletal community structure is drawn. Between communities and within communities there was and is considerable variation. Nevertheless, there do appear to be significant regularities which this chapter attempts to summarise.

In considering to what extent in Durham mining communities social changes are currently taking place, a note of caution should be sounded. For just as there is today such facile talk about the new, 'classless', Britain, without any reference to the large amount of sociological evidence on the subject (much of which does not support such a view), so there may be a tendency to exaggerate change in mining communities without carefully looking at the evidence. In reviewing what material is available, one is struck as much by the persistence of traditional social patterns as by the extent of social change. In reviewing here the problem of the degree of change, as much emphasis will be placed upon the particular questions needing investigation as upon findings which are established.

Change in the physical environment of mining and former mining communities is discussed in chapter 12. It is worth noting that the sociologist does not infer *a priori* from physical decay of buildings that the patterns of social relationships in that community have necessarily changed markedly. A physical dilapidated pit village may have more vigorous and active communal social life than a modern housing development. Moreover, the modern trend toward concentrated settlement, often encouraged by planners, tends to ignore some of the advantages of dispersal. Do the inhabitants of Durham mining communities not derive some advantage from having the countryside on their very doorstep?

The most striking fact of course, which was shown in the frontispiece, is the decline of coal-mining as a source of employment; this is discussed in chapter 11. Relatively little sociological work has been done on this problem, and there are a number of specific questions to be tackled. In the first place, how significant are current technological changes in mining itself for those who remain in the industry? The introduction of machines to carry out extractive operations previously done by physical labour may produce different patterns of social relationships within the enterprise than did the older longwall method of coal-getting. Will the change to minding machines in the pit break down the solidarity and cohesion of work groups previously characteristic of mining? What influence will the shift from sheer physical strength toward greater technical (especially mechanical) expertise have on the internal organisation of the work-force, and on the status of the different grades of miners in relation to each other? Secondly, what has been and is the experience of the large number of ex-miners in the country who have moved into manufacturing industry? How striking is the change from working in a two-foot seam to working in a modern factory? What changes, if any, follow from the absence of constant physical danger and liability to serious injury? What kinds of work group develop? How adaptable is the miner, whose skills are peculiar to one industry, in a quite different situation? Some answers are suggested in chapter 16.

Thirdly, what is the situation of the ex-miner who is unable to find alternative work and becomes permanently or semi-permanently unemployed? How far do the various social benefits meet the needs of these men and their families? What are the effects upon social and family life of a permanent fall in income ten or fifteen years before retirement? Even if income is maintained, what are the effects of not working on a man used all his life to hard and constant physical labour? In what ways do patterns of leisure activity and family relationships change under long term unemployment? Some answers to these questions are suggested by a recent study by House and Knight in northern Durham.[27] Among redundant miners they found that 87 per cent had suffered a decline in income, and significant economies were necessary for these families. Social life and leisure were impaired, and among those seeking work resentment was high and self-respect hard to keep. Yet many families also accepted with resignation and even cheerfulness the lower standards of living after redundancy and unemployment.

The course and effects of mining redundancy have caried according to the local situation of the mining industry. Both the studies by House and Knight and the DEP team at Ryhope[28] took place at a time when there were still local vacancies in mining in the closure areas. A subsequent study of a redundancy in west Durham showed that absence of local vacancies was a significant factor in encouraging men to leave the industry.[29]

The sociological implications for community structure of long journeys to work needs further attention.[30] While the Durham miner could not always walk to work, most lived within a few miles and a short travelling distance of their pit until ten years ago. For those who remain in the industry, long journeys to work from west to east across the county are common, and for ex-miners and non-miners in manufacturing industry, some travelling to work is usual, since factory development is more clustered than was coal-mining. Among transferred miners studied by House and Knight, four-fifths had a longer journey to work than previously, half had a decrease in leisure time (in some cases affecting the quality of leisure pursuits), and half had lost contact with former workmates, without this being replaced by contacts in the new workplace. The result of this is that where place of work and place of residence no longer coincide, the extent of an individual's social contacts and involvement in the place where he lives may be reduced.

The more general question about the results of industrial change is indeed what effects has it on the overlapping networks of work and non-work relationships? The integration and cohesion of the traditional mining community is based upon this; if the economic structure changes, does the community structure change or does it persist in spite of the economic change? There is certainly no warrant for assuming *a priori* that economic change leads to the disintegration of long-established and inter-locked social ties. R.C. Taylor's study of migration of miners from west Durham to other parts of the country, under a scheme run by the NCB, suggests that about half of 240 families studied moved because of possible redundancy in mining in West Durham.[31] Had it not been for economic insecurity, these families would not have considered leaving the area. The effect of economic change is by no means direct, and nearly half the migrants moved for non-economic reasons. A fifth he characterises as 'dislocated', being for a variety of reasons less fully integrated into their primary and secondary groups in the villages. A further fifth he characterises as 'dissenting' families who viewed the social life of a west Durham village as both irrelevant and inadequate, and having a strong sense of the nuclear family. The effect of such migration, moreover, may be to reinforce the traditional pattern as much as to lead to change. Taylor points out that, although migration opens up new perspectives on the world to these Durham communities through the migrants who leave, and leads to newcomers moving into vacated houses, migration also tends to remove the dissenting members from the community, and this increases the social cohesiveness of those who remain.[32]

Reference to migration leads on to a question bearing on industrial development. It is sometimes regarded as odd or unreasonable that men in former mining communities should be so unwilling to move to places where there is work available for them. Bowden found in his study of Newton Aycliffe (see chapter 13) that 45 per cent of the men in his sample employed on the Industrial Estate and three-fifths of the new recruits to industry there lived outside the New Town. Moreover, half of those in the sample resident outside the town stated that they were not willing to move to Newton Aycliffe under any circumstances. This phenomenon requires much further study, but some points are clear.

Consciousness of having lived in a place for a long time, in relative isolation, reinforces the sense of participating in a close-knit network of social relations. To leave this community is to cut oneself off from one's roots. Moreover, housing is cheap. Much of the housing in mining areas was built and owned by the coal-owners, as noted earlier. At nationalisation in 1947, for example, the National Coal Board took over 32,000 dwellings in the county, approximately one-eighth of the total housing stock. In 1969 it still owned 19,000 of these, heavily concentrated in small and medium-sized communities. For the miner or ex-miner the rent of such a house is low in comparison to council housing, and with a little capital they can be bought cheaply or very cheaply. This is a further incentive not to move.

The study of political change in the county is difficult since so little is known about the workings of the political structure. In Durham's rich and unusual political tradition, the effects of working-class hegemony and one-party control over several decades are largely unknown. An attempt to tackle these questions is made in chapters 6 and 9, but it can only be regarded as a start. Relatively little is known, either, about the inter-relations between local politics at the urban and rural district level (where housing is the principle issue), politics at the county level (where the issues centre around education, planning, and the social services), and national politics. The traditional community appears to have enjoyed a fair degree of autonomy in its political organisation; to what extent is this still so, and to what extent is control exercised predominantly at the county and national level?

Housing, further discussed in chapter 7, is obviously one very important political resource, as demonstrated by the proportion of the housing in the county which is municipally owned. Whereas nationally, in 1971, approximately 49 per cent of all houses were owner-occupied (with or without a mortgage) and 30 per cent were rented from a local authority or new town, in County Durham these proportions were nearly reversed; 47 per cent of housing was rented from a local authority or new town only 36 per cent was owned-occupied.[33] Durham was unusual, too, in still having a large proportion of housing rented by virtue of employment. Table 2.3 shows the position in 1961 for sub-divisions of the county, compared to the national picture.

What stands out is the predominance of council and colliery housing, and the lower proportion of owner occupation. In one or two areas the proportion of council housing is double the national figure; for employment-linked housing three or four times the national average.

Since 1961, the development of New Towns and of 'growth points' in older settlements such as Spennymoor and Stanley (see chapter 12) has involved further new housing on a very large scale indeed. There are thus very good opportunities for a comparative study of the structure of community relations in different types of housing, old and new, within a short distance of each other. Such studies must inevitably consider the preference of people for these different kinds of housing, and their availability in relation to income, stage in the life cycle, and other qualifications. Clearly housing conditions have improved out of all recognition compared to the inter-war period; this is one of the major achievements of local government.

The central focus of research upon the mining community remains, however, upon those activities which are shared by all or most of its members – such as those carried on in leisure time. There is no evidence to suggest that the Working Men's Club is diminishing in importance, although in some Clubs professional entertainers and variety artists are increasingly featured on popular nights. Nationally, clubs continue to play an important part in leisure activities. Evidence gathered for the Maud Commission showed the types of organisation belonged to a national sample. Apart from membership of trades unions and professional associations, clubs were rivalled only by sport as a centre of activity. Among social clubs, the Working Men's Club was the most important, nearly one in ten respondents in a national sample of 2,000 belonging to one.[34]

Table 2.3 Housing Tenure by Households, County Durham, 1961

	Owner-Occupied	Rented from local authority or new town	Occupied by virtue of employment**	Rented unfurnished	Other	Total
N.W. Durham	29%	34%	20%	15%	2%	100%
S.W. Durham (part*)	31%	37%	11%	19%	2%	100%
E. Durham within which	26%	47%	15%	11%	1%	100%
Authority A	27%	45%	19%	8%	1%	100%
Authority B	24%	53%	11%	10%	2%	100%
Authority C	17%	59%	13%	11%	–	100%
North-East	33%	33%	8%	23%	3%	100%
Great Britain	41%	25%	5%	24%	5%	100%

*including only Bishop Auckland U.D., Crook U.D., Sedgefield, R.D., Shildon U.D., Spennymoor U.D., and Tow Law U.D. The sub-divisions are defined in G. Wilson, op. cit.

**of which the very large proportions was housing for employees in the coal-mining industry.

Source: 1961 *Census of England and Wales,* analysed in G. Wilson, *Social and Economic Statistics of North East England* (University of Durham Rowntree Research Unit 1966); North-East and Great Britain from E. Hammond; *An Analysis of Regional Economic and Social Statistics,* (University of Durham, Rowntree Research Unit, 1968).

Sillitoe, in a major study of leisure patterns, provides complementary evidence shown in Table 2.4. Again the importance of social clubs is demonstrated, though it is not possible to determine exactly the proportion who are members of Working Men's Clubs.

Of four sociological studies which deal in any detail with social clubs, two are of mining areas. D. Rich, in her pioneering study 'Spare Time in the Black Country',[35] examined the role played by the club in the lives of her sample (interviewed in 1948-49). In their study of Ashton, Dennis,

Henriques and Slaughter consider the role of the Working Men's Club in the miners' lives.[36] More recently, Jackson has discussed the role of the Club in Huddersfield.[37] Taylor, in his thesis on five Durham villages,[38] discusses the important continuing role played by the Working Men's Clubs in village life, and provides a fascinating ethnographic desription of a Saturday night at one of them.

Table 2.4 Club Membership in a National Sample

	Men	Women
None	45%	67%
Sports or social club in a place of employment	14%	3%
Club mainly for physical or outdoor recreation	15%	4%
Club mainly for *other* games or hobbies (e.g. darts, dancing)	12%	5%
Club mainly for young people	5%	3%
Club mainly for 'social' activities	17%	12%
Club connected with church or other religious organisation	7%	11%
Political organisation	5%	3%
Other	7%	5%
N	= 2,824	3,451

Source: K.K. Sillitoe, *Planning for Leisure,* HMSO, Government Social Survey, 1969.

Further local evidence of the importance of social clubs was obtained if the course of research in Spennymoor further described in chapters 15 and 16. Four Working Men's Clubs were visited; their total paid-up membership amounted to nearly 4,000 men and 1,800 women, in an urban district (centred on the town) with a total population in 1966 over the age of 19 of about 12,000. In interviews with factory workers, three-fifths of the sample said they went out regularly at least once a week and among this group seven-tenths said they went usually to local clubs. The next most common place visited was a pub (one-fifth). Too much weight should not be put on this small sample, and the matter requires further investigation, but it is consistent with other local evidence. For instance, Elkins has documented the history of the Federation Brewery in Newcastle, with which many of the clubs are linked, and its financial success is proof of the continuing health of the Club movement.[39]

However, much remains to be investigated. What is the degree of participation in community activities of various kinds? What are the effects on these activities of the mass media, and particularly of television? Are the traditional voluntary organisations still as popular as they were? Are new organisations taking their place? Who assumes leadership in such organisations? Is recreation still segregated primarily along sexual lines, or are these divisions breaking down?

Family structure is of continuing research interest. To what extent are the extended family, and the sharp division of roles between husband and wife, being replaced by greater emphasis on the nuclear family and on conjugal roles? There is little evidence on this, although Taylor comments on the 'true masculine character' of the west Durham mining village, and that there is less evidence in his villages of a move towards a companion-type relationship than elsewhere in the county. This is a matter for further investigation; it is obviously bound up with changes in leisure patterns, the proximity or dispersal of the extended family, and geographical mobility.

No general conclusions are possible. There are, however, pointers towards significant general features.[40] One is the decline of occupational homogeneity and the fact that work and residence no longer coincide in all cases. The breakdown of geographical and social isolation is also important, the former through easier travel, the latter through education. Indeed, social and geographical mobility is linked; the longer a child remains in education, the more likely it is that he or she will leave his home community. In a study by House, Thomas and Willis, with a sample drawn from four north-east towns, nearly half of those who had been to technical college were living and working away from home, whereas only 12 per cent of those who had been to secondary modern school were doing so.[41] The social effects of economic change remain problematic, to be investigated in relation to the rationale of community. What is the nature of people's attachments, in the contemporary world, to particular places and areas? What does it mean to people to live in a particular place, rather than in another place? Interesting evidence about this is provided in two recent papers by C. Taylor and A. Townsend.[42] Based on a 1973 survey into local sense of place in four areas within the North-east (Tynemouth, Sunderland, Spennymoor and Stockton), they find that there is significant continuity in the Spennymoor sample (the only one from a mining area) between past and present. In general, the results for the

Spennymoor sample

> suggest that the social patterns and attitudes of a single-occupation community have outlasted the extinction of coal-mining (in the town) since the war; this is evidenced in the more localised kinship and friendship network, the communication of local information relatively more through conversation than through newspapers, and the continuing importance and popularity of the Working Men's Clubs. In addition, Spennymoor is the exception in relation to some of our political hypotheses; we find for instance a greater knowledge of who the local councillors are and a greater faith in the local Council. Great stress is placed on the friendliness of the people in Spennymoor, and in addition we find a more specific survival of certain items of local 'folk culture'. Such regional cultural traits as painting eggs at Easter, wearing a flat cap and scarf, pigeon fancying and whippet racing were participated in more here by family members in the past and survive more here now. The very slow diffusion of more modern cultural elements to the area may result from the relative lack of gross migration. Indeed, when our results are standardised for population size, we find that the Spennymoor sample is the most self-contained on such biographical variables as place of birth, upbringing, previous residence, father or mother's upbringing, and father's workplace . . . The strong attachment and identity with Spennymoor seems to be connected with behaviour patterns associated with a long established traditional, socially homogenous 'community'.[43]

'Community' is both a social scientific concept (it has been used in that sense in the preceding analysis) and a moral concept or metaphor for valued types of human association. The study of the social structure of mining settlements, like the study of the history of mining trade-unionism, is inevitably normatively-toned. In social science since Ferdinand Toennies' famous work on *Gemeinschaft und Gesellschaft (Community and Society)*[44] and before, the concept has had these overtones:

> Community is both empirically descriptive of a social structure and normatively toned. It refers both to the unit of a society as it is and to the aspects of the unit that are valued if they exist, desired in their absence. Community is indivisible from human actions, purposes and values. It expresses our vague yearnings for a

> commonality of desire, a communion with those around us, an extension of the bonds of kin and friend to all who share a common fate with us . . . Looking at this double nature of the term, empirically descriptive and normatively prescriptive, leads us to the basic question: what do we want?[45]

The strong associations of the term are also stressed by Robert Nisbet. His comment recalls some of the commonsense uses of the term 'community' referred to earlier, as well as its history in social thought:

> In many spheres of thought, the ties of community – real or contrived – come to form the image of the good society. Community becomes the means of denoting legitimacy in associations as diverse as state, church, trade unions, revolutionary movement, profession and co-operative . . . The word, as we find it in much nineteenth and twentieth century thought, encompasses all forms of relationship which are characterised by a high degree of personal intimacy, emotional depth, moral commitment, social cohesion and continuity in time. Community is founded on man conceived in his wholeness rather than in one or another of the roles, taken separately, that he may hold in a social order . . . Community is a fusion of feeling and thought . . . It may be found in, or given symbolic expression by locality, region, nation, race, occupation or crusade. Its archetype, both historically and symbolically, is the family and in almost every type of genuine community the nomenclature of family is prominent. Fundamental to the strength of the bond of community is the real or imagined antithesis formed in the same social setting by the non-communal relations of competition or conflict, utility or contractual assent. These, by their relative impersonality and anonymity, highlight the close personal ties of community.[46]

Yet in relation to mining settlements, which are communities of local residence *par excellence,* this positive evaluation has often been lacking. To some extent this has been a matter of class perspective. Middle-class observers for at least the last two hundred years have tended to look down with hostile condescension or merely distance upon the condition and way of life of a distinctive occupational group, without clear justification for doing so. Perhaps this was due to a sense that miners were somehow a group apart from the rest of society. Colls has recently argued that 'every observer of the colliery communities (of Northumberland and Durham) in the first half of the nineteenth century and well after, makes the immediate homage to the pitman as "a peculiar race" '.[47] He quotes, for example, J.R. Leifchild, who carried out an important investigation of child employment in the area in the 1840s. Leifchild was so confused at first by local speech that he considered asking for an interpreter. When he did become familiar with the area (and his work is regarded as an important source) he was struck by the fact that 'the pitmen often display a feeling of being special and belonging to a hereditary closed shop'.[48] A hundred years later, an acute observer such as Mark Benney, quoted on page 49 makes a similar comment on miners' distinctive way of life.

The critical perspective upon mining settlements received some impetus, paradoxically, from the reforming middle-class conscience. Particularly in the inter-war period, a black picture of social conditions in mining areas was presented to a wider public. Some of this evidence will be reviewed in chapters 11 and 12, but its importance should not be underestimated. The combination of poor housing, insanitary conditions and high incidence of ill-health marked out mining districts from other areas. In certain villages in Durham in 1919, four out of every ten persons were living in over-crowded conditions (i.e. more than two persons per room) compared with one in ten for the country as a whole. By 1936, Durham had the highest percentage of working-class families over-crowded in the country.[49] Inadequate water supplies and sanitation are described in chapter 6; many villages lacked basic public health amenities enjoyed by city-dwellers of the period. Social commentators traced a direct connection between these conditions and the incidence of disease and death. The infant mortality rate in England and Wales in 1935 was 57 per thousand. In the Home Counties it was 42, in the South-East as a whole 47, in the North 68, in County Durham 76, in Scotland 77.[50] After adjusting for the age structure of the population, the total death rate in Durham and Northumberland in 1935 was 36 per cent higher than the national average.[51] Titmuss, for example, demonstrated that mortality in Durham was double that for the 0-4 age group compared to Surrey, 83 per cent higher for the 5-14 age group and 48 per cent higher for the 15-25 age group.[52] As Sid Chaplin observes, there was this negative side to the traditional mining community: 'The corrective is to remember the harshness, the disease, the filth, above all the smells . . . For many, the village was a prison'.

This last comment also deserves to be further explored. The idea of the community as a prison implies both constraint and lack of opportunity. If everyone knew everyone else, then there was a fair probability that they knew something about everyone else's business;

close-knit highly integrated collectivities can exercise powerful social control over their members as well as being highly integrated and *gemeinschaftlich.* For those with social, educational or cultural aspirations, moreover, the village could not necessarily provide. As Moore has emphasised, social mobility out of the village, particularly via education, was characteristic of the aspiring Methodist families he studied.[53] They and others clearly felt that the homgeneous working-class community failed to provide opportunities which, if they could not achieve themselves, they could aspire to for their children.

A further extension of these views is that the particular character of mining communities arose out of economic adversity, notably the experience of inter-war unemployment discussed in chapters 10 and 11. The very collective solidarity of mining communities is seen to be due to the prolonged experience of economic disadvantage, bitter industrial conflict and damagingly inferior social conditions before 1945. The industrial relations history of 1972 and 1974 suggests that this is an inadequate explanation for the characteristics of mining as an occupation, as indeed do studies of pit work itself.

Nevertheless, there is a sense in which some of the more positive aspects of mining communities derive from negative features of local social life. As David Harvey has suggested, reciprocity in local social relations stems from a common fate and common life chances:

> Reciprocity comes closest to performing its traditional function in the neighbourhood and in the local community. It became particularly important, for example, in the early years of the industrial revolution when working-class communities typically evolved a neighbourly warm-hearted reciprocity that did much to assuage the worst ravages of an insensate wage system. The sense of community has been significant as a protective fence in the industrial city ever since. In the early stages of industrial urbanisation, reciprocity was typically based on extended kinship relations, ethnic or religious identifications, or on the coming together of particular population groups under some threat (the sense of community is very strong in mining areas, for example) . . . Spatial propinquity, geographical immobility and reciprocity in the community are undoubtedly related.[54]

The social scientist writing about mining has to try to keep distinct the metaphorical and moral connotations of 'community' from the scientific ones. The scientific approach is most clearly embodied in chapter 7 and chapter 9 onwards. The discussion of the planning literature in chapter 12 indeed suggests the considerable danger in allowing moral considerations to stray into objective analyses. In that case the negative evaluation of the small mining settlement is used as a questionable basis for policies for which on other grounds (for example, economic efficiency in the provision of services) there might be a quite reasonable case.

Nevertheless, moral elements do enter in to earlier chapters, particularly some of the personal documents. It is therefore appropriate to emphasise that the aim of this work is in part to serve as a corrective to the predominantly negative evaluation of the social character of mining areas made by many commentators. Durham is not just *different,* it is representative of a way of life which may be valued as well as devalued:

> Village life can only in the most facile sense be understood by assessing the number of indoor taps per pit row. Areas of community life were literally invisible to the nineteenth century outside observer. To know them demanded an intimacy with the community itself . . . The colliery village as a place to live meant a network of meeting places . . . The working-class territorial imperative, 'next door', 'our street', 'wor toon', was rarely visible to the outside eye, it could only assume shape and form when that eye was tutored by a cultural rapport; without it, significant aspects of the miners' village were as ghosts to be walked through. Cultural problems of this sort have produced technical problems of evidence for the social historian, but this is no reason either to ignore the dimension or surrender the battle.[55]

Mining communities have often been seen as the embodiment of a particular type of working-class society with a strong trade union and political base. Strong elements of moral approval are present in the descriptions of the Big Meeting by Dalton and Lawson quoted above. In Sid Chaplin's and Mark Benney's personal documents, the positive elements of mining life are strongly stressed. Among academic commentators, John Rex has suggested that:

> there are two or perhaps three worthwhile ideals regarding community life-styles which might inform our thinking, as we take decisions which could perpetuate or destroy the communities we have known in the past in Britain. At one extreme is the urban ideal, based upon

> the ideas of differentiation and complementarity . . . At the other is the idea of industrial and social homogeneity, where the fullness of life lies in the strength of overlapping social ties which give such communities, not merely a kind of snugness, but also a vigour which urban society can rarely recapture.[56]

Such a perspective seems at least as fruitful as a negative one for an understanding of the character of mining settlements as communities. The policy implications are moreover important, and more so today than in the past. Thirty and forty years ago the social goals were improvement in standards of water supply and sanitation, housing and health, which were obvious, straightforward and easily measurable. Housing and health remain important problems today, but with no longer the same saliency. In County Durham, problems of employment, town planning and population movement are perhaps of greater local import. In these fields the goals are less clear, less directly achievable, and less easily evaluated. To assist in this difficult task, the present collection of papers is offered as an aid to an understanding of (and a contribution to debate about) social change in one area of Britain, County Durham.

Notes

1. S. Chaplin, *A Tree with Rosy Apples,* Newcastle, Frank Graham, 1972, p.88.
2. R.E. Pahl, 'The Rural-Urban Continuum', *Sociologia Ruralis,* VI, 3-4, 1966, p.322.
3. A.E. Smailes, *North England,* London, Nelson, 1968; J.W. House, *Industrial Britain: the North-East,* Newton Abbott, David & Chalres, 1969; K. Warren, *North-East England,* Oxford University Press, 1973.
4. Lady Bell, *At the Works: a study of a manufacturing town,* London, Arnold, 1907.
5. A.L. Bowley and A.R. Burnett-Hurst, *Livelihood and Poverty: a study in the economic conditions of working-class households in Northampton, Warrington, Stanley and Reading,* London, Bell, 1915; see also A.L. Bowley and M.H. Hogg, *Has Poverty Diminished? A sequel to Livelihood and Poverty,* London, King, 1925.
6. The classic sociological description of a coal-mining community in Britain (in West Yorkshire) is: N. Dennis, C. Slaughter, and F. Henriques, *Coal is Our Life,* London, Eyre & Spottiswoode, 1956. On Durham the main social scientific studies are: R.C. Taylor, 'The implications of migration from the Durham Coalfield', unpublished Ph.D. thesis, University of Durham, 1966; J.W. House and E.M. Knight, *Pit Closure and the Community,* Geography Department, Newcastle University, 1967; DEP, *Ryhope: a pit closes,* HMSO, 1970: M.I.A. Bulmer, 'Mining Redundancy: a case study of the working of the Redundancy Payments Act, 1965, in the Durham coalfield', *Industrial Relations Journal,* Vol.2, No.4, December 1971, pp.3-21. On the technical side of mining work,

see E. Trist, *Organisational Choice,* London, Tavistock, 1963. See also the research reports by E. Thorpe and M. Bulmer referred to at the beginning of chapters 7 and 15.

7. Cf. G. Parkinson, *True Stories of Durham Pit Life,* London, Kelly, 1912; J. Newsom, *Out of the Pit,* Oxford, Blackwell, 1936; M. Benney, *Charity Main: a coalfield chronicle,* London, Allen & Unwin, 1946; J. Lawson, *A Man's Life,* London, Hodder, 1932; D. Douglass, *Pit Talk in County Durham,* Oxford, Ruskin College, 1972, republished in R. Samuel (ed.) *Miners, Quarrymen and Saltworkers,* London, Routledge, 1977 pp.297-348.
8. S. Chaplin, *The Thin Seam,* Oxford, Pergamon, 1968 (First published 1950).
9. See the descriptive account and comparison with mining in J. Tunstall, *The Fishermen,* London, McGibbon, 1962.
10. R.W. Grainger and J.W. Hurst, *A Report on the incidence of disability among Durham miners,* Department of Economics, Durham University, 1969, mimeo.
11. J. Rex, 'Images of Community', p.56, in J. Rex, *Race, Colonialism and the City,* London, Routledge, 1973.
12. E. Trist, *Organisational Choice.*
13. Benney, *Charity Main.*
14. W.R. Garside, *The Durham Miners, 1919-60,* London, Allen and Unwin, 1971. An entertaining, light-hearted and yet pointed play describes the course of these struggles among Durham miners 'who created a revolutionary weapon without having a revolutionary intention'. A. Plater, S. Chaplin, and A. Glasgow, *Close the Coalhouse Door,* London, Methuen, 1969.
15. D. Douglass, *Pit Life in County Durham* (1971), republished in R. Samuel (ed.), *op. cit.*, pp.205-96.
16. Ned Cowen, *Of Mining Life and Aal its Ways,* Durham, privately printed 1973, p.55
17. Ernest Armstrong, MP for north-west Durham.
18. H. Dalton, *Memoirs: Call Back Yesterday, 1887-1931,* London, Muller, 1953.
19. J. Lawson, *Peter Lee,* London, The Epworth Press, 1951, p.168.
20. J. Gorman, *Banner Bright,* London, Allen Lane, 1973.
21. W.A. Moyes, *Banner Parade,* Newcastle, Frank Graham, 1973, and the much fuller W.A. Moyes, *The Banner Book: a study of the banners of the Lodges of the Durham Miners' Association,* Newcastle, Frank Graham, 1974.
22. W.R. Garside, *The Durham Miners,* pp.287-8.
23. Ibid., p.289.
24. Cf. M.I.A. Bulmer, 'Sociological Models of the Mining Community', *The Sociological Review,* 23, 1975, pp.61-92, esp. p.85.
25. R.S. Moore, *Pitmen, Preachers and Politics: the effects of Methodism in a Durham mining community,* Cambridge University Press, 1974.
26. 'The Trimdon Grange Explosion' in *Come All Ye Bold Miners: Ballads and Songs of the Coalfield,* compiled by A.L. Lloyd, London, 1952. Much of the material is drawn from the Northumberland and Durham coalfield. See also R. Colls, *The Collier's Rant,* London, Croom Helm, 1977.
27. J.W. House and E.M. Knight, *Pit Closure and the Community.*
28. DEP, *Ryhope: a pit closes.*
29. M.I.A. Bulmer, 'Mining Redundancy'.
30. Basic data is contained in: J.C. Dewdney, 'The Daily Journey to Work in County Durham,' *Town Planning Review,* 31(2), 1960. A small sociological study by P. Jephcott is reported in: G.H.J. Daysh *et al, West Durham, a problem area in North-East England,* Oxford, Blackwell, 1953, Ch.9.
31. R.C. Taylor, unpublished Ph.D. thesis.
32. See also R.C. Taylor, 'Migration and Motivation', in J.A. Jackson (ed.), *Migration,* Cambridge University Press, 1969, pp. 99-133.
33. Data obtained from 1971, *Census of Population.*
34. Royal Commission on Local Government, Research Studies 9, *Community*

Attitude Survey, England, 1969 (London, HMSO), Table 53, p.54.
35. D. Rich, 'Spare Time in the Black Country', in L. Kuper (ed.), *Living in Towns,* London, Cressett, 1953.
36. N. Dennis *et al., Coal is Our Life.*
37. B. Jackson, *Working Class Community,* London, Routledge, 1968, ch. 4, 'The Club'.
38. R.C. Taylor, unpublished Ph.D. thesis.
39. Ted Elkins, Jr., *So They Brewed Their Own Beer: the history of the Northern Clubs Federation Brewery Ltd.,* Sunderland, 1970.
40. See, *inter alia,* Sid Chaplin, 'The Bonnie Pit Laddie', pp.124-131, in S. Chaplin, *A Tree with Rosy Apples,* Newcastle, Frank Graham, 1972.
41. J.W. House *et al, Where did the School-leavers Go?,* University of Newcastle, Geography Department, 1965.
42. A.R. Townsend and C.C. Taylor, 'Regional Culture and Identity in industrialised societies: the case of north-east England', *Regional Studies,* 9, 1975, pp.379-93; C.C. Taylor and A.R. Townsend, 'The Local "Sense of Place" as evidenced in North-East England', *Urban Studies,* 13, 1976, pp. 133-46.
43. Taylor and Townsend, 'Local "Sense of Place", ' pp. 141, 144.
44. F. Toennies, *Community and Society,* London, Routledge (first published 1887).
45. D.W. Minar and Scott Greer, *The Concept of Community: readings with interpretations,* Chicago, Aldine, 1969, p. ix.
46. R.A. Nisbet, *The Sociological Tradition,* London, Heinemann, 1967, pp.47-8.
47. R. Colls, *The Collier's Rant,* London, Croom Helm, 1977, p.54.
48. Ibid., p.54, referring to J.R. Liefchild's evidence to the *Children's Employment Commission,* 1842. See also J.R. Liefchild, *Our Coal and Our Coal Pits,* 1856; 2nd edition, Newcastle, Oriel Press.
49. W.R. Garside, *The Durham Miners* p. 287.
50. R. Titmuss, *Poverty and Population; a factual study of contemporary social waste,* London, Macmillan, 1938, pp.80-1.
51. Ibid., p. 135.
52. Ibid., p.119.
53. R.S. Moore, *Pitmen.*
54. D. Harvey, *Social Justice and the City,* London, Arnold, 1973, pp.281-2.
55. R. Colls, *The Collier's Rant,* p.17.
56. J. Rex, 'Images of Community', in *Race, Colonialism and the City,* London, Routledge, 1973, pp.58-9.

PERSONAL DOCUMENTS ABOUT COUNTY DURHAM

3 THE LEGACY OF MINING

Mark Benney

Writer and social scientist Mark Benney was employed as an Industrial Relations Officer at Newcastle for the Ministry of Fuel and Power at the end of the Second World War, in 1944-45. On the basis of this experience he published in 1946 Charity Main: a coalfield chronicle *(George Allen & Unwin), from which the following extract is taken. Although written in the third person and in fictionalised form ('Johnson' refers to himself), it provides an excellent picture of mining life under private ownership. The publication of the book coincided with the promulgation of legislation for the nationalisation of coalmines, which came into effect in 1947; the situation described here relates to the period when the coal industry was still in private ownership.*

Twenty years later, in 1966, Benney recalled how he arrived at Newcastle, knowing nothing of either the area or the industry, and immersed himself in 'the complicated geology, sociology, technology, economics and politics of the Durham coalfield'. He continues:

> *It was a fascinating study, and it appalled me how little of what I needed was available in print. Here, encamped on a vast raft of coal that outcropped in the Pennine Hills to the west and sloped down under thick Permian rock to the North Sea, was a tribe of Englishmen so distinctive in their way of life that, had they been situated on a remote island in the South Seas, they would have been the subject of a dozen ethnographic monographs . . . A shaft had been sunk to the coal seams wherever economic advantage suggested, and around the shaft the miners and their families lived, an isolated, work-centred, hate ridden, community. On those moors and in those valleys, in an often lovely countryside, were congealed all the grotesque horrors of nineteenth-century industrialism – dwellings regimented in hideous row upon row, vile smoke belching from stacks placed without regard for eye or lung, a railway siding at the foot of a slag-heap where the clangour of freigh cars sounded day and night . . .* (Almost a Gentleman, Peter Davies, 1966 pp.155-6).

It will be recalled that at the time of my appointment, in April of this year, the widespread strikes resulting from the Porter Awards were in process of settlement. The terms of settlement, as embodied in the National Wage Agreement, were generous to the miners: but it was obvious to everyone that, while the Agreement would probably succeed in reducing the number of disputes to the minimum during the four years of its bond, it was unlikely in itself to affect the underlying causes of dispute. Indeed, the coalowners widely predicted that the Agreement would have the direct effect of encouraging absenteeism and restriction, and so reduce output still further. My appointment in an experimental capacity at this time encouraged me to believe that my real duties were to take advantage of the four-year armistice, first to assess the industrial, social and psychological causes responsible for the notoriously bad relations between miners and coalowners, and secondly to experiment with techniques for removing the causes or mitigating their effects.

I was chosen for this work on my record as a trained sociologist with experience both in industrial research and practical labour organisation. My duties, as laid down by Headquarters, were deliberately framed to leave me with the utmost freedom, although I was specifically charged with improving the working of pit production committees and all industrial publicity in the region. Immediately upon taking up my duties, therefore, I reduced my office-work to a bare minimum and devoted my time to as close and intimate a study of the coalfield as was possible. In the first three months of this investigation I visited thirty-four collieries in the county, some of them several times, discussed local conditions, grievances and customs with managers, trade union officials and workmen. During the course of these visits I spent rather more than seventy hours in underground visits at twelve different collieries, on three occasions working full shifts with the men at the coal face and on the haulage ways. I should like here to thank my colleagues in this office, whose advice and assistance on these visits were invaluable, for the trouble they put themselves to on my behalf. My findings have been given in many separate reports and memoranda, but I will give them again here in a correlated form.

This county now produces rather less than one-seventh of the national coal output with rather more than one-seventh of the total number of workers in the industry. Of nearly two hundred pits now working, more than ninety are more than a century old, while several shafts still in use were first sunk more than two hundred years ago. History is the *femme fatale* of the coal trade in more respects than one, and it is necessary to insist from the beginning on the great age, both of the workings and of the traditions, in these parts.

There are a hundred and ten villages and towns with a predominantly mining population scattered fairly equally over the five hundred square miles of this county. Although many of these villages are set in the heart of some of the loveliest country, they represent an extraordinarily uniform picture of bleak ugliness to the stranger with standards set by South of England villages. There is another noteworthy peculiarity in the physical appearance of these villages. Wherever, by chance, the eye rests upon some building more attractive than its neighbours, one almost invariably finds that it owes its existence to the organised efforts of the miners themselves. Their clubs, welfare institutes, co-op. stores are the outstanding institutional buildings. The charming little rows of cottages built for aged miners are also their handiwork; and the occasional less charming but still outstanding housing estates built by local councils in the last twenty years owe their existence to the urgent representations of miners' representatives on these bodies. Conversely, wherever the eye selects some row of cottages as being more squalid and offensive than others, one invariably finds that these are colliery-owned cottages. There can be no question at all that these villages (most of which assumed their present size during the middle years of the nineteenth century) owe all their horror to the colliery-owners who built them, and all their redeeming features to the organisational energies of the people who live in them.

Of the collieries themselves I should perhaps say little, since I am no mining engineer. Yet my knowledge of general engineering processes leaves me in no doubt that all but half a dozen of the largest and newest pits in the county are worked to no very exacting technical standards. There is not a single colliery whose surface layout makes any pretensions either to efficiency or seemliness. The managers and their office staff conduct their complicated affairs in offices and with equipment that have remained unchanged since the last century. Nearly every manager with whom I have spoken has admitted that the underground layout of his pit, after twenty years of snatch working and 'quality grading,' has become an unmanageable honeycomb of ill-kept roads such as to make efficient underground transport impossible. Ventilation is bad, lighting is worse, and research to improve these and other technical deficiencies almost non-existent.

It is inevitable that any technical criticism of the pits should seem to reflect on the capacities of the managers. And it is true that the typical colliery manager in this county is not a very inspiring person. For two generations the industry has become less and less attractive to talented and enterprising young men; the prospect of living in a mining village, with such mines as these to control, has scared away from the industry all but those whose imaginations are too bounded to conceive anything better. Even so, the industry fails to make anything like the best use of the brains left over. The statutory qualifications required of a colliery manager are a sound grounding in mining technology; but the odd development of the industry in recent years leaves him with less and less time to practice his competency in this field. Recently I persuaded two managers, both of medium-sized collieries employing about a thousand people, to make time-studies of their week's work for me. In the first case, 72 per cent of the manager's working-hours (calculated at sixty hours) was spent dealing with labour problems of one sort or another – attendance at production committees, welfare committees, canteen committees, pit committees, absentee tribunals, National Service Officer appeal courts, deputations and sundry complaints; leaving him only a few hours a week for his proper work of technical supervision and planning. In the second case, the manager contrived to delegate some of his committee-duties and so reduce his dealing with labour problems to a mere 60 per cent of his time. While most of this work is necessary, it is absurd that it should be done by a man chosen for his qualifications in other fields. There is an obvious case for personnel managers at all collieries employing more than five hundred workmen: as it is there is not a single personnel manager in the county, even in the case of collieries employing three thousand or more men.

But it is not the colliery managers who administer this industry: it is the coalowners. They are an elusive breed, and therefore hard to study in their natural habitat. The four or five most powerful individual owners still living in the county have diverse interests and *grand seigneur* standards; a minor civil servant does not meet them, and must judge them by their visible works. But lest my worm's eye view of them should seem distorted, let me preface my own remarks by quoting a bishop who stayed in their houses, ate at their tables, shared their counsels and approved their politics. His summing-up runs thus:

> Mineowners, unlike most other great employers of labour, are not normally confronted by a local opinion and tradition which may stimulate the sense of social obligation, and restrain the shortsighted selfishness of acquisition. The minefield seemed to me significantly destitute of those evidences of serious effort by Capital to improve conditions of Labour which so often arrest the attention in great

> cities. Often I heard the question, *Who ever met a poor mineowner?* There may be, probably there is, as much ignorance as reason in the challenge, and not all mineowners are alike; but it cannot be disputed that *the wills of deceased coal magnates, even in bad times, go far to provide a certain justification for the popular belief.*[a]

It is noteworthy that the good bishop assumes absentee ownership as a standard condition of the industry. In this he does something less than strict justice to that handful of local men who administer their interpenetrating interests in coal, steel, shipping, insurance and breweries from this city. But in checking up the place of residence of the twelve largest coalowners in this county I find that only three live inside the county, while no less than seven live in and about the industrial areas of Yorkshire. Of these twelve owners, eight at least are members of families associated with this coalfield for more than a hundred years; and the implication of the admittedly inadequate figures given above would seem to be that profits earned in this coalfield have been gradually reinvested in the newer coalfields and industries to the south.

There can be no question that the coalowners of this county have manifested little sense of social responsibility for the hundred thousand miners from whom their wealth derives. Nor have they shown to any appreciable extent that spirit of enterprise and independence which they themselves advance as the chief justification for their existence. Singularly little fresh capital has been brought into the coalfield in the last two decades (apart from Government grants during the course of this war). What technical advances have been made in the same period have been concentrated entirely on the marketing rather than the production of coal. Sheltered under the price-fixing machinery of the 1930 Coal Act, and using employment benefits to keep an abundance of surplus labour always on hand, all their energies have been bent on price-cutting, i.e., wage reductions.

The long, strong traditions of ownership in these parts, indeed, almost inhibit any other response to economic problems than the attack on wages. The owners have inherited a proud and arrogant conception of their function from their great-grandfathers who made the Industrial Revolution. They remember that the railways of the world were the children of their brain, that the iron foundries of England grew up under their guidance and advice. Our modern industrial civilisation came to school in this part of the world, and in

---

a *Retrospect of an Unimportant Life,* H.H. Henson, vol.2, p.406.

return made oligarchs of the industrialists it found here. Particularly, among the owners of today, the economic dogmas of the nineteenth century have survived almost untouched. Coal still 'tends towards a natural price,' and wages must still be pared 'in accordance with the law of supply and demand.' A long tradition of negotiating wage claims on the basis of the price of coal has made them almost incapable of the intellectual effort required to conceive of methods of reducing costs other than reducing wages. I have before me now a letter from one of the more influential owners, commenting on the reduced output of his collieries:

> I am quite sure [he says] there is no prospect of any increase in the output so long as these high wages obtain. It must not be assumed that I am of the opinion that the men are not entitled to these high wages, as they are not unduly out of proportion to the wages got in other industries, but nevertheless the fact remains that the men generally find they have more than enough to meet their needs and want more leisure or an easier time. When the war is over, if these high wages remain and the present restrictions are removed, absenteeism will increase and there will be a further fall in output.

It is quite clear that the author of this letter has never stopped to ask himself how other industries contrive to pay reasonable wages without suffering a decline of output, or wondered if the response of the miners might not be different if he relied less on manpower and more on horsepower.

The survival of these outmoded attitudes has been helped by the fact that most of the directors of colliery companies are technically unqualified, and are therefore dependent on their managers and agents for advice as to the practicability and profitability of applying new technical methods in their pits. It is natural for any man who depends on others for advice to feel less confident in the outcome than those who gave the advice. It is also natural for any man to give more weight to factors he understands than to those he doesn't, when summing up a situation. Hence the fact that, while the financial and market structure of the industry has been considerably integrated in the past twenty years, the technical picture has remained almost unchanged.

It is not surprising that, in the course of a century and a half during which the coal industry has been of central importance to the development of the country, the coalowners have come to identify the national interest with their own. During the first century of their dominance they asked no more than to be left alone – even though this allowed them to maim children, work men fourteen hours a day in poisonous air, evade inspection of their workings, evict unionists from their homes and avoid paying compensation for injuries and death. But that was during a period of steadily expanding markets. With the contraction of their markets after the last war, their belief in the identity of national and coalowning interests assumed a more positive form. They showed an increasing tendency to reply upon the State to help them out of their difficulties: a twenty-odd million pound grant in 1925; price-fixing legislation in 1930; indirect subsidies of unemployment benefits which enabled them to close their pits for six months at a time and still have a labour-force when they were reopened; and now, since 1942, the generous arrangements of the Coal Charges Account, which empowers them to borrow from the Treasury at 4 per cent in order to pay themselves a standard profit of 10 or 12 per cent. Meanwhile, using the 'future uncertainty of ownership' as their excuse, they are ceasing even to replace the necessary equipment of the pits, blaming the consequent reduction of output on the men, and telling the Government through their associations that huge Government grants will be necessary after the war to bring the industry to a level of competitive efficiency. This, they say, will be necessary in the national interest. Of this there can be no doubt. Nor can there by any doubt that the present coalowners, of this county at least, are constitutionally and technically incapable of handling public monies for any purpose other than their own profit.

In turning to deal with the miners, I want first to call attention to the inherent peculiarities of their work. While only a small percentage of the men employed in the mines are actually engaged in coal-getting, it is the work at and around the coal face that determines the attitude of the whole mining community to mining as an occupation. The hewers, fillers, cutters and putters who work at or near the coal face, and are paid piece-rates for their output, are the most influential sections of the local Lodges, and a great majority of the disputes arising in the pits are on questions solely affecting these sections. Piece-rates, in any industry, are always a fertile source of dispute, and this no doubt contributes to the peculiar unrest and bitterness characterising the relations inside the industry. But more important I am convinced, is a psychological element inseparable from the occupational problems of mining. Operations in the dark and dust and heat of an underground tunnel subjected to tremendous geological pressures afford only a precarious margin of control over working conditions. The skilled factory worker is reasonably certain that, with the use of the appropriate technique, and the expenditure of a given amount of energy, he can produce the results required of him. But the skilled miner works in an incessantly shifting world of variables and incalculables. Seams dip and roll, get thinner or thicker, harder or softer. Roofs cave in without warning, floors heave, roads creep. Gob-fires, floods, gusts of poisonous gas are liable to interrupt work at any moment. The high accident rate of the industry is only the most tragic index to the unpredictable behaviour of nature underground: for every accident that harms a worker, there are a dozen that interfere with his work. No miner, however skilled and energetic, has any assurance that a given expenditure of skill and effort will produce a given quantity of coal.

This element of uncontrol in his work is, I am convinced, of central importance to the understanding of the mineworker's psychology. When conditions are favourable, his work is immensely satisfying. He has, what so few workers have today, a direct and immediate sense of purpose of his every action. But just because the winning of coal can be so psychologically satisfying, the incessant interruptions and hindrances are that much more frustrating. No financial compensation, in the form of payments for exceptionally difficult work, can affect this basic frustration. That the paysheet sums the total of a miner's interest in his work is an error which miners fall into scarcely less often than coalowners: but it is an error nevertheless. No one who has spent a few evenings talking with miners in their clubs can help noticing the pecularly obsessive hold their work has on them. 'They's more cowels won in t'Club than iver they is in t'Pit,' is a comment most miners make at one time or another. It can, I think, be accepted without question that the day-to-day frustrations of mining account for much of this obsessiveness.

It can also, I think, he held to account for something more important. Few laws of human behaviour are more firmly established than that which traced a casual connection between frustration and aggression. Effort that fails to achieve its object in one field of activity seeks, with increased urgency, success in another field. 'If I can't get my own way here, I'll get it there.' We take the reaction so much for granted that half the stock situations of comedy are based on it: the child, denied a second helping of pudding, kicks the table: the henpecked business man bullies his typist; the infirm poet writes swashbuckling verses. In general, if we find people behaving in a peculiarly aggressive fashion, we look for frustration in some other field of their experience. (It is not often that the aggressor himself provides the clue, as when Karl Marx, having finished the first volume of *Das Kapital,* remarked with savage satisfaction: 'That'll give the bourgeoisie cause to remember my carbuncles!')

The stubborn, aggressive character of the miners in their relations with the mineowners has been the subject of constant comment. Disraeli, writing *Sybil* in the 1850s, noticed it:

> Whenever the mining population is disturbed the disorder is obstinate. On the whole they endure less physical suffering than most of the working classes, their wages being considerable; and they are so brutalised that they are more difficult to operate on than our reading and thinking population of the factories. But when they do stir there is always violence and a determined cause.

The Tory Reform Committee uses different language today, but the general tenor of their remarks is the same: 'Mining labour in general has a sour and suspicious outlook. The evidence, if any is needed, is that coal, with one-twentieth of the workpeople in industry, was responsible for two-thirds of the time lost in industrial disputes between the wars.'

Without prejudice to the rights or wrongs of the miners' struggles it must be conceded that they prosecute their fight with a fervour and tenacity far beyond that of other sections of the organised workers with grievances no less cogent. Some explanation of this aggressive character is necessary to a full understanding of the industry, and it is my firm belief that the basic (though not the only) cause is to be found in the occupational frustrations inseparable from work in the mines.

This hypothesis – that the obduracy of the miner is a function of highly variable and uncontrollable working conditions – makes no attempt to account for the particular forms in which aggression dresses itself. For this, examination of the social circumstances of the mining community is necessary. Three factors are of decisive importance here. The social isolation of most mining villages; the industrial isolation, which makes the income of a whole village population dependent on the fortunates of a single pit; and the physical isolation imposed by geography. The combination of these three factors has led the miners' unions to assume direct responsibility for many matters normally considered beyond the scope of trade-unionism. The Union Lodge, in the ordinary mining village, is not just one of a number of social institutions of more or less importance; it is *the* paramount institution, subsuming all others. If a man is elected to a Lodge office, he will also be elected pretty certainly to the local parish council, the Welfare Institute committee, the management committee of the co-op stores, the Workmen's Club committee, the Aged MIners' Homes committee, and as many other bodies as his constitution will stand. If a vicar wants to hold a garden fete, the local Labour Party to nominate a Candidate, the Sports Club to arrange a fixture, the colliery band to accept an engagement, he will be consulted. To think of the miners' unions, therefore, simply as *trade* unions, in the way that one thinks of, say, the transport unions or the AEU, is fundamentally to misunderstand their nature. Their fuctions are much more like those of the local medieval church than any other modern institution.

This development has been made possible by the coalowners' complete severance of industrial from social responsibilities. Up to the late nineteenth century, whenever a new pit was opened, the owner built a few rows of houses around it to house the workers he required, and so called a village into being without any further thought of obligation. Some of these villages quickly became the size of small towns, but from the point of view of social resources they remained worse equipped than rural hamlets. The uniformity of colliery housing and the lack of alternative sources of employment imposed a uniformity of living standards and styles which, crystallising into traditions, has been able to resist influences to which the rest of the country has long succumbed. Nowhere is this more noticeable, or of more immediate importance, than in the consumer-habits of the miners. In spite of all the efforts of modern advertising, the miners' needs remain essentially those of the last century. There is less 'conspicuous consumption,' less competitive parade of acquisitions, in a mining village than in any other community in the country. Even house furnishings are practically identical from one house to another. Thus a sharp increase in wages, as happened last year, does not produce the phenomenon, so repellent to middle-class wives, of working women wearing fur-coats. The only commodity in which there is any wide elasticity of demand is beer. Because of this the owners are undoubtedly right when they claim that increases in wages have an immediately depressing effect on production. The miner will not work at his uncongenial tasks beyond the need of his simple family requirements; or if, from motives of patriotism, he does, his village offers him only one avenue of spending his unwanted earnings – the Club and the pub, where he is apt to drink himself so sick that he is too ill to come to work the following day. The mining community, then, makes its demands on life *as* a community, and not as a collection of individuals.

4 DURHAM MINING VILLAGES

Sid Chaplin

Local writer and novelist Sid Chaplin, who comes from a mining family and is himself an ex-pitman, first gave this account as a talk to the Durham University Sociology Department staff-graduate seminar in 1971. This chapter is an edited version of the transcript. Mr Chaplin is also the author of a novel, The Thin Seam, *first published in 1950, which portrays very vividly life and work in a small Durham pit – a colliery which might be not unlike the drift mine whose closure is described in chapter 15.*

We still have a few pits up here and a few mining villages and there is still some pit humour floating around which I sometimes think is better by far than all the millions of tons of coal that's even been produced in Northumberland and Durham, and the other week a new manager came to a pit in Northumberland – I wish it had been in Durham, but unfortunately I've got to tell the truth, it was in Northumberland, and it was his first visit underground and he went along what is known as the mother gate, that is the main roadway into the workings of a long wall face (which is a method of extracting the coal from the seam on a front anywhere from a hundred to two hundred yards long. Imagine a sort of slit in the earth about a yard thick, about 2-3 ft high, when the coal has been taken out). He went along there, this new manager, and the men were busy working and it wasn't a mechanised face. The coal was simply undercut and then blasted down, and then they simply shovelled it on to a conveyor – a very old-fashioned process today. In the main about 95 per cent of the coal is machine cut and loaded in one simultaneous operation on to a conveyor and carried away out of the pit – soulless and soul-destroying I may tell you, although a little more profitable than the other way.

He went in and the men were working all right. He looked up the face and there were a dozen men at intervals of about ten yards swinging away with their shovels, stripped down to the pit hoggers (these are light flannel trousers), just wearing these hoggers and stockings and boots, shoving their shovels into the coal and swinging the coal on to the conveyor in the yard of space and going away at it. And he got his eye fixed on the man nearest to him: And the man was working in advance of his supports. In the old days, of course, supports were made of wood, pit props, nowadays they're made of steel, based on the principle of the hydraulic retractable undercarriage of aircraft, and are very easy to operate, very easy to move over. But this man had committed the cardinal sin of the pit. Instead of taking a little spanner from his belt and moving a little valve and extending that set of supports forward, he was so intent on getting out coal – which is a very healthy instinct in any miner – that he was working in front of his supports, which meant that the roof was unsupported, and he was in an unsafe area. Now if you want to make yourself known to any man working underground, there is one sure way of doing it, and that is you're wearing your light in your helmet and there are two kinds of light – you change the light. There is a sort of diffused glow, which is the polite thing to do – you turn it on to diffused glow when you are looking at anybody – and there is the spotlight – and this is the one you don't keep on unless you want to irritate a man. This was just what the manager did. He turned his spotlight on and every time that man turned round with a shovel-full of coal to put on to the conveyor his face came round right into the spotlight. However he took no notice, he just went on shovelling. At last the manager said 'Hey lad' – getting hold of the shovel – 'Hey lad, does thou knaa whe aa is?' (Do you know who I am is a rough translation) – and the man stopped – you can just imagine this black figure, the sweat rolling down him, a big, strong, powerful figure of a man – and he just stopped and without a change of expression turned up to the face and shouted up to marra 'How Geordie, thou wants te have a luk down here, there's a fella dusn't knaa whe he is '.

Well, the one thing about being born into a mining community is that 'ye knaa whe ye are'. You know who you spring from, you know who you belong to, your roots are firmly embedded. In fact at times you feel imprisoned in a past that isn't entirely yours, a past that belongs to the community. In a strange sort of way it's almost like being a member of a great aristocratic family. It's something you've got to put up with and something you've got to fight. To a great many people, I've no doubt at all, it's been a source of strength, to a great many people it's been a source of pain and they've never been happy until they've licked the living daylights out of it and got away.

There are two sides to the mining life and the mining tradition. Personally, now that I'm clear of it, I can draw on all its richness very freely and I wouldn't have missed it for anything. But at the same time I recognise that had I gone down pit at the age of 15, as I did, with the prospect of working till I was 65 at the same sort of work it would have been a pretty grim sort of prospect whatever the leisure time pursuits I might have taken up. So always bear that in mind, whatever I say to you.

My earliest memory is of absolute darkness, and being jogged along on my dad's shoulders, comfortable, jogging motion along the high road of a more isolated spot in County Durham between Binchester Blocks and Todhills, the high point of the Wear valley where Weardale in fact gives way to the Wear valley. Where the narrow dale gives way to the open valley. I didn't know it at the time, of course, I was just three or four. I can't date the memory precisely, but I can remember distinctly the pit telephone wires singing as the wind hit them, and I can remember my dad talking to my mother, and I can remember a wonderful feeling of security and comfort in the night, and then suddenly we came over the top and it was as if the heavens had dropped down from the sky and all the Milky Way was spread out on the ground and this was the Wear valley by night. They were the pits of the Wear valley spread out with their electric lights. Very few of the villages themselves had any electric lighting. In the little village where I lived the electric street lighting didn't come until I was about ten or twelve, that was six or seven years later after the date I'm mentioning. But all the pits had electric light, of course. And in addition they had something much more fascinating – it never ceases to fascinate me – and that was the coke ovens. You know south-west Durham was a great coking coal area. The finest coking coal in the world. There are two kinds of coking coal. A kind of coke that makes good steel, and the kind of coke that foundrymen like. Both are worth their weight in gold – always have been and still are to this day, and so far nobody's found out, although they've tried their damndest, how to do without coke made from coal for making iron and for making iron castings. You know, from some of these castings you get some of the important parts of the machinery that you use in your homes and in industry and the bridges and so on and so forth. This was the Durham that I was born into and it was an Eldorado. It was a sort of Yukon of the North-East. I think very few people get the idea that the Stockton-Darlington railway, for instance, wasn't the whim of a group of far-sighted, enterprising men who saw that one day people would want to travel at immense speeds of 30 or 40 miles an hour from point A to point B, but in fact it was the idea of men who knew there was an Eldorado in south-west Durham of this coking coal. Steelmasters, ironmasters, foundrymen who wanted to get at this coal because it was giving out on the Tyne and Wear, the great old pits there were giving out. And here it was in south-west Durham. Millions and millions of tons of it. And it was an extraordinary sensation for me. It wasn't till I was about 16 and started going to WEA classes that that I discovered for the first time that pits in south-west Durham hadn't existed from time immemorial. As a child I thought pits were like the temple at Jerusalem, sort of created by God and had been there since time began. There was something divinely ordained about them and the mining villages had been there for all time.

Brancepeth Castle, which stood opposite us, the old home of the Nevilles, and Durham Cathedral, which we saw every day as we went to 'skeul', were quite unreal, but the village was the real concrete thing and it meant something and one clung to it. When I went to these classes and I discovered that in fact until 1825 all that there had been in south-west Durham had been up on the Pennine ridges, a few holes in the ground worked by one or two men and the coal conveyed away by mules or donkeys or ponies – maybe a few hundred tons a year – and that in fact all the big pits had been created after 1825, it was a stunning revelation. And this was the meaning of this galaxy on the ground and it was an astonishing world to grow up into. But it went on and on and on – at the height of the coal industry I should think there were, in Durham (this is between 1913 and 1919) somewhere in the region of 350 and 400 pits. The statistics weren't very good in those days so no-one exactly knows. But there they were, and quite apart from the pits that were going at that time, the time when I was born, there were old pits that had gone out of being, but had created villages and traditions, so it was an immense sort of structure which was constantly being born and constantly dying and constantly developing. But, and this was the miraculous thing, one lived in one's own village and it was sufficient. One was hardly aware of the villages next door. There was a tremendous sense of insularity. I moved from Binchester Blocks when I was about six years of age to a little village called Newfield and was immediately accepted, and in between Binchester Blocks and Newfield lay the village of Byers Green, and if any Byers Green boys ventured into our village we'd stone them until they took to their heels. And likewise if we went to the pictures in Byers Green we'd more likely than not be stoned on the way through. And we used to go round the perimeter of the village. The cinema with its tin roof was at top end of the village and we used to sneak away round the hedges at the back of the village and nip into the pictures as quickly as possible and get lost among the audience of about two or three hundred people – tremendously cosmopolitan. We'd be in no danger of being found out. So there was this insularity and isolation and one became terribly attached to one's village and there was very little marrying out – I've noticed that. I've been back to Byers Green and Newfield subsequently and this is just a rough check. I wish somebody would go into the Registers at all these little mining villages, but I notice from tombstones that husbands and wives generally came from the same village, and if not, from not very far away. There was very little cross-breeding.

The villages were built overnight – the Americans are much more realistic about mining than we are. They know it's a short-lived thing, relatively speaking. Even if there is fifty years of coal – what's fifty years? So they talk about mining camps, we talk about villages, which is one of the oldest words in the language. It means a permanent settlement. But most of the Durham villages were, in fact, camps, and they were put down as camps. The first street was Sinkers Row, and an upper and downer. At the best a sort of but-and-ben arrangement. That is a little scullery with a fairly large kitchen and if you wanted a bedroom for the kids, you put planks across the rafters and provided your own ladder up and a trapdoor for the kids to go up. As a child – oral tradition was very strong in these villages incidentally – I often heard of the beginnings of the chapels when the colliery company would simply hand over one of these old cottages and the people would have to mount the ladder – because somebody would be living downstairs, you see – people would have to mount the ladder to get into the garret for the service. The tribulations of the stout ladies, who lived on potatoes and meal bread, when two strong Society Stewards had to get their shoulders beneath them and push them through the trapdoor! Well they were very poor and the sanitation was very poor as well. You know, those were the days of the 'netty'. Generally two 'netties' (to serve two adjacent houses) stood across the street or at the bottom of the common yard – it's funny how you get the Norman French. My grandmother had a lot of Norman French expressions. She came from Cockfield and I suppose it came from the Nevilles of Raby and their Squires. But netty is, I suppose, a corruption of cabinet. They were in twos and they were about ten yards away from the house and in full view of the kitchen window and everybody saw everybody going across and it provided an eternal source of gossip – 'Se-and-se's been ower the yard fower or five times this morning, something must hev happened te them'. And 'Ee our se-and-se has been in the netty there half an oor and he didn't tek a paper either'. Of course this was a great thing, to take the paper over to read in the 'netty'. Housewives used to take a great pride in their netties: they were white-washed inside and kept very clean, the seats were scrubbed, and they were very proud of the design. That little American book *The Specialist* had nothing on these people. The ventilation was provided by either a cut-out star or a diamond, but it had to be of sufficient size to admit the light so that when the old man got his sporting pink on a summer's night, round about seven o'clock he could retire to the netty away from the kids – the seven kids – and look up his results in peace. Or the old lady could go there. I know of a girl who went to Training College and became a teacher from this little village next to us, Byers Green, and she had a very rough upbringing. Her father was a drunkhard, it was a large family, a family of about eight of them, and most of her studying was done in the netty. I dare say these pit villages were Primitive Methodist villages, they were very religious communities and I suppose a lot of praying and a lot of serman composing also went on in the netty. They played a very large, a very vital part, quite apart from the hygienic function, in the lives of the communities.

One of my earliest memories is of the grinding noise of the wheels of the midden carts – two wheeled cowps or tipping carts. You can still see the odd one about. Drawn by a big shire horse, the grind of their metal-shod wheels, the jangle of the bucket full of some kind of antiseptic dusting powder hung on the back, and then the scrape of the shovel as the arduous job was done, would often waken us kids at night. You can read the life of Dr John Wilson, of Tommy Burt, of Parkinson – go into the memoirs of all these pioneer mining people – and there is nothing about this kind of arrangement, and yet of course it was vital. It had a lot to do with what happened in those days. I suppose about fifteen pit villages in that area had all their night soil led away to a mighty heap which was a Mount Etna, only more noisome, at the opposite side of the Wear, and it stood absolutely central – by arrangement with all the Councils, I suppose – so that no-one had any further to go than anybody else, and there they all led the night soil. Everybody was praying for the wind, that the wind would blow in the opposite direction – fifteen villages simultaneously praying to the same God that the wind would blow in the opposite direction! I know it was a terrifying smell, and that was the kind of sanitation we had.

I remember Challies Street, which was a lovely street from the point of view of the people who inhabited it, wonderful characters. Challies Street: probably sixty or seventy houses, a long meandering street, and one tap for every ten houses and the women would queue up to get the water. The more modern houses, you know, the more posh houses for the deputies whatever the proper name given to it, was always 'Quality Row'. They would have a washbasin – a rough earthenware washbasin

– inside, but no running hot water of course, except for the boiler attached to the kitchen range, of limited capacity, just the ordinary cold water tap, and all the slops would go straight down into an open sort of drain that was common to the whole street. They would run down this open drain to the bottom of the street and into a sink and away. And of course, as a result of this, and as a result of the scrimshank construction of most of the houses, you had an awful lot of TB – 'he's gone into a decline' or 'she's gone into a decline' was the expression, and it was terrifying, the number of families decimated by declines in those days. There were also intermittent – I am talking about the late twenties when I first became aware of this – epidemics of scarlet fever and measles and finally smallpox, which took away in South Durham scores and scores of people, and all this of course was the result of the bad sanitation.

I think one ought to talk about the kind of arrangements inside the house, particularly when families were so large – those were the days when all mining was based on coal hewing and the thing was to have sons, and everybody went in for large families, and if you had seven sons so much the better, because before your seven sons got married they'd be bringing the money home, and that would be capital for your old age, so there was a period of affluence in middle life for most people from these strong lads. As I remember it, most families were large so the fecundity must have been pretty high in Durham, and certainly feeding was good. There was contempt for those who lived 'hand to mouth'. I never knew until recently that the term 'hand to mouth' was first invented for people who went once a week to a shop to get the groceries. Anybody who was anybody got supplies in by the quarter or half year. They got their flour by the sack; I can remember my grandmother getting it by the sack, and I can remember my mother certainly getting her flour by the stone – eight loaves and a fudge from one stone of Daisy White flour for 1s. 8d. plus three-pennyworth of yeast. And I can remember the great baking days twice a week, and the poss-tub with that instrument of torture the poss-stick, because I had to use it and I had to wind the mangle. And many a braying I've had too over the poss-tub. The poss-tub was in the yard, you see, and it was handy.

I remember there was a jazz song of the period called 'Bye-bye Blackbird'. We were very innocent in those days really: we were country children, I mean it was rural mining, and we knew very little of the facts of life – I knew nothing about them. This song was prevalent at school, this parody of 'Bye-bye Blackbird', and I came in one day singing, 'There was a man, he was no good, he took his wife into the wood.

Bye-bye Blackbird'. The next thing I knew my mother got hold of me and head first I went into the poss-tub and got my backside belted. 'There,' she said, 'that'll learn you to come singing your dirty songs'.

And there was boot alley. At least that's what it was called in our house. There was a family of five lads of us. Boot alley was where the boots were kept, and that was a horrible place as well, especially if dad and five or six sons worked at the pits, because most of the pits were shallow and wet and that meant there was a sort of peculiar, sticky ('claggy' we used to call it) clay which was awful stuff. It used to burden you down – burden your boots down, burden your clothes down and get into your very pores. The boots would go into boot alley in the passage and before your started work, of course, it was your job – and we were a fairly democratic household, so it went on a rota system – to look after boot alley every day. So that meant about five or six pairs of boots to clean and blacken. But there was great pride in the house and there was a turning-out every Friday when all the proddy mats were taken up. (Incidentally, all the mats were made at home out of odd bits of cloth cut up and put in with peculiar little instruments of torture – I've done that many a time as well. It was a winter time occupation.) These very attractive and very beautiful mats were taken up on the Friday and the range – the iron range – was black-leaded (after it had been cleaned out of course, after all the soot had been taken out of the catchment area), and the big steel fender and the fire irons and the pretty betty (or tidy betty, I should say) that kept the ashes from coming out too far, and the kettles were polished till they shone, and all the furniture was dusted. Pretty often the furniture consisted of a box bed, an extra bed which folded up during the day time and was kept in the kitchen, and a big chest of drawers with a kind of cupboard above, generally with long mirror doors on it with all sorts of fantastic figures on the mirrors. All the bed linen and tableclothes were kept in this. A sideboard and table completed the kitchen furnishings. The houseproud housewife put the old pit stockings on the legs of her sideboard and table. One comes across sneering references in books about the Victorians being so modest as to put stockings on the legs because they were unmentionable, because they were too modest to see the legs of a table. But, of course, this is absolute nonsense. It was just to save the legs from being knocked about because people were much more careful about things in those days. And every week of course, these stockings were taken off, the legs were polished and new stockings were put on and the old ones were washed. Friday was turning-out day for my Grandma and – oh, it was hell. I used to get as far away as possible.

It was absolute hell. But it was marvellous when it was finished because the house shone. In addition there were all sorts of brass ornaments. They weren't the sort of fancy fal-a-lals you get now, the manufactured brass ornaments that have become all the rage, but real brass things. I mean brass holders for the fire irons and the brass rod to dry the pit duds (the pit clothes) over the fire place. And that brass rod shone until you could see your face in it practically. The whole house shone and it was a marvellous sensation to come into, it was worth everything, and I remember Grandma standing like this and saying 'Well everything's points device', you know, one of her Norman French words again from Cockfield; meaning, of course, that everything was all correct and to her liking. So that however bad the housing was, people's personal standards lifted them out of the trough.

The first pit I knew was not only central but small. This was Newfield. Originally the pit shaft by the riverside had drawn the coal, then those reserves had been exhausted. So they drove adits, or drift mines, into the river banks. The main drift was about a quarter of a mile from the shaft (and screens), the rolleyway or tubway running parallel with a sheer cliff 60-70 feet high for a quarter of a mile, then disappearing into the base of the cliff, where it turned with a bend of the river. Low seams, low tubs (holding 8 cwts), low-stooping walk for the men. Some had more than a mile to walk in only tub-height, and naturally there was a great temptation to ride the sets – a terrifying sensation. Once you were inside the tub there was no getting out until you arrived in- or out-bye.

We used to lie on the edge of the cliff, on our bellies, and wait for a set to come out. Intensely dramatic. First a distant muffled thunder with the black rope running smoothly on the rolleys which carried it, then it would begin to tighten like a bow-string and stot (bounce) furiously, then at last the midget train would emerge, tub after tub brimming with roundies like blackberries. Those were the days of hand hewers and bord and pillar, a highly selective mining system. The first machines were murder in those low seams from which the water fell like rain. I've seen the men come out so disciplined to the stooped walk that they'd walk doubled up twenty yards, maybe more, before realising that their roof was the sky.

The token cabin, where the men picked up the little discs which verified each tub to them and left their pipes and tabs (fags, cigs), was just down there. Sometimes we'd shout to a man going in, 'Leave us your tab, Mister', and would scramble down to pick it up, damp-ended, from the rolley wall. We knew if they'd forgotten their tokens, marked every man that carried a ring of picks (spares for his hewing, sharpened every day by the smith), knew which lads were drivers, which putters. Tubs were our toys (at weekends) and we soon learned how to couple, dreg (drag) them with a wooden stake, yoke a pony to them. We watched the shoers (farriers) at work, the smiths (there was a distinction), watched the brick-making (the segger, or clay, bed of the seam made firebricks for furnaces), and over at Vinovium, where the riding shaft was, we watched our fathers ride to bank at weekends. As long as you kept the rules (never crossed the rope, never chased the ponies or pinched coal or pitwood, never set your lip up to man or gaffer) you were free to come and go as you chose. There was no boundary between the pit and village, as at the larger collieries.

Coal soaked into your being, if only from the interminable coal talk, good and bad cavils, coal wet, coal dry, coal you could push down with the toeplate of your boot, coal a diamond drill wouldn't touch, how many score this one got, how many this didn't. . . There, as elsewhere, it was reckoned an extra barman was employed at weekends at the club to shift the loose coal.

And from our older brothers, the lads that had just left school, we learned names of seams, districts, variations (faults, hitches, washouts, nips, etc.), the names of the ponies and their nature, and the knack of getting tubs through the low. Swimming down by the river, they'd expose their scarred and knobby backs with pride. There was an overall power picture of coal trade and Durham Miners' Association, but within the village structure of power (manager and lodge) there was a hierarchy with its skills, traditions and degrees of prestige and, for the growing boy, initiation leading to the ceremonial of being a 'new starter' (screener, driver, putter, coal-hewer or stoneman).

Our dream and whole life's ambition was to be high-ranking putters, favoured by the big hewers as we ourselves would cherish and favour our ponies. That is, if our ponies were good.

Still when I was a boy, every coal hewer worth his salt took a Yule Doo (a cake in the shape of a little man) to work for his putter every Christmas, with at least half a dollar (2s 6d) embedded in the head or body. My brother says the money, but not the cake, survived in the Main Coal, Dean and Chapter, until about 1950.

Everything had a name and place and belonged: the seams, High and Low Mains, Harvey, Hutton, Busty, the dips, inclines, swalleys, engine-planes, flats, and 'places'; the tools, dregs, sockets, shackles, limbers, cows, bulls, rolleys and rolleyways, switches, bends, turns, curves, points, dillies and gantries, the clothes. The pitman put on his duds and wore hoggers, carried a Jimmie Midgie (open flame) lamp; the gaffer, knee-breeches, skull-cap, yardstick, and shining safety lamp.

As with things, so with men and boys. Everywhere you carried your rank (or father's rank) with you. A bit rough if it was low. A man was always identified by his job; Mick the Pumpman, Ikey the Electrician, Jackie the Banksman. A stoneman heading a set of men attained the dizzy heights of having a place named after him. I used to imagine 'Just fancy, Chaplin's Fifth West!' The mind boggled at the thought. You had your job; you had your nickname also, sometimes inherited, sometimes for some skill or idiosyncracy ('Bebber', 'Cowboy', 'Boxer', 'Soldier').

Interesting to trace incidence of mental disorders in the coalfield. I have a hunch that few were neurotic. You knew where you were; you were known and named. At the very least, if you didn't like it, you could lump it. At any rate, the pit was softened and personalised by this process. The process survived even intensive longwall working, and I suppose it survives into this power-loading age. In *The Thin Seam* there is a passage where the hero goes through a trap-door into some workings disused for many years:

> I walked into the past with a queer kind of expectant dread, as if the ghost of me 13 years lost might be waiting round the next bend. The place was standing well, I must say. Anderson's set had driven it straight and true and well-girdered and lagged . . . Thirteen years, and excepting for thick layers of dust, you might swear the place was ready to start coal-work again . . . I walked into the district until I came to the end of the winning, the abandoned stone-face, as Anderson had left it. On the last girder was chalked, 'Eight yards paid'. The chalk was as fresh as if put on yesterday. I stood there a moment, uneasily. After a while I heard voices.

For me, reading this passage after twenty years, the pitman's terminology stands out. 'Bend', 'place', 'set', 'lagged', 'coal-work', 'district', 'winning' – these words breathe life.

A wrought place, the pit was as real and as intimate in its associations as the house where you were born, but more importantly it was the arena and testing ground where, for good or for ill, you found your rank and integrity. It's not for nothing that for every miner the pit is 'she'; possibly one reason why women have always had the thick end of the stick in mining villages – there was a sensual satisfaction in holding your place down there against *her*.

For some – amongst whom must be included the women – being born in a pit village must have meant lifelong suffering and frustration. It must have seemed a prison. For many it offered most of the things men seek – identity, the recognition of their peers, a place, carefully defined boundaries, richness in work and leisure. If the clever lad made his way up the ladder from deputy to under-manager to manager, even managing director or coal-owner, that was all right. They most found what they wanted in the home-pit and village. Sustaining evidence of a sort: in my boyhood and early manhood the recognised ways to 'get out' were up the Union ladder or by getting into Parliament, and there was something contemptible in becoming a clerk (which anyway involved going over to *them),* or in buying an insurance book. I can vividly remember being ashamed and secretive about my early writing efforts. Note how in the thirties the folk who'd gone down to Leicester or Evesham brought their dead back here; how they still stream back from the new coalfields to the old village during the holidays. After all, I can remember my pride in my father because the men considered him a good electrician; the thrill that ran through me when a man stopped me, and said: 'Thou's Joe Charlton's grandson, isn't tha? The man that could cut through a cage rope in three bats (blows)!' Skill and physical strength, you see.

And very satisfying. My Grandad and the town intellectuals used to foregather in 'The Surtees' at Shildon, in the Snug. There was no question of it ever being reserved to them. That was their rank. Naturally, most of the 'intellectuals' were gaffers, but there were quite a few pitmen and craftsmen amongst them. Their rank took them there. The man who shouldered his way past the Snug and along the passage into the bar would never dream of gate-crashing. He was looking for his own.

All this was poised, as I was to discover, precisely and exactly balanced on a power structure, which went on and on in steps and stairs. While there was an undying antagonism between ours and the next village (Byers Green), which was kept alive by lads, the two Lodges raised their banners together in times of trouble and the men were bonded together just as certainly as the two pits were linked underground. And just as certainly as we linked up with Byers Green, and Westerton, and Willington, we all linked up together with the DMA at Red Hills, Red Hills facing Coal Trade Hall across the Tyne.

I have to guard myself against waxing poetic on the theme of this great galaxy of villages, each with the pit as its focal point, and each nurturing a sort of semi-tribal community which, in the light of present-day urban society, seems almost a dream of paradise – a sort of pitman's *Paradiso,* safely set in the remote past. The corrective is to remember the harshness, the disease, the filth, above all the smells. At the same time, their achievements cry out for celebration. Against all the odds, they and the folk who inhabited them built up communities prepared for every contingency, little societies of great strength and resilience and full of vigour and humour. Almost by accident, as it were the pattern engendered an education in the humanities and initiation for the child. Like every other industrial settlement, the pit village had its quota of brutes and bullies, but it also produced some of the finest human beings it has been my great good fortune to know. For many the village certainly was a prison: it became such a prison to me that in the end I just had to break out. But perhaps there was much to be learned from that also. I broke out, only to find myself so shaped and moulded by the village that in many ways I remained inextricably its prisoner – inextricably, but willingly, and for life.

There was a great stress on outdoor life, and I suppose it was simply because the houses were so small. It was just a practical thing that one got out. Though there is great talk about drinking today, there was much more drinking when I was a boy. There was all hell let loose on Friday night and Saturday night, and there was fighting. I mean, ours was a little village of about, I suppose, never more than a thousand people, and at ten o'clock on Saturday night it sounded like Newcastle at midday. There were fights going on here, there and everywhere. It was hard drinking and weekly drinking, and then they were off and at work again. Then there were the pigeons. One of my earliest memories, in fact, is an old man I called grandad, who played an extraordinarily influential part in my life, taking me into his pigeon cree and saying 'There, lad, that was only laid today'. Incidentally, this was during the 1920-1 strike, just before I started school and it was the first time I ever tasted margarine, and margarine was hellish stuff in those days. It's relatively civilised today, although nobody will ever convince me it's as good as butter. You could smell it a mile away, and during that strike was the first time we were ever reduced to eating it. And this old man gave me the pigeon's egg, he must have known that times were a little bit hard, and he said 'Tak that hyam and get thee mother to boil it'. One little pigeon's egg, and I took it home and my mother boiled it, and it was just as he said. It turned out to be as sweet as the nut he said it would be. I've never forgotten that pigeon's egg. I don't think I've ever had another one since, but it was lovely.

The games of childhood – of which there were dozens and dozens from booler-ing to top-whipping, about thirty games of marbles (tally-ho, follow-me-leader, and so on) – all encouraged, it seems to me, the idea of rank of hierarchy. Men played marbles, tipcat, throwing fag cards, as well. It's tempting to pose that the games (adult and child) were practised and held in high regard not only as modes of entertainment, but because they trained the reflex and motor skills at a premium in mining. I don't think this was the case. Rural mining (as it was then) took over complete many of the games, as it did speech, customs, traditions, from the country folk – and then bent them to its needs.

There were the pigeons, and there was cricket and there was football, and there was quoits – quoit playing everywhere. The most familiar sound, I think, of my boyhood, next to the sound of the drivers shouting at the ponies as the tubs were pulled along the pitheap top – you know these conical heaps that you see nowadays, well they're a comparatively recent development. The old pits had long, ridged heaps, because the grade had to be in favour of the load so they were just constantly extended. The stones were brought out of the cage and the pony-lads drove the tubs along the heap top and tipped them at the end by hand, and that was a familiar sound of my boyhood. But the other one was the ring of quoits – a beautiful, clear-ringing sound. And the arguments that went on, and the way they measured up with their fingers, 'I've a finger ahead of thou', or 'I've two fingers ahead of thou', or measuring up with – it got to such a fine point – a piece of straw. Of course a great deal depended on it – maybe a two-penny packet of Woodbines, which was an awful lot in those days. Because nobody ever played for nothing, this is something that you must remember. The great outdoor occupation and the basis of all sport, which was infinitely rich in those days, was gambling. And gambling wasn't something organised by bookmakers or by the horse-racing industry or the greyhound-racing industry, it was something organised by the people themselves. And everything was an occasion for gambling.

I can remember the last of the great handball games. I think the last handball game I saw was round about 1927, and I never saw another one until two years ago, and I saw it in Dublin Castle yard where they've got a handball court, and very clever they were at it. It's a wonderful game. A wonderful hard, fast game. The back of every pub had a clear space and it was marked out, an area marked out where the ball had to 'stot' from was the word used (it's an expressive enough word, I don't have to explain it) and these men stripped to the waist. Two men stripped to the waist would have a game with a very hard rubber ball and the game was to keep the ball going within the appropriate spaces on the wall. And of course the one who kept it going longest, just as in tennis, was the one who won. And it was a great occasion for gambling. As a matter of fact there was one occasion in our village where one man was by way of becoming virtually champion of south-west Durham, and a syndicate got together to support him, and everybody wondered why he was flourishing because these were fairly hard times. The local farmer was wondering what was happening to his mobile mutton, because as they were running out of meat for the champion they were taking a lamb or a sheep.

On another occasion in a nearby village, one of the champions, just to give an occasion for a match, he was so unbeatable, took on another chap with one arm tied behind his back, and he played one-handed. And he beat the other fellow. But the whole basis of it was the side bets, and probably there were bookies there, but most people did their side-betting themselves and people would bet on everything.

You went out walking during the week and you could pick up the sign – I mean, chocolate paper among the whin bushes was where the courting couples had been, but woodbine ends was where the lads had been playing cards, and where there was a clear space, like a circular ring, flattened out, that was the pitch and toss school. And by gum that was wonderfully organised because they had their watchers, the men who watched out, they had the bebber (that was the man who tested the pennies and declared them good and true) and the man who watched the pennies thrown because they hadn't to go any higher than ten feet, and he judged them with his eye. And if he said they went higher than ten feet than the bet was off. And then there was the man who took the bets. And of course there were various grades of schools, and you could go into the shilling school, or you could go into the half-crown school, or you could go into the quid-a-time school.

I knew a chap who went out one Sunday morning with his last half-crown. He had been on the booze the day before, and he graduated through three schools in a day, and went home with £120 in his pocket, which was a small fortune in those days, only to be told by his wife when he was setting off to go to the pub that night, 'Is there somebody waiting for you outside, Jack?' 'What do you mean?' 'Well, there's a couple of fellows sort of been looking at the house', and he had a look outside, of course, and it was a couple of chaps from Newcastle way who had been involved in this big school – the big-money school, as they called it. And he decided he wouldn't go out. But thirst got too much for him and he went out the back way, but they had two men watching the back way as well, and they stripped him of everything, even his shirt – by a savage quirk of wit, I suppose – and left him lying there, and took his £120 away with them. Of course, he wasn't going to leave £120 in the house, the wife might have found it!

One sport I haven't mentioned was bare-fist fighting. The school-yard was tough. This again ties up with the idea of hierarchy. You fought for place. Then you held it by force. The schoolmaster would no more think twice about skelping you about the legs than the village slop hesitate to kick your backside out of it, or the overman to raise his yardstick to you. But this isn't to say that the weak went to the wall (outside the playground!). Moral force went a long way. Combined with physical strength and the gift of tongues it was irresistible. I've heard of Jim Robson, in the early days of the Union at West Auckland, standing in his shirt-sleeves on the village green to take in contributions, the set of his chin and shoulders telling men they'd better cought up or else. . . A man who in a crowded Council meeting had just to slap the table with his hand to get immediate silence and attention from more than three hundred brawling delegates. I can remember meeting Peter Lee marching up to Westcott Chapel (Ferryhill) to preach, and automatically stepping off the pavement to make way for him.

The part the chapel played in the life of our little village was very important. It was a Primitive Methodist Chapel, and contrary to all the superstitions about Methodism, Wesley had very little impact on the miners in the North-East. It was the Primitive Methodists who came between 1821 and 1840, who had the greatest impact on the miners, and who gradually worked out that influence first in a great spiritual revival which went to the building of chapels and congregations and so on, and then the great social awakening which led to the building of the trade unions and the Labour Party and then died and withered away. I count myself fortunate that in a little isolated village I saw remnants of all these – the earliest phases and the final phases. It was an extraordinary situation because these people came in 1821 and they seemed to touch some sort of deep psychic need because you read about John Nelson, for instance, preaching at Sunderland in the open air to thousands. And this was their great thing, of course, preaching in the open air, and this became the camp meeting. Then there was the love feast, which was a sort of faith tea, everybody brought food and if you didn't have food, well you could go anyway because there would be sure to be food – there would be food for everybody, you could bet your boots on that. The prayer meeting was based on this and was held largely in the open air. They even had a camp meeting on the top of Cross Fell. I don't know if any of you have ever been on top of Cross Fell, but one of the roughest winds in Britain starts off there – the Helm wind, which is reckoned to be so powerful that it can rip in half the neb of a steg (that is the bill of a goose) – and these people had a camp meeting on the top of Cross Fell.

A strange psychic phenomenon. I've seen it. I've seen it at work. They used to have fallers – people who fell under conviction. They used to have standers – people who stood up and spoke out. And they used to have walkers – and apparently (this is something I'd really like to have seen) – people who would walk all round the chapel along the pew edges and never fall down, they had such a tremendous sense of balance. But quite part from this they had this tremendous moral influence – and remember this was the time of the gin mill and very bitter harsh times when, I suppose, for the majority of people life was so bloody awful the only way out of it seemed the moment you got out of the pit to get into the nearest gin mill and sup gin, or whatever. But these people had a tremendous moral influence, and one of the reasons there are very few rapper dancers left in the North-East is the fact that most of the rapper dancers were converted *en masse*. I think it was at Old Haswell where an entire team of eight were converted and they took their rappers to the blacksmith and had them turned into gullies (that's bread knives) and sold them in aid of the chapel.

Well, it wasn't like this at all when I was young. I wouldn't say this for a moment. But they were very devout, very simple and very plain people. And wonderful preachers. A wonderful feeling for, and gift of, the Word, and before ever I was able to read adequately, and certainly long before I thought about writing, I got the elements of real literature from the last of the ranters who, pretty often, without being able to read – some of them were so illiterate that they'd learned their lessons by heart – become wonderful preachers. I knew one old man who, until 1940 – he lived until 1940 – Jack Bedonfield, who memorised his reading for the night. His wife read it over to him time and time again until he had it word perfect. He would open the bible – an innocent little deception – and proceed to read it. But preach – wonderful preachers, you know. And it was all story telling. Marvellous story telling. And the whole life of the community was centred around the chapel, and I suppose at Anniversary time all the kids went there. Even in 1926 and 1921 – the hard times – all the little lassies got new dresses for Anniversary time, and this was one occasion when the Primitive Methodists went on the streets again and did a circuit of the village and sang hymns, and everybody went to chapel and it was packed out that night. It was a wonderful feeling, and they had their camp meetings too. I can remember the men of the chapel pulling the hay wain to the top of the little eminence in the meadow near the chapel, and preacher after preacher getting up. But there were not very many people there, I'm afraid. What did used to draw the people was in fact the annual chapel picnic. And there were two farmers in great rivalry. They were both called Hutchinson. There were the poor Hutchinsons and the rich Hutchinsons, and I'm afraid the rich Hutchinsons always got the edge over the poor Hutchinsons. I can remember on one occasion the men of the chapel decided to go one year to the poor Hutchinsons, to their meadow, and one year to the rich Hutchinsons, and make it fair. I can remember one year, the men of the chapel shouldering the trestles and the boards and all of us kids following with our mugs, and what have you, and marching along with our Sunday School teachers, and this great hay wain coming along pulled by two draught horses and we went along in style, and we considered that a great treat.

There was a great social life and a great feeling, and I have in fact seen as a child many occasions when, at the end of the service, the entire congregation would rise to their feet, and with one accord, nobody would tell them to do it, sing the Doxology, 'Praise God from whom all blessings flow'. And it was very moving. But as I saw, it found its best expression in the trade union movement. Five of the seven men transported to Botany Bay from Jarrow after the great strike of 1832, for instance, were Primitive Methodists. This happened time and time again: in West Cramlington in 1860, of the eleven who went to jail, nine were local preachers or Sunday School Superintendents. At the same time, mind you, it is fair to report that when a Primitive Methodist Evangelist round about 1830, called Gelley, who was apparently the whiz kid of the times, came up, the coal-owners of Northumberland and Durham engaged him, and paid him to go round the colliery villages. So it worked both ways. But the outcome finally was that the energies of Primitive Methodism, and one saw all this as a child, went in to the trade union side, went into a Lodge. But not by a long shot into the Labour Party. Most of the Primitive Methodists were Liberals to a man and there followed a great Lib/Lab cleavage which is never talked about today.

Of course, one went out – the first thing one did when one got out of chapel on a Sunday evening was to go for a long walk. There were walks across the fields that one knew well. One walked everywhere. As the eldest child, I was often walked to stay with my maternal grandparents at Shildon. It was one of the economic as well as loving facts of family life that very often the first-born male child was virtually adopted by the grandparents. In some cases truly adopted. In Ashington you will find to this day men with two names. One name on the colliery books, and one name they go under – the name on the colliery books is their own name, their parents' name; the name they go by is their grandparents' name. They are elder sons who were wholly adopted. I was an eldest son and I was virtually adopted, and I was away with my grandparents every holiday that came. And we always walked, it was about five or six miles. I would set off with dad and it meant nothing because there was this great place at the end of it. My grandad and my grandma and these five great uncles who would take me out mushrooming and getting wasps' nests and taking me fishing. Then I would get to Shildon Show, or there would be a pig killing, or something like that, you know. And it was a great thing.

I can remember once being terribly homesick for my grandma's, and my granda meant much more to me, I've got to admit to my shame, than my mother. I was so homesick that one night I actually set off walking and I got halfway there, and I suddenly realised they would be wondering about me at home, the commotion it would cause, and I turned back. I got a right hiding for my pains, of course. They didn't know what had happened, I never told them. This was another thing, of course, reticence. I suppose it was another part of the realism of the times. One rarely showed affection. You never kissed your mother, or even your grandparents. You never talked about your innermost feelings.

This was something, I suppose, for which the Primitive Methodists were responsible, because they departmentalised this, you know, they put it inside the chapel.

The very nature of pit work made most women slaves, wives and daughters all. Shifts split up the family so that men would be coming in at all hours of the day, waiting for the bath-tin and the water and a woman to wash their backs. Then clean the boots and wash and/or dry the duds. 'Service' was the only escape and amelioration of that black tragedy of the mining family – too many daughters. (Lads not only brought in money but added to status). Between Newfield and Leeds, for example, there was a long attachment. The treatment by Jewish folk of Durham lasses was always civilised and often generous to a degree. I knew of one family where five daughters in turn served the same family, each receiving a handsome gift on marrying. Not so locally. The aunt of a friend of mine went as maid-servant to the pit manager's wife. 'Lily's too good a name for a servant,' said the lady, 'I'll call you Jane'. And Jane she was, till she went elsewhere.

Methodism softened the lot of women in the pit villages enormously;

the factory brought final liberation; but how I ache for the pin-cleanliness, the wealth of homely wisdom and home-cooking of the older pit villages! Then women made homes; now they buy comfort. Of course, the shine and glitter of the colliery house must have concealed many a fathomless hell of sexual, spiritual and mental deprivation. But not, I suspect, much. That sort of thing comes through.

More misery came from 'keeping back' most of the weekly pay than from any other factor. But on the whole there was nothing but contempt for the kind of man such as one who lived many years next door to us, marching up the back street and muttering 'That's for her, that's for me' as he shoved the lion's share of his pay into his waistcoat pocket. You see, there were too many sacntions against wholesale 'keeping back' (safe though it was), the strongest being rank. A man had to keep his end up, no matter what.

I seem to remember more women running the home and ruling their husbands than the reverse; but in between I'd say was a sizeable majority who split the responsibility, she the running of the home and the family, he the pit and his own leisure, meeting all reasonable demands. The shift system made more opportunities for illicit affairs than were ever taken. The village was too small and had too many eyes. It was then, and is today, I suspect, astonishingly restricted.

Looking at the gravestones in Newfield churchyard some years ago, I was struck by the fact that Newfield lads had on the whole married Newfield lasses (also by the astonishing proportion of deaths, both male and female, in early middle life). It strikes me that the insularity in marriage is due not so much to lack of enterprise as simple *nous* on the part of a girl. The majority married when they 'got into trouble'; easier to pin down your man in your own village where all the sanctions worked in the woman's favour. It could be a profitable line of study.

The ceremonial of the seasons, the kitchen, of birth, marriage and death, all were bent to the usage of the village. Bidders went out two by two before a funeral and knocked at doors; 'You are invited to the burial of So-and-so, tomorrow, Wednesday. Mourners gather at No.22, High Row at half-past one; coffin lifts at two'. As a child, you were expected to go and see the deceased playmate. I never saw a coffin on trestles outdoors, with the four glasses of wine or spirits on a napkin for the refreshment of the bearers. As near as possible, friends would be bearers; often sons in the case of a father. People would walk in twos behind the hearse, black ebony and glass, drawn by two plumed horses, and the mourners' cabs. The bereaved wore black if females, or black ties and caps, until after a memorial service held a fortnight later. The teas were grand. Not only the food, but the crack was good. There was an enormous sense of release.

Weddings were held Saturdays, so that the couple could spend their honeymoon (the weekend) with relatives in the nearby town or village.

Only the very 'posh' went on a proper honeymoon. Although there were still plenty of big families around in the twenties when I went to school, the change had already set in. Perhaps other, more powerful, factors were at work, but the pit pattern of bord and pillar, in which hundreds of hewers per shift in the larger pits worked the narrow 'bords' or headings on the perimeter of the pillars, and were supplied with tubs by drivers, putters and pit ponies, was fast going, and this meant that a large family of sons was no longer a social and economic asset. On the contrary, the cutting machines came faster and in large numbers to the North-East than to any other coalfield, reducing the need for both men and boys. This must have helped to change attitudes to a degree. We were a family of six, but long before the last baby arrived I can remember my mother complaining of 'being looked down upon' for having so many. Lockout, Strike and Depression completed the job.

In the meantime, I can recall Mrs Matthews two doors down from my Grandmother's call in the family by their first names at bedtime – a feat of memory as well as breath. And stories stick in my mind of one father chalking off his bairns on the caller's slate by the door as they arrived; another putting a neighbour's bairn to bed with the rest. How they slept in two-bedroomed houses is a miracle – a big bed, or it may be two, occupying the whole room; the children sometimes alternating head to foot. Think of the old days when there was only the garret with a ladder up to it, and the wind and the rain blowing or soaking through the straw in the holes! Families of 13, 16 and 21! Incidentally, in the older villages you can mark along the colliery rows where the second storey was added to make proper bedrooms, bricks on top of stone.

I have been told that a bottle of whiskey was bought for Mrs Moses, the good neighbour who delivered me; that she insisted on a second bottle for the christening led to 'words' between my parents. A friend of the family carried the bairn to church for the christening, and the first person you met of the opposite sex to the child on leaving the house was presented with silver and a piece of christening cake – I know, because as a child it once happened to me. The houses on Adelaide's Bank have long been pulled down, along with the pit headgear and engine house, and I often wonder what luck I brought that baby girl. After the christening, there were the traditional gifts from all of silver, salt and a box of matches. My wife still gives silver to a new-born baby, often to the great embarrassment of the Southron. In those days, of course, a wife wouldn't dream of being seen out of the house after having had a baby before she had been churched.

All the seasons were rich in domestic ceremony and celebration – the Yule log to carry the fire through into the real new year, which went from Christmas to Christmas; pace egg rolling and jarping (the latter a great occasion for betting); your new suit or dress always at Whit or an Anniversary Day, whichever came first. I mustn't forget First Footing, Guising at Christmastide, Carling, Pancake, Palm and Pace Egg Days, or Harvest Festival. Or the way people rushed out to hear what the crake-man had to say – Lodge meeting or whatever.

In my boyhood there were still pitmen who'd turn back home if they met a woman on the way to work in foreshift, and pitwives who put the cat in the oven on cavilling day (when the lots were drawn for the quarter's place of work). Baby's fingernails were bitten, not cut with scissors, up to their first birthday. If you were on your way to work and discovered you'd left something, your mother always made you sit down for a while before you left (a relic of the times when folk engaged in prayer before a journey?). And so on, and so on. The women maintained these traditions and superstitions. They were the memory of the community. The one traditional song I can remember was 'Down the Waggonway', used by my mother as a cradle song.

I think that if seeing the pits spread out at night was my first great memory, the second was at five years of age being lifted on to ample shoulders, and seeing the banner being lifted for the first time to go off to the Gala. The odd thing was that belonging to a family of pit craftsmen (and becoming one myself) I missed the experience of the big meeting in childhood, something I shall always regret. So I never saw the big meeting until I was 16, and it so happend that year they allowed us the day off. We didn't work any overtime, and I went to Durham. And what a sight that was! It's just pathetic to see the two or three dozen banners parade today, because that morning, at about 7.30, a pal and I came in by train, and we stood at the top and we saw the first banner start, and we saw banner after banner pass by and the bands playing. And all those serried ranks of men – because they were proud of being in the union. Those serried ranks of men with their 24-inch bottoms to their trousers, all swinging as they marched, going down the field. And they were coming in – we marched with about the thirtieth banner – down from the County, and there they were coming in from the New Inn as well, and we went up to Elvet, and they were coming in from that side, and they were coming down from the Sunderland side. In those days there were about 150 pits, of course, 150 bands, 150 banners, and it was a great and glorious sight. Each one represented the village, and each village was very much like my own. And each village was, in fact, a sort of self-constructed, do-it-yourself counter-environment, you might dub it. The people had built it themselves. There was everything there, in the pit village. The Lodge was there to look after the interests of the men at the pit, and they had built up a kind of equipoise with the coal owners. They had fought them to a standstill. And this remained true until roughly 1926, and then the break-up came.

But in addition to this you had a sort of complete welfare system. You had your Sons of Temperance, and you had your Reccabites and you had sick clubs. You had your Hearts of Oak, which was traditionally for the mechanics and you had your Workmen's Club, which also had its social and educational side. Very much stronger than it is now. And you had your aged miners' homes, and you had your hospital scheme, which was run through the union. And there was the Lodge secretary with his galluses (that's his braces) hanging down his side. And his door was never shut, his door was always open. Jug Goundry, as rough a diamond as you could ever wish to meet, blind drunk every Friday or Saturday night and pretty often on a Sunday night as well, but an encyclopaedia of social welfare. If you were in trouble, if you had an accident down pit, if you were negotiating a new agreement, if you wanted an aged miner's home, if you had trouble with your coal – that is, your concessionary coal – if you wanted some roof repairs doing on your colliery house, if your lad had to go to hospital and you needed the ambulance, well you went to Jug. So the banner, which was so beautiful, represented something very solid and very substantial indeed, and while one recognises that all things have to go, and mining as it was in the North-East has gone, and perhaps in many ways has gone for good, one also has to recognise that there was a great achievement and that the greatest of these achievements was that with the poorest of materials, in the poorest of circumstances, fighting a battle underground and fighting a battle against bad housing and bad sanitation on the surface and poor wages, people banded together and built in their villages little communities which were quite something to live for.

I know as a child I felt very very secure, very very secure indeed. When later in life I went to London I found the one thing that distressed me was that it was about ten degrees hotter than it was in the North-East. Another thing that distressed me above all was that as I was walking down the Strand or Fleet Street there was neebody to say

'What chay, Sid', and in a pit village, of course, there was always somebody to say that. You were known, you were named, you had your place, you could make your mark in life. And there's not very much more than this you can ask of life. So the mining villages were quite something in Durham. The pattern as I knew it has gone now, of course, but I think its folk deserve a place in our history, if only for the extraordinary ties of kinship they created and the way they made an occupation into a tolerable way of life. Rough and ready it may have been – but I am still glad to warm my hands at the living memory of what it had to offer.

5 THE LEEK

Bill Williamson

My father is a leek judge, and a deadly serious one at that, and so was my grandfather. It was only when I'd been away from the area for some years that I really began to appreciate the importance of big leeks and leek shows in the North-East of England. Before that, the big leeks were part of the everyday world which I had come to take for granted. It was my grandfather who started off the judging in the family and I was apprenticed to it at the age of 18. In a family like that it would have been difficult to think of leek-growing as in any way curious. But over the whole region – in the pubs and workingmen's clubs – leeks are an important topic of conversation.

From a very early age you simply accept that leek-growing and the paraphernalia which goes with it are important, that leeks and leek shows have a place in the scheme of things, just like weddings, funerals, christenings and Poppy Day. Nothing curious about them at all – especially when you know that something of the order of a million pounds is spent on leek-show prizes each year, and in a good show the winner might get anything from a refrigerator to a motorcar, though the fridge is more likely. Prizes like that are worth working for, but the reasons for growing leeks are too complex to be reduced to the simple 'donkey and carrot' theory of why men do things. The big leeks are the symbol of the whole regional culture.

For most people the leek is simply a vegetable – small, green, related to the onion – and one that isn't eaten very often. Southerners may know that it grows wild on the Welsh hillsides, but that's the limit of their knowledge. Show leeks have leaves, or, as they say here, 'flags', which may be over three feet long and whose 'bulb' or white part, measures six inches from button to beard, the button being the dividing point between the white of the leek and its leaves. Three leeks like this are put together to make a 'stand' for showing, and their collective volume, by and large, settles their place in the show. But once again, it's not so simple. Leek-judging has its technology – tapes, gauges and ready-reckoners – but it hasn't been rationalised into a mechanical operation.

Those leeks are of a special breed. An Aberdeen botanist – a friend of the author Sid Chaplin, to whom I owe this piece of information – carried out an analysis of leek genetics and found the breed to be peculiar to the North-East. And although September is the Month of the Leek, leek-growing goes on all the year round. It begins immediately after the show with the selection of seed pods from the 'good breeds': this can often mean trekking over the region to purchase a leek or two from the winners of well-known shows like the 'Durham News of the World'. In January the pods are 'boxed' and the seedlings reared until May, when they're 'trenched', and 'fed up' for the show.

Some things are rarely understood fully, and this is true of the leek. Success at the show seems to depend firstly on access to the good breeds (through a finely-graded hierarchy of 'big growers'), and secondly on one's knowledge of 'leek-feeding'. Human childbirth and rearing has its rich folklore, and so does leek-growing. Leeks are known to have been fed on beer, urine, blood, human waste (in one case I know of a whole family which was barred from the lavatory for a fortnight to provide a good supply of feeding material; in another case a Northumberland pitman fed his leeks on the scrapings of the baby's nappy, and swore blind that his leeks won because they'd been fed on 'pure mother's milk'). Sophisticated chemical solutions are also available. A chemist in Stanley, County Durham, sells a mixture for ailing leeks at 50p a bottle. It's a privilege to be able to report these prescriptions for growing leeks, for they're jealously guarded secrets. Pitmen usually conceal their modifications of leek genetics in a gentle folklore of cultivation, denying that they'd do more than manipulate the blessings of the Lord himself – water, sunshine and manure.

The range of leek potions available is a testimony to human ingenuity and defies full documentation. Leek-growers conceal their knowledge from the world. To do otherwise would violate the secret contract which the grower has with his leek. Indeed, to reveal one's techniques is to admit defeat in the annual battle of horticultural wits, to write off, perhaps, years of carefully sifted experience. Asked what he feeds his leeks on, a typical grower would normally reply: 'Nowt, hinny – wey, nowt special. Aa just keeps the soil loose and watters them regular'.

Leek-growing takes time. It involves long hours loosening the soil in the trench; feeding; watering; and, so it's been recommended, talking to the leeks. Given the increase in 'nobbling' which takes place now, as much as four months before the show, a great deal of time must also be spent virtually on guard, and certainly men do sit up with their leeks overnight before the show and patrol the allotments.

On the morning of the show, immediately after breakfast, the leeks are lifted. Often as many as ten have to be lifted to find a good stand of three. Their flags are stripped off to lengthen the white part of the leek or to find a firm button. The experience is painful and exciting, for it's only now that the quality of the leeks can be assessed realistically. The pain of the situation comes from the knowledge that some leeks will be wasted, or that some have been savaged by sub-soil infections, or even discoloured by injections of artificial feeders. Each leek will be greeted with a mixture of astonishment an remorse: 'Wey– luk at that. Wad ya believe it: it's ower lang'. Or: 'These are a bonny breed'. Each is lifted, and eased out of the trench to avoid damage: they're all treated as if they're perfect examples of the species. Next, they're gently washed in milk or oil, their beards combed and cleaned, and finally they're wrapped in a clean, damp cloth. The delicate care of this operation brings the pitman closer to an understanding of childbirth and mother hood than he'd even allow himself to come in the confines of his family life. The point may escape the pitman, and almost certainly he's repress the analogy, but it's not insignificant that the growth cycle of the leek covers a full nine months!

Just before noon the leeks are placed in a bucket and with continuing care are carried to the Club. The children 'help' in this, seizing their first, or their annual (and illicit), drink of beer from their father's glass. At this point the pitman is still in his working clothes: baggy pants, white collarless shirt and boots. The casual observer might be forgiven if he mistook the procession of staid uniforms and bucketed leeks for the activities of a religious cult.

The care and control exercised by the grower is paralleled by the care and control which is a part of the show itself, its rules and its judging. Decisions to show must be registered by March and fees of £2 paid. Judging is carried out by an independent practitioner locked in the room where the leeks have been 'benched'. He in turn may be controlled by his membership of the Northern Leek-Growers Association, which seeks to standardise judging and protect competitors. Leeks must be 'freshly pulled with firm button', and to ensure that huge leeks do not go the rounds and win a number of shows, all the leeks are stamped at least a week before the show. Judging itself is a hazardous process. The judge has to look for old leeks, for split buttons, and for incredible violations of the rules ranging from the case of the Wooden Leek to the leek which has been filled with a hypodermic injection of milk. Judges decide the distribution of prizes, sometimes worth hundreds of pounds, as well as the annual pecking order of champions (normally an annual reshuffle of the placings of a handful of big growers, who care little for the prize, since their homes are already furnished from the shows anyway).

Unlike many other judges or referees they are called to account for every decision made. The social status of the judge is high and can be measured by the attitudes towards him adopted by the club officials and helpers. Everything is engineered to ensure that the judge is segregated from the growers. He's offered no advice. Even the judges' secretaries are careful not to intrude upon his concentration and sole right to make decisions. He's paid a fee, which he himself determines, and which can be as much as a week's wages. He's truly professional, even if it's only for one afternoon.

When you enter the showroom the first thing you notice is the distinctive odour of leeks, a cross between boiled cabbage and fresh onions. The room itself is ornate with prizes ranged in expensive tiers around the walls, arrangements of flowers and gaudy shreds of tinsel woven around the tables. The judge brings to this situation a unique knowledge of other clubs and growers' tricks, and a distinctive northern aesthetic appreciation of leek quality. The bigger and more opulent the show the greater the intensity of his concern, since later in the evening he'll find himself defending his decisions against disgruntled growers. It is, in fact, expected that, for a brief period at least, the judge will be available to explain the reasons behind his decisions in a ritualistic encounter with big growers. These encounters reveal a number of techniques which the judge uses to defend the validity of his choice. He is encircled by club officials and growers, and they're all drinking by this time, each one looking for the vindication of his own argument. There's little a grower can do to change his position in the show. The judge, after all, is an experienced practitioner. Even if he was wrong, he wouldn't admit it. In fact, if he were ever forced to change a decision he wouldn't be asked to come again the next year to judge the show. But his reasons for being steadfast are still more complicated than this.

Part of the attraction of growing leeks is to have one's views and theories about leek technology (which growers talk about knowingly and evasively all the year round) vindicated by a respected, independent judge. Any dent in the image of himself which the judge can project would not only ruin his own reputation but would leave a trail of disappointment among the growers. Their arguments about who was right would not be settled, victory itself would leave a sour taste.

One technique used by the judge to secure his position, and easily the most interesting to watch, is that of 'cooling out' the grower:

forcing him to accept a new definition of his position, although he may initially be reluctant to do so. In this case the judge always refers to the onlooking committee men:

> Yiv got ti agree that the leek's got feeda burns on't. And look at that button: it's var' nye split reet across. And Aa aalways say that you shud fancy eatin a gud-quality leek. Noo luk at that. Wad ye fancy heving that for your suppa? Wey, Aa shud think not – ne bugga would. It wud born holes in yor belley . . . In fact, ye knaa what? If Aa was startin to judge all ower again Aa think Aa wud hev ti knock them buggas back farther. So think yasel lucky and let's hev ne mair complainin!

The case is now secure.

The judge invariably gains esteem from these encounters, and, apart from the fee to be collected at the end, his greatest reward (which he actively seeks) is to hear the Leek Club secretary confirm to him that the judging has been good and fair. 'Well done, hinny. Yev dun a gud job thair. Nivva mind aboot them buggas complainin, they're always the same. Aa's satisfied and we'll hev ye back agin next year.'

As he goes around examining the exhibits – which to the uninitiated look indistinguishable from one another – the finely cultivated perceptions of the judge are themselves on show:

> Ah, that's a bonny stand . . . Here's some canny leeks, bluddy smashers . . . Luk at them buggas, great whoppers, fed on shite and shunshine by the luks on it . . . Thisun's badly blenched: it's a pity cos it's well-shaped . . . An auld leek here, hinny. Ne doot it was shown at Blucher last week . . .Feel that: well-blenched, firm, just like silk . . . These buggas hevn't been washed proper . . . Noo luk at that: eh, that's a find stand.

If show leeks could be bought like ordinary leek seedlings, then all this would be totally irrelevant, but they are not in fact acquired this way. Although leek-growing does have its commercial side (men do make money from the growing and selling of leeks), the market for leeks is entrenched in a local network of growers, and access to the market does not depend upon money. Rather, it depends upon relationships cultivated over the years through work, through leek-growing and through visiting other clubs. The big growers who effectively, though not intentionally, control the distribution of leeks, particularly the better breeds, are not in leek-growing for the money – which is a further aspect of the situation which makes a market model of the system inappropriate.

The complex technology of the leek is paralleled by an equally complex system of social relationships among the big growers. They are few in number and well-known throughout the region: they dominate the system. They alternate as judges and sages; in practice they control the quality of the breeds available. Their involvement in the shows stems primarily from a concern to protect status rather than to win prizes. The involvement of younger growers, on the other hand, is partly pecuniary but also represents an attempt to break into the older community of the Club, to establish an adult masculine identity. The involvement of young people is much less certain than it used to be, however. The mining labour-force is no longer recruited entirely from the sons of miners: changing patterns of industry and commerce are everywhere in the region changing this traditional self-recruitment. The young find their pleasure and identity less in the village than in the town, and one consequence of this is that leek-growing has become even more the pastime of older men. Such changes will inevitably work themselves through the mining communities, although it's much less certain that leek shows will disappear as rapidly as the pits. Arguably, the show could gain in strength as people cling to the shreds of a declining culture.

Exactly why leek-growing has been and still is central to the community life of the North-East isn't easy to explain. However tempting it may be to advance a Freudian explanation of why grown men of practical bent vie to grow the longest and fattest leek, the answer must be sought elsewhere. While leeks have been grown since the last century, it was only in the Depression that leek shows with big prizes became the dominant pattern. In the thirties the North-East was among the worst-hit areas, and the men had far too much time on their hands. Gardening in general was a common release, combining as it does hard economic sense with a nostalgic rural strain that still runs through the area. The leeks took up lots of time, and the awarding of prizes offered a hope of financial relief to competitors. In better times, growing leeks fitted harmoniously into the daily lives of the miner or even the shipyard worker. It's cheap, certainly compared with hobbies like photography or sailing. The activity is out-of-doors and not strenuous, so that it's compatible with the men's hard occupational lives. For the man of the house it provides a quiet relaxing release from family life (as well as entry into an all-male group), and yet wives are placated because prizes can be large and are universally something for the house.

But the leek offers more than just an individual reward to the grower. Leek-growing is a community thing: while wives and children may be peripheral to it most of the time (as indeed they are to that central institution, the Club), its significance for the men cannot be overstated. The lore of leeks and leek-growing can be exchanged between the keenest rivals throughout the year. The show itself offers the high point of community life and co-operation. The leek club is usually an offshoot of the Club: the leek provides another reason for the Club's existence, while the Club provides the organisational resources to ensure annual continuity.

After the judging at the show, the winners receive public recognition as the exhibits and the prizes are inspected, and in some cases, like the West End Club in Ashington, a communal leek broth is made and doled out to be eaten on 'Leek Monday'. The broth is made in galvanised dustbins and stirred with broom handles. The recipes vary from Mrs Beeton's to concoctions equalled only by the weird sisters in Macbeth. In Ashington, 'Leeky Broth' is made with sheep's heads, sackfuls of potatoes and carrots, and, not least, a selection of the best leeks from the better stands in the show. The leeks are no longer wanted: they've fulfilled their function and they're eaten, served in bowls from the stage to a procession of eager men who are used to standing in queues.

POLITICS IN COUNTY DURHAM

INTRODUCTION

Martin Bulmer

Durham County today, both in Parliament and local government, is dominated by the Labour Party. Durham is indeed a stronghold of Labour. But it was not always so. At the turn of the century, Durham miners, forming one of the strongest and best organised working-class electorates in the country, were staunchly Liberal. One in three men employed in any occupation in the geographical County were miners, so the miners' Liberal allegiance (outside the boroughs on its edge) strongly influenced the political complexion of the area.[1]

There were various reasons for this strong link with Liberalism. Hostility to landlords enjoying unearned mining royalties ensured few vestiges of support for Conservatism. The strength of Methodism in the coalfield from the mid-nineteenth century also helped to ally miners to Liberalism. Anglicanism was weak in mining areas; the Church was directly represented by – and resented as – the Bishopric of Durham enjoying coal royalties. The coal industry feared tariffs, which would damage their export trade. And from 1885, the miners' leaders had come to an arrangement with the Liberal Party to share control of industrial constituencies, a trend foreshadowed by Thomas Burt's election for Morpeth in 1874. The union link was of particular importance in an area such as Northumberland and Durham, which by the 1890s was the most strongly unionised in the whole of the country, with over 11 per cent of the entire population belonging to some union or other.[2]

By the early years of the century, Durham parliamentary constituencies were largely dominated by an electorate working in mining. The DMA was thus able to secure political representation without setting up a new political party. The statues of men such as John Wilson, which stand at the entrance to Redhills (the DMA headquarters), are a visible reminder of the strength of the Liberal-mining link, which until the 1920s provided a solid counterweight to the rise of the Labour Party. The history of this influence in relation to Methodism has been traced by Robert Moore for four west Durham villages at this period.[3]

The Miners' Federation of Great Britain joined the Labour Party in 1910, but the Durham Association did not become politically active until after 1918, when it began to give the Labour Party support in a consistent and organised fashion.[4] This conservatism, reflected also in their earlier slowness in joining the MFGB, was partly due to the greater success in Durham in obtaining higher pay and shorter hours. In the early years of the century, Durham miners at the face were on a seven-hour shift; there was therefore little support for the campaign being waged in other mining areas for legislation to limit the working day to eight hours. The history of the transition from Liberalism to Labour in mining areas at this period has been analysed by Roy Gregory.[5] He estimated that it was not until 1910 that socialists formed even a small majority on the DMA Executive; in terms of parliamentary seats this change did not become apparent until after 1918.

In the period before 1918, there were only three Labour members of Parliament for seats in Durham County (excluding the boroughs on the edge). These were Arthur Henderson, who won the by-election in 1904 which followed the death of Sir Joseph Pease (of the Darlington coal-owning family), MP for Barnard Castle; J.W. Taylor, MP for Chester-le-Street from 1906 following the raising of the local liberal coal-owner MP James Joicey to the peerage; and Pete Curran, MP for Jarrow from 1907 to 1910. At the 1910 elections only two Labour members were returned. Even in 1918, the change was more real than apparent. Two out of eleven county seats returned Labour members; both were miners, R. Richardson and J. Lawson.[6]

The seeds of change had nevertheless been sown. The older generation of Lib-Lab MPs were dying off or retiring. The Labour Party nationally was becoming a larger and better-known political force. Its new 1918 Constitution and reorganisation brought in both the growing number of trade unionists and individual members for the first time. The expansion of the electorate from 7½ million in December 1910 to 21 million in 1918 – with the enfranchisement of all women over 30 who were householders, married to householders or graduates, and all males over the age of 21 who were not already voters – increased the size of the electorate in the County threefold.[7] The deteriorating industrial situation in mining and sharpened conflict after 1918 also brought firmer support for Labour from mining areas, and growing allegiance from newly enfranchised voters. This is not a history of the rise of Labour or an explanation of its occurrence; it is sufficient to note that Labour Party dominance in parliamentary terms was established in the 1920s. By 1929 all eleven county seats were Labour;

although only two (Spennymoor and Chester-le-Street) were retained in 1931, all eleven were won by Labour in 1935 and Ramsay MacDonald (who had succeeded Sidney Webb as MP for Seaham and held the seat in 1931) was defeated. Detailed accounts of the changing fortunes of Labour in the county are provided by Garside and M. Callcott.[8]

An outline account such as the above conceals local variation. In some seats the DMA played a more important role than in others. The MP was an important force at the grass-roots. The Liberal vote in the county was not negligible. But the trend in Labour support overall was clear, and different strands coalesced under the banner of party allegiance.

Nowhere was this more important than on the County Council. Labour gained control of Durham County Council in 1919, lost it in 1922, regained it in 1925 and has held it ever since. Durham was the first county council in Britain to become Labour-controlled; it is remarkable today for the period of continuous one-party control for over 50 years. Yet what is today taken for granted was far from the case in 1919. Social conditions, in particular, were very different, as will be described in chapters 11 and 12.

The influence of the coal-owners and their managers was still felt in every community: much of the local housing was colliery-owned; there was little council housing; few public services in many villages; and not even a unified water supply throughout the area. The impact of the first leader of the Labour Council, Peter Lee, was therefore particularly important. In the chapter which follows, an impression is given of the influence he had on the county, from his biography by Jack Lawson. The history of local politics is as yet unwritten; the extract, though tinged with sentimentality, is a vivid picture of an important leader.

A different perspective upon the same phenomenon is provided in Ellis Thorpe's study of politics and local housing in Coalport, which follows. After water and public transport, the most important resource which local politicians could develop in the inter-war period was local authority housing. Mr Thorpe chronicles this in one medium-sized Durham town, and shows how control of housing remained of cardinal political importance in the post-war period. He also highlights the political dominance of the local area by the Labour Party after it gained control of this local Council in 1930.

Apart from studies of elections and of particular localities, there are unfortunately no contemporary academic studies of politics in County Durham which characterise the political system in general terms. Following the study of Coalport, a short chapter is included by journalist Graham Turner, attempting to provide an overview of the post-1945 political scene. The limitations of such an account should be borne in mind; see Appendix C. Turner's account is based on fairly brief acquaintance with the area, and may be read by some as relatively unsympathetic and even hostile to the character of local politics. How far such views are reflected in the population is of course not known, although one particular controversial planning issue is discussed in chapter 12. In extenuation, it should be noted that Turner draws on extensive conversations with local people both within and outside County Durham. In the absence of more scholarly material, he provides some hypotheses about politics in twentieth-century County Durham which deserve to be tested by further research.

This section on local politics is concluded by a short chapter by the editor, summarising local electoral statistics, discussing the impact of the Poulson affair and examining the applicability of more general models of political structure to the political system. But first Jack Lawson takes us back over half a century, to the General Election of November 1918.

Notes

1. H. Pelling, *Social Geography of British Elections 1885-1910,* London, Macmillan, 1967, Ch. 14; R.S. Moore, *Pitmen, Preachers and Politics,* Cambridge University Press, 1974, Ch. 1.
2. Pelling, *Social Geography*; Moore, *Pitmen.*
3. Moore, *Pitmen.*
4. R. Garside, *The Durham Miners, 1919-60,* London, Allen & Unwin, 1971, Ch. 8; M. Callcott, 'Parliamentary Elections in County Durham between the wars: the making of a Labour stronghold', *Bulletin of the N.E. Group for the study of Labour History,* 8, October 1974, pp.15-19.
5. R. Gregory, *The Miners and British Politics 1906-14,* Oxford University Press, 1968. For a discussion of the meaning of 'radicalism' in mining, see J.H.M. Laslett, 'Why some do and some don't: some determinants of radicalism among British and American coal-miners 1872-1924', *Bulletin of the Society for the Study of Labour History,* No.28, Spring 1974.
6. R. Garside, *The Durham Miners.*
7. Cf. C. Chamberlain, 'The growth of support for the Labour Party in Britain', *British Journal of Sociology,* 24, 1973, pp.474-89.
8. R. Garside; M. Callcott, *op. cit.,* for a fuller account, see also M. Callcott, *Parliamentary Elections in County Durham 1929-35,* unpublished M. Litt. thesis, University of Newcastle-on-Tyne, 1973.

6 THE INFLUENCE OF PETER LEE*

Jack Lawson

November 11, 1918 brought relief to millions who had lived in misery for years. In Britain people were delirious with joy and easy to play upon – as they were played upon by the few powerful ones who had willed a General Election, lest the electors were in different mood when more composed.

Peter Lee took part in that election. In the morning he put a sandwich in his pocket, mounted his cycle and rode to some distant colliery where he thought he was needed. From door to door he went, talking to the people, trying to persuade them that better homes, food, wages, education, clothes, boots, and all those things of which mothers and fathers dream for their children were the real things to vote for – the rest meaningless. Some listened and agreed; most of them disagreed. Now and then one invited him in and gave him tea. Whether they agreed with him or not they saw what manner of man he was. But he who was soon to become known and loved of them all was a complete stranger to them, except in Wheatley Hill, Thornley, and Wingate, where he was known to adults and children.

When the day's work was done he cycled to a meeting in some part of that Parliamentary division to speak to crowds. Day after day, for nearly three weeks, he went from door to door in different colliery villages, not for himself but for his Cause. He was not a candidate; he was just a voice for Labour. And his Cause was overwhelmingly defeated throughout Durham County.

The county council elections came in the following March. These meant little, for County councils had not yet arrived at that stage in the minds of the masses when they were taken seriously. In Durham, as elsewhere, Labour did what it could but expected little, in the light of past experience, and particularly in view of the General Election just over. But a deeper change had taken place than anyone dreamed, a change so great that when it found full expression it left the Britain of pre-war days a century away.

Durham had the first knowledge of the change in the whole of Britain. When the county council elections began Labour had less than

*From J. Lawson, *Peter Lee* (London, The Epworth Press, 1949), pp. 119-23, 125-31, 144-50 and 192-5.

a dozen seats. When they ended it had four times that number. That meant an overwhelming majority, and the first county council Labour majority in the whole of Great Britain. *And more than this. It was the first time working men had been called to govern in Britain,* for throughout the whole range of local government there was not one council which had ever had a Labour majority, and of course, it was not until some years after that Labour formed a Government in Parliament. Indeed throughout a great part of British local government it was considered an achievement for the workers to win an odd seat on the council, while a negligible minority was the rulc under the most hopeful conditions, as far as Labour was concerned.

Labour majorities on councils are now so commonplace that this may seem almost unbelievable, but the fact is that if anyone had suggested the possibility of the present order of things in 1918 he would have been considered an impracticable dreamer. A few were optimistic enough to proclaim the coming of a great revolution, and went wild with enthusiasm when they gained a handful of votes. They sang the 'Red Flag' for a moral victory in which their opponent had won the seat by a ten to one majority!

The meeting of the successful workers' candidates in the Durham Miners' Hall after the March elections in 1919 was thus an historic gathering in the annals of British government. It was also an incohesive, wondering gathering, for the idea of a firm, decisive Labour government had not yet gripped them as a whole. A few individuals had no shadow of doubt upon the matter; but it was clear the meeting did not take this for granted. The writer had been a member of the County Council for some years and was present at the gathering concerned. It is no criticism but a statement of plain fact that the meeting was not too sure of its mind. Hitherto there had been 'Progressives' and 'Moderates' in the Council as in others – and Labour had always been grouped with the Progressives. Should that continue? There was a trade-union member or two who had been elected as such, though they were really Liberal-Labour. Should the new majority compromise by being called the Trade Union Party? There was some debate, but the few who knew their minds easily carried the meeting. It was decided to take the reins of government firmly as a Labour Party.

The question then arose as to the chairman. This was no light matter, for no man among them had even been chairman of a committee of the Council. Indeed, so few hitherto had been the Labour members that it was only by the grace of the dominant sections that one or two had been given a place on the more important committees. They were almost without experience of responsible administration as far as the County Council was concerned. And every public man knows there is a vast difference between being a member of a committee and a chairman who must give time and thought to the shaping of its administration, and also make very serious decisions. Who, then, in such an assembly could be relied on to lead a Council with the social destiny of a million people in its keeping?

There was only one man. That was Peter Lee. It was unanimously decided to nominate him as Chairman at the coming meeting of the Council.

But he was not the man to jump at such an invitation, being too wise in the ways of the world and experienced in the responsible administration of lesser councils to underrate the task to which he was being called. There were also other grave questions requiring consideration. He depended for his livelihood upon his work at the pit. The men of Wheatley Hill had always been generous in giving time off, but this was practically a full-time job. To accept this invitation was a great risk to a man with a wife and dependent family. Once upon a time such a risk would have been nothing to Peter Lee, but now he was fifty-five years of age, with no other resources whatever than his week's pay to maintain a wife, family, and himself. Always the men who had filled this position had been men of independent means, and indeed that was why such posts had been utterly beyond the worker. No financial provision whatever had been made for a man lacking a good income to fulfil the duties of chairman of a county council. And, even if there had, the office was but for a year, and it might demand such time as to threaten his livelihood. That it would be exacting in the face of the overwhelming arrears of the war years, when things had stood still, never worried him for a moment. But facts had to be faced and thought given to such a position. So he asked the meeting to give him time to think over the invitation, and the request was granted. He went home and talked the matter over with Mrs Lee, took counsel with the Miners' Lodge, and finally decided to accept the nomination.

In his speech accepting the responsible office, he left no one under any illusion as to the colossal task before the new Council and the drastic changes it implied.

During the four years of the war the work of the Council had stood still. Roads, health, education, and everything concerning the social life of the county were in arrears. There was general deterioration. In an industrial area such as Durham the 'standstill' had only intensified the great problems, which were the inheritance of long neglect. In that slow, measured style peculiar to him the Chairman delivered his first speech, and none could say the warning of things to come was lacking in clarity or emphasis, however quiet the manner of the man.

It is hardly an exaggeration to say that in those days Peter Lee lived in the Shire Hall. He was Chairman of the Council and also Chairman of the Finance Committee. As usual he settled down to master every phase of the administration to the least detail. Within a few months he was such an armoury of facts and figures that he dominated meetings and won the unqualified praise of friend and opponent alike for his efficiency. Whether it was the cost of the projected new reservoir, the legal details of taking over the water supply from the private company, or the cost of a shovel compared with that of 1914, he was ready to answer the question.

Big projects were afoot, but an infinite knowledge of little things was necessary to bring them to life. Meanwhile he was almost without means.

There were no expenses for travelling or food at that time, as far as the Chairman of the Council was concerned. Work was lost to do the job in Shire Hall. The men at his colliery were considerate, but they could not meet the full charge under such conditions. No one ever heard a word from Peter Lee, and he discouraged questions even from his intimate friends; but things could not continue in this way.

The new County Council of Durham had a giant task before it, testing all the powers of its elected heads and their staffs, and none more than the Chairman. Something had to be done. A motion was placed on the Order Paper that a certain sum should be voted for his expenses in carrying out the duties of his office. While it was discussed the Chairman left the chamber. Let it be said to the credit of opponents that they agreed. One of their number, the late Sir Francis Arthur Pease, a coal-owner, made a generous speech in which he stated it was imperative that this should be done in view of the prevailing conditions. He also moved a much bigger sum than that on the Order Paper. Finally, the Council passed the motion unanimously as it was on the paper. When the Chairman returned he made it clear that though he was compelled by circumstances to accept expenses, he would not accept more than half the amount granted by the Council. Within the writer's knowledge he not only discouraged the proposal, but it had to be made in spite of him. He had lived so sparingly and been so jealous of his personal independence all his days that he felt he was lowering his flag in this matter. And it was difficult to make him realise that the expenses were voted not for Peter Lee, but for the Chairman of the

County Council. Since that time the practice has become common; facts compelled county councils to courses members never dreamed of in the old days.

Durham was not alone in its social go-as-you-please standards, but there, conditions were accentuated by particular industrial circumstances. Throughout the country, standards of life were low for the masses. Literature, from Dickens to Wells, has pictured these as they prevailed throughout the nineteenth century. Evil housing slums, and low wages meant ill-shod, ill-clothed, ill-fed, unhealthy men, women, and children by the thousand. Scathing attacks by literary artists might be counted largely imaginary; the propaganda of socialists discounted as reason warped by bitterness. But none could evade the terrible facts revealed by the war. When hundreds of thousands were judged by doctors as too far below the low physical minimum standard required for soliders, then stage by stage mental disturbance mounted to alarm. A new term was coined – a C_3 nation. That was the category of rejects. The grim facts below the socially obtuse out of their mental trenches.

This was one of the problems Durham had to face in common with the rest of the country. That meant drastic changes in health services.

There were also arrears of school building, for not only had no building been done during the war, but a long list of condemmed schools was in existence. Added to this was the national demand, expressed in the Act of 1918, for smaller classes and more advanced education. This meant more schools and better schools.

Roads had been made for horse traffic, but now motors were coming on a great scale, and the highways had to be widened, properly surfaced, and extended to meet an expanding new travelling population and transport of goods. Lighting, too, needed attention.

Housing was not directly the work of the county councils, but health was, and proper living accommodation is one of its primary conditions. A revolution in this respect was needed in Durham.

Water is one of the first conditions of health. Private companies had hitherto served the county, but generally speaking they had broken down and had long been unable to meet the needs. Whole communities were without a water supply for days – and in some cases weeks. Water carriage for sanitation purposes was almost non-existent. This problem had to be met and was one of extreme urgency. As for Infant Welfare and Maternity Clinics, they were hardly existent.

These were only a few of the problems before the new Durham County Council. Some of them were all too sharply outlined, grimly forbidding by reason of long-standing neglect; some of them loomed vaguely uncertain in their limitations. In 1918 we stood, as a nation, with our backs to an age in which we had been content to meet by individualistic hand-to-mouth methods social conditions totally beyond us. The first industrial revolution had given us social production on a vast scale, bringing together close-packed communities to carry on its functions. But after a century we had failed to apprehend that social production demands social services equal in efficiency, to the end that the community should be kept in the proper condition to carry out its functions. And even this takes no heed of the fact that men work to live rather than live to work. We had paid dearly for our failure socially: in the future it would be cheaper to succeed.

We were also to pay in cost of material. The war had raised the price of everything to two, three, and sometimes four times that of 1914. The wages and salaries of staffs needed attention. Salaries of teachers and police were fixed by national bodies outside of the counties. The prices of bricks and timber for schools and other buildings and of material for roads as well as tools were beyond control.

This is only the thin outline of conditions under which the first Labour county council began its task of undoing the evil of the old conditions and trying to meet the new age. Peter Lee had not only become Chairman of the county council: he was chief of the civic life of Durham and leader of its people. In every mining village and to all its people his name and figure alike were now familiar. He could fill any hall and hold his audience rapt, not with triumphant oratory; but by a plain statementof immediate problems and methods of solving them. To be capable of illuminating fact and figure by disciplined social passion, at such a time as that, was a rare gift. Instinctively the people understood that and were proud of him. But he possessed himself too. For neither cheers nor loyalty ever troubled that inner loyalty to truth and right as he saw them. He never was led, he never led from behind. That was why he was a born leader. Dogmatic, intolerantly so, if you like, but with a sureness based firmly on conviction.

There was another side, too, of this giant figure now silhouetted on the social skyline. He could be seen clearly by opponents as well as friends. If he led his people by calm reason, mobilized factual argument, and fortified them with transparent sincerity, he was all the greater danger to opponents. That was crystal clear. The extent of his power to calm or sway elected or elector was also that of his power to damage reaction.

It took those who had previously ruled unquestioned some time to realise the danger and to mobilise to meet it. But they did, finally, a personal as well as a public campaign. The political charge was waste of public money; but that was dwarfed by other things. Few were free from attack. Peter Lee was the head and front of offence. It was the most forthright kind of thing which any man in public life in Britain can have known.

Peter Lee was a paradox since he himself was of the very stuff of which dictators are made. He could listen, weigh, and balance reasons before he arrived at conclusions, but once his mind was made up he could be intolerant of other views if it was a matter of deep import. It was also true that he was a stern disciplinarian, but he demanded of others no more than he imposed upon himself. Further, he had a high conception of a citizen's duty to the State. And he had the courage to fight for, and the driving energy to give effect to, the things he held to be of worth. Take the story of bringing water to supply all our needs under the crowded, complex conditions of modern society, water for drinking, preparation of food, personal cleansing, keeping disease at a distance and driving it out of existence; water for the making of houses which shelter, us, and for clothes which warm us; hardly a thing we need, an article we touch, but would be impossible were it not for this great gift. The water taps and the sewerage of modern communities have behind them and in them the world's great untold stories.

In the year 1860, a few gentlemen formed what is known as the Consett Waterworks Company, mainly to supply water to the three ironworks in the Consett district and to serve the inhabitants, which at the time comprised just over twenty thousand people. By 1872 the Smiddy Shaw Reservoir was completed, and in 1906 the Hisehope Reservoir was in commission. Another small company had, in 1865, begun to exploit the great water resources of those rising moors, stretching up to the west. The Waskerley and Tunstall Reservoirs were constructed in 1879-80. By 1902 the separate companies were amalgamated into what became known as the Weardale and Consett Water Company, and by 1914 the operations of this company extended over an area of approximately four hundred and twelve square miles, including one hundred and eleven parishes, twenty-two rural and urban councils, and the City of Durham.

Owing to the large increase of population and trade demands the company was not able to give an adequate supply, and in 1914 serious curtailment occurred in the Consett district. As far as the population was concerned 'curtailment' is a feeble word to express prevailing conditions. Water had to be carried from springs and wells.

The writer speaks with feeling as he remembers the many experiences of balancing full pails of water over long distances. And this went on for weeks at a time. But the domestic problem was the least of the trouble. Water closets in schools stood unflushed for many days. An impasse had been reached in that great area as far as the water supply was concerned. The private company had rendered useful service, but the situation was now utterly beyond it. In these circumstances the Durham County Council passed a resolution to the effect that it had become impossible for such a large population to be supplied by a private company, and that public enterprise was necessary to supply the need. In July 1919 negotiations began which finally wound up the old company and brought into being the Durham County Water Board, composed of representatives from the county council as well as rural and urban councils within the area.

It would be a long story to tell what was done and how it was done but it is plain fact that the task was done so well that, at this moment, no one in the area of that Water Board knows what it is to want water. Tens of thousands of houses have had water laid on for sanitary purposes. Water is today used on a scale, and for purposes, by the people in the area of the Water Board that would have staggered the old company which was legally responsible for the supply. If it was incapable of meeting the needs in 1919, it would have been infinitely more helpless before the demands of today.

Meanwhile, the construction of the Board, obtaining legal powers, satisfying opposing interests – all these tasks laid upon Peter Lee long, strenuous days of labour and thought. The great work was the construction of the Burnhope Reservoir. It was to be ten years before it started – for there was the financial problem, and the construction of this great new work was to cost nearly a million pounds. The delay was not absolutely necessary, but the Chairman was as far-seeing as the shrewdest business man, and he could wait as well as act. He knew well that a Labour government would be in office sooner or later, and that it was pledged to carry out public works on a large scale. That meant generous grants, so he waited. One or maybe two hundred thousand pounds extra were worth waiting for.

There was always plenty to do carrying on this great business in its ordinary concerns as well as its minor developments. The finance, detailed work, the area from which water was drawn, and that which it supplied, became as well known to Peter Lee as his own hand. Also he was familiar with the purposes of the supply and watched the increasing demand with pleasure, which is not usually the way of those responsible for the supply of water. Water meant health, more water better health, and this was no small part of his life's work. So Durham saw the miracle of a responsible Water Board official urging the increasing use of that which he supplied, instead of pleading for limitation. He talked 'water' to local authorities and to public meetings, and he made his subject so entrancing to the simplest audiences that this ordinary gift became a thing of romance. When the Water Board was mentioned in Durham, people thought of Peter Lee.

Looking back at the development of County Durham in the nineteenth century, it is clear that many were blind to the social effects of industrialism and to the conditions arising from the swift growth of communities in new places where there were only primitive sanitary arrangements. It was bad enough in hamlet and village in the late-eighteenth and early-nineteenth centuries, though these were small, scattered, and in close touch with nature, but when it came to pass that a population of thousands was often termed a village, and where hirtherto lonely fell and valley had now many such aggregations of people, the old sanitary ways became a menace. In the late-nineteenth and early-twentieth centuries fevers and diseases of all kinds swept through such places, leaving death and misery in their wake. Durham County, as one of the great coal producing areas in the land, had fared badly in comparison with the rest of the country. That was in part because it was one of the first large-scale products of the new order – had masses of old houses, and with them the crude ideas of the period in regard to sanitation.

Durham was also mainly an area from which coal was sent abroad at a very low price, and price governed life. From boyhood onward every miner had the need of cheap coal for export driven into his mind, and every family knew when prices rose or fell a few coppers. For the rise or fall was reflected in wages. Durham paid dearly for Britain's imports, of which it got a meagre share. Low wages and poor social conditions were the price of cheap coal. From time to time a reduction of wages was the price of a contract. Sometimes conditions became unbearable and a strike followed. It was a century of mining conflict. 'Give us just wages and decent conditions and fix the price afterwards', was continually the cry, but ever was coal sold at the price got 'in the haggling of the market'; and everything else was dependent on that.

It was a cheap life for which Durham people paid dearly. Whole villages in which the houses were hardly decent stables were the result, and when winter snows came, rows of low-roofed houses stood in a morass. Some companies, owning more modern collieries, did build better class houses, but even under the best conditions street lighting was practically non-existent and streets were quagmires in winter. Many a boat the writer has sailed, when a boy, on one of the large lakes in the centre of the colliery village, after the rains. Sewage was in its infancy and sanitation there was none. If we had missed our annual fever, diphtheria, and other epidemics, we should have thought something had gone wrong with the seasons. Misery and heartbreak came so often that they were commonplace. The company owned the colliery, and manned the council with its officials all to the end that money should not be wasted on social improvement. Men living today remember the time when a workman candidate for the council in a colliery district would have been an offence beyond pardon; and the lesson he received would have been sufficient to ensure that the offence was not repeated. Our local rulers had more undisputed power than a Prime Minister has today. Let it be said that he would be foolish and unjust who did not recognize that there *were* good citizens who were alarmed at this state of things. There were a few able and courageous men who served the County well, previous to the coming of the Labour administration. These were known as Progressives; but it is a significant fact that there was no marked inroad on the state of things here described until the Labour 'victory'.

When Labour came to power in the County of Durham in 1919, the annual death-rate for children stood at 115 per thousand: for 1947 it was 44 per thousand. For the five years 1916-20 it stood at an average of 114, for the five years 1941-5 it was 62 per thousand. It must be emphasised that water played a great part in this change. Peter Lee's insistence on water and more water for sanitatary and cleansing purposes had its effect. If he gave himself to the work of the Water Board with a passion that was almost religious, if he dreamed of diverting wasting waters, until he made a fetish of the new reservoir, if he loved the Pennines down which the water ran, it was because these things meant life to his people.

This is not the whole story. Free Secondary education, new schools, Maternity and Child Welfare Centres, Maternity Homes, a new Central Hospital, an Agricultural College – fierce winds blew through the administration of Durham County Council when Peter Lee and his colleagues arrived.

7 POLITICS AND HOUSING IN A DURHAM MINING TOWN

Ellis Thorpe

This chapter is taken from a larger community study of 'Coalport' (a pseudonym) conducted by the author between 1968 and 1970 at Durham University, with the support of the Joseph Rowntree Memorial Trust. Two reports by Ellis Thorpe on this project are available in the Library of Durham University. Coalport: an interpretation of community in a mining town *(280 pages) contains chapters discussing the problems of 'community' research, the development and growth of the town under private ownership, nationalisation and its social effects, and patterns of local voluntary association activity.* The Miner and the Locality, *(a preliminary report of a pilot survey) is a 190-page analysis of a pilot survey in Coalport of a small sample of miners and their wives, containing data on family and kinship, work, neighbourhood and friendship patterns, and trade union and political activity. The theoretical discussion uses* Coal is Our Life *in conjunction with* The Affluent Worker *research as a base line.*

Introduction

Coalport is a mining town located between the sea and the countryside on the Durham coast. The town was the focus for a study of the development of community social relations and a collective consciousness expressed in Labour Party domination of the town from 1930 until the present-day reorganisation of local government.

The development of the area began in the 1820s with the construction of a port for shipping coal from the North-East to markets in the South of England. But the most significant economic factor was the commercial exploitation of coal in the 1840s and the subsequent sinking of two more pits in the late-nineteenth and early-twentieth century. The area developed in terms of population as the pits became productive, but in the period just prior to this study a decline in population was becoming noticeable. For example, according to the 1931 Census, there were 27,325 people in the Coalport area, but by the time of the 1966 Sample Census this had fallen to 25,870.

The economic and social basis of the community was firmly rooted in the pits, but by 1966 the roots were being shaken loose by changes in national economic and energy policy (described in chapter 11) even though the decline of mining did not affect the coastal collieries in the short-term. For instance, according to Census data in 1931, 70 per cent of workers employed in the area were in the pits, in 1951 75 per cent, but by 1961 only 50 per cent. In 1966 the proportion of workers in mining who were resident in Coalport was as low as 42 per cent.

Given this development of Coalport as a mining town, it is of great sociological interest to examine the ways in which community social relations and a collective consciousness developed over a period of time, in particular in relation to the provision of housing. Moreover, it is of significance to note how a collective consciousness or a sense of collective identification can persist in time, even though the 'material' basis for such an identification may have weakened, changed and indeed have been transformed as a result of the very collective consciousness. It may survive and be sustained as an ideology justifying a monopoly of political domination.

In order to reveal these social processes, it is useful to focus upon a key dimension of social, economic and political life, namely the struggle for the provision of adequate housing in a situation of deprivation and conflict. It is this dimension of community relations and the meaning of such relationships related to the development of Labour party political dominance in Coalport, that will be described and analysed in this chapter.

Housing Deprivation in the Context of Relations Between Pit Owner and Pit Men

Taking the period between the sinking of the first pit in Coalport in the 1840s and the Nationalisation Act 1948 as a convenient unit of history, we can say that for one hundred years the local noble family was the capitalist institution in Coalport. In the period of history spanning a hundred years there were a number of holders of the title Lord —, but the family as an institution was characterised by its power based upon the ownership and control of industrial capital, and by its influence on social, political and economic life in Coalport. As an institution it was responsible for all the pits, for all the jobs in the pits and many subsidiary industries dependent upon the pits. It owned the harbour, ships, bottle factory, railway wagons and a range of other ancillary economic enterprises.

The use of the concept of an *institution* to summarise the rules and conduct of successive Lords of the town and their families is quite justified by the second characteristic, namely that for most of the time any one individual holder of the title was an absentee owner. The institution then in a sense is absentee ownership of land and industrial capital. The routine everyday life of commercial and industrial command was placed in the hands of a succession of paid agents, all of whom carried out the policies of the institution with commendable efficiency; that is, if the profitability of the institution is the standard of measurement or the misery of the inhabitants of Coalport is a basis for judgment. Every year from September to December the family was in residence at one or other of their two houses in the North-East but the rest of the time was spent either in London or in Ireland.

This well established capitalist institution that dominated the lives, the well-being, the destiny of Coalport people was characterised by tremendous power. But it was power ultimately separate and remote from the point of contact where it was exercised, that is, the social relations of the community. The agents of the institution were the points of contact but yet the agents were an essential part of the institution, as the mediators and exercisers of power and authority in the control of human and physical resources. Hence opportunities for work; opportunities for leisure; opportunities for housing in Coalport depended on the institution.

This is not to say that a capitalist institution of the kind epitomised by the noble family was able to exercise unbridled and naked power. Other institutions, like the law, religion and trade unionism provided some form of legal, social and political restraint. Moreover, a legitimating ideology of duty and obligation attached to feudal institutions like the landed aristocracy, still provided some moral restraint and furnished the titled family with 'community oriented' roles like 'doing good works' of a charitable kind. However, having said this, the realities are most sharply revealed by reflecting on the facts that Lord — controlled the 'opportunity to work' and the 'opportunity to be housed'. Most crucially these aspects of life in an industrial community are the key dimensions of the relationship termed market-situation and life-chances in any analysis of class structure. In the context of the community-situation of Coalport, it meant for miners and their families the difference between eating or starving, between being sheltered or being homeless.

The early years of the twentieth century saw little improvement in the situation. In 1921 the Census of County Durham pointed out that housing conditions were the worst in the country, the ration of 0.77 rooms per person being lower than any similar county.[1] In 1924 in Coalport, according to the Medical Officer of Health's reports, large areas of slum property had been condemned as along ago as 1911. Quite bluntly the report states: 'Seeing that this question affected the public health of a large section of the community we had an interview with Mr. V.C.S.W. Corbett, agent to Lord —— and that gentleman very kindly undertook to consider the whole matter'.[2] The report does not state that all the slum property in Coalport belonged to Lord —— but the inference is that because of the dominant institutional position of the —— family with regard to land and housing provision, a considerable measure of responsibility lay with them. That the role of the ownership of land and housing played a significant part in the lives of Coalport people can be gathered from the fact that at this time the infant mortality rate in Coalport was 103 compared to a rate of 85 in the County of Durham as a whole, and 69 in England and Wales.[3]

Local newspapers provide one source on housing in the locality. Throughout this period there are references to the problem of ownership of land and the provision of adequate housing for the fast growing population of Coalport consequent upon the sinking of new pits in the area.[4] This is exemplified by the contents of a letter sent early this century to the local press by Mr and Mrs Crawford, who wanted land in Coalport to build a seven-roomed house. Because of constant delays in negotiations with Lord ——'s agents, the Crawfords wrote a letter to the local newspaper.[5] Mrs Crawford writes:

> Perhaps it is news to your Lordship that including your official residences there are not more than three dozen houses in Coalport with fitted baths . . . Four and a half years of negotiation are insufficient to obtain by lease or by purchase from an English lord, a plot of British soil sufficient to accommodate a seven-roomed house. Could there by any better argument in favour of land reform?[6]

There are more details given which are of interest with respect to the ownership, and control of land in Coalport. First, the Crawfords were dealing with Mr Corbett, the agent referred to in the Medical Officer's reference to slum property in Coalport in 1911. Secondly, in twelve years, only five sites were released by Lord —— for private house building and these were described as the 'worst sites in Coalport'. Thirdly, it can be noted that the price for building purposes was 7s 2d per yard [sic], the same as 'any large town', but because his Lordship was a 'kind benefactor' he charged charitable institutions only 5s per yard [sic].

In order to present a balanced picture of the housing situation in

Coalport prior to the commencement of local authority house building on any scale, attention must be drawn to the provision of housing both for rent and for purchase by the —— institution. Again as parts of this institution, there had been established a property company and building society. For example, one of the activities of the institution was the building of a 'model village' surrounding the new pit opened in the first decade of the twentieth century. This scheme was described as the 'plum of the —— workmen's dwellings' by the writer of the letter above, but the writer went on to add that it should be an offence to retain land wanted for building, punishable by fourteen to twenty-eight day's stay, not in gaol, which would be too easy and comfortable, but 'in one of the worst slums which their action was helping to perpetrate', and they should have an allowance of £1 per week, 'on which they would be obliged to live and pay all their expenses including rent'.

Further evidence of the effects that the institution had on the life chances of Coalport people is provided by the comments made in The Northern Echo in 1907:

> Through the commencement of new works people came into the town. This created a demand for houses. Immediately Lord —— asked a higher ground rent for all building sites, with the result that although there was a great demand for and plenty of money to invest in house building, people refused to do so because it was impossible to do so . . . The supply of houses being considerably less than demand . . . my rent was raised by 26/- a year, consequently I had that much less to spend on food and clothes.[7]

Another critical letter in a local newspaper on the occasion of the opening of an extension of the Sunderland District Nursing Association's Home, shows again the social distance that lay between the —— institution and the working folk of Coalport. Lady —— said in her speech that 'illness should be nipped in the bud'. The writer then says:

> I cannot but think that Lady —— is taking hold of the wrong end of the stick. *As a very humble member of society to an exalted one,* I venture to remind her Ladyship of the old saying 'prevention is better than cure', and to suggest that her ladyship should use her great influence on Lord —— to induce him by opening out more building land on easy terms, to encourage building and thereby eventually either lead to the most squalid slums in the town being left untenanted or force the owners to make them habitable . . .

> In this town some of the worst property is leased to the —— collieries as dwellings for their workmen . . . There are in the town blocks of buildings where over twenty tenants use one yard.[8]

This last comment refers to the use of a lavatory and a tap outside in the yard by twenty tenants, which meant typically twenty families.

It was noted above that Lord —— opposed the Land Tenure Bill because he said it interfered with a landlord's right to do what he will with his own property. In this connection it should be noted that the 'opportunity for work and the opportunity for housing' form an important dimension of everyday life in Coalport because they are fundamental to life itself in the local community and also because everyday life was dominated by the agents of the landed family. The agent for Lord —— (that is the controller and administrator of the —— family estate) and the pit managers were powerful figures in the lives of all Coalport people. Hence work and housing were used by the agent and by colliery managers to control or at least attempt to control the criticisms and the organisation of opposition among Coalport working men.

For example in a strike of 1912, it is reported that there was a lengthy stoppage because of a dispute over the allocation of housing surrounding a recently opened pit. It was claimed by the union that 'strangers' were getting colliery houses in preference to local miners. The agent and colliery manager claimed that there were undesirables among the local men – men who do not keep clean houses. The Union denied this and said that clean and honourable workmen were waiting for houses while four hundred had been filled. When their men did succeed in evading the policeman at the office door and were interviewed, some were told that they had too many children, some too few, others told to adopt children; another was told he had no right to adopt a child to get a house.[9]

The above illustrations from local press reports and letters to local newspapers reveal the problems facing miners and their families in a community characterised by the dominance of a capitalist institution which owned and controlled access to life-chances so effectively. The actual historical chronology of the titled family is not described in detail. What is important is the realisation that the titled family was an institution in Coalport. It was the ownership and control of human and material resources (including the rules governing their allocation) that is sociologically important. This ownership and control stretched almost unbroken, though not unchallenged, and to some extent mitigated, for one hundred years.

It is important to note the operation of the 'ideology of rights and duties' that was also a feature of the institution, and then after the 1914-18 War the operation of national government legislation, albeit tentative at first, in the housing market. Firstly, the influence of the operation of the 'ideology of rights and duties' had led to some provision of housing by the institution. The 'model village' that accompanied the sinking of a new pit in 1899 began to influence the provision of housing in the first decade of the twentieth century and as was noted above was the centre of a strike in 1912. Secondly, the 'ideology of rights and duties' also embraced the notion of a 'property owning democracy' and as the —— institution was framed around the Tory Party and the Church of England, it was a strong advocate for giving people the 'right' to own their own home, and it was the 'duty' of the dominant institution to provide the means by which this might be achieved.

In 1923, at the same time that Lord —— opened twelve houses for retired miners to celebrate his son's twenty-first birthday (the houses were paid for by the institution but were to be maintained by the Miners' Union), an experiment to build houses for sale to miners was begun by the family. In all forty houses were laid down at a cost of £350 each less £75 government subsidy. A house could be bought for £5 deposit and the balance on loan at 3 per cent was paid at '10/- per week for fourteen years'.[10]

However, the notion of a 'property owning democracy' did not extend to any other body seeking to meet the demand for houses, outside that is the —— property company and building society. The Coalport Co-operative Society were prepared to invest funds in house building but Lord —— asked the Co-op to pay £2,000.16.4d per acre for land in Coalport and the project was abandoned. The report on the negotiations for land states: 'for two years not a house was built owing to the action of Lord —— though the population continued to increase'.[11]

A continuous increase in population because of the demand for labour produced by the sinking of new pits for Lord ——, meant a constant demand for housing and hence a high demand for land owned by the —— institution. Hence a perfectly circular system of supply and demand in the economic sector of Coalport formed the basis for the power of the landed family as a social institution in Coalport. Even if one begins with the ownership and control of land, the circle is completed by following another route. For instance, the ownership of land enabled the titled family to limit other kinds of industrial and commercial development, hence, the monopoly in the extraction of coal was maintained and also its distribution and sale because no other enterprise could buy or lease land to establish an office in Coalport.

However, a well documented sociological concomitant of the ownership and control of land and the dominance of a capitalist institution in determining life-chances, is the development of collective consciousness. And its occurrence in Coalport was in time to alter drastically the pattern of housing development in the community. Sociologically, it might be suggested that because of the dominant institution of the —— family, the oppositional institutions of trade unionism and Labour Party politics developed, but ironically it was because of the —— institution's beliefs in 'rights and duties', and their policy of letting charities have land cheaply, that organisations were established which provided the setting and the means by which politics of opposition could flourish – that is, the workingmen's clubs.

In 1906 when the miners of New Winning pit asked for a site to build a club Lord —— offered one on condition that no intoxicating liquor was sold. Both he and his wife were active in the Temperance Movement. The miners found a plot of their own but because it was near a Non-Conformist Church his Lordship was petitioned to prevent the club opening. After receiving guarantees from the miners that the sale of alcohol was to be carried on under restriction, he gave the club his support. Later, in the period after the opening of the 'model village', Lord —— gave a site for a workingmen's club 'on the lowest terms that could be arranged to satisfy the law'.[12]

This action, supporting the miners and the granting of land for a further club, in the context of the way in which the family owned and controlled most of the economic opportunities for work and for housing, may seem insignificant or indeed trivial. However, as studies like *Coal is our Life* reveal, the importance of workingmen's clubs lies in providing a setting and a means for the development of a collective consciousness. Class and political consciousness in a community like Coalport cannot be over-estimated.[13]

In 1925 when Lord —— visited the workingmen's clubs in Coalport it is reported he said then that 'His earnest wish was not to increase the profits which went into his pockets, but to assist the community to which he had the honour and privilege to belong.'[14] Perhaps this was another of the 'institution's ideological smoke screens' because there is no doubt that the landed family institution made a lot of money from their ownership and control of land in Coalport. Or perhaps by 1925, social, economic and political changes (these it will be seen later are reflected in the housing pattern) were occurring to such an extent that the leopard was changing its spots, but a writer in the *Darlington Echo* does not give much credence to this theory: 'Lord —— is in Coalport what would in Ireland be termed an absentee landlord. It is many years since he resided at the Hall. He only pays occasional visits to the town in a motor car'.[15] What is important is the pattern of housing development in the context of the development of the 'collective consciousness' of Coalport miners and their families.

The Growth of Collective Consciousness and the Pattern of Housing Development

The crucial point in the long-term pattern of housing development in Coalport came in 1919, when because of the formation of a collective consciousness, the Coalport Urban District Council made use of the Housing Act of 1919 and laid down a scheme for 127 Council Houses. The sociological basis of collective consciousness, rooted as it was in community relations of opposition and antagonism to the local landed family institution enjoying private ownership of economic and housing resources, need not be explored here. Suffice it to say that in the period after the First World War up until 1948, local political opposition to private enterprise was manifest in the emergence of the Labour Party as the second party nationally and as the only party in Coalport by 1948.

In 1920 in Coalport there were seven Moderates (Tories) and six Labour members of the local council. Previously there had been only two Labour members. In 1930 the Labour Party gained control of the urban district council and so it remained until this study ended in 1970 (in 1948 all the seats on the council were taken by Labour). In national politics Coalport secured a place in history because of its members of parliament, who were leading figures in the Labour Party, holding senior office in the minority governments of 1924 and 1929-31. Labour gained control of the parliamentary seat in the early 1920s before it controlled the local council, and has held it ever since, with the exception of 1931-35.

The pattern of Labour party dominance in Coalport dating from 1919 not only reflects, but could be said to have been shaped by, the collective consciousness of the community in its struggle with the —— institution.

In the 1920s Lord —— laid down schemes for further housing development in private estates and a number of other local private builders also began housing development. But compared to the number of houses found injurious to health in 1924 (one hundred) and those unfit for human habitation (seventy-five) the number that could be provided by private enterprise to meet the large demand for housing was meagre. The attempt to alleviate housing problems in Coalport by Local Authority housing were hindered by the 1923 Housing Act which reduced government expenditure by Exchequer contributions to local authorities. However, even with this handicap, Coalport local council built a further 283 houses. In 1924 a new Housing Act was passed and a further 900 houses were built, including 150 on an estate which now provides housing for old people in Coalport.

The major problems facing the community during this period were unemployment and slum clearance, but the collective consciousness of Coalport, expressed as it was in 1930 by the Labour party capturing the local council, determined the building of more council houses. The Slum Clearance Act of 1936 enabled the council to build 748 houses and under the 1938 Act relating to overcrowding a further 366 houses were built. (See Table 7.1 at end of chapter.)

The post-war pattern of housing development in Coalport (shown in Table 7.2) again reflect the collective consciousness of the community as manifest in the continuation of the dominance of the local council by the Labour Party. The switch from the private ownership and control of housing resources in Coalport was consolidated after the war. In particular this was accelerated by the Nationalisation of Mines Act 1948, when the power and influence of the —— institution was finally broken by the Labour government. Not it might be added cheaply. It is said that the titled family received £900,000 compensation for the loss of the three pits in Coalport. (The changed pattern of housing ownership can be seen Table 7.3.) in 1966 Coalport UDC owned 5000 houses out of a total of 8,132 nearly two-thirds of all dwellings in the town. The National Coal Board owned over 1,000 houses. The remainder were distributed between owner-occupied and privately rented houses, which accounted together for only one-quarter of the housing stock.

A feature of housing provision in Coalport is that the local council have followed a deliberate policy of maintaining low rents for council houses. This is not unexpected given the development of a collective consciousness in the struggle for control of opportunities for work and opportunities to be decently housed. (The distribution of pre-war and post-war council housing can be seen in Tables 7.4 and 7.5 and the differential pattern of rent charges can be seen in Table 7.6.)

The opponents of the Labour Party in Coalport in the period of this study (1968-70) frequently said that council rents were 'ridiculously low'. What these critics perhaps were unaware of was that the high degree of council houseownership and the pattern of low rents is a manifestation of collective consciousness developed in one hundred years of struggle. It expresses in the present the control that local workingmen gained over decision-taking in the past. It is a control over key resources in the local community that will not be relinquished by local workingmen in the future without a considerable struggle.

An example of the kind of struggle that might occur is provided by the relationship between private house building and public authority house building in Coalport, bearing in mind the struggle that went on historically between one dominant land owner and the community for adequate housing provision. Prior to 1968 it was announced in the Coalport local press that a firm of private builders were to build private houses on a site near Coalport town centre. Late in 1968 it was reported that because of financial restrictions the private builder had withdrawn the scheme. The Council then decided to use the site for council houses. The critics of this decision were Independent (Tory) councillors who claimed that there was no land being released by the Council for private building. It appeared to be the reverse of the situation of the early 1900s when the complaint was that the landed family (Tory) would not release land for house building for the community (Labour). The critic claimed that financial restrictions were not the reason why the private builder had withdrawn but because the Council insisted on extremely high standards of house building.

In March 1969 a similar situation arose when a scheme for 68 private houses in the north part of Coalport was deferred because of proposed mining operations. Again an independent councillor (Tory) made the point that private house building sites were difficult if not impossible to obtain in Coalport. The Labour majority pointed out that there were private housing schemes in Coalport. They did not state how many schemes there were or how small a proportion of private housing there was in Coalport.

From the data presented for the pattern of housing development in Coalport since the turn of the century, it would seem that the collective consciousness, forged in the struggle with a private enterprise institution like the titled family, is still firmly rooted and strong in Coalport. In January 1969 plans were announced for the approval in principle of a several hundred thousand pound town centre redevelopment scheme, which included up until that time a considerable amount of 'slum property'. Again the critics were independent councillors (Tories) complaining of the cost to the rate-payers and so on. In reply the Chairman of the Council said, evoking the collective consciousness, 'remember the slums . . . Coalport has a fine record in building houses'. Given that the first council house building programme began in 1919, by the late 1960s considerable resources were being devoted by the Council to modernisation schemes. In February 1969 plans were announced by the Chairman evoking the collective consciousness again: 'The use of community resources, for the benefit of Coalport people'.

However, 'definitions of situations' are never static and never wholly consensual. A radical socialist critic of Coalport Council, dominated as it was by Labour councillors, considered that many of their measures were not socialist. He considered that rent increases were not socialist measures and that one street in Coalport was a 'ghetto' and used for the dumping of problem families. Both Labour councillors and the Housing Manager denied that this was the case but it is known that it was easier to get a council house in Coalport if a person were willing to live in this particular street rather than elsewhere. In 1969 there were 458 persons waiting for a council house in Coalport.

The political issue of housing provision remains dominant in Coalport despite the disappearance of private enterprise institution like the aristocratic family and despite the monopoly of the Labour Party in Coalport since 1930. In 1970 the Labour Party in Coalport mobilised the collective consciousness with the slogan (aimed at a neighbouring Conservative council) 'There are no low rents in Tory Town'. The controlling Labour group came under attack by independent councillors (Tories) on the grounds that rents were kept low while rates were increased.

At the same time the Labour Council were subjected to local press attack by an unknown person referred to as 'Empty Heads' (M.T. Heads). In February 1969 M.T. Heads called the town centre scheme a 'sheer waste' by not using the land for more houses and keeping people in the town centre, a criticism of much town centre redevelopment that has a great deal of force today. In March 1969 and in August 1969 M.T. Heads criticised the Council in the press, for increasing rates, the shortage of council houses, misuse of public money by the Council in the Civic Centre, the abuse of the Council bonus scheme, waste of money on plans, the cost of councillors going on yearly conference jaunts, and so on and so forth. In October 1969 M.T. Heads returned to the attack on the topic of the local Council and the Maud Report on Local Government Reorganisation. In the letters M.T. Heads said: 'a vast majority (of people), strange as it may seem, have never heard of it, and like some councillors, if they have, they don't understand it.' In February 1970 the same pattern of half truths, veiled innuendoes and contradictions about the Labour Council in Coalport were repeated.

M.T. Heads is more important sociologically than the contents of such letters written to the Press would suggest. The anonymous letter writer symbolises a latent opposition to a monopoly political situation, in which the Labour Party has had control of local community resources since 1930. Whether such opposition can be effectively mobilised within such a one-party system of control is, however, problematic. In Coalport Council elections in the 1960s, the fate of electoral opposition to the Labour Party may be traced.

In 1961 there were 29 Labour councillors, one Independent and one Conservative councillor. Of the 29 Labour councillors, 25 were returned unopposed. In 1964 9 independents contested 5 of the 8 districts in Coalport but only one Independent gained a seat. However, in 1967 the Independents fielded 19 candidates and they gained 5 seats making the Independent representation 6 overall with 33 per cent of the total votes cast. In 1970 when the Independents fielded 29 candidates and gained 36 per cent of the votes cast, they lost every seat except the one gained in 1961. Why should it be the case that Labour always held more than four-fifths of the local council seats and usually more than nine-tenths, throughout the period?

In over one hundred years of social, economic and political history, a drastic transformation of circumstances has been recorded in Coalport. Since the 1840s when the first pit was sunk, industrial and commercial development of Coalport followed classical capitalist lines. With more pits came an increase in population, and the demand for opportunities for work and opportunities for housing provided the focus of struggle between Capital and Labour. The situation was the classic class struggle of the nineteenth and early-twentieth century; the institution of the landed family on the one hand; the trade union and political party of the miners on the other. In the conflict for the right to work and the right to be decently housed the collective consciousness of Coalport developed and a long political struggle ended with the dominance of the Labour Party over the monopoly of the titled family institution. From land for housing and for commercial and industrial activity being owned and controlled by one family, the National Coal Board now owned and controlled industrial activity and the local council owned and controlled the vast bulk of land and housing. It has been suggested that this is an expression of the collective consciousness.

The problem that emerges is to what extent has the monopoly control of the aristocratic family been replaced by the monopoly of the National Coal Board and Coalport Council? Does the collective consciousness evoked by the local council, as for example in the local elections of 1970, now serve the interests of Coalport people in the changed social, economic and political situation of the 1970s, or is it the case that the collective consciousness is now used by a local political elite as an ideology to maintain its own political power?

Table 7.1 Pre-war Council House Building in Coalport

Scheme	No. of Houses
1919	127
1923	283
1924	900
1936	748
1938	366

Source: Housing Records, UDC.

Table 7.2 Post-war Council House Building in Coalport

Scheme	No. of Houses
1946-49 (1946 Act)	1,425
1958 Act	808
1961-69 (1962 & Subsequent Acts)	275

Source: Housing Records, UDC.

Table 7.3 Pattern of Housing Ownership in Coalport, 1966

Type of Ownership	No. of Dwellings	%
Coalport UDC	5,000	62
National Coal Board	1,003	13
Owner-Occupied	1,380	17
Private Rented	630	8
Total Number of Dwellings in Coalport UDC	8,132	100

Source: 1966 Sample Census.

Table 7.4 Distribution of Pre-war Council Houses in Coalport

Area	No. of Houses	Type of Houses
A	1,600	Terraced
B	146	Mainly semi-detached
C	420	Majority terraced
D	60	Mainly terraced
E	116	Terraced
F	14	Semi-detached
C	87	Semi-detached
G		Some terraced

Source: Records of UDC Housing Dept., 1969.

Table 7.5 Distribution of Post-war Council Housing in Coalfort

Area	No. of Houses	Type of Houses
C	440	Half semi; half terraced
H	170	Half semi; half terraced
I	101	Terraced
B	118	96 1 bed flats and old people's bungalows
J	358	Semi
K	226	Semi
L	748	Semi
M	360	Semi
N	4	Old people's bungalows

Source: Records of UDC Housing Dept., 1969.

Table 7.6 Sample of Rents Paid in Coalport Council Housing

Type of Housing	Net Rent*	Gross (Rates and Water)
	Pre-war Housing	
(2 beds)	19 6	£1 10 4
(2 beds)	£1 0 0	£1 10 9
(3 beds)	£1 1 8	£1 13 9
(4 beds)	£1 4 3	£1 17 8
	Post-war Housing	
(2 beds)	£1 8 1	£2 1 4
(2 beds)	£1 13 8	£2 7 3
(3 beds)	£1 18 1	£2 13 3
1 bedroom Bungalows	19 6	£1 5 5
1 bedroom Flats (Heated)	£1 3 0	£1 8 11

*All rents based on a 50 week year.

Source: Records of UDC Housing Dept., 1969.

Notes

1. *Report of the Medical Officer of Health,* 1924.
2. Ibid.
3. Ibid.
4. The data for this paper were obtained from newspaper files and other recorded reports in the Archives of the then Coalport Urban District Council and the Archives of Durham County Council. A number of reports were not dated and a number of cuttings did not give the name of the newspaper from which they had been cut.
5. No source or date is indicated in the file but because of other references in the letter it can be dated as being in the early part of the twentieth century.
6. This reference is to the Land Tenure Bill which the —— family opposed and it gives an indication that the letter is referring to the early part of the twentieth century.
7. *Northern Echo,* January 1907. No day or date.
8. Durham County Archives, —— Family Papers. Fuller references are given in the longer reports on Coalport referred to at the beginning of this chapter.
9. *Sunderland Daily Echo,* 1912 (no day or month given).
10. *Sunderland Daily Echo,* August 29th 1923.
11. Durham County Archives.
12. Ibid.
13. N. Dennis *et al, Coal is Our Life,* London, Eyre & Spottiswoode, 1956.
14. Durham County Archives.
15. Ibid.

8 THE STRONGHOLD OF LABOUR*

Graham Turner

The extraordinary history of the county of Durham – and of the industrial areas which fringe it – has produced a society which is, in many ways, unique in Britain. One of its most unusual features has been the development of a class of city and town bosses, some of whom pursue and exercise power with a frankness which would cause considerable shock in other parts of the country.

Many of them, to begin with, are both ready and eager either to proclaim themselves, or see themselves proclaimed, as symbols of a particular town or area. Alderman Andrew Cunningham, ex-chairman of Durham County Council, is delighted to have been nicknamed 'Mr Felling'; T. Dan Smith has been called 'Mr Newcastle', Alderman Joe Symonds 'the uncrowned King of Jarrow'; and the town centre of Billingham, on Teesside, is sometimes referred to as 'Dawson City' after its energetic Town Clerk, Frederick Maddock Dawson.[1] This type of homage, to both elected and paid officials, is a commonplace of the area. Even if the titles were not bestowed, the men themselves are perfectly frank about the extent of their influence.

The position of many of these men is utterly secure: they seem to be virtually tribal chiefs appointed for life. Their extraordinary power and status has not, of course, developed merely by chance. It is the direct result of the way in which the industrial North-East grew up.

As the nineteenth century went on, scores of entirely new settlements sprang up; existing towns and villages boomed with the rising demand for coal and iron; hundreds of thousands of immigrants poured in, almost burying the old agricultural society. As mining spread, there was a flight from the land and farming was also seriously affected by land subsidence, by smoke and dust pollution and by an increasing trespass on the land. The coal-owners often bought or leased land rather than pay compensation for the damage they did.[2]

The new towns and villages have been caustically described the the Hammonds:

> They were not so much towns as barracks: not the refuse of a civilisation but the barracks of an industry . . . The mediaeval town

*From G. Turner, *The North Country,* London, Eyre & Spottiswoode, 1967, pp.313-20

> had reflected the minds of centuries and the subtle associations of a living society with a history; these towns reflected the violent enterprise of an hour, the single passion that had thrown street on street in a frantic monotony of disorder . . . They were settlements of great masses of people collected in a particular place because their fingers or their muscles were needed on the brink of a stream here or the mouth of a furnace there. These people were not citizens of this or that town, but hands of this or that master.[3]

In communities like these there were, at the outset, no social traditions, no established hierarchy of power. As one of Durham's most illustrious sons, Lord Lawson has written about the colliery communities, there was 'no real government here, no tradition, no leadership, only the personal dominance of the colliery official.'[4] Just as in the early days of the American West, so in Durham a new leadership had to emerge.

This leadership needed to be robust enough to cope with the situations which a tough and brutal environment threw up. Sidney Webb has described how desperately the early mining villages lacked civilising influences: 'There were no Co-operative Societies; no Miners' Hall; no workmen's clubs; no schools; no religious or philanthropic institutes or missions; hardly any Friendly Societies; no insurance and no savings banks; no music, no organized recreation of any sort; nothing but (from 1830 onwards) an absolutely unrestricted number of beer-shops.'[5] This was a rip-roaring frontier society, where men made their living by doing violence to the earth, where drunkenness and lawlessness were common despite the influence of the chapels, where men stood their friends beer by the gallon and where (as in industrial villages like Witton Park) carriers continuously humped great churns of ale into the ironworks throughout the working day.

Only too often, there was also a clearly defined enemy to be faced, in the person of the coal and iron owners. On occasion, they had no compunction whatever about evicting men from their cottages at a day's notice and sending their agents all over the country to bring back replacements. Richard Fynes records that in the strike of 1844 'throughout the counties of Durham and Northumberland there were thousands of cottages tenantless, whilst their late inmates were camping in the open air, exposed to the inclemency of the weather.'[6] In that same strike, the then Marquis of Londonderry told the shopkeepers on his estate, that, if they gave credit to the striking miners, he would simply withdraw his own custom.[7] He was supported by an Anglican clergymen, who told the strikers in a broadsheet: 'You are resisting not the oppression of your employers, but the Will of Your Maker.'

The men who aspired to leadership in a society like this had to have both moral and physical courage, they had to be local men – because these isolated communities rapidly became extremely ingrown – and they had to have the right pedigrees. They must work in the pits, they must belong to the union and – as the Labour movement grew in power – they must be members of the Party. Any other lineage was unsatisfactory and could even prove a disqualification. One alderman of Durham County told me that he was, in fact, directly descended from a Scottish laird, but begged me not to reveal the fact.

This new, working-class leadership came triumphantly to power immediately after the First World War. Durham was the first British county to elect a Labour majority, in March 1919. 'It was the first time,' wrote Lord Lawson, 'that working men had been called to govern in Britain.' Typically, the first chairman of the Council, Peter Lee, consulted his miners' lodge before accepting the office.[8]

But, despite Labour's accession to power, conditions in the North-East between the wars merely confirmed the traditions of tough political leadership in the industrial areas of the region. Not only did local bosses have to deal with the coal-owners, they also had to try to hold together men and communities slowly falling apart under the demoralising impact of the years of Depression.

All over the area, in towns like Jarrow and Stockton and in the more isolated mining communities of the West, there were thousands upon thousands of men who, as the slump persisted, lost all hope. Now, more than ever, they looked desperately for somebody who would speak out for them, somebody who would put their case in those distant places in the South where decisions might be made which would save them. Where such a man emerged, enormous trust was placed in him. He often became the focus of the community's will to survive, the guardian of the communal guts. As Dick Atkinson, the Durham County planning officer, explained: 'In Wiltshire, the squire may be a perfectly adequate figure-head, but it was no good having "nice" chaps with the sort of problems this area had.'

The Depression also served to deepen Durham's parochialism. Communities shrank in on themselves as the economic crisis slowly wore down their morale: many of the more enterprising simply took the road south, never to return. Durham's sense of separateness was confirmed: it became more inbred, sensitive to any intrusion from outside. Outsiders were (and still are) greeted with suspicion, perhaps partly because they come from a part of the world which has not suffered as Durham has suffered.

So, when the Depression ended, and the war after it, the socialist bosses who had helped Durham survive were left with an extraordinary degree of power. This, more than any other in Britain, is now a county totally dominated by one party and one class. One of the senior Labour aldermen told me in 1965 that his party held 119 seats out of 130 on the County Council. Something like eighty were, he said, either miners or connected in some way with mining. The other eleven seats belonged to the Moderate Party.

The seat of Labour power is the magnificent new County Hall in Durham City, a palace of which any of the Prince Bishops might have been proud. It cost £2½ million to build, stands six storeys high, has expensively landscaped grounds and an artificial lake, and the steps to its main entrance hall are heated to prevent councillors slipping on snow or ice. It also boasts a hairdressing salon, recreation and games rooms and a restaurant block. The reception rooms are spacious and splendidly decorated, but its real glory is the Council Chamber, hexagonal, tiered and furnished with walnut benches. County Hall, like the majority of other local authorities in the area (with the notable exception of Newcastle) is also virtually a closed shop.

As for the old class of power, the landed gentry, they have virtually all left the county. Lord Gort owns Hamsterley Hall, but his estate is in Canada, and the present Lord Londonderry does not exercise any great influence in the area. Most of the big houses now belong to the County, and some Labour men rub their hands at being in control of the seats of those who were once mighty: 'we have taken their castles,' said one alderman triumphantly. Whitworth House is now a day-school for the educationally sub-normal; Windlestone Hall (formerly the seat of the Eden family), Redworth Hall, Walworth Castle and Elemore Hall are all special schools of one sort or another. Lumley Castle belongs to the university, and the old home of the Bowes family is now a museum.[9]

Outsiders who come to live in Durham are also struck by the marked absence of a strong middle-class (See Table 2.1). Bishop Henson had a good deal to say about Durham's lack of social and political balance. He wrote in his memoirs of the 'dullness and drabness of life in the Durham pit villages,' and added: 'There is less variety of social type and economic condition, less healthy competition of political parties, less acquaintance with the larger ranges of national life . . . I cannot but think that the secure dominance of a single political party has not assisted the development of a healthy citizenship.'[10] Some of the most intelligent clergymen at present in the area take a similar view of the effects of the Labour Party's unshakable power. 'There is absolutely no counter-balance to depomp them,' said one. 'Many find it quite impossible to think that any Tory may be even well-meaning or honest.'

Certainly the profoundly parochial attitudes of the area, combined with the bitterness which has been handed down from the past, has helped to keep Durham an in-grown little enclave. The principle of Durham jobs for Durham men or, to put it more crudely, jobs for the boys, has been, and to a large extent still is, a feature of life there. As one leading county alderman put it: 'I have so much confidence in the people of this county that I don't believe in going out of it for anything that I can get in it.'

The application of this principle has encouraged a degree of in-breeding which is patently unhealthy. The stories about the way in which appointments committees work in the county are legion.

The classic tale goes something like this. A committee of local worthies is sitting to make an appointment. They call in the next applicant. He read history at Trinity College, Oxford, did a post-graduate degree at the Sorbonne, and subsequently held a string of distinguished positions.

The candidate sits down. 'Now,' says one of the committee. 'Where does your wife shop – the Co-op?' The Oxford man looks astonished. 'No,' he replies, 'she usually goes to Harrods.' (The members of the committee raise their eyebrows.) 'Are you a member of the Party then?' 'No,' says the candidate, 'I am above politics.' (A chorus of 'Ohs' from the committee.) 'Have you any relations on the County Council?' 'No.' (More 'Ohs'.) 'Are you a member of a union?' 'No.' (Glum silence for a moment from the committee.) Then the chairman: 'Well, would you just wait outside?', and after the candidate is safely out of the room: 'Who put that bugger on the short-list – he's got nae qualifications at all.'

The story may be a heavy parody of the truth, and selection committees may be a great deal more impartial than they were, but there is also plenty of evidence that the bias towards local men is still strong. Open canvassing for posts was also banned a few years ago, but it still seems to go on. 'If you were born in the county, you've a bloody sight better chance than if you are an outsider,' said one official. 'If you're in the Party, that helps too. As for the canvassing, that's disguised but it still goes on at a rapid rate.' A headmaster at a school in the southern part of the county took a similar view: 'If you're Labour, it definitely helps to get the job, and people other than local chaps known by the committee stand very little chance. There is immense parochialism round here.'

Critics allege that this state of affairs stretches far beyond the schools. Some say that the County Council really wants the university to act simply as a county university; their answer is to encourage Durham applicants for places to go to universities outside the county. It is also alleged that the County Council did not really want the new towns of Newton Aycliffe and Peterlee, because they would not be under its thumb, and that some councillors felt bitter because so many of the jobs on the first Boards of Management went to businessmen when they regarded the posts as their own perquisites. Finally, the critics point to the County Council, and deplore what they see as the excessive influence of a small number of really powerful men over the top jobs.

Needless to say, the county's present leadership are proud of their power and of the quality of their administration. 'Out of privation and suffering,' said one senior alderman, 'has been born a new type of leadership in this county, not the aristocracy, not the titled aristocracy, but the dominant people of our own class, the aristocracy of Labour.' Yet, curiously enough, and partly because of their attachment to the past, some of the county's Labour leadership seems to have taken on characteristics of the class which they have replaced. The result is that they sometimes project a surprisingly conservative image.

Notes

1. Quoted in the *Northern Echo,* 15 September 1965.
2. *Durham County Development Plan, 1951, Written Analysis,* p.19.
3. J.L. and B. Hammond, *The Town Labourer 1760-1832,* London, Longmans, 1936, p.39.
4. J. Lawson, *Peter Lee,* London, Epworth Press, 1949, pp.78-9.
5. S. Webb, *The Story of the Durham Miners 1662-1921,* London, Fabian Society, 1921, p.17.
6. R. Fynes, *The Miners of Northumberland and Durham,* Sunderland, Summerbell, 1923, p.71.
7. Coal owners frequently kept 'tommy shops' close to the pits, which stocked basic food and clothing for the men. The men were obliged to buy from these shops and the money was stopped out of their pay. Eventually, the 'tommy shops' were ousted by Co-operative Societies.
8. J. Lawson, *Peter Lee,* pp. 120-1.
9. For a bitter lament on the decline of the gentry, see Sir Timothy Eden's *Durham,* Robert Hale, 1952.
10. Bishop Henson, *Retrospect of an Unimportant Life,* Oxford University Press, 1942, Vol.2., pp.406-7.

9 THE CHARACTER OF LOCAL POLITICS

Martin Bulmer

The three preceding chapters have described the work of Durham County Council's first Labour leader, examined politics and housing as a political resource in one locality, and presented an impressionistic picture of Durham politics in the 1960s. In 1975, Durham County Council celebrated 50 years of continuous Labour control. If not unique, Durham local politics present rather unusual features for a large English local authority. This chapter will consider recent electoral statistics, the Poulson affair in historical context, and generalisations about single-party dominance. But its purpose is as much to raise questions for further research as to present finished results. Local politics in Durham is largely an academic *terra incognita.* What follows are hypotheses to be tested in future research.

One source of data is local electoral statistics. Voting figures for County Council elections from 1946 to 1970 are shown in Tables 9.1 and 9.2.[1] These show, firstly, the overall dominance of Labour in the Council, varying from 10.6 to 1 over all other parties in 1958 to an unusually low ratio of 5.8 to 1 in 1967. Within the overall majority, all aldermen (elected by the County Council itself) were Labour throughout the period. Among councillors, Labour dominance was slightly less marked than in the Council as a whole, but nevertheless overwhelming. At its lowest it was four to one in 1967.

A remarkable feature of the election of councillors was that a significant proportion, averaging 56 per cent over all parties in the nine elections, were elected unopposed without a contest. This proportion was significantly higher for Labour councillors, ranging from 82 per cent in 1964 to 34 per cent in 1970 (average, 61 per cent). It was much lower for councillors of other parties, ranging from 43 per cent in 1964 to 9 per cent in 1946 (average, 27 per cent). This atrophy of the democratic process meant taking aldermen and unopposed councillors together, a substantial proportion of the council were not directly elected by the electorate (as distinct from the party) at all. This reached its peak in 1964, when 92 out of 106 Labour members of the County Council (87 per cent) were either aldermen or unopposed councillors; its low points was 1970, when only 49 out of 92 Labour Aldermen and councillors (53 per cent) were not directly elected.

Table 9.1 Aldermen and Councillors of Durham County Council 1946-70

	1946		1949		1952		1955		1958		1961		1964		1967		1970**	
	Labour*	Other	L.	Other	L.	Other	L.	Other	L.	Other	L.	Other	L.	Other	L.	Other	L.	Other
Aldermen	29	–	29	–	29	–	29	–	29	–	30	–	30	–	30	–	26	–
Councillors	76	12	75	12	77	11	74	14	77	10	77	13	76	14	69	17	67	10
Returned unopposed	38	1	33	3	38	2	48	5	56	3	58	4	62	6	54	5	23	2
Contested elections	38	11	42	9	39	9	26	9	21	7	19	9	14	8	15	12	44	8
Party Balance:																		
Councillors Plus Aldermen	105	12	104	12	106	11	103	14	106	10	107	13	106	14	99	17	93	10
Total No. of Aldermen and Councillors (All Parties)	117		116†		117		117		116†		120		120		116		103†	

*Official Labour.
†Plus one vacancy.
**County Council reduced in size following formation of Teesside County Borough in 1968

Source: Durham County Council, Electoral Registration Office.[1]

Table 9.2 Contested and Uncontested County Council Elections, 1946-70*

	1946	1949	1952	1955	1958	1961	1964	1967	1970
Percentage of County Councillors elected unopposed:									
Labour	50%	44%	48%	65%	73%	75%	82%	78%	34%
Other parties	9%	25%	18%	36%	30%	31%	43%	29%	20%
All parties	44%	41%	45%	60%	68%	69%	76%	68%	32%
Percentage of County Councillors elected in contested election:									
Labour	50%	56%	52%	35%	27%	25%	18%	22%	66%
Other parties	91%	75%	82%	64%	70%	69%	57%	71%	80%
All parties	56%	59%	55%	40%	32%	31%	24%	32%	68%

*Based on figures in previous Table.

A further measure of the political character of the dominant group is provided by an analysis of the 26 Labour aldermen elected in 1970.[2] Several members had been members of the County Council for over 30 years, and two had been County aldermen for over 20. What is particularly striking is the length of continuous service on the County Council. Although of course aldermen tended to be the most senior members of councils, it is nonetheless remarkable that all 26 aldermen had been members of the County Council for periods ranging between 18 and more than 33 years. The average length of service on the council for this group was about 24 years each, nearly a quarter of a century.

More detailed data over time are needed on the social composition of the County Council since 1918. Its structure in terms of age, sex and occupation is important. The links between trade union and Labour Party activism (particularly in relation to the Durham Miners' Association) are crucial; it is surely significant that two men who could certainly have entered Parliament as Labour MPs and probably achieved ministerial office – Peter Lee and Samuel Watson – both steadfastly refused to do so and remained firmly loyal to their local roots. Both were Agents of the Durham Miners' Association, Peter Lee from 1919 to 1935, Samuel Watson from 1936 to 1963. But both were also active in the Labour Party, Peter Lee as Chairman of the County Council, Watson as a long-serving member of the National Executive Committee of the Labour Party, and a leading figure in its regional councils.

The links between county council and district councils are also important to trace. Urban and rural district councils often provided the first opportunity for the politically active to undertake public service; most county councillors had previous experience on district councils, and therefore careers in public service spanned an even greater length of time than the average figure of 24 years for County aldermen suggests.

The way in which these two could become interwoven is illustrated by the parallel involvement of Alderman N. Cowen in mining and county council service (see overleaf.) We know this because Alderman Cowen has written his own invaluable autobiography,[3] describing a full and active life in the Labour and trade union movements reaching back to before the General Strike. We do not know how far it is typical of Durham councillors as a whole; further research is needed.

Another important consequence of council and trade union eminence was appointment to offices on statutory and voluntary bodies in county and region, for example on the Boards of Local Co-operative Societies, New Towns, Water and Airport authorities, governing bodies of colleges and schools, administrative tribunals, and so on. Only detailed biographical investigations could fill in this picture.

Alderman Cowen's trade union and political offices

	Mining	*Council*
1925 (Age 34)	Elected chairman of Lodge of Bewick Main Colliery	
1930	Elected Lodge delegate at Betty Pit, Ravensworth Colliery (to which he had moved)	
		1931 Elected to Lamesley Parish Council
1933	Elected compensation secretary there	
		1934 Elected to Chester-le-Street RDC
1935	Elected to Executive Committee of DMA	
1944	Elected to Executive of MFGB	
		1946 Elected to Durham County Council
1957	Elected to NUM Executive	
1958	Retired from mining	
		1962 Elected alderman of Durham County Council

For the Labour movement as a whole some of these particulars are beginning to be provided by the Dictionary of Labour Biography,[4] so that for a few individuals in County Durham, usually the most prominent, some more detailed information is available. But there is a particular danger in generalisation from an individual to the character of local politics or of a county council as a whole. One may not assume that particular individuals are typical or representative of the Council as a whole.[5]

This is particularly true of events in the early 1970s which have come to be known as the Poulson affair, which involved prominent members of the Labour Party in the North-East in legal proceedings. These events are too near for detached analysis, and most of the protagonists have still to tell their side of the story. The chronicle can best be told by the Royal Commission on Standards of Conduct in Public Life, 1974-76:

> The main reason for our appointment was, no doubt, public anxiety aroused by the Poulson affair . . . Mr J.G.L. Poulson set himself up in practice as an architect in 1932 . . . By the late 1960s, Mr Poulson owned and controlled what was claimed to be the largest architectural practice in Europe. The main selling point of the service that he offered was that his organisation combined under one roof expertise in architecture and related professions such as engineering and surveying . . . a large part of the organisation's work was in the public sector – local authority housing, hospitals and municipal work of one kind or another.[6]

In January 1972 a receiving order was made against Mr Poulson for bankruptcy, placing his estate, including books and papers, in the custody and control of the bankruptcy court through the Official Receiver. His public examination in bankruptcy which began in June 1972, revealed that Mr Poulson had used improper influence to secure contracts:

> We do not know exactly when Mr Poulson first resorted to corrupt methods in order to obtain work, but we have reason to believe that it was as early as 1949/50. In 1961 he came into contact with Mr. T. Dan Smith, who was at that time leader of the majority Labour group and chairman of the planning and housing committees of Newcastle-on-Tyne City Council . . . Between 1962 and 1970, Mr Smith incorporated 14 public relations companies. The basic way in which he operated on Mr Poulson's behalf was, quite simply, to appoint councillors on various local authorities as paid 'consultants' to one or another of these companies. The councillors would then be expected, without declaring their interest, to use their influence on Mr Poulson's behalf. This they did.[7]

On 11 February 1974 Mr Poulson and Mr Pottinger (the Secretary of the

Department of Agriculture and Fisheries in Edinburgh, one of the most senior civil servants in Scotland) were convicted of various offences under the Prevention of Corruption Acts.[8] Over the next three months, a further six people were also convicted of corruption arising from the affair, including:

> Mr. T. Dan Smith (Mr Smith was convicted of various of the offences charged against Mr Andrew Cunningham, and also of conspiracy with Mr Poulson in respect of building projects of the Peterlee and Aycliffe Development Corporations). Mr Andrew Cunningham (former member of Durham County Council, chairman of the North-East Joint Regional Airport Committee, member of the Felling Urban District Council, member of the Peterlee and Aycliffe Development Corporations, chairman of the Tyneside Passenger Transport Authority, chairman of the Northumbrian River Authority, member of the National Executive of the Labour Party, and regional secretary of the Northern region of General and Municipal Workers' Union. Mr Cunningham was convicted on various charges of conspiracy and corruption involving building projects of the Felling Urban District Council, the Northumbrian River Authority, the Durham County Police Authority and the General and Municipal Workers' Union).[9]

Mr Poulson also pleaded guilty to various charges arising from his involvement in the offences charged against Mr Smith and Mr Cunningham.

Those who achieve notoriety (and fame) are often untypical. Does the Poulson affair have any wider significance for an understanding of local politics? Perhaps it has clouded the issue rather than clarified it. In the first place, the conviction of certain individuals tells us nothing about councillors as a group, who suffer guilt by association. This is quite improper. If a *few* people in a *few* areas depart from a strict interpretation of their responsibilities as public servants, the majority of dedicated elected representatives suffer unjustly.

Secondly, comment on the Poulson affair at the time played down the very strong tradition of rectitude and probity in public service in the Labour movement nationally. Peter Lee's uncertainty about whether to accept an honorarium, as County Council Chairman, is a local example. The biography of Labour's most eminent figure in local government in the first half of the century, Herbert Morrison, is another. Morrison from the beginning of his political career as Mayor of Hackney:

> had a keen eye for anything that smacked of graft . . . His concern for clean government seemed to some almost the obsession of a man who had started from nothing, was fearful that he might be tempted and allow himself to be bought and so kept announcing that he was not for sale . . . His view was that local government offered to working men and women with their low wages great temptations . . . Morrison was most anxious that Labour's reputation should not be tarnished. Whenever a whiff of such activities arose in Hackney, he was to the fore in exposing it.[10]

When, in 1934, he became the Leader of the controlling Labour group of the London County Council, he followed the same principles. Labour members were warned off over-familiarity with officials:

> Above all, members (of the Council) had to be free from the least suspicion of personal interest in making appointments or promotions . . . He advised members to stay beyond an arm's length from contractors who provided services to the council . . . He was determined that no scandal should besmirch Labour's reputation . . . The only reward for a member was a sense of public service, and perhaps the pride in seeing his name publicised.[11]

Thirdly, the extent of such corruption is impossible to establish and becomes the subject of guess or rumour. The Royal Commission undertook a thorough analysis of the conditions which made possible the Poulson affair. 'There is no objective way of making a true assessment of the amount of public sector corruption [they concluded] that exists now or whether the amount has changed over recent decades . . . corrupt dealings are secretive; few, if any, crimes are harder to prove'.[12] Nor is it possible to determine the extent of actual malpractice in one-party, Labour, working-class areas as compared to one-party, usually Conservative, middle-class areas with equally long periods of unopposed rule. There may be little difference; we do not know.

Fourthly, there is evidence that the most serious offences occurred in one particular area of local government activity. The Royal Commission concluded that:

> most of the serious crime has centred around planning decisions and local government housing and development contracts. These are the fields in which the stakes are the greatest during the 1960s, and . . . we expect them to remain amongst the most vulnerable . . . In the

> cases that have come to light councillors and officials have entered into corrupt relations with private individuals or commercial interests. Without making the slightest excuse for anybody, we nevertheless feel that the conditions created by Parliament in the field of planning law and in urban and housing development have put greater strain than has generally been realised upon our system of locally-elected councils, whose members may enter public life with little preparation and may find themselves handling matters on a financial scale quite beyond their experience in private life. The power to make decisions which lead to large capital gains or business profits has given rise to obvious temptations on both sides.[13]

One can appreciate the character of local Durham politics more justly by reference to the record of the Labour-controlled County Council. This would require detailed study of the policies pursued in different fields – education, social services, planning, and so on – and a comparison with the performance of other authorities facing comparable problems elsewhere in the county. Such a very large task cannot be attempted here. In the earlier period, Jack Lawson provides a picture of the very great strides which were made under Peter Lee's leadership. The controversial village categorisation policy is discussed in chapter 12, but this is clearly a policy of principle believed to be in the best interests of the county as a whole, which does not serve particular interests.

One must also underline the effects of one-party control demonstrated at the beginning of this chapter. As the Royal Commission notes:

> The local authorities most vulnerable to corruption have tended to be those in which one political party has unchallenged dominance. Not only are such authorities at particular risk because of the absence of an effective opposition which can scrutinise their decisions, but investigations and the making of complaints in such areas may also be inhibited by the feeling that there is no way round the local 'party machine'.[14]

The absence of effective opposition in the pre-1974 County Council did much to give local politics its particular character. In this respect, Durham did not follow Herbert Morrison, who in his work as Secretary of the London Labour Party, 'advised councils with huge, sometimes hundred per cent, Labour majorities to appoint as aldermen members from the opposing parties. He found councils without an opposition appalling'.[15] Speaking to the miners of Blyth in 1935 about the new experience of controlling the LCC, he said: 'The only trouble with the Tories on the council is that we cannot get them to stand up. You have heard of the fellow who was dead and would not lie down. There are people who are alive and won't stand up to us'.[16] But Morrison did face real opposition and the possibility of electoral defeat, and always had his eye on the next election. The other extreme is illustrated by the description above of politics in Coalport in the 1960s.

Robert Michels's classic analysis of oligarchic tendencies in modern political parties, even those with a democratic constitution, is also relevant, and such tendencies are reinforced by the lack of change in leadership: 'Long tenure of office involves dangers for democracy . . . the longer the tenure of office, the greater becomes the influence of the leader over the masses, and the greater therefore his independence'.[17] Michels also emphasised the extent to which the leadership of a political party, once established, could become entrenched in control. Though the old ought to give way to the new, he says:

> the sentiment of tradition, in co-operation with an instinctive need for stability, has as its result that the leadership represents always the past rather than the present. Leadership is indefinitely retained not because it is the tangible expression of the forces existing in the party at any given moment, but simply because it is already constituted.[18]

In an area with strong tradition of class struggle with mine-owners, powerful trade-unionism and effective working-class solidarity, loyalty to the party is possibly accorded more importance then elsewhere.

Not that the trade union base has been static. The influence of the NUM Durham Area upon local politics was, by the 1970s, fast disappearing, and the proportion of NUM sponsored local MPs in particular was but a shadow of the past. Some observers consider that the General and Municipal Workers Union has taken over the role formerly played by the NUM. Certainly organised trade-unionism remains a powerful force within the local political arena. In the absence of effective opposition, such tendencies might be expected to be greatly enhanced. However, generalisations of this type are merely hypotheses, and detailed research into the sociology of politics in County Durham would be needed to test them.

These structural features of the political system are of much greater importance than particular individual offences described earlier. The structure may partially explain why those who engaged in malpractice were able to do so, and why the duties and rights of high office were abused. But individuals alone do not make a system.

There is a tendency in characterising such a local political system to resort to American comparisons. Morrison's biographers, for example, argue that 'his passion for clean government indicates that he was far removed from the legendary Tammany boss with which he was so often compared.'[19] Mr Edward Milne in a controversial account of his life as a public critic of corruption in the Labour Party in the North-East, has referred to 'Durham's long years of Tammany Hall type politics'.[20] Is a hypothesis that there are parallels between Labour power in County Durham and boss politics in America tenable?

Such a comparison is probably erroneous. The social conditions of mass immigration which nurtured the American political machine are not reproduced in County Durham in the twentieth century. The political structure in the two countries is different. Britain is a more centralised system, Parliament and the civil service exercise a far greater degree of local control than in the United States, important functions such as social security, the health services, and the nationalised industries are not in the hands of local government in Britain.

Moreover, British political culture is different from the United States. To give just one example, public life is, by international standards, a model of probity and rectitude. Where lapses occur they achieve great, even exaggerated, prominence. Robert Michels summed up the predominant reaction to such revelations among supporters of Labour:

> The accumulation of power in the hands of a restricted number of persons, such as ensues in the Labour movement today, necessarily gives rise to numerous abuses . . . If at length the eyes of the masses are opened to the crimes against the democratic ideal which are committed by their party leaders, their astonishment and stupor are unbounded.[21]

Nevertheless, the comparison with America may at least highlight significant differences.

The main characteristic of the American city political machine was that it existed:

> to secure and perpetuate power in the hands of a known organisation. And that power [was] primarily used for the enrichment or gratification in some form, of the owners of the machine . . . Its object [was] political control; its means the control of nominations and of

> elections . . . its rulers owe their power to the control of the machine. Nominations, elections, offices, these are the sources of the power that the machine wields and so often sells.[22]

A political machine exists in Durham to the extent that the Labour Party may control nominations to public offices. Since 1925, however, this control has not had to be fought for against effective opposition as in the American city. Indeed, in the present century the social conditions in the two societies are quite dissimilar. The American machine developed alongside mass immigration; providing for the needs of immigrants was one of its main supports. In a fluid and uncertain world, the machine offered a degree of stability, but it had to be prepared to fight off hostile political opponents, some with higher standards of public virtue. In the end, this battle was lost; the American machine is now virtually extinct. Contrast this with continuity in Durham, where Labour hegemony, once established, seems never to have been effectively challenged at the ballot box. This is due largely to the social homogeneity and one-class character of the area, not to the efficiency or influence of the Labour Party machine.

What were the American machine's functions? Robert Merton identified three; The machine was:

1. A means of satisfying wants for lower-class groups not provided for by the legitimate social structure.
2. A means of providing political privileges to business which result in immediate economic gains.
3. A channel for social mobility for groups otherwise disadvantaged in society.[23]

There is virtually no evidence for the third point from County Durham. The alleged ingrown nature of the local educational system might be interpreted in that way, but it might equally well be interpreted as merely a rather well-developed form of parochialism in teacher-selection.

On the second point, the Poulson affair revealed business connections where hitherto none had been suspected. But there is no evidence, as the Royal Commission pointed out, that corruption exists on a significant scale. Indeed, the very reaction to the revelations in the bankruptcy proceedings is an indication of their rarity. In American cities, on the hand, 'graft' was very widespread and endemic. It took place on a large scale, was known to thousands of city officials, and included several varieties of graft; some forms of corruption were more 'honest' than others.

Merton's first point perhaps raises the most interesting questions, also in relation to other chapters in this book. The American political machine provided many and varied services. Its members:

> gave away coal and food, got the sick into hospitals, the unlucky out of jail. They got jobs for the boys leaving school, not only with the municipal or state agencies, but with the businesses that dealt with city and state. They made peace between husband and wife, or arranged a quiet divorce if that was thought better. They were always at hand.[24]

The personal and particularistic ties of the machine distinguish it from other political systems.

> Public issues are abstract and remote: private problems are extremely concrete and immediate. It is not through the generalised appeal to large public concerns that the machine operates, but through the direct, quasi-feudal relationships between local representatives of the machine and voters in the neighbourhood . . . The machine welds its link with ordinary men and women by elaborate networks of personal relations. Politics is transformed into personal ties . . . One source of strength of the political machine derives from its roots, in the local community and neighbourhood.[25]

The last statement is undoubtedly true of County Durham, though it has yet to be supported by local research. How far do the values and practices of Durham politics stem from the pattern of local community life? Close-knit communities facing adverse economic and social conditions emphasised mutual aid and self-help as a means of survival. The parallel between Durham and America surely exaggerates the extent to which in Durham jobs, for example, might be used as a reward for services rendered to the machine. Turner's picture, if it were to any extent substantiated, surely points much more to a kind of inbreeding and preference for one's own kind. The affective social ties of the community find expression in the local political system.

Nor is there substantial evidence of nepotism as such in political appointments, rather a suggestion of preference for people with a local background. Social network analysis would be fruitful here. How far are there inter-locking patterns of influence? To what extent do Labour Party, trade union, and co-operative society membership overlap or not overlap; to what extent are there links between Methodism or Roman

Catholicism and the Labour Party; or between those prominent in the Club movement and the Party? Moore's study of Methodism suggests cleavage as well as cohesion within his communities, to some extent along political lines.[26]

Even if an extensive Labour Party network were revealed, which it has not been, how many *services* did the latter provide? As noted earlier, many government activities in America controlled by the city, in Britain are not controlled by local government but either by central government or autonomous public bodies. Even the police, functionally independent in day-to-day matters anyway, are subject to central government regulation and inspection.

Where the political system did provide services, many of these (such as improved water supplies or better standards and availability of housing) were distributed to everyone as a general benefit, rather than distributed as rewards in return to votes. After all, in a sense the votes were not needed.

The model of American boss politics cannot be made to fit, yet County Durham retains a political distinctiveness and tradition all its own. Its achievements and limitations in the half century after 1925 will be for future historians to determine. If he came back today, one wonders what Peter Lee would think.

Notes

1. I am greatly indebted to Mr Philip Corrigan, who gathered these data as part of an undergraduate social research methods project in the Sociology Department, Durham University.
2. Again, I am indebted for these data to Mr Corrigan. The source is the Minutes of the Durham County Council for 22 April 1970.
3. Alderman Ned Cowen, *Of Mining Life and aal its Ways,* Durham County Hall, mimeo, 1973, p.50.
4. J. Saville and J. Bellamy, *Dictionary of Labour Biography,* 3 vols. to date, London, Macmillan, 1970, 1974, 1976.
5. Contrast Alderman Cowen, op. cit., with the interview with Alderman Middlewood in G. Turner, *The North Country,* London, Eyre & Spottiswoode, 1967, pp.320-2.
6. *Royal Commission on Standards of Conduct in Public Life, 1974-6* (The Salmon Report), Cmnd. 6524. 1976. p.5.
7. Ibid., p.5.
8. Ibid., p.6.
9. Ibid., p.6-7.
10. B. Donoughue and G.W. Jones, *Herbert Morrison: Portrait of a Politician,* London, Weidenfeld, 1973, pp.59-60.
11. Ibid., pp. 196-7. An illuminating comparison could be made between Labour Party control of the LCC., County Durham and Glasgow (on the latter see S.G. Checkland, *The Upas Tree: Glasgow 1875-1975,* University of Glasgow Press, 1975).

12. *Royal Commission on Standard of Conducts in Public Life.* p.11.
13. Ibid., p.11-12.
14. Ibid., p.12.
15. Donoughue and Jones, *Herbert Morrison,* p.215.
16. Ibid., p.198.
17. R. Michels, *Political Parties: a sociological study of the oligarchical tendencies in modern democracy,* New York, Free Press, 1962, p.120 (first published 1911).
18. Ibid., p.121.
19. Donoughue and Jones, *Herbert Morrison,* p.215.
20. E. Milne, *No Shining Armour: the story of one man's fight against corruption in public life,* London, John Calder, 1976, p.142. For a description of American political machines, see D. Brogan, *The American Political System,* London, H. Hamilton, 1947, pp.217-95.
21. R. Michels, *Political Parties,* p.166.
22. D.W. Brogan, *Politics in America,* New York, Harper, 1960, pp.104-5. See also A.B. Callow (ed.), *The City Boss in America,* New York, Oxford University Press, 1976, and J.A. Gardiner and D.J. Olson (eds.), *Theft of the City,* Indiana University Press, 1974.
23. R.K. Merton, *Social Theory and Social Structure,* New York, Free Press, 1957, p.73-4.
24. Brogan, *Politics in America,* p.113.
25. Merton, *Social Theory,* p.73-4.
26. R.S. Moore, *Pitmen, Preachers and Politics,* Cambridge University Press, 1974, pp. 187, 216.

10 INTER-WAR UNEMPLOYMENT IN WEST DURHAM, 1929-39*

G.H.J. Daysh, J.S. Symonds, *et al*

No description of West Durham can be complete which ignores the unemployment experience of the area, for it was unemployment that so strongly influenced the course of West Durham's industrial history during the 1930s. Throughout the pre-war decade there was serious unemployment in West Durham, and this inevitably caused unrest and a movement out of the area. The effects of the unemployment are still obvious today in the poor condition and appearance of the area, and lack of what may be called social capital. In July 1929 there were 14,090 persons unemployed in West Durham, 14.7 per cent of the insured population. By July 1932 the number of unemployed had risen to 44,699, 45.8 per cent of West Durham's insured population. These figures plainly indicate the state of industrial paralysis which pervaded the area. Even when the Depression had passed there were still 17,605

Table 10.1 Unemployment – (West Durham, North East, Great Britain)

	1929	1932	1939	1947	1950
West Durham	14,090 14.7%	44,699 45.8%	15,558 15.8%	3,047 3.0%	2,879
North East	97,161 14.0%	280,132 37.4%	110,491 11.4%	28,956 3.2%	29,783
Great Britain	9.9%	22.7%	8.8%	1.5%	1.3% (approx.)

The unemployment figures are those recorded for July of the year concerned and are only necessarily accurate for that month. Unemployment rates are obtained by expressing the numbers unemployed as a percentage of the total insured. This again may involve slight inaccuracies, since the number of insured persons generally relates to those whose *workplaces* are within the area whereas the unemployed figure tends to show the number of *residents* of the area who are unemployed. These, however are small limitations which are not likely to alter the general significance of the figures.

*From G.H.J. Daysh, J.S. Symonds *et al*, *West Durham*, Blackwell, 1953, pp.37-42.

persons unemployed in July 1937, 17.6 per cent of the number insured in West Durham, and it was not until the war and the subsequent boom period that West Durham ceased to have an unemployment problem.

West Durham's unemployment experience relative to the North-East and the whole country is shown in Table 10.1. This gives comparable figures for 1929, a pre-dpression year; 1932, during the worst of the slump; 1939, when recovery was almost complete; 1947, a year of full employment; and 1950.

It is clear from the above figures that the North-East suffered far more heavily than most parts of the country before the war, and that West Durham was one of the most badly affected areas within the North-East. Despite heavy unemployment in the shipbuilding areas of the region, the average unemployment for the North-East was lower than that for the mining communities of West Durham. Since the war there has been a big improvement but both West Durham and the North-East still show rates of unemployment above the national level.

The extent of the unemployment among individual exchange areas within West Durham is shown below (Table 10.2).

Table 10.2 Unemployment Rates (%) by Exchange Area – West Durham

Exchange Area	1929	1932	1937	1947
Blaydon	15.0	37.8	16.5	6.0
Chopwell	21.2	42.9	18.7	8.9
Dunston	13.0	35.4	13.0	1.8
Total	15.3	37.8	15.7	4.4
Consett	6.0	19.6	4.7	1.0
Lanchester	14.2	63.4	11.9	3.2
Stanley	13.4	64.3	12.8	3.3
Total	10.4	45.7	9.1	2.2
Bishop Auckland	27.1	60.2	36.6	3.9
Spennymoor	12.2	41.5	20.8	2.9
Crook	17.1	49.0	23.2	3.6
Shildon	24.4	63.3	33.2	2.4
Wolsingham	7.6	51.5	2.9	1.6
Total	18.7	51.7	27.2	3.3
Barnard Castle	17.1	23.1	11.2	1.6
Cockfield	16.5	45.4	25.7	1.4
Stanhope	4.4	38.0	14.8	4.9
Middleton-in-Teesdale	8.2	23.6	3.2	1.9
Gainford	10.2	31.7	5.9	1.3
Total	12.4	37.4	15.4	2.1
Total – West Durham	14.7	45.8	17.6	3.0

Even in the fairly settled conditions of 1929, the main part of south-west Durham was showing an unemployment rate of nearly 19 per cent, almost twice the national average, and was noticeably less fortunate than other parts of West Durham. In north-west Durham the unemployment figure was kept down by the prosperity of Consett's industries, but in the northern district unemployment was distinctly higher than in the country generally, and was slightly greater than the regional average.

It was in the 1930s, however, that the unemployment problem became serious. In 1932, the worst year of the depression, more than half of south-west Durham's insured population were unemployed, and only Consett's ability to withstand the depression prevented the unemployment in north-west Durham from averaging over 60 per cent. The northern district of north-west Durham and the dale area of south-west Durham had unemployment rates similar to the region as a whole, but even here there were particular districts which suffered excessively, such as Cockfield and Chopwell. It will be seen that four exchange areas (Stanley, Lanchester, Shildon and Bishop Auckland) had an unemployment rate exceeding 60 per cent in 1932, and five others (Wolsingham, Crook, Cockfield, Chopwell and Spennymoor) had rates exceeding 40 per cent. Consett alone had an unemployment rate less than the national average. It requires little imagination to translate these figures into living terms, and to visualise the magnitude of the unemployment problem in West Durham.

By 1937 there was a big improvement in the situation, particularly in north-west Durham, and, although unemployment was still high, the worst of it was confined to south-west Durham. The worst areas were Bishop Auckland, Shildon, Cockfield, Crook and Spennymoor, all with more than 20 per cent unemployed. Although Lanchester and Stanley in north-west Durham had experienced very severe unemployment they recovered much quicker than the districts of south-west Durham.

This question of speed of recovery or, in other words, duration of unemployment, is important not only in its effect on the individuals concerned and social conditions generally, but as an indication of the extent and nature of the unemployment problem.

If the duration of the high unemployment is to be examined closely it is obviously necessary to know the course of unemployment in the West Durham exchanges year by year for the pre-war decade. Unfortunately the Ministry of Labour appears to have no records whatsoever of unemployment for several of the depression years, and it has thus not been possible to confirm the figures. It is thought, however, that the figures are accurate to within 1 per cent or 2 per cent, but, rather than print figures which may not be strictly accurate, the course of unemployment has been shown in the form of a moving average (see Table 10.3). In this way the general trend can be presented with confidence in its capacity to show what is claimed of it – the general trend (but not necessarily a rigid accuracy). A moving average table also has the advantage of smoothing out fluctuations so that the course of the unemployment is easily recognisable, and is free from the disturbing irrelevancies (in this instance at least) of year to year oscillations.

Table 10.3 3-Year Moving Average of Unemployment %s – 1929-1939

Exchange Area	1930	1931	1932	1933	1934	1935	1936	1937	1938
Blaydon	25	32	35	30	28	25	22	17	15
Chopwell	27	35	39	37	32	29	25	21	18
Sunston	27	34	30	31	28	24	19	16	14
Consett	12	16	18	14	10	6	5	6	6
Lanchester	41	57	60	56	50	42	30	25	17
Stanley	20	37	47	46	36	33	26	24	17
Bishop Auckland	42	53	54	55	52	48	42	36	31
Spennymoor	25	34	38	34	30	28	25	23	21
Crook	30	41	44	45	42	37	32	29	24
Shildon	34	47	60	58	53	46	41	34	29
Cockfield	24	34	43	45	43	37	33	31	29
Great Britain	16	20	21	19	17	15	13	12	11

Figures are 3-year moving average of July unemployment rates. Figures are not available for the smaller, less important districts. Cockfield has in this instance been included within the south-west Durham group. Chopwell's unemployment in July 1935 has been assumed at 30 per cent, a more representative figure, taking the year as a whole, than the actual.

A glance at Table 10.3 or the graph (Figure 10.1) which has been constructed from the figures given in Table 10.3 shows that the trend of unemployment was the same throughout West Durham – rising, generally fairly steeply, up to around 1932 and then falling off more gradually, right up to the war. The three northern district exchanges all reacted similarly, each showing unemployment around 25 per cent at the beginning of the Depression (the period centred on 1930), rising to 35 per cent – 40 per cent during the worst of the slump, and then recovering steadily to little more than the national figure. In north-west

Durham Consett stands alone in its ability to withstand the slump and to enjoy several years of very low unemployment. Lanchester was quick to suffer the force of the Depression, whilst in Stanley the full impact was longer delayed, but both suffered heavily in the 1931-1933 period. An improvement followed, more rapid in Lanchester than Stanley, and both localities ended the period, not indeed in prosperity, but in a far better position than their 1932 record, and the experience of neighbouring areas, would have suggested.

Figure 10.1 West Durham Unemployment Percentages, three-year moving average 1929-1939

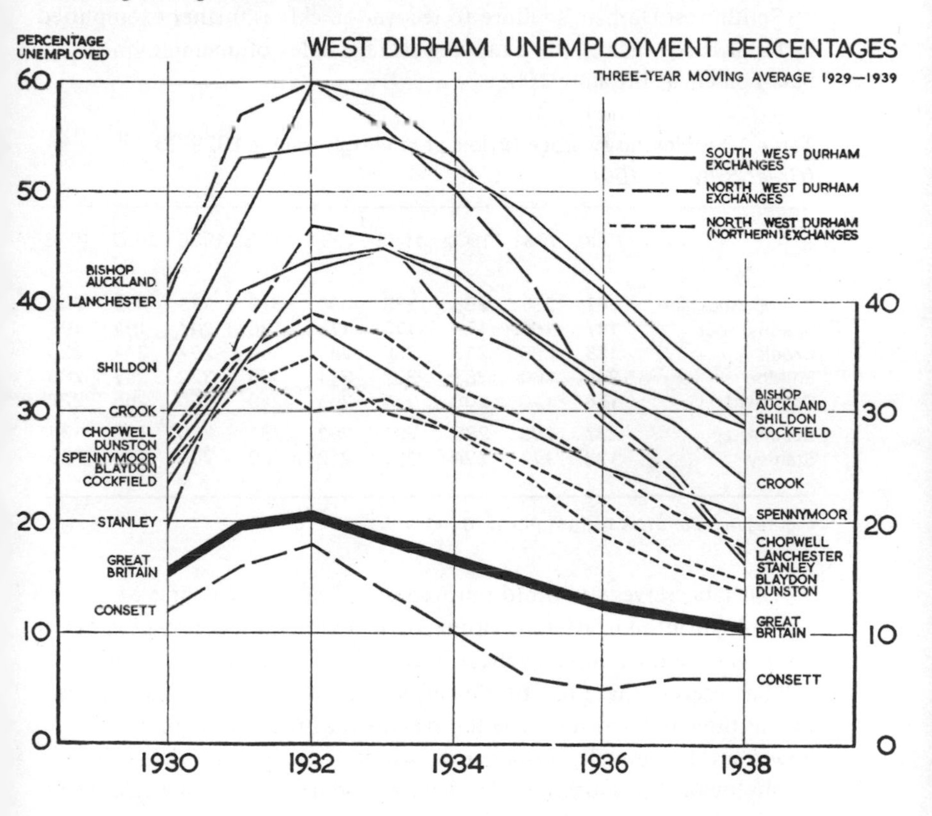

In south-west Durham fairly heavy unemployment was experienced at the first approach of depression, particularly in Bishop Auckland and Shildon, and the position worsened in all areas up to 1932-1933. Unemployment lessened around 1933-1935, but the rate of improvement was slow, and the figures show that unemployment was persisting in all areas of south-west Durham at a higher level than elsewhere in West Durham. This is shown clearly in the graph (Figure 10.1). The south-west Durham exchanges, together with Lanchester and Stanley, had very high unemployment during the worst of the depression but by the end of the inter-war period it is the five south-west Durham exchanges which stand out alone in the misery of their unemployment.

South-west Durham's failure to recover quickly is further exemplified in Table 10.4 which shows a moving average index of unemployment, based on Great Britain = 100.

Table 10.4 Moving Average Index of Unemployment 1929-39
(Great Britain = 100)

	1930	1931	1932	1933	1934	1935	1936	1937	1938
Bishop Auckland	267	268	258	288	306	319	*333*	302	294
Spennymoor	147	169	179	173	175	186	*201*	191	198
Crook	188	206	213	235	247	250	*251*	241	220
Shildon	245	260	288	302	311	308	*322*	287	283
Cockfield	155	170	208	234	255	249	260	255	*272*
Lanchester	237	286	288	291	*292*	281	225	199	164
Stanley	123	177	224	*231*	212	220	200	196	156

Figures *in italic* show highest point of index

This table serves a twofold purpose of indicating the course of unemployment in relation to Britain as a whole, and also revealing the position once the normal cyclical fluctuations are eliminated. Thus, it will be observed that unemployment in West Durham was, in many cases, two or three times as severe as the average for Britain, and, more important, for several years after the worst of the slump in 1932, unemployment in south-west Durham was actually increasing relative to Britain. Recovery was slower than for the country generally so that, *compared with Britain, unemployment was rising steadily up to around 1937 in all the south-west Durham exchange areas.* This trend is very marked, and has few deviations. Lanchester and Stanley, on the other hand had both begun to improve at more than the national rate by

1933 or 1934. In interpreting these facts, revealed by the figures in Table 10.4, it must be remembered that the table has been further designed to show the unemployment position after the national cyclical unemployment has been eliminated. All figures over 100 show, therefore, an excess employment which must be attributable to either special cyclical unemployment peculiar to the area concerned or structural unemployment. Local cyclical unemployment which is of sufficient intensity to cause the trend to be rising steadily for six or seven years, as in south-west Durham, must, however, be regarded as so abnormal as to justify the broader remedies which are usually applied to structural unemployment. There can be but one conclusion – that under the impact of the general depression the whole economy of south-west Durham had collapsed, and it could only be re-built with the aid of external measures.

The collapse of the south-west Durham economy was brought about by the closing down of many of the pits. Details of the unemployment in different industries are not available before 1938, but the rapid movement of insured workers away from the mining industry is sufficient indication that it was the collapse of this industry which led to most of the area's troubles. Between 1929 and 1938 nearly 9000 miners in south-west Durham left the industry, and in spite of this, there were still 22.7 per cent or 4087 of south-west Durham's mining population unemployed in 1938. It is safe to suppose that the number of miners actually in employment in south-west Durham in 1938 (13,865) was little more than 60 per cent of the 1929 figure. In the case of south-west Durham external help was extended and, together with the rise of a war economy which produced national full employment, the revival of south-west Durham was effected, as the 1947 unemployment figures show (Table 10.2).

11 EMPLOYMENT AND UNEMPLOYMENT IN MINING 1920-70

Martin Bulmer

The previous chapter has described the traumatic impact of the Great Depression upon the western part of the county, from which it did not recover in employment terms until 1947. This chapter seeks to expand that analysis in two ways, firstly by locating the 1930s in the context of employment trends in mining over the last 50 years, and secondly by looking briefly at some of the social consequences of unemployment, particularly in the 1920s, and 1930s.

The overall employment picture in mining in County Durham since 1913 is summarised in the frontispiece and Table 11.1. It shows a period of declining employment between 1924 and 1934, relative stability from 1934 to 1957, and very rapid decline since then. The period can conveniently be separated into two parts, before and after the Second World War.

The decline of mining has been a national phenomenon, but because of the region's dependence on the coal industry it had more serious effects in the north-east. Until after the First World War coal was the backbone of the region's economy. In 1914, at the historic peak of UK coal production, the North-East produced about twenty per cent of this country's coal and (after South Wales) was the region with the largest production. In 1938 it produced the same proportion of the nation's coal and produced more than South Wales. Since 1945, the North-East's proportion of national production had fallen only marginally up to 1970, from 20 per cent to 17 per cent. Thus, the contraction of the coal industry in the region was not a phenomenon peculiar to the North-east; it is an aspect of the national contraction of the industry.

It is important to emphasise that the history of the industry is not simply one of long-term secular decline at a steady rate. The contraction apparent between 1913 and 1939 conceals very wide cyclical fluctuations in mining employment, due not only to the economic recession of the early 1930s, but to the collapse of the coal export trade in the 1920s and stagnating domestic consumption. In 1913 Britain produced 25 per cent of world coal production and 55 per cent of world coal exports. By 1937, these had fallen to 19 per cent and 40

Table 11.1 Employment in Coal-Mining , 1913-1975

Year	National	County Durham	County Durham Mining Employment Index 1913=1000
1913		165,807	1000
1922	1,095,000	154,837	934
1923	1,137,000	170,181	1026
1924	1,171,896	169,142	1020
1925	1,086,103	147,022	887
1926		National Stoppage	
1927	999,941	128,283	774
1928	923,092	126,762	765
1929	932,330	136,413	823
1930	916,809	131,197	791
1931	848,455	112,968	681
1932	802,705	103,768	626
1933	790,868	101,129	610
1934	774,866	106,814	644
1935	758,587	105,698	637
1936	756,232	107,426	648
1937	777,791	114,480	090
1938	781,865	114,472	690
1939	777,950	112,182	677
1947	711,400	108,900	657
1948	724,000	110,900	669
1949	719,500	110,700	668
1950	687,900	108,300	653
1951	697,100	107,100	646
1952	718,900	107,200	647
1953	706,500	103,400	624
1954	705,500	101,200	610
1955	700,200	101,500	612
1956	703,700	101,400	612
1957	710,000	100,900	609
1958	687,400	97,900	590
1959	640,200	93,000	561
1960	587,500	87,200	526
1961	565,900	83,700	505
1962	540,900	77,900	470
1963-64	509,600	70,800	427
1964-65	481,200	65,900	397
1965-66	439,600	58,400	352
1966-67	412,700	52,800	318
1967-68	367,500	44,200	267
1968-69	321,100	37,900	229
1969-70	297,800	34,500	208
1970-71	286,400	34,200	206
1971-72	274,000	33,100	200
1972-73	263,600	30,000	181
1973-74	242,500	27,100	163
1974-75	248,800	26,500	160
1975-76	243,700	25,500	154

The County Durham Mining Employment Index expresses employment in coal-mining in County Durham in any one year as a proportion of employment in coal-mining in County Durham in 1913, taking 1913=1000.

Sources: 1913-1949: W.R. Garside, *The Durham Miners 1919-1960*, London, Allen & Unwin, 1971, pp.18, 313, 430.

1950-1976: (National) Ministry of Technology, Digest of Energy Statistics 1976, HMSO, London, 1976, (County Durham) *NCB Annual Reports, HMSO, London.*

per cent respectively. Domestic consumption in 1913 was 184 million tons, in 1937-8, 185 million tons. In County Durham the effects of these fluctuations were felt most acutely between 1924 and 1934, when coalfield employment fell from 170,000 to 106,000.

A common picture of the inter-war years, reinforced by evidence in the previous chapter, is that the Great Depression caused the misfortunes of the area in general and the mining industry in particular. It certainly was a most important influence, and mining was one of the industries which bore the brunt. In 1932, 34 per cent of all coalminers in Britain were unemployed, a proportion exceeded only by shipbuilding workers, iron-workers and dock-workers. By 1937 this had fallen to 14 per cent, but was still high in comparison to the general employment picture.[1] The figures for mining unemployment in County Durham at this period are shown in Table 11.2. Apart from its very high level absolutely, what is remarkable is the high level of unemployment *before* the onset of the Depression in 1929.

Nationally, cyclical unemployment arising from the world depression was highest in the period 1929-33. The problems of unemployment in the coal-mining industry in Durham, however, were at least as much structural as cyclical, due to the fortunes of the coal industry in the 1920s, already referred to. Even without the Great Depression, mining in Durham would have experienced severe unemployment in the 1930s – and it did experience it in the 1920s.

Economic historians currently debate how to characterise the inter-war years. Several commentators have emphasised that this was a period of economic growth nationally, and even during the Depression one of increasing prosperity and better housing and health in the South and Midlands.[2] This was paralleled by a quite different picture in the depressed areas (further discussed in the next chapter), which were 'separate enclaves' of unemployment, material deprivation and ill-health in an increasingly prosperous country. No occupation exemplifies these conditions in Wales, Scotland and the north of England better than the Durham miners. Measured in terms of unemployment rates, the incidence of death and disease, housing, or conditions of income maintenance, County Durham was a depressed, deprived and distressed area between the wars.

This process began, moreover, in the 1920s. Garside has graphically described the consequences of contraction and industrial conflict upon employment and income in the industry.[3] During the decade conditions got worse, as employers forced wage cuts and longer hours on the miners. Unemployment Insurance regulations became more stringent, the

Durham Miners' Association exhausted its own funds to provide relief to strikers, and increasingly greater burdens were placed on local Boards of Guardians. The course of industrial conflict, culminating in the General Strike of 1926, is described by Garside and is a well-known story. Perhaps less well-known were some of the other conflicts of the period.

Table 11.2 Proportion of Work-force of Coal Industry Unemployed*
1928-38

	Great Britain	County Durham
1928	22%	22%
1929	16%	21%
1930	20%	19%
1931	28%	30%
1932	34%	35%
1933	33%	34%
1934	28%	26%
1935	25%	25%
1936	21%	19%
1937	14%	11%
1938	15%	12%

**Unemployed* included both 'wholly unemployed' and 'temporarily unemployed'.

Source: W.R. Garside, *The Durham Miners, 1919-60,* London, Allen & Unwin, 1971, p.268.

One lay between central and local government over the administration of poor relief. Although most Boards of Guardians in Durham followed Ministry of Health instructions, the Chester-le-Street Board stepped out of line. Forty-seven of the fifty-nine members were Labour, of whom thirty-nine were miner's officials, miners or miners' wives. In 1925-6 the Board made payments against Ministry instructions to unmarried miners on strike. During the General Strike it was alleged to have continued to disburse funds beyond its powers, and was dismissed after hurried legislation in August 1926.[4]

Boards of Guardians were superseded by Public Assistance Committees in 1929 under the Local Government Act. The PACs had autonomy in fixing scales of benefits according to need, permitting the continuation of 'Poplarism', over-spending by local councils in working-class areas against the wishes of central government. Matters reached a head in

County Durham in 1932. The Durham PAC in 1931-2 disallowed only 1% of claims (the lowest in the country) and allowed 90 per cent at the maximum rate of benefit, an indication of the extent of distress in the area. The Durham PAC became increasingly critical of the Government's insistence on a means test and in September 1932, with the support of the County Council, decided to ignore instructions from Whitehall. This led to its replacement by government appointed commissioners.[5]

The subsequent 1934 Unemployment Act led to nationwide protest, described by Runciman.[6] But the earlier opposition from Chester-le-Street Guardians and the Durham PAC is an indication both of the hardship being suffered by a very large proportion of the population, and a strong political will to do something about it.

Employment and unemployment, earnings and family incomes, can to an extent be quantified for the period. But what lay behind these figures? What were the human and wider social consequences of unemployment? The impact of the experience of the 1920s and 1930s upon County Durham cannot be exaggerated, whether in terms of future employment, industrial relations, political action or wider social change. For the generations active in leadership in the 1940s, 1950s and 1960s, the 1920s and 1930s provided a continual point of reference.

By the early 1930s, the severity of adverse social and environmental conditions brought home to a wider public what was being endured by some sectors of the population. One observer, John Newsom, wrote:

> 'Two million unemployed', what does such a statement mean to nine out of ten citizens of Great Britain, two million is too great a number for most of us, like the Trobriand islanders we would rather think of it as 'many, many'. 'Unemployed' – we conjure up a picture of sullen figures in cap and choker brooding sedition and capable of effort only in the avoidance of work.
>
> There is no 'unemployed man', he is as much an abstraction as his predecessor of a century ago – the 'economic man'. There are in fact a very large number of people whose personal lives are deeply influenced by actual or potential unemployment . . . the most important facet of the problem . . . is personal and individual. It is a question affecting *men* and *women* with individual needs who react to the fate of unemployment in as many ways as there are different persons . . .
>
> If it is agreed that unemployment is a normal concomitant of our present industrial organisation, that because of its complexity there will always be 'labour in the wrong places', even if there is a lack of it

> somewhere else, some measures are urgently required to remove from what is in effect an economic dislocation, any suspicion of moral or functional disability. It is difficult to appreciate why one section of the population should bear the shocks of a system from which others are benefiting.[7]

Adverse social and environmental conditions aroused shock and horror among some middle-class observers; the incidence of disease and ill-health, referred to in chapter 2, led to inquiries and improvement. But the well-documented social deprivation and waste of the period remains rooted also in the memories of those who endured it. Social conditions in County Durham await their historian. Contemporary documents by Bowley and Hogg, Newsom, The Pilgrim Trust, Lambert and Beales, the Unemployed Workers' movement, Ellen Wilkinson, and Richard Titmuss provide rich sources on the county and the urban centres on its fringe.[8] Later commentaries by Garside, Branson and Heineman, Runciman, Glynn and Oxborrow, and Stevenson underline the social conditions in 'industrial graveyards'.[9] From these sources one may start to build up a picture of the social and psychological consequences of endemic and prolonged unemployment, briefly referred to in the next chapter. Though some migrated, why did more not do so? What was the explanation of people's apparent rootedness in the area?

As argued in chapter 2, one should not exaggerate the negative features of this experience. The Pilgrim Trust's nationwide study of unemployment included Crook in West Durham among towns investigated in detail. It noted that coal mining in the town was at its peak in the years 1851-1871, and that the industry there was already depressed at the end of the nineteenth century. There was little coal being worked in the town, but the investigators were impressed by the vitality of its social life:

> In many respects we felt that 'the atmosphere' in the homes visited in Crook was more satisfactory than anywhere else. There was little of the desperate poverty of Liverpool, there was more determination not to give way to unemployment and not to subsist on self-pity than there was in Wales. This is the more striking since on the whole unemployment has lasted longer here than in any other of the places visited. 71 per cent (of the unemployed) had had no work for five years or more as compared with 45 per cent in the Rhondda, 23 per cent in Liverpool and only 3 per cent in Deptford. The Durham miner who has been out of work for five years has not a perpetual

> sense of grievance but rather a determination to make the best of things; to make his allotment or his poultry holding a life for himself; not as an alternative to employment but rather to keep himself fit for employment, to help at the family budget, and to retain active interests.[10]

More significant for the future were consequences of this experience not realised until during or after the Second World War. The importance of a strong mining trade union was underlined. Political support for the Labour Party as a means of improving social conditions and representing the interests of the working class was strongly reinforced, to achieve implementation in mines Nationalisation, social insurance and the National Health Service after 1945. Social attitudes changed too. Runciman emphasises 'the non-correlation of hardship and grievance',[11] but one might also point both to the surviving consciousness of the period among those who lived through it, and its impact upon more fortunate, particularly middle-class, observers, for whom it provided a political and social education. 'Traditions' are socially constructed;[12] this experience of Durham mining communities in the 1920s and 1930s is central to understanding a variety of post-war developments, including the planning field discussed in the next chapter.

Durham and coal-mining survived the 1930s. The recovery in the industry begun in the late 1930s was maintained during and after the Second World War, and throughout the first decade after Nationalisation in 1947. In terms of mining employment in County Durham, however, this did not lead to a return to employment levels of the early 1920s. This was partly due to local factors such as the permanent flooding of a large number of workings in south-west Durham. Mining employment was 106,000 in 1933, 103,000 in 1943, 109,000 in 1948, 103,400 in 1953 and 100,900 in 1957. Similar relative stability is observed in the north-east regional figures: 161,200 were employed in mining in 1938, 142,500 in 1957. These figures, however, conceal a relative decline in the proportion of the insured male population of north-east England who were miners. In 1938, 20.8 per cent were miners, by 1948 this had fallen to 15.3 per cent, around which figure it remained for a decade.[13] While mining employment remained stable, the total insured male population was increasing, and this increase was concentrated in the manufacturing and service sectors of employment.

The turning-point for employment in the coal mining industry in County Durham came in 1957-8, as Sam Watson, General Secretary of the Durham Area NUM wrote in his Annual Report for 1957. Did he know what his words portended?

> It is evident that the coal industries of Germany, Holland, Belgium and France are beginning to feel the effects of competition, and while at the moment (January 1958) we are still maintaining our position, there is no doubt that the economic sky is darkening and less coal (at least for a period) will be required.

The effects on employment of this change in demand for coal are shown in Table 11.1. Over twenty years, 100,000 miners have fallen to 25,000. For local residents, the decline is symbolised by the shrinking number of banners, bands and people who attend the Miners' Gala (or Big Meeting) in Durham City every July, which is but a shadow of its former glory. Mining in County Durham has been steadily on the wane for two decades.

The reasons for this decline are complex. A number of factors have combined to reduce coal production in this country to a figure less than 60 per cent of what is was in 1950. National trends in primary energy consumption (that is, fuels which are not produced from other fuels, like electricity from coal- and oil-fired power stations) are shown in tables 11.3 and 11.4. A major reason for the onset of the decline of mining employment after 1957 was competition from oil, which steadily increased its share of the domestic fuel market up to 1972. Natural gas is also now offering fierce competition, and coal today supplies less than two-fifths of the nation's fuel needs, compared to over four-fifths in 1957.

Both industrial and domestic consumers changed to other fuels over the last 20 years. It is true that, in part, the Government's insistence that coal pay its way contributed to this – the 1967 Fuel Policy White Paper was quite explicit that its aim was cheap energy, not the buttressing of a declining industry. The earlier 1965 White Paper stated: 'The size of the industry within the framework set by the general fuel policy will depend significantly on its success in reducing costs.'[14] This should not conceal, however, the increasing competition to which coal has been exposed. Two very large industrial users, the gas and steel industries, turned to other fuels. The gas industry had stagnated until in the early 1960s it developed a process for making gas from oil instead of coal, which reduced significantly costs of production. Later in the decade the discovery of large quantities of *natural* gas in the North Sea has changed the situation more radically by introducing another primary fuel to compete directly with coal in the home market.

The 1967 White Paper recognised these trends by stating the Government's determination to expand nuclear energy electricity and natural gas as primary fuels and move from a two-fuel to a four-fuel economy. Trends in national fuel consumption between 1950 and 1975 are shown in Table 11.4. The Government envisaged a rapid build-up of natural gas and an acceleration of the production of electricity from nuclear energy. Natural gas consumption has indeed risen to 1975 in line with estimates in the 1967 White Paper, and oil and coal consumption are broadly at the levels then estimated. Nuclear electricity had, however, notably failed to provide significant extra primary energy resources; there was no sign at all of the promise held out in 1967 of nuclear energy meeting one quarter of *all* energy requirements in the late 1970s being fulfilled.

Besides market trends, physical conditions of mining have had an important part to play in determining the size of the coal industry. Decisions about which coalfields to develop, and within coalfields which pits to expand and which to run down or close, depend upon geological conditions, thickness of seams, ease of working, and quality of the coal being produced. Sheer physical factors like these have played a considerable part in the contraction of the Durham coalfield. In the western part of the Durham coalfield, opened up earliest and with coal measures nearer the surface than to the east of the county, by the early 1960s many pits had reached, or were approaching, exhaustion. For many pits, closure was dictated by geological conditions which rendered the colliery no longer efficiently workable. Linked with geological conditions, much of the decline is explicable in terms of the application of criteria of profit and loss to the pits of the coalfield. In assessing the viability of a pit, account would be taken not only of its present economic situation but of its future potential for mechanisation. By and large, the pits in the western part of the coalfield had a lower output than those in the east, made a much greater loss and were unsuitable for mechanisation, physically and economically.

Coupled with the governmental requirement that the NCB did as well financially as it could, this led to the severe cutting back in the 1960s of uneconomic pits. One should not, however, exaggerate the inevitability of such a contraction. The economic criteria which the NCB applied to particular pits' operations themselves reflected the economic conditions under which the government required the NCB to operate as a nationalised industry. In theory it would have been possible to maintain any pit in operation, given a constant demand for coal and a high enough degree of governmental subsidy, until all the coal that could

Table 11.3 Total Annual Fuel Consumption in the United Kingdom, 1950-1976

	PRIMARY FUEL					Total
Year	Coal	Oil	Natural Gas	Nuclear Electricity	Hydro Electricity	Gross Inland Energy Consumption
1950	202.6	22.2			0.9	225.7
1951	207.8	24.8			1.0	223.6
1952	206.8	25.7			1.0	233.5
1953	207.8	27.8			1.0	236.6
1954	213.8	30.9			1.3	246.0
1955	215.2	34.5			1.0	250.7
1956	217.5	37.5			1.3	256.3
1957	212.9	36.7		0.2	1.6	251.0
1958	202.4	47.2	0.1	0.1	1.5	251.3
1959	189.4	56.1	0.1	0.5	1.5	247.6
1960	196.7	65.5	0.1	0.9	1.7	264.9
1961	191.8	71.0	0.1	1.1	2.1	266.1
1962	191.2	78.6	0.1	1.5	2.1	273.5
1963	194.0	85.3	0.2	2.5	1.8	283.8
1964	187.2	93.3	0.4	3.2	1.9	286.0
1965	184.6	102.8	1.3	6.0	2.3	297.0
1966	174.7	111.7	1.2	7.8	2.4	297.8
1967	163.8	119.3	2.1	8.9	2.7	296.8
1968	164.5	125.9	4.7	10.1	2.2	307.4
1969	161.1	135.7	9.2	10.5	2.0	318.5
1970	154.4	145.6	17.6	9.4	2.6	329.6
1971	138.7	147.3	28.4	9.7	1.8	325.9
1972	120.9	157.6	40.3	10.5	2.0	331.3
1973	131.3	159.4	43.5	9.9	2.0	346.1
1974	115.9	150.1	52.1	11.9	2.1	332.2
1975	118.1	134.4	54.5	10.8	1.9	319.7
1976*	120.5	132.0	57.6	12.7	1.9	324.7

All Figures are expressed in *million tons coal equivalent.*
* Provisional

Source: United Kingdom *Digest of Energy Statistics,* 1970, 1974, 1975 (London, HMSO); DOE *Energy Trends* (Dept. of the Environment, February 1977).

Table 11.4 Total Annual Fuel Consumption in the United Kingdom, 1964-76; showing percentage shares of primary fuels

	Coal	Oil	Natural gas	Nuclear electricity	Hydro electricity
1964	66.2%	32.1%	0.1%	1.0%	0.6%
1965	63.0%	34.1%	0.4%	1.8%	0.7%
1966	59.6%	36.9%	0.4%	2.4%	0.7%
1967	56.2%	39.6%	0.7%	2.7%	0.8%
1968	54.1%	40.7%	1.5%	3.0%	0.7%
1969	51.0%	42.5%	2.9%	3.0%	0.6%
1970	46.9%	44.4%	5.4%	2.6%	0.7%
1971	42.6%	45.4%	8.7%	2.8%	0.5%
1972	36.4%	47.9%	12.2%	2.9%	0.6%
1973	37.7%	46.5%	12.6%	2.7%	0.5%
1974	34.8%	45.4%	15.9%	3.3%	0.6%
1975	36.9%	42.1%	17.0%	3.4%	0.6%
1976	37.1%	40.7%	17.7%	3.9%	0.6%

Sources: *United Kingdom Digest of Energy Statistics,* London, HMSO, 1975, p.14; *Energy Trends,* Dept. of the Environment, February 1977.

be worked was exhausted. In practice, the crucial economic and political arguments turned on what is a reasonable degree of subsidy, either from the government to the NCB, or within the Coal Board between its economic and uneconomic collieries. The opaqueness of the latter consideration is one reason why in general there is no simple explanation of the decision to close a particular pit. Indeed, closure often appeared to be the result of compounded difficulties, and closures were not announced more than three or four months before their actual date. However, the general trend in the county is clear; it has been portrayed graphically by geographers J.W. House[15] and W. Moyes.[16] Closures have occurred at a much more rapid rate in west than in east Durham, reflecting the age, size, geological difficulties and profitability of pits. The effects of this are illustrated in Table 11.5.

The location of mining activity in the county in 1970 is shown in Figure 11.1, which indicates closures in the previous decade and emphasises the extent to which the contraction of the coalfield has taken place from west to east. Mining today in County Durham is concentrated on the large and coastal collieries. The consequences of

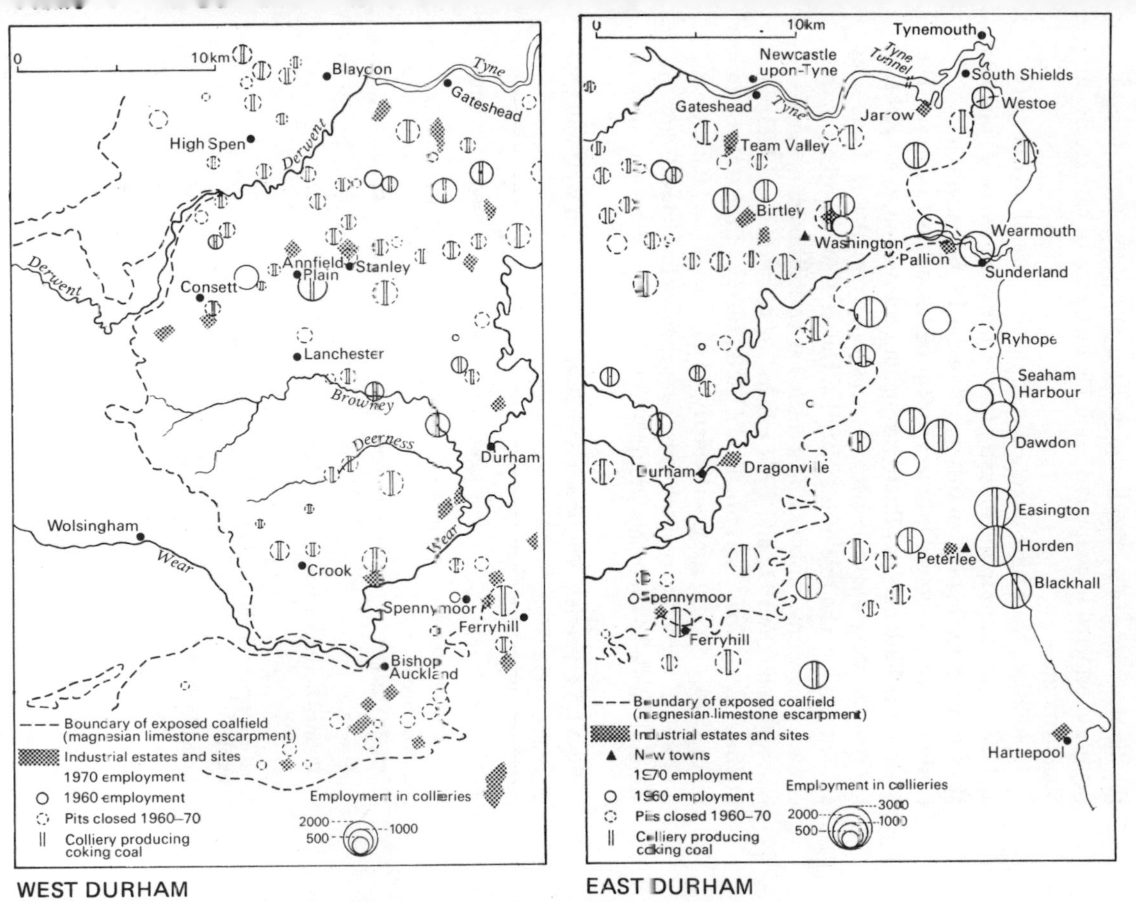

WEST DURHAM

EAST DURHAM

Reproduced with permission from K. Warren, *North East England* (OUP, 1973)

the disappearance of mining in the western part of the coalfield are further considered in chapters 15 and 16, by means of case studies in Spennymoor.

In addition, the future of coal turned on the state of productivity and labour relations in the industry (particularly the levels of voluntary absenteeism). Fuel policy in this regard in the 1960s remains a contentious and involved problem for future historians to unravel. The head of the National Coal Board throughout this period, Lord Robens, has told the story of the 1960s as he sees it in a remarkable if one-sided autobiography. The role of the National Union of Mineworkers in the closure programme remains unchronicled as yet, although material is available on the 1972 and 1974 miners' strikes.[17] Michael Jackson in *The Price of Coal*[18] has provided a useful survey of the state of mining up to 1974, concentrating particularly on changes in the 'market position' of the industry, problems these changes had caused, and attempts made to overcome them.

Table 11.5 Collieries, Manpower and Saleable Output in West and East Durham, 1953-67

	1953	1965	1966	1967
No. of collieries				
West Durham	86	49	41	35
East Durham	35	29	26	24
County Durham Total	121	78	67	57
Wage earners on colliery books ('000s)				
West Durham	53.5	26.0	21.7	18.2
East Durham	50.0	39.9	36.7	34.6
County Durham Total	103.5	65.9	58.4	52.8
Saleable output (million tons)				
West Durham	12.7	7.2	6.0	4.8
East Durham	13.0	13.2	13.1	13.3
County Durham Total	25.7	20.4	19.1	18.1

Source: NCB Annual Reports for 1952-3, 1965-6 and 1966-7.

Both sides of the industry agree that far from being a 'natural' or 'inevitable' process, the contraction of the mining industry could be influenced by government action. Prior to the oil crisis of 1973, the argument raged back and forth as to what had hastened the closure programme. The White Paper of 1967[19] attributed the decline to falling demand from consumers, the chairman of the NCB to a policy being forced on the industry by the Government.[20] There is some truth in both views. The Government manipulated consumption of coal by the amount it induced the Central Electricity Generating Board to buy. The amount of coal bought by the CEGB increased from 46m tons in 1956 to 65m in 1970-71, over one-third of Britain's coal production. Negotiations between the NCB and the CEGB were not immune from political pressures from the government of the day, who could also influence matters by allowing the CEGB to build power stations using other fuels than coal. The decision to allow the construction of nuclear power station at Seaton Carew, south of West Hartlepool, in the late 1960s, is a local example of this kind of governmental influence. The government also affected the price at which coal was sold by the financial protection it gave the industry. The protection had been substantial, by means of a ban on coal imports for many years and a 2d per gallon excise duty on fuel oil, coal's main competitor. The financial targets which the Government set the industry have already been mentioned. The 1967 White Paper said that these various measures would continue but ruled out entirely any general subsidy to the coal industry as uneconomic.[21]

How rapidly and how far mining would contract in Durham was not at first appreciated. Sam Watson's 'at least for a period' turned out to be permanent and of increasing intensity. There was, moreover, a persistent tendency to err on the side of over-optimism in forward planning for the coal industry. The Pepler MacFarlane Plan of 1949 (further discussed in chapter 12) estimated a gross reduction of manpower in coal-mining in the county of 23,500 over 25 to 30 years.[22] (The actual reduction in the 25 years to 1974 was 83,600.) The NCB *National Plan for Coal* of 1950 estimated total national production in 1961-65 would average 240m tons per annum. (In1965 actual production was 183m tons.) The NCB in 1958 produced figures, quoted in the County Development Plan Amendment of 1964, which gave the following estimates for manpower employed in the county: 1967, 100,000; in 1968-82, an average of 89,000; in 1983-2008 an annual average of 72,000. (The actual 1968-75 annual average was 31,900.) Both the 1965 National Plan and the 1965 White Paper over-estimated total national coal production at 170-180m tons in 1970. By 1967 total production had already fallen below this level; by 1976 it was at 120m tons.

Only Lord Robens's estimates in response to the 1967 Fuel White Paper erred on the over-pessimistic side. He suggested that if the government's projections for coal production in it were turned into manpower (assuming rising productivity and normal wastage and retirement), the coal industry would require a labour force of only 65,000 in 1980.[20] (In 1968 manpower was 364,000 nationally.) Assuming 10 per cent of these miners were in County Durham, there would be 6,500 miners in the county in 1980, or less than one-fifth of the number of miners in the county in March 1969. Although this appears in 1977 to have been over-pessimistic, by 1970 the Durham mining labour force had been reduced to one-third of its size in 1957; by 1975 to one-quarter.

Looked at nationally, Durham's share in the industry's contraction was not exceptional, though the area lacked the longer-term expansion prospects of the Midlands coalfields in particular. The Scottish, West Midlands, and North-Western divisions of the NCB all contracted in the 1960s more sharply than the North-Eastern division.[23] The decline in terms of manpower had proceeded rather faster than the national rate, the Durham percentage of national manpower falling from 14.2 per cent in 1957 to 11.6 per cent in 1969-70 and to 10.5 per cent in 1975-76. Paralleling this fall in manpower had been a slight decline in the proportion of the nation's deep mined coal won in the county from 12.2 per cent in 1953 to 11.1 per cent in 1965 and 1967, to 9.9 per cent in March 1969.[24] But in Durham the effects were even more serious because of the county's dependance on coal for employment.

Notes

1. S. Glynn and J. Oxborrow, *Inter-War Britain: a Social and Economic History,* London, Allen & Unwin, 1976, pp.150-1.
2. Cf. D.H. Aldcroft, *The Inter-War Economy: Britain 1919-39,* London, Batsford, 1970, esp. ch. 3; A.E. Booth and S. Glynn, 'Unemployment in the inter-war period: a multiple problem', *Journal of Contemporary History,* 10, 1975, pp.611-36; S. Glynn and J. Oxborrow, *Inter-War Britain.*
3. W.R. Garside, *The Durham Miners 1919-60,* London, Allen & Unwin, 1971, ch.7.
4. W.G. Runciman, *Relative Deprivation and Social Justice, London, Routledge,* 1966, p.66; W.R. Garside, *The Durham Miners,* p.272-3.
5. W.R. Garside, *The Durham Miners,* p.279-80.
6. W.G. Runciman, *Relative Deprivation,* p.66-7.
7. John Newsom, *Out of the Pit: a challenge to the comfortable,* Oxford, Blackwell 1936, pp.xii, 107.
8. H.A. Mess, *Industrial Tyneside: a social survey,* Newcastle, 1928; A.L. Bowley

and M. Hogg, *Has Poverty Diminished?* London, King, 1925; J. Newsom, *Out of the Pit;* Pilgrim Trust, *Men Without Work,* Cambridge University Press, 1938; H.L. Beales and R.S. Lambert (eds.), *Memoirs of the Unemployed,* London, Gollancz, 1934; W. Harrington, *Unemployed Struggles, 1919-36,* London, 1936; Ellen Wilkinson, *The Town that was Murdered: the life-story of Jarrow,* London, Gollancz, 1939; R.M. Titmuss, *Poverty and Population: a factual study of contemporary social waste,* London, Macmillan, 1938; D.M. Goodfellow, *Tyneside: the social facts,* 1940. On the social effects of unemployment nationally and internationally, see also E.W. Bakke, *The Unemployed Man,* London, Nisbet, 1933. The most famous study is on Austria: M. Jahoda, P.F. Lazarsfeld and H. Zeisel, *Die Arbeitlosen von Marienthal,* Leipzig, Hirzel, 1933; translated as M. Jahoda *et al., Marienthal: the sociography of an unemployed community,* London, Tavistock, 1972. On the United States see R.C. Angell, *The Family Encounters the Depression,* New York, Scribner, 1936 and M. Komarovsky, *The Unemployed Man and His Family,* New York, Dryden, 1940.

9. W.R. Garside, *The Durham Miners;* N. Branson and M. Heinemann, *Britain in the 1930s,* London, Weidenfeld, 1971; W.G. Runciman, *Relative Deprivation;* Glynn and Oxborrow, *Inter-war Britain;* J. Stevenson, *Social Conditions in Britain between the Wars,* London, Penguin, 1977. The latter contains a selection of extracts from contemporary documents.
10. Pilgrim Trust, *Men Without Work.*
11. W.G. Runciman, *Relative Deprivation,* p.65.
12. J. Gusfield, *Community,* Oxford, Blackwell, 1976. pp.37-9.
13. P. Bowden and A.A. Gibb, *Economic Growth in the North East of England* – a study undertaken by the Business Research Unit, University of Durham, for the Department of Economic Affairs. (Interim Report, Durham, 1967), ch.1, p.25.
14. White Paper on *Fuel Policy,* Cmnd. 2798, October 1965, p.19. In this the Labour Government set out its policy objectives. Their second White Paper, *Fuel Policy* (Cmnd. 3438, November 1967), did not review these but aimed 'to reassess the balance between the available primary fuels' (p.1).
15. J.W. House and E.M. Knight, *Pit Closure and the Community,* University of Newcastle Geography Department, 1967, Figures 1 to 4.
16. W. Moyes, *Contracting Coalfield,* Newcastle, Frank Graham, 1972.
17. Lord Robens, *Ten Years Stint,* London, Cassell, 1972; J. Hughes and R. Moore (eds.), *A Special Case? Social Justice and the Miner,* Harmondsworth, Penguin, 1972; M. Wilson, 'Case-study of the mineworker's national strikes of 1972 and 1974', Open University, course D203, *Decision-Making in Britain,* Block IV, *Government and Industry,* Milton Keynes, Open University Press, 1976.
18. M.P. Jackson, *The Price of Coal,* London, Croom Helm, 1974.
19. Cmnd. 3438, *Fuel Policy.*
20. Lord Robens, quoted in *Keesings Contemporary Archives,* 22470 A, January 1968.
21. Cmnd. 3438: 'The Government's basic objective can be summarised as cheap energy' (p.38). 'In order to alter relative prices in favour of coal sufficiently to slow down its decline significantly, it would be necessary to protect it at a level which would lead to misuse of resources and would put British industry at a disadvantage with its competitors' (p.36).
22. Sir George Pepler and F.W. MacFarlane, *North East Area Development Plan; Interim Report,* Ministry of Town and Country Planning, 1949.
23. J.W. House and E.M. Knight, *Pit Closure,* p.1.
24. See *National Coal Board,* Annual Report 1966-67 (House of Commons Papers 611-2) and Annual Report 1967-68 (House of Commons Papers 401-2).

PLANNING IN THE COUNTY

12 CHANGE, POLICY AND PLANNING SINCE 1918

Martin Bulmer

In a real sense the economic and social problems of north-east England in the period since the First World War are a result of its past economic success as an economic growth area in the nineteenth century, with a prosperity founded on coal, iron and steel, shipbuilding and heavy engineering.[1] Structural changes in the national and world economies, and in world markets, were eroding the predominance of these staple industries from 1914 onwards, and regions such as the North-East dependent on these industries suffered particularly severely during the world economic recession of the 1930s.[2] The impact of the recession was felt evenly throughout the United Kingdom, but hit the older industrial areas of the north and west of Britain particulary hard.[3] One of the prime social consequences of this depression was, of course, massive unemployment in the region throughout the 1930s, concentrated particularly in the areas dependent on coal and shipbuilding, described in the two preceding chapters.

This traumatic historical experience had many consequences. It led to the first faltering steps toward a government policy to help economically disadvantaged regions of the country. It heavily underlined the social costs of the experience in a multitude of ways – perhaps symbolised most tellingly by the Jarrow March.[4] It helped to bring into being an 'image' of regions of the country – including the North-East – that was markedly unfavourable and centred around a stereotype of pervasive industrial and social waste and bleakness. It had unknown social and psychological consequences for the families of those who experienced unemployment. And in sheer numerical terms the impact was often devastating.

Economically, the effects of unemployment were very serious, both for individual families, for communities, and for large areas of the region. The decay in the already poor economic infrastructure – the lack of resources to repair or replace the houses, schools, hospitals and other public buildings of the nineteenth century – left a legacy of neglect for the future.[5] Socially, contemporary interpretations of the unemployment experience stressed its disorganising effects on social life, although the Pilgrim Trust report on Crook strikes a slightly optimistic note.[6] There can be no doubt, however, that the experience of the 1930s in the North-East made its mark not only on those who lived through it, but on the political and economic structure of Britain. For it brought home, to even the more vigorous advocates of *laissez-faire* and non-intervention in the workings of the market, that the state had to make some effort to remedy chronic regional imbalances in employment and economic well-being generally.[7]

Any account of economic changes is not divisible in a clear-cut manner from political trends. The history of the coal-mining industry between the wars, for example, was one of a series of attempts by governments to grapple with the chronic problems which faced a fragmented, under-mechanised, under capitalised strife-torn industry. It was marked also by a reluctance on the part of government to come to terms with and seek a solution to the fierce and bitter clash of economic interest throughout the inter-war period between coal-owners and miners, which did not end until mines nationalisation in 1947.[8]

Even so, direct intervention in a particular industry was open to governments, using various means. Although the economic problems of the North-East were due more to world economic trends – especially the decline of export markets and then the collapse of world trade – than to short-term economic policies, governments lacked the willingness to use tools of economic analysis to tackle the problems at their root. The scale of the human problems involved meant that in the long run some kind of political intervention of a more *ad hoc* kind became necessary to deal with the problems of the 'industrial graveyard' areas.[9] The planned intervention of central and local government in economic and social issues in the North-East over the last 40 years may, in its origin, be traced back to this searing experience of economic adversity in the inter-war period.

In the North-East the number of workers attached to the coal mining, shipbuilding and marine engineering industries declined by approximately one-third over the inter-war period as a whole, while employment in the iron and steel and general engineering industries was subject to sharp cyclical fluctuations. At times the collapse in activity was so considerable that certain coal-producing and shipbuilding districts were reduced to almost complete idleness. In 1932, the worst year of the slump, the unemployment rate in the North-East reached 40 per cent of the insured population. The level of unemployment would have been even higher had it not been for a large and continuing movement of labour from the region throughout the inter-war years, amounting to approximately nine per cent of the total population per decade. This movement was given official encouragement, the Ministry of Labour offering financial assistance to those willing to move. The unemployment problem, however, was too great to be solved by this means alone, and as a remedy migration found little support among local authorities adversely affected by the loss of population. Accordingly, attention was turned to the possibility of attracting some of the newer expanding industries to the North-East and other severely depressed areas.

The first sign of this political concern in central government may be traced to the appointment in 1934 of investigators to examine and report upon social conditions in the North-East, South Wales, Central Scotland and West Cumberland.[10] The report on Durham and Tyneside, by a Conservative MP, Captain D.E. Wallace, showed that at the time of the investigation there were still 165,000 unemployed in the area. Of these, 63,000 had been out of work for two years, 40,000 for more than three years, 18,000 for over four years, and 9,000 over five years. Since four or more days' work constituted a break in unemployment the actual number of long-term unemployed who had had only a few days' work in three or four years was certainly greater than these figures suggest.

Captain Wallace recommended among his conclusions, although 'with considerable reserve', the setting up of a governing body with resources at its disposal to provide on a large scale for the establishment of new industrial developments in the area. Such a cautious recommendation merely reflected what others had been arguing for some time, that the chronic unemployment problems of the depressed areas could not be remedied without large-scale government commitment of money to help establish new industry there. These strong political pressures were among the reasons for the passing, following the publication of the reports, of the Special Areas (Development and Improvement) Act 1934, which appointed two full-time Commissioners for the Special Areas, one in England and Wales and one in Scotland.[11] Up to £2 million was advanced to the Commissioners initially for their work.

Three main points emerge from the experience of the Special Commissioners, who continued to labour throughout the 1930s, and whose trials are recorded in their annual reports. Firstly, the scale and scope of the aid they were allowed to give was quite inadequate to the scale of the problem. Not only were their financial resources severely limited, but stringent conditions were attached to the way in which they could be exercised. Many different schemes for public works were turned down, since the Commissioners' support was permitted only if the scheme contributed to the economic development of the area. The Commissioners could not supplement a grant given by another government department, nor could they provide support for a scheme eligible for a government grant but not receiving it. Secondly, the Commissioners' experience led to a move increasingly away from *laissez-faire* toward taking active steps to attract industry to the Special Areas. Although the restrictive conditions under which they worked limited what they could do, a sign of the change was the passage in 1937 of amending legislation to allow them to give subsidies to private firms, a policy very strongly opposed by Parliament three years previously. Thirdly, the Commissioners' main impact was in the establishment of a number of industrial estates in the depressed areas. In terms of employment creation these were rather insignificant. In the North-East the largest development, the Team Valley Trading Estate on the outskirts of Gateshead, had in May 1939 98 units in production, employing altogether 2,250 workers. Two small developments, at Pallion in Sunderland (three factories) and at St. Helens near Bishop Auckland (three factories) provided employment for a total of 590 workers at that time.[12] Three thousand jobs made a scarcely perceptible dent upon the problem of unemployment, and is a measure of the inadequacy of the resources allowed the Commissioners. More than half of the total employed were females, many of whom were under 18 years of age. Before the war, therefore, distribution of industry policy could claim very modest success indeed. It had brought a limited addition to female employment opportunities in areas where they were lacking, but in relation to the problem of large-scale unemployment, particularly among males, its effects had been negligible. It was, however, significant as providing a pointer within government to the direction in which policies might be developed in the future.

Recognition of the scale of the problems involved had led to the establishment of the Royal Commission on the Distribution of the Industrial Population, which reported in January 1940.[13] The importance of this seminal report lies in the *imprimatur* which it gave to state intervention in matters of industrial location, in striking contrast to the doctrines of non-interference which continue to predominate in, for example, the United States:

> The choice of location for industry in the past has been mainly at the discretion of the employer or entrepreneur: the State has not directly intervened to control or direct it. Industry in Great Britain,

> as in other industrialised countries, both in Europe and the West, has prospered exceedingly during the period of unfettered control . . . It is true that some intervention or influence by the State on the choice of industrial location had not been unknown in recent years . . . but such influence or control has been indirect and limited in character. So far Government has not attempted to control directly the industrialist's choice of location . . .
> Undoubtedly a principal national consideration is the successful conduct of industry; any control which fatally hampered or handicapped industry would in any Western nation, especially in one so highly industrialised and so dependent on manufacture as Great Britain, deal a blow of the gravest character to the national existence . . . But while making all necessary allowances on that account, when conditions affecting the health or well-being rather than the wealth of the State demand attention, when slums, defective sanitation, noise, air pollution and traffic congestion are found to constitute disadvantages, if not dangers, to the community, when the problem, in fact, becomes social in texture rather than economic, then modern civilisation may well require a regulating authority of some kind to step in and take reasonable measures for the protection of the general and national interests . . .
> It is not possible from the evidence submitted to us to avoid the conclusion that the disadvantages in many, if not in most of the great industrial concentrations, alike on the strategical, the social, and the economic side, do constitute serious handicaps and even in some respects dangers to the nation's life and development, and we are of the opinion that definite action should be taken by the Government towards remedying them.[14]

The means adopted to carry out this broad aim, the Commission suggested, should be the dispersal of both industrial undertakings and the industrial population from the large urban centres where they were concentrated. Particular concern was expressed about the drift of population to London and the South-East, but the efforts to stem this would contribute to the broader aims of achieving population balance. The report suggested that the objectives of national action should include not only the decentralisation and dispersal of industries and the industrial population, but the encouragement of a reasonable balance of industrial development, so far as possible, throughout the various regions of Britain, coupled with industrial diversification within each region. The new authority which the report proposed should be established would examine the case for developing garden cites or garden suburbs, satellite towns, trading estates, and existing small towns as a means of implementing the policy. It should have the power to regulate industrial development over much of London and the Home Counties, as one means of encouraging new industrial development in the depressed areas.

A minority report, signed by the Professor of Town Planning at London University, Patrick Abercrombie, and two others, argued for the establishment of a more powerful authority – namely a government department – which would take over the responsibilities of the Commissioners for Special Areas – and for the use of more stringent controls over the industrial development in congested areas. Their differences with the majority report lay very largely in this area of implementation, rather than in their analysis of the origin and nature of the problems involved.

The recommendations of the Barlow Report were based upon economic and social analysis, and only secondarily upon strategic considerations of wartime. Its influence upon subsequent policy is shown by the White Paper of 1944 on 'Employment Policy' looking forward to the end of the war and after.[15] This proposed that the Special Areas legislation would be replaced by an active policy to secure a balanced distribution of industry, by means of control of new factory developments by private firms, continuing to build certain factories in the (newly designated) 'development areas', and providing financial assistance in the form of short- and long-term loans for industrial development. These proposals were embodied in the Distribution of Industry Act of 1945 which empowered the Board of Trade to build factories in the development areas and to acquire land for this purpose, if necessary by compulsory purchase, as well as exercising control nationally over new factory developments above a certain size.

A review of the policy in 1948[16] noted that unemployment in the North-Eastern Development Area had fallen to 3 per cent of the insured population, compared to 15 per cent in 1937 and 39 per cent in 1932. Although not providing a precise estimate of the number of new jobs created on industrial estates it referred to industrial estates and group sites being established at Aycliffe, Spennymoor, North-Tees, Hartlepool, Jarrow, East Middlesbrough, Skelton-in-Cleveland, Shildon, Sherburn, Crook, Langley Moor, Bedlington, Houghton-le-Spring, Ashington, West Chirton, Castleside and Newburn. Although the main reduction in the unemployment rate was attributable to the expansion of the national economy, the number of new jobs created were significant compared to the pre-war totals. For example, between 1945 and June 1950, a total of 37,052 new jobs were created in Durham geographic county, largely in new or existing industrial estates;[17] this compares very favourably with three thousand jobs created at Team Valley, Pallion and St Helens Auckland between 1934 and 1939.

The post-war development of this policy has been examined elsewhere,[18] and although it has played an important part in moulding the regional picture, its detailed history will not be recounted here. The whole question of government intervention to affect the distribution of industry in the county and to redistribute the population requires a study in itself. All that may be done at this point is to indicate formally the main political agencies of intervention in the distribution of industry and population. before going on to examine more closely the policies pursued in this area within County Durham.

The other form of government intervention has been the creation of new towns, of which there are three in the county, Newton Aycliffe, Peterlee and Washington. The origins of Newton Aycliffe (designated in 1947) and Peterlee (1948) are discussed in detail in chapters 13 and 14 immediately following.[19] Both have populations at present of about 20,000 and have developed to this size from greenfield sites in twenty years. Washington New Town, between Sunderland and the Tyneside conurbation, was designated in 1964, with a population of 20,000 already resident within the area. It is intended to grow to four times that size. All three towns are governed by New Town Corporations (appointed by the Government) which manage the town and control its housing. They are thus outside the usual local authority structure, although local authorities provide the new towns in their areas with certain services. Newton Aycliffe was built adjacent to the Industrial Estate, although the two are under separate management. (This contrasts with the Team Valley estate, which has no new linked settlement.) Peterlee was originally envisaged as a residential town but industrial development is now taking place. At Washington, industrial and residental development are taking place together, both under the aegis of the corporation.

Looking analytically at the impact of industrial and population policy as it has developed in the area, three levels of intervention may be distinguished: central government action (both directly and through bodies which it has created); county action through Durham County Council; and local government action through Urban and Rural District Councils. There are three types of action which these bodies undertake that are relevant here. Firstly, action to redistribute industry and bring new industry to the county – thus creating new employment. Secondly, creating new centres of population through the creation of either new settlements or rejuvenated older settlements. Thirdly, the limitation of the growth of certain older settlements which are not judged suitable for development. There is thus a combination of measures, shown in Figure 12.1. This diagram is highly schematic and leaves a good deal out. The links between different aspects of policy, pursued in different spheres, are not adequately shown. Nor do the various regional authorities appear, although they perform important functions. The Northern Economic Development Council and the Northern Economic Planning Council undertake promotional activities similar to those undertaken by the county council and other local authorities. In addition the Planning Council keeps a watching brief on government regional policy and formulates regional planning strategy. Implementation, however, depends upon central and local government.

Figure 12.1 Industrial Development and the Settlement Pattern in County Durham

		POLITICAL AGENCY		
		CENTRAL GOVERNMENT	COUNTY COUNCIL	LOCAL AUTHORITY
TYPE OF ACTION	DISTRIBUTION OF INDUSTRY	FISCAL & OTHER FINANCIAL MEASURES Board of Trade Advance Factories EIEC	DEVELOPMENT OF INDUSTRIAL ESTATES both jointly and separately PROVISION of the necessary ancillary services	
	DEVELOPMENT OF CENTRES OF POPULATION GROWTH	NEW TOWNS	'GROWTH POINT' POLICY	SUPPORT FOR 'GROWTH POINT' POLICY BUILDING NEW HOUSES TO IMPLEMENT IT
	LIMITATION OF DEVELOPMENT OF OTHER SETTLEMENTS	RATIFICATION 'CATEGORY D' POLICY AS SUPREME PLANNING AUTHORITY	'CATEGORY D' POLICY	SUPPORT FOR OR OPPOSITION TO 'CATEGORY D' POLICY

Central Government has used fiscal and other financial inducements of various kinds to try to attract industry to the North-East. These are outside our remit here. The development of industrial estates has already been mentioned. The large established industrial estates include the Team Valley Trading Estate in Gateshead and the Aycliffe Industrial Estate to the south of the new town of Newton Aycliffe. The Board of Trade has also established a considerable number of Advance Factories; for example there is a flourishing development at Crook in west Durham. All these factory developments are carried out and managed on behalf of the Department of Trade and Industry by the English Industrial Estates Corporation.

Government policy in physical terms has, therefore, concentrated upon the provision of industrial estates and advance factories and the building of new towns. Although the latter policy has encouraged the concentration of population, it is fair to say that government policy on industrial development, taken together with fiscal policy, has tended to favour a blanket policy, to promote development throughout the industrial areas and particularly in areas of high unemployment. The exception to this was the period 1963-65, when the Government pursued a more vigorous policy of encouraging 'growth points' within the region. Thus the effect has been to maintain the existing distribution of population rather than to redistribute it; the classic case of this is probably the Team Valley Estate, to which very many people travel to work from north-west Durham.

This brief overview of government regional policy may exaggerate its coherence, since it has been subject to many variations over the years, with changes of party, of minister and of departmental responsibility. By contrast, the County Council planning policy has been much more clear-cut and consistent. One element in the County Council policy has been to foster industrial development in the county, not only by promotional schemes but by the purchase and equipment of its own industrial estates, in partnership with local authorities. Hand in hand with this has gone the concern with amenity and visual improvement to clear up industrial and commercial dereliction. This policy has been pursued in the context of an existing dispersed settlement pattern of a large number of small and medium-sized population units, based in many cases originally on mining. The core of the County Council's settlement policy has, therefore, aimed to adjust this dispersed settlement pattern to changed economic circumstances. Industrial development has been enlisted as a necessary element in this policy but the actual location of the industry has been decided in terms of these long-term aims, not in terms of short run considerations such as the level of unemployment in a particular place. The aim has been to adjust the settlement pattern to a changed economic structure and to plan industrial development (itself an integral part of structural economic change) in order to create and sustain the new settlement pattern. The two elements thus both contribute to a new distribution of the population. And it is these changes which are of especial interest here, particularly from the point of view of change in mining communities.

The historical origins of County Council policy are of some interest, since these may throw light on the assumptions on which it is based. Tracing the genesis of ideas about how to tackle the problems of a declining mining area is not easy in the abstract, and the regional development documents examined above do not pay particular attention to the balance of settlement within such areas. One author who did so, at least by implication, was Dennison in a book published in 1939. In the course of an economist's assessment of industrial location policies, contrasting one of large-scale migration with one of taking work to the workers, he points out that it is necessary to differentiate between areas in terms of their economic characteristics. His prognosis for areas whose livelihood was based on a declining mining industry was pessimistic:

> There are some areas which must, under present conditions, be classed as derelict; they are mostly places which depended for their existence on coal-mining, and are now without any industrial significance because the coal measures are exhausted. Unless it is desired to give an entirely new direction to the siting of industry, such as is implied in the construction of large numbers of 'garden cities', it is manifestly an inappropriate policy to attempt to attract new industries to such places, for they are mostly somewhat isolated, have little economic life apart from that which originally depended upon their one industry, and are indeed not at all suitable for the location of expanding industries. Thus the appropriate policy here appears to be one of transference; it has been suggested that such places be 'evacuated'; and perhaps the communities transplanted as individual entities.[20]

Dennison recognised that there would be resistance to such a policy and that compulsion would be necessary. The human difficulties this might create would be surmounted by distinguishing between those who had, and those who had not, 'potentially high employment value'. The former should be encouraged to transfer to other areas, with the support of greatly extended industrial training facilities. The latter would not, being recognised as belonging:

> to a declining community on which transference of the 'best' elements of the population has placed an additional burden. Here then is an appropriate field for the application of those measures which are usually classed as 'palliatives' . . . Schemes such as land settlement or 'subsistence production' add greatly to individual well-being and as such are appropriate under conditions for which it must be recognised that for the present at least, there is no 'complete' solution.[21]

On the other hand, in areas which were 'depressed, but not derelict', a policy of encouraging new industrial development, by means of inducement and facilities provided for those moving into the area, was suggested. This policy might even be extended to those areas *'least* derelict', as distinct from more derelict areas which would not be centres for new industrial development. Here, in embryo, is a policy for concentrating upon 'growth points' in declining areas, with a parallel policy of population concentration.

The criteria by which to distinguish between a 'derelict' and a 'depressed' area were not specified, but a study carried out by T. Sharp four years previously suggests the kinds of considerations which would be involved. Sharp noted that industrial north-east England as a whole was merely 'distressed' (although to an extreme degree), in contrast to the 'dereliction' of individual towns and villages within the area. The S.W. Durham area, the particular focus of Sharp's attention, betrayed considerable evidence of dereliction. The six small towns near Bishop Auckland 'are just long straggling collections of streets; bare, featureless streets of grim little houses. A few shops, one or two rather seedy cinemas, a score of pubs, half-a-dozen chapels, and an urban district council, constitute the sum of their civic amenities'.[22]

As an example of the grim view taken of these places, one may quote his description of a part of Spennymoor:

> It has within its boundaries, and separated from the main body by three or four fields, a typical pit village, Tudhoe Colliery. Two long streets stretch out on either side of the main road. Between these and the sprawling mass of the pit and the pit heaps run two more streets, bare, bleak, with neither yard-space nor garden space, just blocks of

> houses run up to keep the weather off the heads of that indispensable part of the pit's productive machinery, the workmen. A typical pit village and a nightmare of a place.[23]

In recommending a general policy of population transfer for the area, Sharp is clear that the physical conditions of the place is the main criterion of dereliction, taken together with the decline of mining:

> These towns and villages are not such as civilized men should be expected to live in. They were ugly and mean from the very beginning and now most of them are outworn. It they are still to be inhabited, large parts of them will need to be rebuilt during the next few decades. Theoretically the simplest plan is to evacuate the whole territory.[24]

Similar views are expressed in A. Temple's thesis, presented in 1940. The author distinguished five stages of dereliction: (i) the abandonment of the settlement by industry; (ii) its abandonment by the best elements among the population; (iii) the experience of prolonged unemployment for those who remain; (iv) the physical and mental deterioration of the population; (v) the ending of the utility of the village as a viable entity. As a policy recommendation, she concluded: 'Now that the pits are dismantled, the smaller colliery villages are entirely without purpose. Most of them have very little in the way of social amenities and further, consist only of out of date houses, but whether this is the case or not, their removal would do much to tidy-up South-West Durham.'[25]

The first major statement of industrial development and settlement policy in County Durham was that prepared in 1949 by Sir George Pepler and F. W. MacFarlane, two Planning Consultants, for the Minister of Town and Country Planning.[26] Instructed to prepare an Outline Plan and Report for the Physical Development and Conservation of the North-East Development Area, they summed up their aims, referring explicity to Patrick Geddes, as the co-ordination of 'Folk, Work and Place'.

> Our aim has been to make possible for its people the best way of life of their own choosing. Their livelihood, however, depends upon industry and the framing of industrial policy is outside our province. All that we can do is to endeavour to fit that policy to the facts

> of the land in a manner which will serve the needs of industry and, at the same time, secure for the people an environment for good living.[27]

They sought to plan for a distribution of population based primarily upon convenient access to industrial opportunity. They refer to 'an equalization of opportunity for employment', which will bring people 'within comfortable reach of work'.[28]

They painted a searing picture of the problems of the coalfield settlements, echoing the grim picture painted by Sharp and Temple:

> The swift, almost 'mushroom' growth of small towns and villages on the coalfield during the rapid expansion of the mining industry culminated in a countryside of isolated or straggling communities housed in terraces totally devoid of reasonable amenities and overshadowed by the black, evil-smelling tips of coal-waste. The conditions are worst in the villages of S.W. Durham, where the mines are smaller and even more scattered than elsewhere but the whole of the coalfield is littered with isolated pit-head villages and ribbon-developed straggling settlements nucleated at intervals by several larger but equally depressing units such as Spennymoor, Crook, Houghton-le-Spring or Stanley. During the heavy post-1918 mining slump and the working out or flooding of many pits in the south-west of the coalfield, employment throughout the area became progressively scarce. The closing-down of the local pit meant total unemployment for nearly every man in the village, with the consequences that all the progressive workers moved out. Some houses fell derelict and the remainder were occupied by the older settled folk, or people attracted by the cheap rents and being content to live in conditions of backwardness and decay. Such a state of affairs exists today to a greater and lesser degree in communities throughout the coalfield.[29]

Discussing mining in West Durham, they explicitly reject the case for 'taking work to the workers'. In their opinion, 'the prospects of introducing under any foreseeable political and economic conditions male-employing industry into West Durham in sufficient volume to compensate for the coming decline in mining are remote in the extreme'.[30] Their case for this rested on the nature of the area, 'bleak and unattractive to those unused to it'. In addition, poor communications, the 'scarred and defaced landscape', minerally unstable sites, and an unskilled labour force, all made the introduction of new industry there uneconomic.

Their analysis of housing and labour mobility reinforced the economic and physical arguments: 'To make some of (the mining villages) in West Durham really habitable would cost a great deal of money and would be a disservice to the inhabitants, as it would tend to anchor them where, either now or before long, they would have no prospects of earning their livelihood'.[31] The concomitant of this policy, therefore, is population movement: – 'the well-being of the area's inhabitants requires a redistribution of population within it. Redistribution is necessary in order to secure an equalisation of the opportunity for employment and homes in pleasant and healthy surroundings, within comfortable reach of work, . . . the whole object being to secure for all the population the best possible opportunities for a good life.'[32]

The authors were optimistic that such a plan could readily be implemented:

> The evidence suggests that labour will move, subject to the two essentials of good work and decent houses, though we do not wish to underrate or be unsympathetic to the social upheavals and broken family ties, which these changes so often produce. Few families move without good cause; sometimes it may be for personal motives but mostly it is the urge for work or improved prospects. Help man in his search for work by pointing out the areas of expanding industry; offer him a home in attractive surroundings near his work and one can hope for his co-operation.[33]

They envisaged its implementation by means of two main proposals. The first was the creation of new centres (of both employment and housing) at places in central Durham such as Team Valley, Birtley, Langley Moor and Aycliffe, to take population from west Durham. Such centres would be 'sites for industry where it can be expected to flourish, with new houses in up-to-date communities nearby, into which the populations from the dying coalfield can progressively move'.[34]

Their second proposal was for the concentration of settlement within west Durham. In relation to long-life pits, they envisaged a recentring of village communities so that a group of them could be re-formed, conveniently placed in relation to the pits and offering better opportunities for a communal life and much improved amenities:

> It will simply mean that instead of treating each village as an isolated unit to be patched up and added to, regardless of the daily journey

> to work or to school, and the impossibility of affording adequate amenities, a series of small communities will be brought together where they can support and enjoy a far wider range of social activities and recreation, where a greater number will be handy for their work and where the children will have a short and safe walk to school.[35]

The influence of the Pepler-MacFarlane Report on the Durham County Development Plan of 1951 (and its Revised Version of 1964) is evident. There is the same concern with the dynamic relationship between new industrial development and changes in the population structure. 'The first task is to adjust the whole fabric of the settlement pattern to the likely future changes in employment.'[36] The authors of the plan, like Pepler and MacFarlane, correctly anticipated the further rapid decline of mining employment in the county after 1957, shown in the lower half of Table 11.1 and sought to adapt the size and location of settlements to this coming change.

The authors of the plan point out that, historically, the settlement pattern of County Durham has been characteristically one of large numbers of dispersed settlements with an economic base rooted in coal-mining. Unlike the general trend towards concentration of populations in large urban centres, which produces a fairly clean division between rural and urban-industrial areas, in County Durham there is a persistence of the dispersed settlement pattern and of the small industrial settlement. This pattern of settlement persists even after its industrial base has disappeared, with the result that work and residence do not coincide and large numbers of people are required to travel out from their place of residence to pursue their economic activity. This is evident for coal miners, factory and administrative workers. New factories (e.g. the Newton Aycliffe Industrial Estate) drawn their work force from considerable distances. Following an analysis of industrial trends and population forecasts for different parts of the county, the Plan sets out the aims of the County Council in respect of the future pattern of settlement. This policy is of great importance and is quoted in full below:

> If new industry does come, then the reason for some of the villages will have gone and a new pattern of settlements will be needed to link up with the new distribution of employment. If the industry does not come, then there may well be a movement of population away from certain areas as the employment available in the heavy industry

decreases. The future is uncertain but whatever happens there is likely to be some change in the function and distribution of settlements. It is the purpose of this plan to anticipate and plan for these changes, to suggest a policy which will be successful whatever the future may hold and to ensure as far as possible that capital is invested in the right places in such a way as to build up satisfactory communities.

An attempt has been made to estimate the future of each settlement in the county and to estimate whether the population of each settlement is likely to increase, remain at its present level or fall. This assessment is based upon the employment prospects in the vicinity, the physical condition of property and services and the siting of the settlement. On this basis all settlements in the County have been placed in one of four categories:

'A' Those in which the investment of considerable further amounts of capital is envisaged because of an expected future re-grouping of population or because it is anticipated that the future natural increase in population will be retained.

'B' Those in which it is believed that the population will remain at approximately the present level for many years to come. It is felt that sufficient capital should be invested in these communities to cater for approximately the present population.

'C' Those from which it is believed that there may be an outward movement of some part of the population. In these cases it is felt that only sufficient capital should be invested to cater for the needs of a reduced population.

'D' Those from which a considerable loss of population may be expected. In these cases it is felt that there should be no further investment of capital on any considerable scale and that any proposal to invest capital should be carefully examined. This generally means that when the existing houses become uninhabitable, they should be replaced elsewhere and that any expenditure on facilities and services in these communities which would involve public money should be limited to what appears to be the possible future life of existing property in the community.[37]

This policy of settlement categorisation is subsequently argued out in greater detail in the plan. The most salient element, it is clear from the Revised Plan of 1964[38] and from public controversy since 1951, has been the proposal to limit development in certain villages categorised 'D'. The 'Category D' issue has aroused a great deal of heat locally and is still a burning political question, as well as being a good example of the problems of involving (or not involving) members of the public in the planning process.[39] It remains, however, a major element in local planning policy, despite a modification of the categorisation from four to six groups in 1964, and the lifting of the 'D' designation from certain villages on appeal to the Minister. Less attention, however, has been paid to its converse, the policy of concentrating settlement in larger centres, those categorised 'A'.

The 1964 Amendment makes clear, however, that this aim is of paramount importance:

> The basic and dominant problem of the county remains the attraction of new industry. Experience has shown how difficult it is to interest industrialists in developing in the coalfield area . . . Concentration of development in selected areas will allow the provision of new houses in better surroundings and in larger units to support more and better social facilities. It will also increase modern urban units, expanding communities and groups of labour and attract industry by providing a modern industrial environment . . . The policy of concentrating development in selected centres are the best possible conditions for attracting new industry.[40]

Government fiscal policies to influence the distribution of industry have tended to cover the whole of the development areas, and not to discriminate between places within them. The notable exception to this is the 1963 White Paper,[41] which endorsed a policy of concentrating resources in 'growth zones' within the region. A later general pronouncement of the Northern Economic Planning Council[42] also advocated a growth zone policy, although it is not entirely clear from the very broad definition adopted which parts of County Durham are excluded from the growth zone. In general, therefore, the 'growth-point' policy has been pursued most diligently by the County Council with only intermittent support from central government.

It has, however, been endorsed by outside specialists associated with the County Council. The policy has been taken to its logically furthest extent by Dr Bowden and Mr Gibb, who argue for the creation of new centres of population within the county, apart from the present conurbations, with populations of not less than 250,000 people. They argue the case for their proposal on straight economic grounds:

> Since the provision of social capital (public as well as private) is very often an economic proposition only in large urban areas, the sensible policy would be to facilitate the development of a few selected centres of growth. These should be in economically attractive locations, in order to encourage industrial expansion and should be large enough to provide an adequate range of manpower skills and ancillary services for industry, a desirable physical environment in which to live and a sufficient variety of cultural amenities to cater for all tastes. It seems unlikely that all these requirements could be met in urban centres of less than 250,000 people, which would appear to indicate the need for some fundamental changes in the present settlement pattern of the North-East.[43]

More recently, Mr Derek Senior, a member of the Maud Commission on Local Government Reorganisation, has given an account of the County Council's policy.[44] He sets it in the context of the need for industrial development following the decline of mining and stresses the deleterious effects on the county of the migration of young people out of the area altogether. Once again, the dynamic relationship between industrial development and a changing settlement pattern is evident:

> The County Council will continue its own efforts to attract new industry, and to prevent the resources available for the improvement of selected centres from being wasted in a vain attempt to prolong the habitation of palaeotechnic settlements. Even if it fails in the short term to stabilize West Durham's population, it will at least have helped to gather it into well-located, compact units that can be economically viable and socially functional.

What should be made sociologically of this very brief account of political responses to the consequences of economic change? One area of fruitful investigation would be the social bases of support of elected representatives in central and local government, and the influence of this upon the policies pursued. This very large question cannot be dealt with here, but there are certain obvious features. In central government, the very substantial working-class support received by the Labour Party from mining areas in particular, and from industrial areas in general, has made it sensitive to the need to assist declining industries and promote regional development. The periods 1945-51 and 1964-70 therefore saw considerable emphasis placed upon measures to promote industrial development in the regions, and sizeable financial resources directed to that end. The Conservative Party, however, has not been inactive when faced with issues of regional development, particularly when these were politically salient, and Lord Hailsham's activities during 1963 are an instance of this. Developments in the early 1970s such as the establishment of the Industrial Development Executive of the Department of Trade and Industry are another. It would be a mistake, moreover, to posit any sharp discontinuity between the policies pursued by different governments. Many of the measures enacted by the 1945-51 Labour government were anticipated both in the Barlow Report and in the White Paper of the coalition government of 1944, and were by no means new policies. Moreover one of the more opaque areas of political sociology is the role played by central administration in the development of government policies. One may surmise that in the case of regional development, this role has not been insignificant.

At the more local level, also, the political structure of government in County Durham (discussed in Chapters 6 to 9) is of considerable interest. Continuous Labour Party control of Durham County Council since the 1920s, without interruption, is in marked contrast to changes of control in central government. It may be more illuminating, however, to concentrate here upon the sociological content of the documents discussed above, and ask what account they give of local social structure and the effects upon it of industrial change. The striking influence of the ideas of Patrick Geddes[45] and his emphasis upon 'Work', 'Place' and 'Folk' is evident in several places; the question can be rephrased by pointing to the overriding emphasis upon 'Work' and 'Place', and asking: Where do 'Folk' enter in?

One of the notable themes of these documents and of discussions of regional development policy and unemployment is that they are pervaded by what might be called a general diffuse humanitarianism, a 'concern' for people, which is shared by all except the hardhearted, short-term-profit maximising, economic rationalist. There is a notable lack, however, of any amplification of such feelings. More seriously, from a sociological point of view, there is very little or no reference to the social structure of the area.

This is evident in the treatment of two problems of the area, unemployment and physical deterioration of buildings and environment. One of the minor consequences of the experience of mass unemployment was the recognition that unemployment cannot be explained as a psychological phenomenon, but must be treated as a social problem. It was one of the virtues of the social service movement in the 1930s that they sought to do this, but it is notable how old stereotypes and elements of moralising crept into supposedly academic economic analyses. Dennison, for example, in the book discussed above, posited a distinction between those out of work who had 'potentially high employment value' and those who did not. How would this be established? If one contrasts the pre-war unemployment figures of 30 or 40 per cent with post-war figures of 3 per cent, is this not evidence that the very large majority of those out of work had 'potentially high employment value'? The discussion is a little redolent of contemporary suggestions that certain workers are 'untrainable' (whatever that means), whereas evidence from several sources suggests that well-run industrial training schemes are capable of helping many if not most unskilled workers made redundant in traditional industries.[46]

If one turns to the discussion of 'derelict villages', a caricature of social life in a mining community is presented. Hugh Dalton, in the preface to Sharp's pamphlet, is compelled to suggest that 'perhaps Mr Sharp does a little less than justice to the qualities of the Durham people, to their sturdiness, their sense of comradeship, the amazing sacrifices made by the women, in particular, on behalf of their children, the achievements, despite overwhelming financial difficulties, of their local authorities in maintaining their social services at a worthy level.'[47] The gloomy picture which Sharp paints in fact is entirely in terms of the physical state of a place, and has no reference to patterns of social relations existing there. Temple's thesis is even more explicit. The five stages of 'dereliction' include, without any apparent warrant, social characteristics of a most curious kind. The second stage of dereliction, for example, is characterised by the abandonment of the village by the 'best elements among the inhabitants'. Here reappears a notion current in analyses of unemployment in the 1930s, of hidden excellence among those out of work, the chimercial search for the 'best elements' among the mass. Temple's fourth stage is even more alarming, since it posits the physical and mental deterioration of the population in declining villages. No evidence is provided for this assertion apart from references to the 'rapid deterioration of community spirit', and to villages which are 'dumps for the most inferior and least desirable elements of a population'. Is it unfair to suggest that these kinds of statements are instances of social stereotyping and social caricature of a gross kind?

There is in fact evidence that in the author's zeal to 'tidy up South-West Durham' the inhabitants have been caricatured where they are not left out altogether. Captain Wallace, for example, a most cautious observer, commented in 1934 on the deleterious effects of unemployment upon the region:

> The vitality of the whole body (of the area) has been sapped by depression. This condition appears to be markedly worse in the larger towns than it is in the coalmining villages, in spite of the fact that in the latter the proportion of unemployed workers is often larger and the duration of unemployment has been in many cases longer. The reasons are not far to seek. The unemployed pitman inhabiting a village with a population of a few thousands is within easy reach of open fields . . . The unemployed man who resides in an industrial borough lives in conditions which are both physically and mentally much less healthy and more depressing.[48]

This conclusion is the exact opposite of those reached by Sharp and Temple. The evidence of the Pilgrim Trust regarding Crook, that the atmosphere in many homes was better than in other towns visited supports Captain Wallace's observations. Newsom's first-hand account of Durham villages in the 1930s provides no evidence of exceptional 'physical and mental deterioration' in west Durham villages, in fact tends to suggest the contrary. In short, the analysis of 'dereliction' confuses totally the physical structure of a place and the system of ongoing social relationships in that place. It argues without any warrant from the former to the latter, and in doing so caricatures the social reality.

Two points should be made at this point. It was not intended to suggest that the consequences of unemployment were not psychologically, socially, and physically harmful; undoubtedly they were. The question is whether there is any evidence of *exceptionally* harmful effects in areas of physical dereliction, and it is suggested that the connection is not established. Secondly, it may be thought this whole discussion is irrelevant to contemporary concerns having taken place over 30 years ago. Its significance lies in the continuity between the ideas of Sharp. Dennison and Temple writing in the late 1930s and the appearance of very similar ideas in the formative Pepler-MacFarlane plan of 1949. This in turn influenced the Durham County Development Plan of 1951.

The Pepler-MacFarlane Plan certainly contains some curious statements about the 'folk' for whom it was planning. It suggests, for instance, that during the inter-war period, 'all the progressive workers' moved out of west Durham villages affected by unemployment, leaving behind 'people content to live in conditions of backwardness and decay'.[49] Migration from these areas had drained the vital stock of these communities. This is one of the grounds they advance for re-settlement in new communities in central Durham. Such judgements, however, are not only vague but unsociological – or at best echo the Geddesian rhetoric of 'Work, Place and Folk'. There is certainly evidence of outward migration from west Durham and some influence upon the age-structure but there is no warrant whatever, on sociological grounds, for arguing that either 'all the progressive workers moved out' (what is the evidence?) or that the 'vital stock' of the communities has been drained. Indeed, *prima facie,* one might argue the exact contrary – what is striking in parts of west Durham is the continuation of a vigorous community life despite the effects of economic change.[50] However, the question is primarily one for further empirical investigation, and such sweeping judgements about the social structure and, thence, the quality of life in west Durham are unilluminating.

One may note also the optimistic view of the process of change taken by Pepler-MacFarlane and the confident tone in which it is proclaimed: 'Help man in his search for work by pointing out the area of expanding industry; offer him a house in attractive surroundings near his work and one can hope for his co-operation.'[51] Such a view begs a whole series of major sociological questions about patterns of work and residence and the views which people take of the desirability of living near their work. Yet the whole tenor of the report is to assume that it is a self-evident fact that people will desire to live near where they work.

The 1951 County Development Plan, which first enuciated the categorisation policy, took a less sanguine view of the course of change and devotes a chapter to the discussion of social characteristics. The inspiration comes direct from Geddes: 'Work, Place and Folk are interdependent and the act and react with one another'.[52] The main problem is seen in terms of an individualistic spirit. 'It will be necessary to adopt and steer a steady course to deal comprehensively with the problems ahead. To do this successfully there will need to be a revaluation of ideas, past grievances and oppressions will need to be forgotten and the individualistic spirit must be co-ordinated.'[53]

The Plan argues that long-term trends must override short-term residues from the past: 'Because of the sturdy, independent and united spirit of each community, there may be resistance to the discontinuance of development in certain villages; but this loyalty, born of adversity, this tradition must not, in the short term, blind us to the hard facts of long-term trends.'[54] What this means is spelled out in the Conclusion of the Plan, in a quotation from Keir Hardie: 'The weight of the dead past in the miner's mind, behaviour, customs and habit is very considerable and it proves a great obstacle to progress and further development. The cerements of the dead past have to be removed and no-one can do it but the miners themselves.'[55] Thus the vague sociological awareness of the strength and solidarity of mining communities is over-laid by invocations of 'progress and further development' and condemnation of the 'cerements of a dead past'. There is a basic lack of sociological understanding. For instance, one of the most striking features of community life in County Durham is that in the minds of those who have lived there all their lives, the past is not dead but very much alive. To deny or ignore this is to obfuscate the planning issues from a social-scientific point of view.

The 1964 Amendment to the Plan does not differ in major respects from the earlier version but it does make clear how the 'social' element is defined. This is pre-eminently in terms of *facilities,* not of social relationships. The aim of concentration of population in larger settlements is the provision of a bigger range and higher quality of facilities in these places: 'Many of the mining and industrial villages now have facilities and activities of some kind but they are usually limited in range and often housed in poor quality buildings.'[56] Once again, a major sociological statement appears without any supporting data. 'Activities of some kind' is hardly an accurate characterisation of the vigorous and continuing strength of the Club movement in County Durham, discussed and briefly documented in chapter 2. More generally, the confusion of social *facilities* with patterns of social relationships leads to statements about category 'D' villages which imply that they lack an adequate social life. In fact all that is referred to is communal buildings but such statements have a spurious sociological tone.

Opposition to the policy by those affected cannot simply be explained as traditionalism or resistance to change: 'Opponents of the Plan contend that many of the threatened settlements are not merely an assemblage of buildings occupied by people but contain closely knit communities bound together by ties of kinship, class and common origins. Shared hardships in the past and the prospect of eventual extinction have reinforced their community self-consciousness'.[57] The support obtained by the County Redevelopment of Villages Action Committee (CROVAC), set up in 1967 in south-west Durham, indicated that there was strong local feeling. Several notable publicity successes were obtained, including stealing the Minister of Housing's thunder when he opened Bessemer Park in Spennymoor in 1969, and demonstrating in Bishop Auckland so that Mr Arthur Skeffington, MP (author of a report on public participation in planning), had to leave the Town Hall by a side entrance.

The overall political effectiveness of this opposition was of necessity limited since 'D' villages contained only 6 per cent of the population of County Durham. Although at the county level, there was political unanimity in public about pursuing the policy, at the district level there was some dissent. One authority, Blaydon UD, for example, commented: 'It is on the human side that the policy is failing. It is unsatisfactory to simply argue that one must look at the overall picture; certainly this has to be done, but not enough is being done to make people feel a part of the overall picture'.[58] Research into the issue showed that some county councillors who were also members of district councils voted *against* the policy as it affected their area (at the district council) but *for* the policy at the county level (in county council), where party control through the Whip was perhaps stronger.[59]

The policy undoubtedly suffered because a plan for population was justified also on social grounds. The only county planning document which faces squarely what 'community' means in the context of the 'D' policy is one commissioned specially by the Council from Derek Senior. The other documents referred to earlier use the word 'community' when 'settlement' would convey exactly the same meaning without any suggestion of social solidarity or shared experience. Senior, however, recognises that one argument against the 'D' policy is that the people in these villages have a strong sense of community:

> So indeed they have; but this is an attribute of the people, a spirit tempered by the shared perils of their former work underground, not a characteristic of the bricks and mortar and spoil-heaps among which they live. It will not be lost when that unworthy environment is finally obliterated; it is a flame the people will take with them wherever they go. But it may well burn more brightly if they go to live among their own folk in one of their own district centres than if local reluctance to develop such a centre leaves them at the end of the day with no choice but to move south and live among strangers.[60]

This argument is in a sense more sociological than most of those advanced in the other planning documents. It explicitly dissociates 'community' from the physical structure of a place. However, in its place 'community' is defined as a 'spirit' which is not spatially bound at all! With that ease and what ignorance of the large sociological literature on the subject,[61] the problem of rehousing people is glided over! The implication is that the spirit of community will burn more brightly in a good physical environment than in a bad, as if new housing is the oil which feeds the wick of the lamp. Once again, any reference to patterns of social relationships is absent.

This is not to deny the economic arguments for the policy. The settlement pattern of County Durham is both distinctive and, in an age when mining has declined, problematic.[62] The official case for the category 'D' policy, when it has been restated,[63] has rested on rational economic argument, coupled with a recognition that the policy is bound to provoke conflict. The then County Planning Officer is quoted in a broadly sympathetic survey in 1969 as saying: 'there is no way of modernising the county which avoids all hardship and difficulty'.[64]

Many social policies involve sharp political conflict. In County Durham the political system did not adequately provide an avenue for those opposed to the planners' policies, although the Labour Party lost control of Bishop Auckland UD Council to a coalition including CROVAC members at one stage. There may well have been sharp private debates within the Labour Group on the County Council, particularly when the policy was introduced, but these are lost to us. The record consists mainly of the published planning documents, some material by their critics, and Senior's apologia. His pamphlet concludes with a reference to 'economically viable and socially functional . . . compact units.'[65] Can one, in the light of the above discussion, be confident that there is any satisfactory criterion for the determination of '*social* functionality'? If the sins of the earlier discussion of dereliction are those of commission – of producing a caricature – those of the later planning documents are rather those of omission – of the lack of any sociological content, of any attempt to treat structure and enduring patterns of social relationships as of independent importance. To point out the lack of sociological content in the formulation of planning policies in County Durham is not to say that the arguments put forward are unsound in themselves. Indeed, the theory or working model of the socio-spatial structure which lies behind these documents can be readily analysed and consists of three main elements.

Firstly, the approach is quite explicitly in terms of economic determinism. Industry is not only the life-blood of the area but the basis from which other characteristics derive:

> A brief analysis of the past will show how the present characteristics of the people have been influenced by changes in the economic basis and in the settlement pattern. It may then be possible to see what changes in outlook will be necessary if we are to adapt ourselves to the anticipated future changes in the economic basis and in the settlement pattern.[66]

An analysis of changes in the categorisation of settlements between 1951 and 1964 suggests that this has tended to take place where there had been a change in the local employment situation (whether an improvement or a deterioration).

Secondly, the primacy of economic factors is closely inter-twined with the physical distribution of people and buildings, Geddes's 'Work' and 'Place'. This is evident through all the document; development is to take place through a dynamic relationship between the two. The converse of this is that change is needed where the distribution of population no longer fits the industrial distribution. Decay of buildings makes renewal necessary but only in places where industrial prospects justify it.

Thirdly, there is a continuing concern with aesthetics. This is a continuing theme, in all the documents: 'black, evil-smelling tips of coal waste'; 'larger but equally depressing units such as Spennymoor'; 'conditions of backwardness and decay'; and so on. The concern to obliterate the industrial legacy of coal mining is shown in a revealing – and very curious – statement in the 1964 Plan in response to critics of the 'D' policy: 'There is no question of destroying true village life. Those traditional villages with an agricultural base are being preserved'.[67] The suggestion can only be that mining villages are not 'true villages'.

It seems not unreasonable to suggest that 'folk' are given insufficient attention. The nature of the economic and physical structure and aesthetic considerations usefully direct attention to certain constraints upon social action by the spatial distribution of the population and the employment and housing markets. Major features of social structure, however, are neglected. Three of these are worth mentioning, as illustrating analytical possibilities which are not brought to bear upon the planning process in the county.

There is a curious paradox whereby large-scale inward migration into County Durham in the nineteenth century has been succeeded by relative population stability in the present century. In 1871, for example, only 73 per cent of the inhabitants of County Durham had been born in Northumberland and Durham, whereas 27 per cent had been born elsewhere. In the latter group Yorkshire people (26 per cent), Irish (20 per cent), and Scots (12 per cent) predominated.[68] In the twentieth century, on the other hand, an increasing proportion of the population of the county has been born within it. At the Censuses of 1931 and 1951 Durham was the county with the highest proportion of its population born within the county in England and Wales – 84 per cent in 1931 and 83 per cent in 1951.[69] Precisely comparable figures cannot be calculated from the 1961 Census, but broadly comparable figures are provided in the 1966 Census. Within Durham geographical county at that time, 91.5 per cent of the population had been born within the Northern region, a much higher figure than other counties elsewhere. In Cheshire, for example, 79.5 per cent of the population had been born within the N.W. region, in Kent 81.6 per cent within the S.E. region, in Cornwall only 72.8 per cent within the S.W. region.[70]

Although these figures are directly a function of the rates of internal migration (the lower the rate of inward migration, the higher the proportion of the population born within the area), they are also suggestive of long and continuous attachment of the majority of the population to a particular area. From a very diverse population (in terms of origin) in the nineteenth century, there has been a shift to a much more homogeneous population in the twentieth (in terms of origin). To what extent must planning policy be adapted to take account of relative geographical immobility among a population, and what are the possible social consequences of such immobility?

This relates to the second feature of note, the question of the nature of people's attachment to particular places in the contemporary world. What *meaning* does living in a particular place have for different groups of people? How do people who live in a particular place define their social situation? Why do they choose to live in one place rather than another? What are the patterns of enduring social relationships in which these various definitions of their social situation are embedded? None of these questions is adequately dealt with in the planning documents, where the emphasis is upon the extent to which people must be expected to move in response to changes in employment opportunities and housing provision.

Opposition to such movement is acknowledged, but attributed to the dead weight of tradition. This fails singularly to take account of a most important feature of people's perception of place: the meaningful social world of a majority of the British population is concentrated in the immediate locality in which they live. The mobile middle class are inclined to think that their own experience is common; in fact, as evidence gathered for the recent Royal Commission on Local Government in England shows, the 'home area' which most people identified was extremely limited, defined by a small group of streets in a town, or the area of a parish in a rural area.[71] One-fifth of the sample in that study had been born in their 'home area' (and this proportion was higher for the Northern Region), and nearly two-thirds of the sample had lived within their 'home area' for at least ten years. Moreover in areas of stable or declining population these proportions were higher, so that an area such as County Durham would be expected to show an even greater proportion of its population with long-term residence in one locality. Those of lower socio-economic status, and with less full-time education, also had a greater tendency to have lived in their home area for more than ten years, than those of higher socio-economic status and more education. On the basis of evidence such as this, it becomes less than clear why population mobility within the county should be regarded as 'natural' and opposition to such mobility as 'unnatural' or 'negative'. The surprising feature, perhaps, is why there is not more opposition to plans for large-scale mobility.

The planning documents recognise the existence of resistance but it is not clear that its origins are understood. Pepler and MacFarlane argue that people will move, given good work and decent houses, although 'we do not wish to underrate or be unsympathetic to the social upheavals and broken family ties which these changes so often produce'.[72] But they pass straight on to a very optimistic view of change based on their own criteria of economic and physical redevelopment. There is an unfortunate tendency both to assume that people in general will share the three particular premises of the planner's model, and to attribute non-compliance to 'traditionalism' or the 'cerements of the dead past'.

In fact as argued in chapter 2 such phenomena can be understood much more illuminatingly in terms of enduring patterns of social relationships. If one analyses patterns of local work relationships and employment opportunities sociologically; if one examines non-work relationships between kin, neighbours and friends, both in the home, in the street, in the club and in other leisure-time activities; then the nature of attachment to particular places may become clearer. It may thus be shown that such attachments are not merely 'traditional', but are embedded in the social structure. If this is so, economic change *per se* will not lead automatically to other changes. Indeed, existing patterns will persist and, in some cases, conflict with the aims of the planners.

There is also the suggestion that the creation of new settlements, involving the movement of population, is equated with the creation of new communities. The 1964 Plan Amendment, after discussing the problem of old mining communities, comments: 'The problem here is to create new communities more suited to the modern industrial world without destroying the friendliness of the older villages.'[73] This is followed by a discussion of physical forms – new kinds of housing, the 'Radburn' system of separating vehicles and pedestrians, etc. Yet it is well-established that one of the principal problems in rehousing and developing new towns is the creation from scratch of new patterns of social relationships. The complexity – and indeed the intractability –

Table 12.1 Selected Socio-Economic Groups, 1961

Area	Managerial and Professional	Other Non-Manual	Total Non-Manual	Manual
County Durham	8.5%	11.7%	20.2%	77.7%
(N. Region)	(10.0%)	(13.7%)	(23.7%)	(65.9%)
Northumberland	11.6%	15.9%	27.5%	63.5%
England and Wales	14.3%	16.5%	30.8%	65.5%

Table 12.2 Selected Socio-Economic Groups by Sub Region, 1961

Sub-Region	Managerial and Professional	Other Non-Manual	Total Non-Manual	Manual
West Durham	7.0%	10.5%	17.5%	72.9%
East Durham	7.2%	10.0%	17.2%	78.0%
Central Durham	9.2%	9.9%	19.1%	75.0%
Wearside	8.4%	13.4%	21.8%	70.9%
Teesside (within County Durham)	9.9%	14.5%	23.5%	71.9%

The last two columns do not add up across to 100% because certain categories are excluded.

The sub-regional classification is that adopted by Bowden & Gibb,[43] and comprises the following Employment Exchange areas:

West Durham: Barnard Castle, Bishop Auckland, Consett, Crook, Shildon, Stanley, Lanchester. *Central Durham:* Birtley, Chester-le-Street, Darlington, Durham, Houghton-le-Spring, Spennymoor, Washington. *East Durham:* Hartlepools, Haswell, Hordon, Wingate. *Wearside:* Sunderland, Seaham. *Teeside* (within County Durham): Billingham, Stockton.

Source: Census of England and Wales, 1961.

of the problem is not recognised and solutions to sociological problems associated with population mobility are reduced to physical terms. Some of these issues are taken further in the next two chapters.[74]

A third feature of social structure, the importance of which is neglected, is the class structure of the population of County Durham. The distinctiveness of County Durham is shown in Table 12.1, which makes clear the much higher proportion of manual workers within the county compared with either the Northern Region as a whole, or England and Wales. The distinctiveness of particular sub-regions is shown when these figures are broken down further, as in Table 12.2. Thus, the higher concentration of non-manual groups in the conurbations is balanced by the greater concentration of manual workers in the sub-regions of Durham. The predominance of the working class in west, central and east Durham is associated with particular forms of settlement and possibly with particular patterns of social interaction (though this is a matter for further investigation). This in turn has important implications for planning policy, since the policies envisaged by the planners may have the unintended consequence of striking at the root of certain central features of working-class institutions and culture. The lack of reference to class structure and class divisions in British society is a major weakness in Durham planning documents. It is by no means evident that physical renewal entails the reduction of social inequalities in society, and indeed the contrary may in some instances be the case. As Pahl, for example, has emphasised, planners need to take much greater account of the impact of their policies upon social conditions and social inequalities existing in the society.[75] Despite much facile discussion of growing 'classlessness', there is considerable evidence of continuing and major inequalities between different social strata in British society.[76] The influence of the planning process upon this pattern of inequality is most evident (often in a negative direction) in cities, but is an important factor in rural-urban areas such as Durham County as well.

This concludes an outline review of some aspects of intervention by central and local government in County Durham. It is not intended to suggest that industrial development or the regrouping of population are sound or unsound policy aims – such a value judgement has no place here, and is a matter for political judgement and decision. Rather the apparent foundations and implications of planning policy have been briefly examined from a sociological point of view and certain comments made. In particular, the necessity of a symbiotic link between new industrial development and a policy of population concentration has been questioned by implication, and the absurdity of making judgements about patterns of ongoing social relationships on the basis of the existence of physical 'dereliction' has been pointed out. County Durham has been taken as a case study. These comments should not be regarded as being directed *particularly* at the development of policy in County Durham, nor to reflect particularly upon *Durham* planners. The working of the planning system has been examined elsewhere in north-east England – by J.G. Davies in Newcastle[77] and most notably by Norman Dennis in Sunderland[78] – and the problems of developing a genuinely responsive and participatory planning system identified. Davies and Dennis have in fact argued for the need to study planning from the inside: 'Politics is about what actually does happen, no less than about what people say happens or believe has happened. Consequently, [our] approach depends less upon reports and reconstructions than on the direct observation of decision-taking. Our main technique, therefore, is participant observation. Our main area is municipal politics'.[79]

The sociological inadequacies of *regional* planning documents in the North-East up to 1970 are even more apparent than in those for the county, being confined either to the expression of general humanitarian sentiments or of vague generalities. ('Change is inevitable – in locations, in jobs, and not least, in attitudes – and change is often an uncomfortable experience. Success will come when the need for change is accepted and the necessary efforts and adjustments have been made.')[80]

What is lacking is not sociological *information* but sociological *analysis,* any understanding of the nature of contemporary social structure and of the types of social relationship which constitute it. As Rex, Pahl, and others have emphasised, the role of sociology in the planning process is not one of 'fact-gathering' or superior market research (which planning departments can do anyway if they devote the resources to it) but is essentially critical, in the sense of looking at the social setting within which planners work from a broader, more sociological, perspective than that of professional day-to-day planning activity.[81] The most valuable contribution which sociology can make to discussions of planning policy is to direct attention to the wider context of social change and persistence within which the planner is working, even if this necessarily involves drawing attention to the limitations of some of the social assumptions which planners may make. In doing this, the sociologist seeks to enlarge understanding, but *not* to usurp either the role of the professional planner or the necessity for political choice in planning matters.

Planners – and clergymen – have been known to approach sociologists for advice rather as if they were somehow the bearers of a panacea for society's problems. It must be strongly emphasised that the analysis of the social consequences of economic change is not intended to produce either a programme for the future management of the social consequences of economic decline, or an alternative utopia to that envisaged in the Durham County Development Plan. Its contribution (if any) to the formulation of economic and social policies is entirely indirect, through enlargement of general understanding of the social processes at work in society. It cannot, either, resolve conflicts between different economic and social values that become apparent in the planning process – such as are implicit in the 'Category D' controversy – and which are political questions. The main aim of the present chapter has been to redress the balance in favour of the 'folk', as against the predominant emphasis upon 'work' and 'place' (or industrial location and population distribution), which has been so salient in the recent economic and political history of north-east England in general, and of Durham County in particular.

Notes

1. Cf. J.W. House, *Industrial Britain: the North-East,* Newton Abbott, David and Charles, 1969.
2. D.H. Aldcroft, *The Inter-War Economy: Britain 1919-39,* London, Batsford, 1970, Chapter 3, 'Regional Patterns of Development'.
3. Cf. chapter 11 above.
4. E. Wilkinson, *The Town that was Murdered,* London, Gollancz, 1939.
5. Cf. W.R. Garside, *The Durham Miners, 1919-60,* London, Allen & Unwin, 1971, chapter 7, 'Living and Working Conditions 1918-39'.
6. Pilgrim Trust, *Men Without Work,* Cambridge University Press, 1938.
7. Cf. G. McCrone, *Regional Policy in Britain,* London, Allen & Unwin, 1969.
8. W.R. Garside, *The Durham Miners* is both the official history of the Durham Miners' Association throughout this period, and a definitive account of the course and outcome of this struggle. An alternative perspective, that of the rank-and-file union member, is presented in D. Douglass, *Pit Life in County Durham: Rank and File Movements and Workers Control,* Oxford, Ruskin College History Workshop, 1971.
9. Cf. N. Branson and M. Heineman, *Britain in the Nineteen Thirties,* London, Weidenfeld, 1971, esp. Chs. 3 and 4.
10. Ministry of Labour, *Reports of Investigations into the Industrial Conditions in Certain Depressed Areas of I-West Cumberland, II-Durham and Tyneside, III-South Wales and Monmouthshire, IV-Scotland,* Cmnd. 4728. November 1934.
11. Note the absurd euphemism. Like the phenomena of poverty and inequalities existing between developed and undeveloped and exploited parts of the world, pseudo-gentility seems to afflict public discussions and the terminology

employed. Cf. 'disadvantaged', 'less prosperous', 'underdeveloped', 'developing', and so on.

12. *Royal Commission on the Distribution of the Industrial Population* (Barlow *Report),* Cmnd. 6153. Appendix III-II, Trading Estates.
13. Barlow Report.
14. Ibid., pp.188-89, 193, 194, 195.
15. Ministry of Reconstruction, *Employment Policy,* Cmnd. 6527, 1944.
16. Board of Trade, *Distribution of Industry,* Cmnd. 7540, October 1948.
17. County Council of Durham, *County Development Plan 1951,* p.32.
18. Cf. G. McCrone, *Regional Policy in Britain,* London, Allen & Unwin, 1969, esp. Chs. IV to VI.
19. See, in addition to chapters 13 and 14, P. Bowden, 'Newton Aycliffe', in J.C. Dewdney (ed.), *Durham County and City with Teesside,* Durham, British Association, 1970, pp.454-463; and R. Thomas, *Aycliffe to Cumbernauld: A Study of Seven Towns in their Regions,* London, PEP, 1969.
20. S.R. Dennison, *The Location of Industry and the Depressed Areas,* Oxford University Press, 1939, pp.199-200.
21. Ibid., p.201.
22. T. Sharp, *A Derelict Area: a study of the South-West Durham coalfield,* London, Hogarth Press Day-to-Day Pamphlet, 1935.
23. Ibid., p.29.
24. Ibid., pp.43-4.
25. A. Temple, 'The Derelict Villages of South West Durham', Unpublished thesis presented for the degree of M.Litt., University of Durham, 1940.
26. G. Pepler and F.W. MacFarlane, *North-East Area Development Plan.* Interim Report presented to the Minister of Town and County Planning 1949 (copy in Durham City Reference Library, South Street, Durham).
27. Ibid., p.2.
28. Ibid., p.39.
29. Ibid., p.18.
30. Ibid., p.57.
31. Ibid., p.167.
32. Ibid., p.39.
33. Ibid., p.63.
34. Ibid., p.188.
35. Ibid., pp.167-8.
36. County Council of Durham, *County Development Plan, Draft Written Analysis,* January, 1951, p.108.
37. Ibid., pp.69-70.
38. County Council of Durham, *County Development Plan Amendment* 1964.
39. A reading of, for instance, the files of the *Auckland Chronicle* (published by North of England Newspapers Ltd., Darlington) for the year 1969 will make evident the concern with which the policy is regarded by some of those affected.
40. 1964 Amendment, pp.41-42.
41. *The North-East: a programme for regional development and growth,* Cmnd. 2006, November 1963.
42. *Outline Strategy for the North: an outline strategy of development to 1981,* Newcastle, Northern Economic Planning Council, 1969. See also the earlier *Challenge of the Changing North,* Northern Economic Planning Council, HMSO, 1966.
43. P. Bowden and A.A. Gibb, *Economic Growth in the North-East England,* a study undertaken by the Business Research Unit, University of Durham, for

the Department of Economic Affairs, Durham, 1967. (Copy in Durham University Business School Library), chapter 1, pp.43-4.
44. *Growth Points for Durham,* A Durham County Council pamphlet written by D. Senior; no date.
45. Cf. P. Abrams, *The Origins of British Sociology 1834-1914,* University of Chicago Press, 1968, pp.63-66 and 113-118.
46. See chapter 16.
47. H. Dalton, in T. Sharp, *A Derelict Area,* p.8.
48. Ministry of Labour, *Reports of Investigations into the Industrial Conditions in Certain Depressed Areas,* Cmnd. 4728, p.74.
49. Pepler and MacFarlane, *North-East Area Development Area,* p.8.
50. See the evidence contained in R.C. Taylor, *The Implications of Migration from the Durham Coalfield,* (Unpublished thesis presented for the degree of Ph.D., Durham, 1966). See also R.C. Taylor, 'Migration and Motivation', in J. Jackson (ed.), *Migration,* Cambridge University Press, 1969, pp. 99-133.
51. Pepler and MacFarlane, *North-East Area Development Plan,* p.63.
52. County Development Plan 1951, p.102.
53. Ibid., p.102.
54. Ibid., p.108.
55. Quoted ibid., pp.185-6.
56. Development Plan Amendment, 1964, p.40.
57. Open University Course D281, *Human Geography,* Block 3, Unit 12, 'The declining villages of County Durham', by A. Blowers, Milton Keynes, Open University Press, 1972, pp.150-1. This Unit includes a detailed case study of the policy as it affects the Gurney Valley, Ferryhill Station, Chilton Lane and East Howle. Associated with it is an Open University film on the subject, No. D281/05, entitled 'Communities and Change: Mining Villages in County Durham', dealing particularly with the problems of Ferryhill Station.
58. Ibid., p.150.
59. K. Patton, quoted in the *Auckland Chronicle,* 10th September 1970. The files of the *Durham Advertiser Series* (published by North of England Newspapers in Darlington) particularly those editions covering south-west Durham in the late 1960s, provide one of the best available sources for a study of local opposition to the Category 'D' policy.
60. Senior, *Growth Points,* p.11.
61. Cf. the brief discussion in chapter 2, and F. Toennies, *Gemeinschaft und Gesellschaft,* 1887, translated as *Community and Society,* New York, Harper, 1963; and R.E. Park, *Human Communities,* Glencoe, The Free Press, 1952. Lucid textbook discussions are to be found in: R.E. Pahl, *Patterns of Urban Life,* Longmans, 1970, Ch.7; C. Bell and H. Newby, *Community Studies,* London, Allen and Unwin, 1972, esp. Ch.2. On social relationships on new housing estates, see G.D. Mitchell *et. al., Neighbourhood and Community,* Liverpool University Press, 1954; H. Orans, *Stevenage: a sociological study of a new town,* London, Routledge, 1952; J. Spencer *et. al.,* Stress and Release in an Urban Estate, London, Tavistock, 1964.
62. D. Thorpe, 'Modern Settlement', in J.C. Dewdney (ed.), *Durham County and City, with Teesside,* Durham, British Association, 1970, pp.392-416.
63. J.R. Atkinson, 'Planning Problems in County Durham', in J.C. Dewdney (ed.), *Durham County,* pp.433-42.
64. J. Barr, 'Durham's Murdered Villages', *New Society,* 3 April 1969.
65. Senior, Growth Points, p.16.
66. County Development Plan 1951, p.102.
67. 1964 Amendment p.43.
68. Cf. J.W. House, *North-East England: Population Movement and Landscape*

since the early 19th century, Newcastle, Dept. of Geography 1954, esp. Table 10, p.62.

69. D.C. Marsh, *The Changing Social Structure of England and Wales 1871-1961,* London, Routledge, 1961, pp.89-92.
70. Figures calculated from the 1966 Sample Census of England and Wales.
71. Cf. Royal Commission on Local Government in England: *Research Studies 9, Community Attitudes Survey: England,* HMSO, 1969.
72. Pepler and MacFarlane, p.188.
73. 1964 Amendment.
74. See also: N. Dennis, 'The Popularity of the Neighbourhood Community Idea', first published in 1958, reprinted in R.E. Pahl (ed.), *Readings in Urban Sociology,* Oxford, Pergamon, 1968, pp.74-92; H.E. Bracey, *Neighbours,* London, Routledge, 1964; R.N. Morris and J. Mogey, *The Sociology of Housing,* London, Routledge, 1965.
75. Cf. R.E. Pahl, *Whose City? and other essays on sociology and planning,* London, Longman, 1970, esp. Chs. 12, 13 and 14.
76. Cf. J.H. Westerguard and H. Rester, *Class in a Capitalist Society,* London, *Heinemann, 1975;* J.H. Goldthorpe *et. al., The Affluent Worker in the Class Structure,* Cambridge U.P., 1969; P. Willmott, 'Some Social Trends', in P. Cowan (ed.), *Developing Patterns of Urbanisation,* Edinburgh, Oliver and Boyd, 1970, pp. 8-30.
77. J.G. Davies, *The Evangelistic Bureaucrat,* London, Tavistock, 1972.
78. N. Dennis, *People and Planning,* London, Faber, 1970; N. Dennis, *Public Participation and Planner's Blight,* London, Faber, 1972.
79. 'Half-beating City Hall: The Duke Street Story', *New Society,* vol.26, No.574, 4 October 1973, p.10.
80. *Challenge of the Changing North,* 1966, p.52.
81. J. Rex, 'Images of Community', in *Race, Colonialism and The City,* London, Routledge, 1973, pp.43-63; R.E. Pahl, 'The Sociologist's Role in Regional Planning', in *Whose City?* Ch.14, pp.227-252. Cf. also T. Burns, 'Sociological Explanation', *British Journal of Sociology,* vol.18, No.4, 1967, pp.353-369.

13 THE ORIGINS OF NEWTON AYCLIFFE

Peter J. Bowden

This chapter is an extract from a longer report of research on Newton Aycliffe undertaken by the author with the support of the Joseph Rowntree Memorial Trust. This two-hundred page study, entitled Newton Aycliffe: a study of a new town, *by Dr P.J. Bowden, comprises four chapters on distribution of industry policy, new towns policy, official policy towards Newton Aycliffe and a survey of firms on the industrial estate. A copy is deposited in the Library of Durham University.*

Towns do not come into being by chance. Most owe their origins to some locational advantage in respect of trade or defence; a few are the result of self-glorification. Not until 1946 in Britain, however, did the planning and building of complete communities first become official government policy, and since then similar projects have been started in many other countries. The main object in establishing the majority of British new towns has been to decentralise population and industry from London and other large conurbations; a few new towns, however, have been designed to provide housing and other social capital for people already employed in existing local industry. Newton Aycliffe falls into the latter category, and owes its existence to the establishment of a Royal Ordnance Factory at Aycliffe, near Darlington, in 1940. After the war the ROF was converted into a government industrial estate administered by North Eastern Trading Estates Limited (now the English Industrial Estates Corporation) on behalf of the Board of Trade. The building of the town, on the other hand, was entrusted to the Aycliffe Development Corporation acting as the agent of the Ministry of Town and Country Planning (now the Department of the Environment). This duality of ministerial control – over workplace and home – is unique among British new towns, the normal practice being for development corporations to exercise responsibility for the administration of industrial sites, as well as for the provision of social assets.[1]

Government measures to influence the distribution of industry date back to the economic depression of the inter-war years, which was particularly severe in its effect on the county's staple export trades and capital goods industries.[2] This is discussed in more detail in chapters 11 and 12. Although the policy of 'bringing work to the workers' began in a small way in the 1930s, by May 1939 only some 5,000 persons were employed on government trading estates in the North-East, half of whom were women. Early distribution of industrial policy made a negligible impact upon large-scale unemployment.

By 1941, however, the unemployment problem had ceased to exist. In the North-East, as elsewhere in the country, manpower resources were seriously depleted by mobilisation for the armed forces, and the main economic problem became one of recruiting sufficient labour to meet the pressing needs of home consumption, essential new investment and maximum war production. In the Special Areas full employment came mainly in the form of a revival in the basic manufacturing industries, such as ship-building and engineering, whose expansion was vital to the war effort. Many thousands were also employed in Royal Ordnance factories, most of which, like the new ROF at Aycliffe, were to be converted for peace-time use after the war.

Meanwhile, the foundations of post-war distribution of industry policy were being laid. The Barlow Commission on the distribution of the industrial population reported in 1940. The Report recognised that there are social and economic advantages, as well as disadvantages, associated with large-scale urbanisation. Among social advantages it included the existence of better educational, medical, recreational and cultural facilities, while it claimed that the main economic advantages for industry in large towns were proximity to markets, reduction of transport costs and availability of a suitable supply of labour.[3] Nevertheless, it laid great weight on the strategic, economic and social disadvantages of urban concentration. The Commissioners argued that the 'disadvantages in many, if not in most of the great industrial concentrations do constitute serious handicaps and even in some respects dangers to the nation's life and development, and definite action should be taken by the Government towards remedying them'.[4] This definite action should have as its objectives: the continued and further redevelopment of congested urban areas; where necessary, decentralisation, or dispersal, both of industries and industrial population, from such areas; and encouragement of a 'reasonable balance of industrial development', so far as possible, throughout the various regions of Britain, coupled with 'appropriate diversification of industry' in each region.[5]

The Report spurred the war-time coalition Government to action. In 1943, it transferred the planning powers of the Ministries of Health and Works[6] to a newly-created Ministry of Town and Country Planning charged with responsibility for physical planning and house building, particularly slum clearance and new town development.[7]

At the same time as the Government was considering the recommendations of the Barlow Commission, it was also giving thought to the methods for maintaining a high and stable level of employment after the war; its proposals for the achievement of these objectives were outlined in the *White Paper on Employment Policy,* 1944. The authors of the White Paper recognised, as J.M. Keynes had done in 1936,[8] that the basic cause of unemployment in the inter-war years had been a deficiency in aggregate demand, and they accepted that, in addition to a general employment policy for the country as a whole, special measures would be needed in regions such as the North-East which were particularly vulnerable to depression. Three solutions were recommended: revival of basic industries, attraction of new industry in these areas to diversify the industrial base, and promotion of geographical and occupational mobility. The Distribution of Industry Act, 1945, which until 1960 was the principal instrument of industrial location policy, put the main emphasis on the second of these aims, where it has remained.

In the years immediately after the war conditions were highly favourable to the movement of industry. Factory construction had been strictly controlled during war-time, and many firms were in antiquated and unsuitable premises. Others, especially in the London area, had suffered bomb damage and wanted to restart or expand production. Demobilised ex-servicemen with gratuities and accumulated capital to invest created a new class of hopeful entrepreneurs. Above all, business confidence was high and firms were eager to expand as quickly as possible to meet the pent-up demand for goods. The main barriers to immediate expansion were shortages of factory space, raw materials and labour. As far as factory space was concerned, the government-controlled system of industrial building licences could be, and was, weighted in favour of the development areas, and a programme of advance factory building was launched by the Board of Trade in these areas offering the prospect of early occupation by tenants. A more immediate consideration was the fact that 13 million square feet of adaptable munition factory space were available in the areas, and these were offered for early occupation to firms which had been refused permission to expand or start production elsewhere. The shortage and control of certain raw materials enabled the Government to give preference in their allocation to factories in the development areas, and to promise such preference to firms becoming established in the areas.

The final shortage was of labour, and the development areas had the main reserves of unemployed of both sexes and of females who had not previously gone out to work. These workers did not always possess the type of skills required by incoming firms, but in most cases the problem could be solved by training. In brief, a combination of circumstances, some of them temporary, made the development areas seem particularly attractive to industrialists in other parts of the country, and this enabled the Government to operate its powers of persuasion and control in favour of the areas with considerable success.

One of the places to benefit from employment creation after 1945 was the former Royal Ordnance Factory at Newton Aycliffe, converted into an industrial estate by the Government in 1945. A characteristic of the depressed areas in the inter-war years had been the scarcity of employment opportunities for women, and the establishment of munition factories in these areas during the Second World War was strongly influenced by this consideration. The decision to establish a Royal Ordnance Factory at Aycliffe was based in the first instance on the presence of substantial reserves of female labour in adjoining localities, especially the mining districts of south-west Durham. However, in these areas difficulties of drainage and mining subsidence severely restricted the amount of land immediately available for industrial development although it had proved possible to locate a ROF at Spennymoor. Moreover, while the network of communications in south-west Durham was adequate for local needs, it was not well adapted for the heavy cross-traffic of workers and materials such as would ensue from the establishment of a major industrial project.[9]

The Aycliffe site was free from these disadvantages. It was situated off the coal measures and comprised approximately one square mile of flat stable land of low agricultural value. As the site lay adjacent to the Al road and was also served by local rail communications, it was easily accessible from other parts of the region. The immediate vicinity was sparsely populated, this being an important consideration in view of the hazardous nature of ordnance production and the risk of aerial attack or explosion. The nearest housing centres were Aycliffe Village (¼ mile), Heighington Village (1 mile), Shildon (5 miles), Darlington (6 miles), Bishop Auckland (7 miles) and Ferryhill (7 miles). Of these, only Darlington and Bishop Auckland contained more than 15,000 inhabitants.

The choice of a site outside the periphery of the south-west Durham coal-field and within the economic orbit of Darlington was to influence significantly the official attitude towards peacetime industrial expansion and new town development. Unlike other large towns in the North-East, Darlington had enjoyed comparative prosperity in the inter-war years; its major industries of railway and constructional engineering were less severely affected by the Depression than economic activities in most other parts of the region. Among these areas, few experienced greater social distress than the coal-mining districts of south-west Durham, where the adverse effects of contracting industrial demand were reinforced by the working out or flooding of many pits. The consequent loss of employment resulted in high outward migration, so that between 1921 and 1939 the population of south-west Durham fell from 134,000 to 99,000.[10] In the worse-hit Spennymoor, Shildon and Brandon and Byshottles areas the loss of population by migration exceeded 30 per cent.[11] Some of the migrants drifted to the Darlington area; others moved south-east to Teesside, where the establishment and expansion of the vast ICI works at Billingham provided a welcome element of growth in a largely stagnant regional economy; yet others travelled further afield, seeking employment in more prosperous parts of the country and even abroad. For those who stayed behind, the hardship of these years could never be forgotten; and it was in an atmosphere charged with memories of massive unemployment and migration that plans for the establishment of the ROF were formulated.

When the new Ordnance Factory at Aycliffe was originally constructed for shell-filling in 1940, its layout was planned with due regard to safety considerations; and over 1,000 buildings, large and small, were scattered widely over the site area. Several of these buildings were built completely beneath mounds (mounded) to minimise damage in the event of explosion and some were virtually built underground to serve as storage magazines. Roads were narrow, lighting inadequate, and the site criss-crossed by elevated walkways and heating pipes. The Government's decision in 1945 to convert this ordnance factory into an industrial estate therefore posed some difficult problems. The ROF buildings had been hastily erected and were not well-suited for peacetime production. Considerable structural adaptations were necessary. The estate today looks different, not least due to a face-lift which began in 1963. Of the 1,000 buildings making up the original ordnance factory, over 400 small units unsuitable for industrial occupation and consisting of external ablution blocks, toilets, decontamination centres, police lodges, control and checkpoints and redundant air-raid shelters, have been demolished and removed. Some of the mounded magazines are not readily adaptable for industrial purposes and continue to be used as stores, both by industrial firms and government departments. The main roads through the estate have been widened. The overhead steam mains and security fences, which so disfigured the original estate, have been removed and many sites cleared and levelled for future development. The appearance of the estate has been further improved by a policy of tree planting and the provision of open spaces with flower beds and shrubs.

Employment for upwards of 16,000 people – using three-shift working – was provided by the ROF during the war on shell-filling. Faced after the war with the shortage of industrial facilities and the barrage of applications to start businesses by men returning from the Armed Forces, the Board of Trade was easily able to fill the Aycliffe premises with enterprises, the great majority of which were new and small. The first industrial tenants began to arrive in the autumn of 1945, and within 18 months over 50 firms were established at Aycliffe, occupuing some 850,000 sq.ft. of space. As most of these enterprises were 'financed on a shoe-string', a major inducement to establishment in many cases was the exceptionally low rents charged for the factory premises by the Industrial Estates Company. This reflected the inferior quality of the buildings, as well as the more general policy of subsidising government factory rentals. By 1948, after its conversion to an industrial estate, the site provided employment for 3,000 which rose to 4,500 in 1962, and then nearly doubled to 8,600 in 1966, due to active industrial promotion by the government. A detailed study of industrial development up to 1966 is available in the longer work referred to on page 202. The main point is that the industrial estate to which Newton Aycliffe owes its existence stems in part from Government policies to influence the distribution of industry, and partly from the choice of Aycliffe as the site of a wartime ordnance factory.

Before discussing in detail the specific origins of the new town of Newton Aycliffe, the genesis of the national new town policy will be sketched. The movement for modern new towns in Britain owes something to the lead given by a few benevolent nineteenth-century industrialists who built model villages for their employees, including Cadbury's Bournville, near Birmingham (1879) and Lever's Port Sunlight, near Birkenhead (1887). These enterprises were on a small scale and were to some extent inspired by enlightened self-interest, but they gave an indication of what could be done to recast the urban environment and pointed the way to bigger things.[12] The greatest stimulus to the new towns movement, however, was provided by Ebenezer Howard, who, in 1898, published, *Tomorrow: a Peaceful Path to Real Reform,*[13] in which he advocated the establishment of garden cities as an alternative to the continued growth of large urban centres such as London. Howard's suggested solution to the economic and social problems of industrialism was the dispersal of population from overcrowded urban centres to relatively self-contained garden cities of limited size, deliberately designed to preserve natural beauty, fresh air and light, while providing everyone with opportunities for work and leisure. Thus, the new towns would combine the advantages of urban and rural life and the disadvantages of neither; a balance would be struck between home and industry and between town and country; while residents would be able to enjoy the benefits of pleasant living conditions, access to the countryside and closeness to work.

He himself promoted his ideas practically by founding the Garden City Association (now the Town and Country Planning Association) in 1899, and by forming private companies which started Letchworth Garden City in 1903 and Welwyn Garden City in 1920. Though these were beset by financial problems, Howard showed that new towns were feasible. Moreover, their standards of planning, landscaping and design were such as to influence urban architecture throughout the world. Garden cities also pioneered the introduction of a number of significant physical planning concepts, including character and density zoning, the ward or neighbourhood planning unit, the agricultural greenbelt to limit urban growth, and unified urban land ownership for the conservation of rising land values. A corpus of knowledge was also acquired which could be drawn upon for carrying out similar developments in the future and for avoiding some of the mistakes of the past.[14]

Planning as we know it today is a post-1945 development. Prior to that, legislative intervention had generally been of an *ad hoc* and piecemeal kind, to tackle specific problems of urban growth such as sub-standard housing, traffic congestion, ribbon development, lack of open spaces or encroachment of the countryside. Emphasis was always on rectifying a particular damage. Powers and techniques for regulating development were also very limited. 'Planning was permissive not mandatory, and the plans that resulted were of negative or restrictive, not positive or constructive, effect – i.e. they secured that development could take place only in certain ways, but not that any area would actually be developed'.[15] A major weakness was the absence of central control over policy-making. Planning powers were fragmented, being wielded by a large number of local authorities whose efforts lacked direction and co-ordination; and it was not until 1932 that county councils were allowed to participate in the planning process. Moreover, before the Second World War only a fraction of the area of Great Britain was actually subject to operative planning schemes, and there were important towns and cities and large county districts for which not even the preliminary steps had been taken.[16] However, in spite of these limitations, some progress was made in the planned reorganisation of urban development, notably in the field of housing. A start was made with slum clearance in the great cities. To overcome the shortage of housing following World War I the central Government adopted a policy of subsidising housing production by private builders and local authorities, and a number of large-scale development schemes were begun.

From time to time, the possibility of establishing garden cities was investigated by official bodies but no government initiative in this direction was taken during the inter-war years. Official reports, such as those of the Unhealthy Areas Committee (1920) and the Marley Committee (1935),[17] which recommended governmental encouragement of garden city development and restraints on factory growth in London, were ineffective in producing any immediate action. It is debatable whether publicly-financed new towns would ever have been built in Britain had it not been for the war, the bombings, and the post-war victory of the Labour Party; but the historic turning point in the official attitude towards urban developments came with the publication of the Barlow Report in 1940.[18] This Report and its aftermath became the cornerstone of post-war British town planning policy and its proposals for relieving overcrowded and congested urban areas strongly supported the arguments of the garden city advocates. 'Such [new town] development,' it noted 'is not likely to proceed successfully if left entirely to private enterprise, on account, mainly, of the magnitude of the financial commitments involved'. Accordingly, it was proposed that local authorities should be encouraged to undertake the task, with financial assistance from central government funds.[19]

Both the Scott and the Uthwatt committees of 1942[20] endorsed the Barlow Commission's recommendations for a central planning authority; and in 1943, the Ministry of Town and Country Planning was established. No immediate measures were taken to implement proposals for the building of garden cities and satellite towns, but legislation in 1943-44 extended planning control to the whole of England and Wales, and conferred upon local planning authorities strong new powers for the acquisition of land in war-damaged and obsolescent urban areas and for comprehensive redevelopment.

The end of the war presented unique opportunities for a national planning programme. The need for extensive reconstruction was urgent and obvious, but other physical conditions were also favourable. The large-scale evacuation of persons, business enterprises and government departments from bomb-threatened areas introduced a degree of fluidity only likely to be repeated in the event of another war. At the same time, the apparatus of wartime emergency controls was not immediately dismantled and could be adapted, in part, for peacetime planning purposes. More intangible than these physical considerations, but hardly less relevant, was a mood of general expectancy created by the feeling that some recompense was due for the years of endurance, sacrifice and suffering. High on the list of social priorities was the maintenance of full employment, and unhappy memories of the Conservative Government's treatment of this problem before the war helped to sweep the Labour Party into power with an overwhelming parliamentary majority in the 1945 General Election.

Once in office the new Labour Government had few qualms about offending private interests, and it proceeded to deal with some of the major issues of physical planning. New procedures were enacted to facilitate the prompt acquisition of land by local authorities for housing and planning schemes; the scale of housing subsidies was increased; and provision was made for the establishment of national parks and the encouragement of local nature reserves. Finally, the enactment of the Town and Country Planning Act, 1947, created a new and stronger framework for the planning system.[21] Under this measure, basic planning powers were consolidated in the hands of the councils of 145 counties and county boroughs. These were required to prepare overall development plans for their areas, such plans to be reviewed by the Ministry of Town and Country Planning and revised every five years. All new developments were made subject to permission from the relevant local planning authority or central government.

The Labour Government had taken office in the summer of 1945, and by October Mr Lewis Silkin, the Minister of Town and Country Planning, appointed a New Towns Committee, chaired by Lord Reith (former Head of the BBC), which in a remarkably short space of time issued three reports.[22] Their goal was the creation of balanced communities enjoying high architectural and engineering standards of layout, landscaping, infra-structure and amenities, and provided with a range of employment opportunities. It was not enough, the committee asserted, 'to avoid the mistakes and omissions of the past. Our responsibility . . . is rather to conduct an essay in civilisation, by seizing an opportunity to design, solve and carry into execution for the benefit of coming generations the means for a happy and gracious way of life'. So far as the Government was concerned, this was preaching to the converted, and in 1946, without waiting for the Reith Committee to complete its investigations, the Minister (Silkin) published the New Towns Bill, which became law in August. Under this Act, the Minister could designate any area of land in Great Britain as the site of a new town, and appoint an *ad hoc* public development corporation, consisting of a chairman, a deputy chairman and not more than seven other members, charged with securing the layout and development of the town. Some such form of central government agency, financed by the Exchequer, had been recommended by the Reith Committee, in preference to a private limited liability company, a local government authority, or a non-profit housing association, as the most suitable type of body to plan and develop a new town.

> A major argument in favour of the form of organisation actually adopted must have been its independence from the pressures and caprices of company shareholders or local electors. In appointing members of a development corporation, the Minister is required to consult with interested local authorities and have regard to the desirability of securing the services of one or more persons resident in or having special knowledge of the locality in which the new town will be situated.

The Minister is not, however, obliged to take the advice proferred, and may refrain from making even the token acknowledgement to local interests which the Act suggested. On the other hand, the autonomy of development corporations *vis-a-vis* the central Government can be – and, in practice, has been – very firmly held in check by the ministerial use of statutory powers and financial controls.

Initiative for the formation of new towns has generally come from local authorities or central government, often encouraged by the proddings of outside observers. Once a specific proposal has gained ministerial acceptance the first practical step is the selection of a suitable site, in accordance with the target population of the town. Following the selection of a site the Minister publishes a draft order indicating the size and proposed character of the new town, and must set up a public local inquiry to consider any objections. The Minister may then make the designation order either as originally set out or subject to modification in the light of objections expressed. After the designation, he then appoints the new town corporation which in turn appoints its own administrative and technical staff. Detailed planning follows, based on a master plan for the new town area often prepared by outside consultants.

Between November 1946 and 1950, twelve new towns were designated in England and Wales and Scotland. Eight were intended to decentralise employment and population from London; Stevenage, Crawley, Hemel Hempstead, Welwyn (already well established), Harlow, Hatfield, Basildon and Bracknell ringed the capital at distances between 18 and 30 miles. In Scotland, the new town of East Kilbride was designed to relieve congestion in the Glasgow conurbation. Of the remaining five towns, two – Peterlee in County Durham and Glenrothes in Fifeshire – were intended to provide better living conditions for populations drawn from nearby scattered mining settlements, although Glenrothes is now playing an increasingly important role in accommodating Glasgow's overspill of population. Newton Aycliffe was established in order to provide housing and community services for workers employed on the adjoining industrial estate, while Cumbran in South Wales and Corby in Northamptonshire are also being built close to existing industrial concentrations in order to reduce travel to work.

The New Town legislation had an immediate effect on the south-west Durham area, central government taking the initiative. Proposals for the development of a new town in the vicinity of Aycliffe were put forward by the Ministry of Town and Country Planning early in August 1946, immediately following the passage of the New Towns Act, by which time the Royal Ordnance Factory had been converted into a Board of Trade industrial estate. Consideration was also given to the possible enlargement of Bishop Auckland, but this solution was rejected on the grounds of the distance of that town from the Aycliffe industrial estate. This left the alternatives of setting up a new town under the New Towns Act, or allowing Darlington County Borough to supply the necessary houses and amenities. Since the latter course would entail a boundary extension and tend to encourage ribbon development, it was officially regarded as undesirable. The Ministry therefore proposed that a new town should be built and suggested a target population of 20,000.

This proposal met with a hostile reception from the south-west Durham local authorities and the Durham County Council. Reviewing the situation, the County Planning Officer argued that a new town was unnecessary: the demand for housing would depend upon the volume of male employment, but only 35 per cent of the workers on the industrial estate were males, and probably half of these would be unwilling to move to Aycliffe; those who wished to move could be accommodated, together with any ancillary workers, in a neighbourhood unit of 1,500 houses, giving a total population of about 5,000 persons. Furthermore, if a new town with a larger population were to be built, this would result in the diversion to Aycliffe of new industries badly needed to widen the range of employment opportunities in mining areas, while the movement of population to the town would 'have a serious effect not only on the prosperity and life of the mining villages but also on the recruitment of labour for the mines'. The County Planning Officer conceded that 'a new town situated within the coalfield and properly placed in relation to future industrial and social policy' might be 'the correct solution', but he thought that a new town away from the coalfield would be 'an error of the greatest significance.'

With these arguments in mind, a deputation from Durham County Council, accompanied by representatives of Darlington Rural District Council, met Mr Silkin, the Minister, on 20 August 1946, determined to contest the establishment of the proposed new town. In the event, the contest was short and one-sided. After welcoming the delegation, the Minister commenced by stating that as some development at Aycliffe was obviously necessary, the question of the extension of Darlington County Borough to include Aycliffe and the industrial estate would have to be considered if a new town was not built under the provisions of the New Towns Act. No further arguments were really necessary to ensure the delegation's agreement to the principle of a new town, though the Minister made some slight concessions in limiting the population of the new settlement.

The technical responsibility for advising on the selection of a site for the new town was entrusted to the planning staff of the County Council and regional officials of the Ministry. Since sites east of the Great North Road (A1) were ruled out because of road safety considerations, and sites west of the ROF were apparently never seriously considered, the practical choice lay between the area immediately south of the industrial estate and the area to the north. The site to the south had a number of points in its favour. It was situated in close proximity to the developed portion of the industrial estate (a large area further north being undeveloped), and was already served by rail communication at Heighington Station. Adequate lighting and power facilities could be provided more readily than elsewhere, while the site was situated wholly within the boundaries of a single local authority, Darlington Rural District. The site to the north of the industrial estate came within the jurisdiction of three local authorities –

Darlington RD, Sedgefield RD, and Shildon UD – although this was an administrative difficulty which could be resolved. Both sites were favourably situated in respect of road communication, while there was little to choose between them in the matter of the provision of water and sewerage facilities.

The site to the south, however, had two major disadvantages. It was situated to the west of an active and working dolomite limestone quarry lying immediately south of Aycliffe village. This presented the prospect of substantial demands from compensation, since the dolomite was of considerable value and the quarry owners possessed a freehold interest in an area of land beyond the working face and an option on further land in the vicinity. In addition, there were the problems of possible shaking of foundations through blasting and of disturbances to inhabitants from the same cause. From the standpoint of Durham County Council, however, the greatest disadvantage of the site to the south of the industrial estate was its nearness to Darlington: a nearness which would make the new town vulnerable to a county borough extension and encourage the movement of population and trade from the administrative county. In rather different terms, the County Planning Officer argued that the tendency to draw towards Darlington 'should be resisted: the new town should not commit the error of tending towards the coalescence of urban units'; every step 'taken towards linking the ties of the new town with the old' would weaken the necessity for the former to provide these 'border line activities' necessary for 'independent urban living'. Moreover, as one of the principle objects of the proposed new town was 'to give a practical encouragement to south-west Durham in its efforts towards rehabilitation', and as a considerable proportion of the town's population would be drawn from this area, it was important that development should be as near to the coalfield as possible. Finally, the County Planning Officer argued that the selection of a site to the north of the industrial estate might permit the utilisation of an estimated 500 acres of unproductive land within the boundaries of the old Royal Ordnance Factory: 'almost enough in itself to house the new town'.

These recommendations were formally conveyed to the Ministry of Town and Country Planning in October 1946, and in November the Ministry informed the County Council that:

> all things considered . . . the site immediately to the north of the Trading Estate, and lying between the present Great North Road and the proposed motor road to the west, is superior to any other.

> The provision of an adequate belt of open space between the new town and Darlington, together with the need to avoid the sterilisation of mineral resources were factors which weighed heavily in favour of the selection of a site to the north of the Trading Estate.

The intention to create a new town at Aycliffe was first publicly announced at a meeting which the Minister had with representatives of interested local authorities on 12 February 1947. In making the announcement the Minister stated that the principal reason for the selection of Aycliffe as the site of a new town was to provide accommodation for some of the workers on the adjoining industrial estate. General agreement to the proposal was given at this meeting by local authorities on the understanding that the population of the new town would not exceed 10,000. The possibility of opposition was also lessened by the small size of the existing population within the designated area and the lack of any firmly-entrenched residential nucleus. The Designation Order was duly made on 19 April 1947, and members of the Aycliffe Development Corporation were appointed on 2 July 1947. At a meeting of the Corporation held in August 1948, a decision was made to call the new town 'Newton Aycliffe', so as to distinguish it from three other localities in the vicinity of the designated area with the suffix or prefix 'Aycliffe' to their names.[23]

The most contentious issues in the early years of the new town's history were the establishment of its legal boundaries within Darlington RDC, Sedgefield RDC and Shildon UDC, and disagreement over the size of the target population for the town. Local authorities in the area resisted expansion above the initial target population of 10,000, while other commentators – for example Pepler and Macfarlane in their 1949 report – recommended that the contemplated population for the new town should be raised to 23,000 in order to provide accommodation for the families of prospective redundant mineworkers and others from the south-westerly part of Durham:

> It is preferable to attract these people to Aycliffe, rather than attempt to keep them in such centres as Crook and Tow Law where prospects for further new industry are doubtful. Aycliffe, on the other hand, with its good road and rail facilities, pleasant surroundings, flat land with ample space for expansion off the coalfields should attract any amount of new industry once housing accommodation is available.[24]

The subsequent development of the New Town and Aycliffe Industrial

Estate has been traced up to 1970 in an earlier article,[25] as well as in the longer report referred to on p.202. The purpose of the present chapter has been simply to explain why and how Newton Aycliffe is where it is.[26] It also highlights, by means of a case study, the interplay between employment policy and settlement policy discussed in the previous chapter.

Notes

1. At Peterlee part of the industrial site within the designated area of the new town has been conveyed to the Board of Trade for factory development.
2. The description in the early part of this chapter leans heavily on the account given in E. Allen, A.J. Odber and P.J. Bowden, *Development Area Policy in the North-East of England,* Newcastle, 1957, pp.1-22.
3. *Report of the Royal Commission on the Distribution of the Industrial Population,* 1940, Cmd. 6153, pp.81-3, 97.
4. Ibid., p.195.
5. Ibid., p.201-2.
6. A new Ministry of Works and Buildings, headed by Lord Reith, was established in 1940. In February 1942, as the Ministry of Works and Planning, it inherited all the functions of the Commissioner of Works and all those of the Ministry of Health under the Town and Country Planning Act, 1932 (except those exercisable under section 32 of the Act). See Harold Orlans, *Stevenage: A Sociological Study of a New Town,* London, Routledge, 1952. p.20, n.1.
7. The Ministry of Town and Country Planning Act, 1943.
8. In *The General Theory of Employment, Interest and Money.*
9. The Grenfell Baines Group, *Newton Aycliffe Original Master Plan: Report on the designation of area,* December 1948, mimeo, p.4.
10. Ibid, p.4. G. Pepler and F.W. MacFarlane, *North-East Development Area Outline Plan,* 1949, Vol.1, p.18.
11. Ibid, p.16.
12. The Bournville Village Trust's *Sixty Years of Planning* (1944) gives the history of Bournville Village.
13. Revised and re-issued in 1902 under the title *Garden Cities of Tomorrow.* A 1945 edition had introductory essays by Sir Frederick Osborn and Lewis Mumford.
14. Sir F. Osborn and A. Whittick, *The New Towns: the answer to megalopolis* London, 1963, p.44-50; Lloyd Rodwin, *The British New Towns Policy,* Cambridge, Mass., 1956, pp.13-15.
15. Orlans, *Stevenage,* p.16.
16. Ministry of Local Government and Planning, *Town and County Planning, 1943-1951,* Cmnd. 8204, 1951, p.4.
17. Ministry of Health, *Interim Report of the Committee to consider and advise on the principles to be followed in dealing with unhealthy areas,* London, HMSO, 1920; *Garden Cities and Satellite Towns: Report of the Departmental Committee.* London, HMSO, 1935.
18. *Report of the Royal Commission on the Distribution of the Industrial Population.* op. cit.
19. Ibid., pp.133, 136, 206, 223.
20. *Committee on Utilisation of Land in Rural Areas: Report,* Cmd, 6378, 1942; *Expert Committee on Compensation and Betterment: Final Report,* Cmd.

6386, 1942.
21. C.M. Haar, *Land Planning Law in a Free Society,* Cambridge, Harvard University Press, 1951; W.Wood, *Planning and the Law,* London, 1949.
22. *Interim Report of the New Towns Committee,* Cmd. 6759, March 1946; *Second Interim Report,* Cmd. 6794, April 1946; *Final Report,* Cmd. 6876 July 1946.
23. *Reports of the Development Corporation,* London, HMSO, 1947-48.
24. *North East Development Area Outline Plan,* pp.60-1, 181.
25. P. Bowden, 'Newton Aycliffe: the politics of new town development', in J.C. Dewdney (ed.), *Durham County and City, with Teesside,* Durham, British Association for the Advancement of Science, 1970, pp.454-63.
26. Part of the latter part of this chapter is based on material contained in the research files of Durham County Planning Department or on personal knowledge of the writer of the events described. These are the sources for statements made in the text for which no references are given.

14 THE FOUNDATION OF PETERLEE NEW TOWN

Ken Patton

Peterlee came into being, not to re-house a massive over-spill population, nor as a counter-magnet to a conurbation, nor to house workers on an industrial estate, but to provide centralised development for a scatter of mining villages in what was then the most heavily populated Rural District in England.[1] The scattered settlement pattern in the Easington district owed its origin almost exclusively to the development of the mining industry there during the nineteenth century and the first decade of the twentieth century. Until the eighteenth century it was poor agricultural land owned by the diocese of Durham and administered from Easington Village (whose church shows clearly its Norman origins).[2] In 1758 Rowland Burdon, a Newcastle barber, bought the Castle Eden estate and began to improve the quality of his land. He too was later responsible for improving the communications in the district by building the Stockton to Sunderland turnpike (now the A19). Others followed the Burdons' example and the prosperity of the area increased considerably as a result, leaving the present day agricultural villages of Warden Law, Sheraton and Shotton as reminders of its former character. Naturally there were other agricultural settlements but the grafting on to them of sizable mining communities has left little of the original untouched.

Whilst coal had been mined for centuries in the shallow seams of west Durham, the thick cap of magnesian limestone which rises to 500 feet above sea level near the coast had deterred the speculators from risking a shaft in east Durham. In 1811, however, Dr William Smith sank a borehole at Haswell and proved the existence of coal in commercial quantities. The ports of the Tyne, Wear and Tees were too distant for the haulage of the coal in commercial quantities and its large scale exploitation had to await the coming of the railway from Hartlepool to Haswell in 1835 – early enough for a relatively inaccessible colliery when it is remembered that the famous Stockton-Darlington railway had only opened in 1825.

From that point onwards coal exploitation expanded rapidly and pits were sunk in rapid succession. South Hetton and Haswell were already in existence (1831 and 1833) and others followed soon after in the same western part of the limestone plateau, encouraged by the advent of the railway. Thornley was sunk in 1936, Murton in 1838, Shotton and Hesleden in 1840, Trimdon in 1842 and Wingate in 1843.

The impact of this sudden upsurge of activity was, of course, enormous. In a decade the district changed from a modest agricultural area to one scarred, yet made prosperous, by the profits of large scale primary industry. The population was swollen beyond recognition by the immigrants from all parts of the British Isles who were attracted by the prospects of employment. The conditions under which they lived and worked were appalling. Not only were the pits dangerous and poorly ventilated but the miners had yearly to sign away their freedom with the 'bond' – an agreement which shackled them lawfully to their employers without the employers incurring reciprocal duties towards their men. The villages themselves were jerry-built under contract by developers and, although usually rent-free, were not an inviting prospect for a family:

> Front doors opened straight onto black, dirty, unmade streets with possibly a concrete footpath edged by an open stone channel communicating with a gully at suitable distances. Back doors opened into a small, sometimes unmade and unenclosed yard, never more than ten feet across and then again on to black, filthy, unmade streets. A stone channel, the sole means of drainage, again ran the full length of the street, with water stand pipes at intervals of sixty yards or so. In the centre of the back street stood detached groups of outhouses, comprising ashpits and middens, later to be converted into W.C.'s. Running usually on one side of this area was the main shopping street, comprising small combined shops or lock-up shops, together with frequent public houses.[3]

The recession in the northern mining industry between 1870 and 1890, caused largely by Midland pits capturing the large and lucrative southern market, resulted in the closure of many pits and the selling off of the village houses. Haswell, Hesleden and Hutton Henry never recovered from this blow and stayed closed, although miners have continued to live in the villages and travel to other pits.

The period between 1890 and 1914 saw the second and last great expansion of the east Durham coalfield. The demand for coal had been increased enormously by the industrial development of the Empire and investment in new and bigger mines grew together with the re-opening of many of the older ones. The new mines were built on the coastal cliffs overlooking the North Sea, beneath which they actually mined their coal. The three great collieries of Easington (1900), Horden (1901) and Blackhall (1907), relied entirely on the coastal railway (the Leeds Northern) from the Tees to Sunderland on the River Wear for shipping their coal; it remains an exciting engineering achievement spanning as it does deep ravines on huge viaducts, always in sight of the sea. The coast road (A1086) arrived in 1924. Up to that time it was said of Horden (at the foot of a steep approach road past Elizabethan Horden Hall) that once a miner moved into the village, there he had to remain. For although the carter could get his furniture down the hill, he was unable to pull the heavy load back up again.[4]

The physical appearance of these three villages and the new sectors of the old mining villages was drastically altered under the bye-laws which came increasingly to shape housing standards and housing layouts from 1870 onwards. The Hammonds refer to the grid-iron terraced rows as the 'barracks of industry'[5] and the architects of Peterlee considered them in 1950 to be 'rigid (and) soulless',[6] yet they represented an enormous improvement on previous standards of accommodation, and, so far as space standards are concerned, were often nor far behind some of the more penny-pinching efforts of the post-war period. It should not be forgotten that whilst they had no gardens and little open space, all the villages in County Durham have open countryside almost (and sometimes literally) at their back doors, whilst the coastal collieries, despite the spoil-covered beaches, could offer fishing for the men and endless play possibilities for the children.

The inter-war period brought extremes of suffering and prosperity to the district. Coal was in demand for some time after the 1914-18 war and in the years leading up to 1939. In fact, Horden by that time had grown to be the largest colliery in the county and the 'village' had expanded to a population of 14,000, but the General Strike of 1926 and the Depression took a terrible toll. In the North-East at least, knowledge of the collective experience of massive unemployment in the late twenties and early thirties is as important to an understanding of the mining community as is knowledge of the activity of mining itself. The modern coastal pits were reduced to part-time work and the inland pits had to lay men off till unemployment sometimes reached 50 per cent. Migration from the area was high (6 per cent from the area between 1931 and 1938[7]) and it was the young men and women who left. In all, the 'slump' left its mark on everyone who lived through it. Just as old men still talk with vivid and total recall of their experiences at the Somme and Ypres, so they and younger men recall in detail the degradation and hardship those years meant for so many of them. Yet there were brighter aspects to life in the thirties. Easington RDC made a determined effort to improve housing and sanitary conditions in the villages. It built 4,700 houses, 2,700 of which replaced the slums from the 1830s and 1840s. Between 1930 and 1932, it constructed a trunk sewage scheme and converted 12,000 privies and middens into flush lavatories. It encouraged private developers to help and they constructed almost as many houses as did the Council. Their combined efforts reduced the proportion of tied colliery houses to 25 per cent of the total housing stock.

This considerable effort nevertheless attracted the criticism of at least one town planner of the time, Thomas Sharpe (whom we met in chapter 12):

> At Horden and Easington [he wrote] a great sprawling town village is being run up by both the local authority and speculative builders. The standard of meanness and disorder shown here seems to me almost incredible in this fourth decade of the twentieth century. Here, above all, is the kind of activity which almost makes one believe that men have lost not only the ability to create what is good but actually to recognise what is evil.[8]

Of course, the villages were dreary and the new additions were not miracles of design and sensitivity but they were an enormous step forward.

Much more important than the physical appearance of the villages was the kind of life which people were able to lead in them. The miners had always, because of their isolation, created their own entertainment in the Workingmens' Clubs and the Miners' Welfare. They had always looked after their own in a host of ways and the row of Aged Miners' Homes in almost every village is only the most obvious of these. All the attributes of the working-class community as described in the classic sociological community studies are present in some measure in the mining communities of County Durham. Yet the first architect planner of the new town, B. Lubetkin, write in 1950 of 'the aridity of the social life in the villages' and the fact tht there was 'little social and less cultural provision in the coalfield. There were no facilities for higher education and none for social advancement. The villages were isolated from the main currents of contemporary life – backwaters of traditional habits and prejudices'.[9]

The gulf between the middle-class values of the planner and those of the people he is planning for is clear. If the case were otherwise, it would not be possible to dismiss out of hand the libraries, the churches, the sports grounds, the multitude of societies and activities which flourished in these villages. Of course, it is very easy to react the other way and conjure up an over-romantic view of cosy, working-class, *gemeinschaftlich* warmth. If some have fallen prey to this, it is arguably nearer to real insight than the unrelenting grimness portrayed by Sharpe and Lubetkin.

At the outbreak of war in 1939 all development naturally came to an end and left one thousand slum dwellings still inhabited, half of the remainder with no bathroom and three quarters with only an outside lavatory. There was still a great deal to do in the housing field and the war years provide the key to the decisions on how they would ultimately be tackled.

The story now turns to the idea of creating a new town in Easington Rural District.[10] Local support for the idea, as distinct from the genesis of national new towns policy described in the previous chapter, appears to have originated with a local council official: 'The inspiration for the idea of having a new town in Easington Rural District can, with all justice, be attributed to the mind of one person, Mr. C.W. Clarke, who was the Council's Engineer and Surveyor'.[11]

Clarke, the son of a colliery manager, trained as a design engineer and had no formal training in town planning, yet he reacted strongly to what he considered to be the piecemeal approach to planning of his predecessors, and as early as 1938 sounded some Council members for their views on centralised new development in the district. Their reaction was unfavourable. He had to wait until 1943 for a further opportunity to promote his ideas on centralisation. Then, in response to the need to plan for new housing and post-war development in the area, he suggested creating central housing estates on a large scale to serve a number of villages, rather than sporadic building of smaller number of houses in every village. Between August 1943 and February 1944 Clarke, in general conversation with councillors, moved to the position of advocating development on a single site[12] and carried the Housing Committee with him.[13] They referred the proposal for truly centralised development to the full Council, which met on 17 February 1944 with 26 out of 41 councillors present.

At this meeting of Easington Council the principle of concentrating all development on one site was adopted, although the post-war programme of building 800 houses was to have first priority, starting as soon as the war ended. Clarke was asked to prepare a report on the longer-term development on a central site, though not as a matter of urgency.

It was not until early in 1946 that Clarke took up his cherished scheme once more. He had read the first Interim Report of the Reith Committee in March and was 'impressed by all those points which are relevant to Easington'.[14] In particular, he noticed the special powers of the Development Corporation and the Committee's view that a new town would be useful to regroup population from scattered communities. While this report provided him with food for thought, he did not have long to ponder upon it, for on 8 May 1946 Mr Lewis Silkin, the Minister of Town and Country Planning, referred in the House of Commons to a new town (to become Newton Aycliffe) he was contemplating for Durham County.[15] This prompted Clarke to write to the Clerk to the Council and request that he write to the Minister:

> Before carrying the work in my department too far, I think it might be advisable, in order to avoid duplication of work or future hold-ups, to contact the Minister . . . on this matter, pointing out that in 1943 the Council decided, on a report from me, that the practice of sporadic building in each and every village be discontinued and that consideration be given to the creating of a new self-contained centre of development, complete with the necessary community facilities, employment being provided by new light industries.[16]

With the help of the Regional Office of the Ministry, Clarke gathered further material to complete his report, *Outline Survey of Easington District with Redevelopment and Development Proposals,* and submitted it to the Council in December 1946.[17]

This report was subsequently revised and expanded and published by Easington RDC in 1947 under the title *Farewell Squalor.*[18] *The Outline Survey* represented a genuine attempt by a local authority to come to terms with a problem which was exercising the Government nationally. It contained a thorough review of all the facts relevant to the area: population, geology, drainage, industry and so on, and proposed the building of 9,320 houses on one central site of 1,500 acres.

> The quickest and most convincing demonstration of the need for centralised development is a tour of the various places in the area. The typical composition of a township, excepting Easington, Horden and Blackhall, is as follows:
> The colliery surface establishments occupy the central feature

> position in what was the original centre of population. This centre of population consists in many cases, shall we say, consisted, of sordid rows of single and double storeyed colliery cottages with walls in random limestone rubble and slated roofs. Where erected on sloping or undulating ground, these rows of twenty or thirty, or even more, cottages followed the natural ground level, so that the ridges, eaves, window and door lines followed parallel with the ground surface . . . [here follows the description of the unmade streets and middens quoted earlier].
> On the outside of this area appeared the development of the early 1900's, terrace-type brick houses by private enterprise, monotonous unrelieved rows of early bye-law type dwellings. Then ringing this area the Council-owned sites of semi-detached houses erected between the wars without any thought to layout or architectural treatment. In addition to all this, we see the sprawling ribbon development of the speculative builders.
> With regard to Easington, Horden and Blackhall, the same description applies, except that since these places developed after 1900, there are no limestone rubble houses with unmade back and front streets. Instead, we have rows of monotonous brick houses . . . without any regard to orderly arrangement or amenity.[19]

In *Farewell Squalor,* Clarke added:

> The density of these dwellings is over thirty to the acre which falls far short of present day standards of twelve to the acre. The people who live in the houses are victims of industrial squalor and have had to be content with this ever present ugliness rearing its grizzly head as if to be in unison with the grimy pit itself, or its belching chimney or the ever present waste heaps with their accompanying poisonous effluvia. They have been bound to live and work amidst this architectural excrescence in an unplanned age; indeed, not only must they live there but strive to eke out such limited pleasures as the sordid groupings and lack of social amenities permit.[20]

A social survey of one in ten households in the villages of Easington in 1948 showed that 30 per cent of houses had no separate kitchen, 46 per cent had no fitted bath, 75 per cent had no indoor lavatory, and 33 per cent were overcrowded on the basis of one room per person.[21]

In the first three months of 1947 events moved fast. Mr Tetlow in the Regional Office of the Ministry convened a meeting of all the relevant bodies, which approved Clarke's proposals in principle, with reservations about agriculture and coal. The newly-formed Northern Region Physical Planning Committee discussed the idea at its first meeting on 28 January and approved the principle (deferring a decision on size and location). On the same day Mr Bates, Durham County Planning Officer, reported to his planning committee in favour of a new town for Easington and a Development Corporation as the agency best suited to achieve it.

Tetlow met the Easington Council on 12 March, persuading them to support the proposal for a single development under a new town corporation. He expressed at this meeting his surprise and pleasure at the initiative of the Council, for 'one finds that it is the Government officials in an area who are pressing the elected representatives to concentrate development.' He played on this point when he pointed out later in the meeting:

> You have a New Town Act . . . but it is having a rough passage in some places, largely because the Government has been trying to use it . . . in Durham we have tried to go about things differently, we do not want the Government to say to an Authority 'Do this' or 'Do that'. Up here we want it to be a case of finding out what the (local) authorities want and then giving them all the assistance possible in helping them to carry it out.[22]

Despite his disagreement with Clarke over the size of the town – he wanted 30,000 as against the latter's 50,000 – Tetlow won the Council over and on 24 March they voted unanimously to put the project in the hands of the Minister. Later events were to show that they did not realise at the time just how much of their own power they were voting away. Housing is one of the principal activities of a local authority and Easington took a step which led to a drastic reduction in the amount they were to be allowed to undertake in the future.

Discussion continued at a variety of levels. Possible sites for the new town were being canvassed until the last moment, when a decision emerged in favour of Clarke's proposed site (put forward in the *Outline Survey* of December 1946) rather than that of the Ministry of Agriculture's, to the north-west, or of the Regional Physical Planning Committee's, which would have linked up Easington Colliery and Horden (see Figure 14.1). This decision was more or less assumed into existence at a meeting of the Regional committee on 28 May 1947[23] and was influenced as much by the fact the the NCB, although hurt

Figure 14.1 Peterlee in 1948

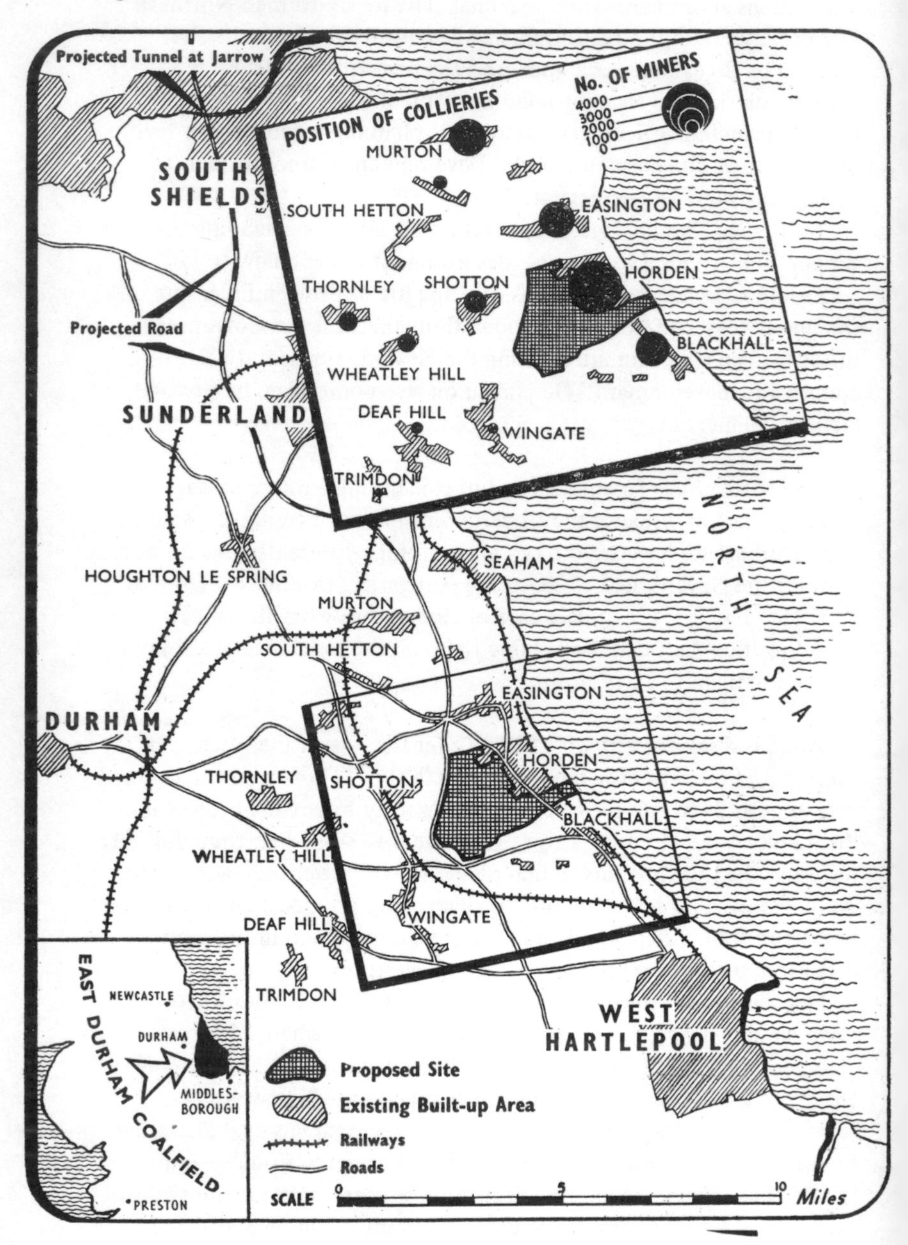

Reproduced from *Current Affairs,* No.75, 5 March 1949

because they had been brought late into the decision, could make 146 acres of stable land available adjoining Horden, as by any other relevant factors. By 11 July Bates was able to report to the County Planning Committee that agreement had been reached with the NCB that: 'where necessary to secure stability, coal will be sterilised (i.e. not mined) so as to develop the first section of the Easington New Town and steps will be taken to co-relate (sic) the mining and surface development in the two future units'.[24]

Now that the major local interests, wittingly or unwittingly, were committed to a new town of between 30,000 and 50,000 inhabitants on a site high above Horden and bounded to the south by a four-mile long and 150 feet deep ravine, the only important step remaining was to convince the Minister that the project was a worthwhile one and that he should adopt it. He was due to visit Newton Aycliffe on 7 July 1947 to examine the progress of what had been intended as the only new town in the North-East, and it was agreed that he should also go to Easington where he met the Council on the 8th. The record of this meeting[25] shows up one of the failings of planning at a national, centralised level, namely, the irrelevant application of generalised solutions to highly particular problems. Apart from asking the Council why they did not build the town themselves, Silkin urged on them the standard model which he had been fighting to establish elsewhere in the country. Despite the fact that Newton Aycliffe was only to have a population of 20,000, he assured Easington that the right size for a new town was 60,000 and that care should be taken to 'balance' this population.

Silkin accepted the site advocated in the *Outline Survey* and on 16 August 1947, the Council received a letter which said that the Minister:

> had in mind the expediency of establishing a town with a population of the order of 30,000 people. The town would be a balanced community, its citizens being drawn in the main from persons now living in unsatisfactory conditions in the Rural District. The existing opportunities of local employment would be supplemented by the introduction of suitable industries.[26]

Since the Council were eager to get some houses on the ground, they urged the Minister to hold his statutory consultations with all the local authorities as soon as possible and proposed 27 August 1947, only a few weeks after his first visit to the district. Surprisingly, he agreed.

The 'consultation' consisted of Silkin addressing the assembled local authority representatives at length and then answering a few questions. The burden of his argument was familiar to those who had read the Reith Reports. He recognised an established need to build some 10,000 houses in the district which would provide for a population of 30,000 people and that these houses should be built on single site rather than in the respective villages.

> There were a number of mining villages [Mr Silkin said] centred all round the area and there was vacant land around the villages, and these houses could be provided there possibly in the proportion in they are required in the villages, partly by infilling and partly by extending the villages themselves; but those who knew the area would [he thought] readily admit that would not be the most desirable course. The villages themselves were not such as to justify their extension, and certainly not such as to provide the kind of life they today regarded as essential for their people. He could not compete with the description given to him when he was at Easington [on 8 July] by some of the men who were present and were Chairmen of some of the Committees of the Council, but he was deeply impressed with what they said. In the main, the villages were mining villages and were all located around existing coal pits, with waste heaps, dilapidated buildings, dilapidated land, all intermingled with the houses, where you get the smell, smoke and noise of the pits all the time and never get away from it. Those who were town dwellers thought that the worst thing that could befall them would be to live on top of their work, but that work was not generally offensive, it did not smell or make noises or emit smoke. Nevertheless, psychologically it was a bad thing to be on top of your work, and how much worse if it was in the conditions of a mining village; and they had not to forget the women and children as well, who were living in these conditions. He was deeply impressed with the view expressed that it was wrong to go on accentuating these conditions for ever when we could do something else. Moreover, the villages did not provide the necessary essential recreational and cultural amenities regarded as necessary today. Shopping was unsatisfactory, and the younger people desiring to get something more than could be provided in the villages had to go into the large towns and occasionally missed the last bus causing great anxiety to parents. He felt as they did, that accepting the requirements of building these 10,000 houses it would be inadvisable to build them

> as an addition to these present unsatisfactory conditions. The only thing was to build them on a new site away from the conditions he had described without the handicaps of any existing buildings, where it would be possible to build up a township of some thirty-odd thousand with the amusements and other essential conditions which were necessary to maintain a good life. The opportunity existed and it seemed to him it would be criminal not to take advantage of that opportunity. Durham was not so rich in fine new towns – or fine old towns either – that it could not do with a new one, and in any case the conditions in which people were living in a place like Easington itself were really more urban than rural but they had the amenities of neither.[27]

Mr Silkin went on the emunciate the principle of 'social balance' which was held to be important in the creation of new towns:

> He thought – and he wanted to speak very frankly in the presence of miners – he thought that it was definitely anti-social that they should have people of one income group and one type of occupation all segregated together, merely able to discuss the events of the pit and the life around the pit, and nothing else. It was anti-social and undesirable and created a particular type of psychology which he thought we wanted to get away from. It was essential that miners should have the opportunity of mixing with people of other occupations and income levels, not only so that they may broaden their own outlook, but in order that they in turn may influence other people who they will come in contact with who would never have had any contact with miners at all. There was no hope of people understanding the miner and his point of view if the miners segregated in their own villages and never got out of them. It was, therefore, most important that they should provide opportunities there for the mining community to mix with other classes of the community and each would enrich the life and experience of the other.[28]

Because of the dependence on mining, the employment opportunities in the district were limited, there was not enough work for women and, as a consequence, the young people were leaving. The future growth of the town beyond the target population was problematic, for it would compel those concerned to decide whether or not to rehouse even larger numbers of tenants of obsolete houses in the new town, or to build in the villages. The 'ideal' population of 60,000 also worried Silkin still, for he resorted to the argument that the new town and Horden (at the foot of a very steep hill) combined to make a total of 45,000 inhabitants: 'getting on to the 60,000 desired'.

The decision to designate 'New Town Number 6' had thus been taken; the local authorities had been consulted and there remained but one important problem unresolved – the name of the town. There had been a certain amount of canvassing but one obvious candidate presented itself. Peter Lee, the miners' leader who died in 1935, had begun his political life in Wheatley Hill in the Rural District and, since the town was predominantly to rehouse miners, the Council felt it would be a fitting memorial if it were to be named after him – Peterlee. Silkin agreed, and the name was adopted.

The Minister's only serious critic in the meeting on 27 August was the Town Clerk of West Hartlepool, who feared the competition which the new town's industrial estate might present. He did not press his objection. The Draft Designation Order was issued in October 1947, followed by a public inquiry in January 1948. At this inquiry objections were raised by the villages of Haswell, Hutton Henry and Thornley, mainly centred on the difficulties of travelling to work in Peterlee. Haswell Parish Council argued that miners worked on a shift system which meant that 'men are proceeding to and from work at all hours of the day and night',[29] and because of the poor bus service, it would be virtually impossible for some men, especially those travelling some distance, to avoid serious hardship and cost. They were fearful too of 'breaking up that community sense of which we are so proud'.[30] Because of this fear: 'The residents of Hutton Henry will reject the idea of having to be moved to the new town'.

The Thornley Miners' Lodge supported their Parish Council and pointed out that the very working of the Lodge and the many activities it organised depended upon men living near to their work. The Labour Party in both Haswell and South Hetton were also vigorously opposed to the new town. Their resolutions read as follows:

> This Labour Party protests against the building of the Easington New Town (Peterlee) as this will prevent the building of much needed houses in the surrounding villages.[31]
> In the opinion of this Labour Party, future building and planning should be carried out in the existing villages; we claim that suitable building sites are available; that there is a crying need for recreational and cultural facilities; that unsightly rubble heaps from demolished

> property have too long been an eyesaw and loudly cry for attention.[32]

In his reply[33] the Minister noted the misgivings in this connexion and: 'share(d) their anxiety to ensure that everything will be done to improve conditions in the coalfield generally and not just in that part of it which he has in mind for development as a new town'.

He was satisfied, however, that the:

> beneficial effect of the new town will not be confined to its own inhabitants but will be felt throughout the Rural District. By providing a modern shopping and recreational centre, and an opportunity to develop the cultural and social activities normally associated with a fair-sized town, the development of the Easington new town will diminish the dependence on larger towns outside the area and, the Minister hopes, help to remove one of the chief causes of the gradual drift of younger people away from the District which has been noticeable during the last twenty years.

He was also reinforced in his conviction by the fact that: 'The Easington Rural District Council, many of whom are miners themselves, have been firm in their support for centralised development on a selected site ever since the possibility was first considered in 1943'.

The Minister indulged in a little embroidery when he added that 'they [the Council] see in it the only means of achieving a more balanced type of community'.[33] It was surely Silkin himself who attached such importance to this aim, despite the contradictions which this exposed in the case of Peterlee. For in an area with a predominantly one-class population (see chapter 12), where were the 'balancing' elements to come from? He had argued in 1946 that 'people of different income levels and classes should all mix and live together if possible in the same neighbourhood unit . . . They must be encouraged to meet and mix and learn to understand one another . . . It is our task, therefore, to break down that slight reserve, and suspicion that exists between people of different classes.'[34] He later commented that 'unless they do mix freely, the whole purpose of a mixed community disappears'.[35]

The Peterlee Draft Designation Order stated that 'it [the new town project] offered an outstanding opportunity for breaking with the unhappy tradition that miners and their families should be obliged to live in ugly over-crowded villages which cluster around the pit-heads, out of contact with other industries'.[36]

Ruth Glass, Harold Orlans and Brian Heraud have examined

sociologically the ideas and achievement of 'balance' in post-war new towns, particularly around London.[37] Ruth Glass draws attention to the fact that the presence of the middle classes in a community adds what might be seen as a desirable element of social control in a situation where a large group of working-class tenants are coming together in a new and unstructured situation. Others must chronicle how far the aim of 'balance' was achieved over the years in Peterlee, beset as it was by the basic handicap of being a miners' town.[38]

Thus, in 1948, Peterlee was born: to get miners away from the squalor of the pit head, yet 'reasonably accessible' to their work; to broaden their social horizons in a 'balanced community'; and to provide a sub-regional centre for the commercial and recreational facilities it was felt the area lacked.

Notes

1. Chesterfield Rural District had, by the late 1960s, overtaken Easington.
2. The following account of the early history of the area draws on pages 2-5, 'The Local Setting of Peterlee', from *Analysis of Planning Problems, Report of the Architect-Planner* (hereafter Analysis), Peterlee Development Corporation, 9 January 1950, p.2.
3. C.W. Clarke, *Outline Survey of Easington District with Redevelopment and Development Proposals,* report to the Easington Rural District Council December 1946, p.37.
4. Cf. J. Lawson, *Peter Lee,* London, The Epworth Press, 1949, which contains an interesting, if sentimental, account of Peter Lee's early life in the rural district.
5. J.L. and B. Hammond, *The Town Labourer 1760-1832,* London, 1917.
6. *Analysis,* p.3.
7. *Analysis,* p.4.
8. T. Sharpe, 'The North-East, Hills and Hells', in 'Britain and the Beast'.
9. *Analysis,* p.4.
10. The following sections draw in part upon D. Steele, 'The Origins of Peterlee New Town', unpublished M.A. thesis, Durham University, 1962.
11. Steel, *The Origins of Peterlee,* p.36.
12. Steele, *The Origins of Peterlee,* p.44.
13. Minutes of Easington RDC Housing Committee 9 February 1944. Clarke's proposals for centralised development were carried by 15 votes to 4.
14. Steele, *The Origins of Peterlee,* p.46.
15. In the Second Reading of the debate on the New Towns Bill, 8 May 1946.
16. Letter from Clarke to Gray, Clerk to the Council, 14 May 1946.
17. Clarke, *Outline Survey of Easington District with Redevelopment and Development Proposals* (hereinafter Outline Survey).
18. Hereafter *Farewell Squalor.*
19. *Outline Survey,* 'The Case for the New Town', p.37.
20. *Farewell Squalor,* pp.63-4.
21. W.A. Moyes, *Mostly Mining: a study of Easington Rural District,* Newcastle, Frank Graham, 1969, p.164, quoting Helen Rankin, 'The Peterlee Social

Survey''*Current Affairs,* 75, March 5, 1949.
22. Notes of the meeting of 12 March 1947, Easington RDC.
23. Notes of the meeting on 28 May 1947, Easington RDC.
24. Report of the Durham County Planning Officer, 11 July 1947.
25. Unheaded report of visit of Minister 8 July 1947, in files of Clerk of Easington RDC, quoted in Steele, p.73.
26. Letter from the Minister to the Clerk to the Council, 16 August 1947.
27. Notes on meeting between local authorities and the Minister, held at Easington 27 August 1947.
28. Ibid.
29. Public local enquiry at Easington on 27 January 1948. Shorthand record taken by Treasury reporter, evidence on behalf of Haswell Parish Council.
30. Ibid., evidence on behalf of Thornley Parish Council.
31. Ibid., letter from Haswell Labour Party, produced by Haswell Parish Council.
32. Ibid., letter from the South Hetton Labour Party to Haswell Parish Council, dated 17 January 1948.
33. Easington New Town (Designation) Orders, Minister's decision letter of 5 March 1948 after the public enquiry.
34. Speech at conference on 'Building New Towns', 12 July 1946.
35. L. Silkin, 'Housing Layout in theory and practice', *Architects' Journal,* 8 July 1948, p.45.
36. Draft Designation Order. Explanatory Memorandum, 1947.
37. R. Glass, 'The Evaluation of Planning: some sociological considerations', *International Social Science Journal,* 11, 1959, pp.402-3; H. Orlans, *Stevenage: A Sociological Study of a New Town,* London, Routledge 1952, pp.81-4; B.J. Heraud, 'Social Class and the New Towns', *Urban Studies,* 5, 1968, pp.33-53.
38. One brief account is contained in W. Moyes, *Mostly Mining,* Chs.12-14. The book as a whole is a useful source of information about the Easington District, both historically and in recent years.

INDUSTRIAL CHANGE

15 THE DECLINE OF MINING: A CASE STUDY IN SPENNYMOOR

Martin Bulmer

This chapter and the next form part of a study of industrial change in County Durham undertaken with the support of the Joseph Rowntree Memorial Trust in 1968-70. A copy of a 280-page report on this work, entitled Collectivities in Change: some sociological reflections on the decline of mining in the Durham coalfield, *by M.I.A. Bulmer, comprising eight chapters on community studies, the regional and local background, the decline of mining and the growth of factory industry, the social role of the workingmen's club and the relationship between industry and locality, is deposited at the Library of Durham University. Policy aspects of the pit closure discussed in this chapter are examined in 'Mining Redundancy: a case study of the workings of the Redundancy Payments Act, 1965, in the Durham coalfield',* Industrial Relations Journal, *Vol.2, No. 4, 1971, pp.3-21.*

The close-knit, industrially homogenous and class-conscious mining community has been immortalised in *Coal is Our Life.*[1] What happens when the industrial underpinning of such a community is knocked away? How do miners experience redeployment, redundancy or early retirement? What is the experience of ex-miners who go to work in new industries? These are very broad questions, of interest to all who live in and know British coal-mining districts. They have, moreover, considerable policy implications for labour mobility and industrial development.

This chapter and the next present two case studies of industrial change, carried out in the town of Spennymoor in south-west Durham in 1969 and 1970, in an area which until the middle of 1960s was still one of significant coal-mining employment. The closure described in this chapter, that in 1969 of Tudhoe Park Colliery on the northern edge of the town, was the latest of a number which signalled the approaching end of coal mining in the Spennymoor area. This contrasted with the position five years previously, when there were nine pits within four miles of Spennymoor town centre. Tudhoe Park was the seventh colliery to close in the local area in just over four years. After its closure only two collieries in the locality, Whitworth Park and Metal Bridge Drift, remained, employing (in June 1970) 520 men. The next nearest collieries, East Hetton (employing 900 men) and Fishburn (1,200 men) lay six miles to the east; neither had the long-life future of the east Durham collieries on the coast. This study is therefore set in an area where coal-mining was fast disappearing, as shown in Table 15.1 (see Figures 2.1 and 11.1, p.19 and 161).

As such, this study differs from several earlier studies of the economic and social consequences of the post-1957 contraction in mining. Both House and Knight's work on the effects of closures in the Houghton-le-Spring area (north Durham) in 1957-65,[2] and the DEP study of the Ryhope closure south of Sunderland in 1967,[3] were carried out in areas where there were still significant mining employment available in the immediate locality of the closing pits. This was not the case in Spennymoor.

Table 15.1 Collieries Closed in the Spennymoor Area, 1965-1974 showing manpower 1947 to closure

Colliery	Date of Closure	Number of men employed			
		1947	1960	March 1968	At closure
Tudhoe Mill Drift, Spennymoor	27.2.65	–	207	–	93
Dean and Chapter, Ferryhill, (including Chilton and Leasingthorne)	15.1.66	4870	2908	–	1367 (March 1965)
Thrislington, West Cornforth ('Doggy')	4.3.67	1091	805	–	210
Bowburn	22.7.67	2296	2080	–	357
Brancepeth, Willington	22.7.67	2211	1473	–	408
Mainsforth, Ferryhill Station	12.12.68	2054	1546	1139	971
Tudhoe Park, Spennymoor	23.5.69	137	236	213	183
Whitworth Park, Spennymoor	27.7.74	243	313	316	218
Metal Bridge Drift	(Still open, 31.3.77)	–	104	221	

Source: National Coal Board, Area Statistician.

Dr R.C. Taylor's excellent social anthropological study of the NCB Inter-Divisional Transfer Scheme, as it affected five west Durham villages in the mid-1960s,[4] was carried out in localities more similar to Spennymoor, but had a different focus – migration out of the area. The present chapter may also be related to studies of the effects of pit closure in west Cumberland by Knight,[5] and in different parts of South Wales in the late 1960s by T.J. Farmer,[6] J. Sewel,[7] and S.W. Town.[8]

The closure of Tudhoe Park Colliery on Whit Friday 1969, marked the end of coal-mining in a part of Spennymoor which had originally begun in the 1860s to supply coal to the Tudhoe iron works. Worked jointly with Croxdale colliery, on the Al, this first pit closed in 1936; several miners interviewed in the present study had lost their job at that time. Tudhoe Park Drift was opened up during the Second World War to work coal measures nearer the surface; the Fore-drift had been opened up in 1946-47 and one respondent recalled cutting the first sod together with his father. This pit, behind and to the east of Front Street in Tudhoe, had its own manager after Nationalisation in 1947, but in the 1950s came under the control of the manager of the other colliery in the town, Whitworth Park. Pithead baths were opened at the colliery in 1956. It closed in 1969.

Tudhoe Park Colliery was typical of a kind of mine at one time common in west Durham. It was a small drift mine, worked not from a vertical shaft but from two 'drifts', passages driven at an incline into the ground. The depth of the pit below ground varied between 100 and 150 feet, the distance from pit-head to coal-face being about two miles before closure. One drift was used exclusively for bringing out coal, using an endless rope driven by a motor on the surface. The other was the means of the men going in and out. Coal seams at the colliery varied in thickness from two feet to three feet thick and those being worked before closure were about two feet thick. Immediately before closure, very wet conditions were experienced at the face. Prior to closure, 183 men were employed and output from the one face being worked at the end was 100 tons per day. (Compare this to Dawdon Colliery in Seaham – producing at the time 10,000 to 12,000 tons per day, with twelve times the labour force and about hundred times the output).

With thin seams, low output and rather poor quality coal, Tudhoe was at the opposite extreme to coal-mining as it survives in the county today – the modern, highly mechanised pits on the coast with thick seams and high output. In Durham in the late 1960s, there was wide variation in size of pit, thickness of seam, and output, though shaft mining was most common. Tudhoe was not, therefore, representative, in general terms of mining in the county. It was, however, not dissimilar to the other surviving *local* pits, Whitworth Park and Metal Bridge. Both were small, both worked thin seams, Metal Bridge was also a drift mine and both had very uncertain futures. Thus Tudhoe Park may be said to be a typical example of the West-Durham drift mine and of the declining fortunes of mining in the Spennymoor area.

The principal aims of this research were to examine the impact of the pit closure and consequent redundancies on the men involved; to investigate the miners' views of the coal industry today in relation to offers of employment at other collieries and alternative employment available in the locality; to follow the experience of men who became unemployed as a result of the closure; and to make a preliminary study of the miner's position in the community. A further aim was to study the workings of the Redundancy Payment Act 1965. (As this last topic has been the subject of a separate article[9] this will not be discussed in detail here.)

The study was originally conducted as a sociological study of work, within an action frame of reference.[10] Although the present account is primarily empirical, the data is analysed within a frame of reference which treats social action as the basic unit of analysis. Action is analysed in terms of external conditions, internalised constraints and normative orientations, as a necessary corrective to theories which postulate free choice of employment, according to criteria of economic rationality, sometimes put forward by economists. Within the action frame of reference, the approach here consists in delineating the course of events leading to the closure of the pit and analysis of the social influences at work. Although some attempt is made to relate the discussion to the wider social structure, it is *primarily* an attempt to analyse a particular situation and course of events.

The conditions of action refer to factors external to the social actor and over which he has no control. They include, firstly, the fact of closure itself. The pit had already been reprieved on at least one previous occasion and it was widely expected to close in the near future. The pit was not productive enough by comparison with others in the county, due to its size, geology and difficult working conditions. The precipitating cause of closure seemed to have been the inferior quality of coal being produced and the consequent marketing problems (a large industrial consumer refused to take Tudhoe coal because of its high ash content).

However, even had marketing and quality problems been overcome, the pit would have closed shortly due to geological conditions. The workings were approaching what the miners termed a 'big hitch' – a break in the strata which would have involed stopping production and driving a new roadway through to the new level of the seam. This was not economic in the precarious financial situation of the pit. This process of closure was one that could not readily be reversed by the management or men of a particular pit (although it might be at national or county level). A threatened closure may be put off for a year or two but small pits like Tudhoe Park would have to close, given the then national fuel policy. Most of the miners interviewed seemed to accept this and almost all had expected the pit to close within two years.

The decision to close the pit was taken by the National Coal Board and communicated to the men at the pit. At Tudhoe, the men had already been warned of the possibility of closure in January 1968, although the position had improved by July of that year. The actual decision was communicated to a mass meeting at the colliery on 11 March 1969 and released to the media the same day. This means of informing the miners did not reach all of them. Half a dozen of the men interviewed mentioned that they first heard the news of the closure on the television.

The second condition of action is the employment context in which closure takes place and what provisions are available for those made 'redundant'. In its original use the word meant 'superfluous', but (particularly in Britain) it has come to be associated with the reduction of the labour force of enterprises by dismissal. The basic meaning of redundancy refers to the rendering of an employee out of work due to circumstances beyond his control culminating in his dismissal,[11] which do not arise from incompetence, unsuitability or misdemeanour.

The record of the National Coal Board in dealing with reductions in man-power was a relatively enlightened one prior to the introduction of government legislation on redundancy in 1965. Before 1965, there was a bilateral agreement between the NCB and the Union whereby cash benefits were given to men made redundant, dependent on age and length of service, and the standard unemployment benefit was made up to two-thirds of the former mining wage for six months. This was worth, in most cases, less than £200, a level of payment more modest than under the subsequent government scheme. The 1965 Redundancy Payments Act established a more solid national scheme with higher levels of payment. The Act, very briefly, put a duty upon the employer in certain circumstances to pay an employee a lump sum if he is made redundant by the firm. The size of the lump sum is dependent on age and length of service with the firm, in relation to average wage before redundancy up to a maximum (at that time) of £40 per week. A man of 55 with over twenty years service was eligible for 27 weeks pay – for a pieceworker in mining at the time earning £22 a week, this would be nearly £600; for a 45-year-old datal worker with 22 weeks entitlement, earning £16 a week, this would be £350 or so. This redundancy payment is only payable, however, in certain circumstances. The Act places upon the employer an obligation to find the employee other work within the organisation if he can do so. If the employee is offered suitable work by his employer, he can accept it or refuse it. If he refuses it, the employer can refuse the redundancy payment. Where employer and employee do not agree, the case passes to the Industrial Tribunal dealing with the workings of the Act; if the employer can show that the employee acted unreasonably in refusing the offer of alternative employment, he will not be obliged to make a redundancy payment.

A further separate aspect of this financial provision was a *special* scheme, introduced in 1968, to pay redundant mineworkers over the age of 55 a further regular sum to bring their weekly income for three years after redundancy up to a level of nine-tenths of their former take home pay.

A third condition of action was the employment situation in mining in the south Durham Area of the NCB, a man in a small concern being in a very different position from one with a large employer like the NCB. Before 1966, approximately seven-tenths of men affected by pit closure were provided with alternative colliery jobs. Of the three-tenths who left the industry some left voluntarily, others retired on age grounds and others retired due to ill-health. A small minority were made redundant.

Wedderburn notes that this system worked quite well:

> The Coal Board's experience shows that with planning, much can be done to control recruitment over a period of time, although with the higher natural wastage in that industry of some ten per cent per annum, there is more flexibility in this direction than in the (Railway) workshops. In the period 1959-63, total (U.K.) colliery manpower fell by 170,000. 5,000 men were transferred to other coal-fields under the transfer scheme. 12,000 men aged 65 and over were retired by agreement with the Unions; 2,350 men have taken pensions before the age of 65; only 7,500 have been described as long-term redundants, most of the rest of the reduction has been secured by natural wastage.[12]

After 1966 this system had not worked so well. There were fewer local pits to which men could be transferred. The pace of closure had increased, so that the problem was quantitatively greater; as a result, more men in any particular closure would have to be made redundant in any case. Moreover, there was a shortage of miners in some grades at some collieries in the area. For despite a rapid run-down in the last few years, miners appeared to have moved to other employment at such a rate that there were vacancies within the Area in most skills. Indeed, for the first time for some years, the NCB was advertising vacancies in the local press during early 1970, not only for craftsmen but also for pieceworkers and datal workers in certain collieries in east Durham. At the time of this study, the NCB Inter-Divisional Transfer scheme described by Taylor[4] was not being publicised.

A fourth condition of action was the availability of employment other than mining in the area. Such a condition has both an economic and a spatial element: whether or not there are vacancies in the area and, if there are, how they are distributed geographically. Evidently, employment opportunities in south-west Durham are likely to be different from those in a conurbation such as Tyneside or Teesside. Within south-west Durham, new employment tends to be heavily concentrated in the towns of the area, Spennymoor, Crook, Bishop Auckland and West Auckland. The fact that there were new factories opening or about to open in the locality, creating vacancies for male operatives, undoubtedly influenced the outcome of this particular closure.

This was the general context of the closure, but how did those involved interpret and respond to what was happening? The two main protagonists were the NCB and the miners employed at the colliery. The manner in which the NCB defined the situation was primarily in terms of employment needs and policies. Their aim initially was to make some 73 men redundant (including those older men kept on salvage) and to persuade another 102 men to transfer to alternative work within the area, out of 183 men employed. The policy of the NCB in the area since the closure programme intensified in the middle sixties had been to fill vacancies by transfer from collieries closing or about to close.

The NCB therefore first gave these 102 men at Tudhoe the opportunity to volunteer for vacancies at other pits. In general, volunteers only came forward for the two local pits. Then, several weeks after closure, all men at the pit not remaining on salvage work received either notice of redundancy from the date of closure or an offer of alternative employment, which was sent to those who had not volunteered to transfer to other collieries. Table 15.2 compares the situation five weeks before closure with that one week before closure.

There was a considerable discrepancy between the aims of the NCB and the final result. The NCB originally wanted to transfer 102 men to other collieries, but of these 43 either refused, left early, or succeeded in being (or were) made redunant (see Table 15.2). The most striking evidence of NCB failure was in trying to transfer men to coastal collieries, for which all the initial offers were made. On a list in the colliery asking for volunteers, there were 50 vacancies shown at South Hetton (compared to less than 10 at any other) and it was the stated intention to try to create a 'little Tudhoe' at this colliery. A whole face was set aside, it was said, where conditions were very similar to those at Tudhoe. In the event, no-one was willing to transfer to South Hetton and no-one did. Out of 58 transferred, 27 went to local pits, 12 to jobs at or based on Tursdale Central Workshops (four miles away), and only 19 to pits further afield – 8 to Fishburn, 5 to East Hetton and 6 to Easington (see Figure 2.1, p.19).

How did it come about that the management singularly failed to achieve what they wanted? How did the miners affected see the situation and why did they resist the initial aim of management? It is necessary to consider first the social context in which action occurs, the internalised parameters of action including social experience, local patterns of social relations, norms and values held. The methodology of the study is described in the appendix at the end of this chapter; data on the closure is derived from interviews with one in four of men working at the colliery; from other interviews and observations concerning employment; and from NCB employment data on age, length of service and employment status; and the 'state of play', over time, with regard to redeployment.

A primary influence was length of service in the mining industry, which was an important influence upon views of alternative work outside mining. Length of service data is shown in Table 15.3 at the end of this chapter. Calculations based on it suggest that Tudhoe miners had spent just under nine-tenths of their working lives in mining, on average.

This is supported by replies from the 44 interviews to questions about experience outside mining. Thirty had had no other employment outside mining and another five had jobs for only a short period after leaving school, before going into the mines. Thus only one-fifth of the sample had had adult experience of work outside mining and only two out of the whole sample for more than ten years. Nor was experience in the Forces any more common. One man had gone into the Forces in the 1930s, five men for the duration of the war and two men on short-service enlistment post-war. The remaining 36 had never served in the Forces (mining, of course, being a Reserved Occupation in World War II).

Table 15.2 Destinations of Tudhoe Miners after Closure

Position Five Weeks Before Closure				Position One Week Before Closure
36	To receive notice of redundancy (and therefore entitlement to lump-sum payment)			56
37	To be kept on salvage. (Mostly over 55 years old)			38
102	men received offers of work at the following collieries:	Of these 102 men:		
		On salvage		1
		To be made redundant		20
		Left of own accord		3
	(a) South Hetton*	Transferred to		
	(b) East Hetton**	Whitworth Park	20	
	Fishburn,	Metal Bridge	7	
	Easington	Tursdale C.W.	4	
	(c) Local collieries,	Area Mobile Team	8	
	for which volunteers			
	had come forward –	Fishburn	8	
	the names were drawn	East Hetton	5	
	out of a hat.	Easington	6	58
		Refused offers of work and told by NCB that application for Redundancy Payment will be contested.		20
8	Left of their own accord prior to closure			11
183	TOTAL			183

* all offers were refused

** a few offers were accepted, more were refused

Source: *NCB Employment Data.*

Similar evidence of the high proportion of the miners' working life spent in mining comes from the study of the Ryhope closure.[13] At that colliery, almost four-fifths of the sample's working life had been spent in the colliery and the total in mining altogether was even higher. In this study, the length of service at Tudhoe Park was not so long on average. This was due to the policy of transferring men between pits. Following the closure of other pits in the area (Table 15.1), men had been transferred to Tudhoe just as the NCB was now seeking to transfer men from Tudhoe to other collieries. Even so, over two-fifths of the sample had worked at Tudhoe for over 10 years, and most of the young recruits under 25 (mainly craftsmen) had started work there.

Substantial length of service at a particular pit, leading to lack of experience of other pits, may lead to a reluctance to move to a place where one is not known. For instance, several men referred to Tudhoe as 'cosmopolitan', meaning that men came from outside the immediate locality. This is an interesting comment, in that three-quarters of the miners came from Tudhoe, Croxdale, Spennymoor or Middlestone Moor, and only one-quarter from beyond the immediate locality. It refers, of course, to men coming from other pits such as Dean and Chapter, but it reinforces the importance of shared experience of working together over a period of time. This occupational experience is illuminated further by replies to questions about why men went into mining originally. When asked: why did you originally go into mining? the replies included the fact that there was no alternative work available (19), family tradition (7), best paid work (5), influenced by people of the same age (4) and the 'natural thing to do' (3). Sample replies were:

> 'Place where I lived there was nothing else'.
>
> 'No work around here. Nothing else at the time'.
>
> 'At that time, nothing else for us to do. When you left school, had to get some work or other. At that time, practically forced to go down the mine'.
>
> 'Like father, like son. In war years, started work with father and brothers. What else was there?'
>
> 'Just the understood thing. Followed our father'.
>
> 'Following your father'.
>
> 'Father a miner, you're a miner'.

Why was this so? It was partly because mining communities have tended to be physically isolated and occupationally homogeneous. Occupational choice is also dependent on the relative prestige of different jobs and mining has usually had higher status (and higher earnings) than comparable jobs in small and medium-sized settlements like those of south-west Durham. Occupational choice too, is culturally conditioned and bound up with educational opportunities (or lack of them).

The views of miners of their industry would seem likely to be influenced by their own family experience. In this respect, the continuity between father and son was very striking. In the case of three-quarters of the sample (32), the man's father had been a miner – in most cases for all his life (except for war service). Of the 32, 21 had worked at pits in the Spennymoor area (6 at Tudhoe itself) and another 9 in the south-west Durham area. One had come from Wallsend and one from South Wales. Moreover, of the 32 whose father had been a miner, in 20 cases their father's father had been a miner and another 5 could not remember. Again this is principally in the local area, very often in pits which have been closed for many years. Clearly this aspect of family history would repay further study, since it is likely that in this part of the country, such a pattern was quite common. However, it would not be reasonable, *ipso facto,* to assume that family tradition is the main reason for men taking up mining.

The extent of kinship relations among the Tudhoe miners was considerable. Seventeen miners in the sample (two-fifths) had, or had had, relatives at Tudhoe. Of these six had in the past, eleven in the present (i.e. one quarter of the sample); eight of these had one relation, one had two relations, one had three relations and one had four relations. Half of these relations were brothers who worked, or who had worked together. Several cited a family of five who had worked at Tudhoe in the past and two out of four brothers in another family who worked there up to closure were interviewed. Such family ties would increase the solidarity of the work on balance.

Another very significant internalised constraint upon freedom of action was the importance attached to locality. Four-fifths of the miners lived within three miles of the pit. One-third could walk to work; two-thirds could get there in less than 15 minutes by various means, four-fifths paid either nothing or less than ten shillings a week for travelling. Of the 44, 33 had lived in the area (i.e. the place where interviewed) all their life since the age of five and only five had lived in that area less than 20 years. Of those who were not born in the district (eight) four moved from elsewhere in south-west Durham and one from the north of the county. Two were from Northumberland and one from South Wales. Here, then, is evidence for strong attachment to the immediate area of residence. A pattern of social relations carried on within a narrow geographical area further limits the extent to which choice is likely to be exercised and has important implications for transfers within the coal industry to coastal collieries.

It was known that a number of miners were related, and the Union Secretary described Tudhoe as a 'family pit'. Respondents were therefore asked, 'It is said that Tudhoe Park is a family pit. Do you think this is true?' Only 3 said it wasn't, 41 said it was. But out of the 41, only 9 mentioned the fact that people there were related. The others by 'family pit' apparently meant a friendly pit, where everybody knew everybody else. Thus:

> 'All pits is family. Good humour'.
> 'Yes, you can say that. Always made welcome.'
> 'Everybody together, everybody knows each other'.
> 'Well, there's a lot of good men there, friends. Friendly little pit'.
> 'Oh yes, aye, very friendly pit. Don't think we've had any disputes there'.
> 'Yes, I would think so. A lot of these small mines are close-knit. People live in a close locality'.
> 'Yes, in a way. John knows Jackie and Jackie knows Jimmy'.
> 'Oh, aye, very sociable pit. Come from all over, more like a cosmopolitan'.

The features of a 'family pit' thus included not only the fact that people had kinship ties, but that everybody knew everybody else, and that miners lived in the locality, which produced a happy atmosphere with easy relations between man and man. This is consistent with considerable evidence in industrial sociology of the 'solidaristic' orientation to work among miners – how working conditions in the pit encourage dependence on and responsibility for fellow-workers and how importance is attached to working among tried and known companions. For example, the study by Trist and others in north-west Durham in the 1950s showed very clearly the great reliance placed on the primary work group.[14] A very vivid local illustration is provided by Sid Chaplin's novel, 'The Thin Seam',[15] the plot of which centres on just such a group of 'marrers'. Indeed, the novel could quite well have been written about Tudhoe Park.

As one would expect from other evidence, work clearly carried over into leisure activities and many of the miners saw other Tudhoe miners out of work. Over half saw miners from Tudhoe regularly, mostly at local Working Men's Clubs. Five saw them occasionally, fourteen saw them rarely or never. Of these latter, seven lived in places where there were few Tudhoe miners and where they could not travel easily to Tudhoe or Spennymoor. However, there were still one-sixth of the sample who did not see miners from Tudhoe outside of work. Therefore, although clearly work ties do carry over into leisure activities, the minority for whom this is not the case should not be lost sight of. How far are these those in supervisory positions; those with aspirations to be upwardly mobile; or those who don't drink? The teetotal miner has perhaps had insufficient attention.

There may, of course be a tendency to idealise what is passing away in describing Tudhoe as a 'family pit'. But it was clearly the case that there was shared consciousness of common work experience, which was threatened by closure. A network of social ties had been built up which could only partially be re-created by marrers going to work together elsewhere.

About one-quarter of the men interviewed had been at Tudhoe more than 15 years and clearly regarded moving to a strange pit with some apprehension. Hence the preference for local pits Those intending to leave the mining industry clearly wished for local employment. It seems possible that factory employment on the doorstep is preferred, not only for convenience but because it is among people one knows, whereas to go to a pit towards the coast is to go among strangers.

A further internalised constraint could be in the miners' view of the closure itself. It was quite clear that the closure had not come as a surprise: 30 had definitely expected it and 10 had more or less expected it, or known it was rumoured. If the pit could have been kept open, 30 gave it a life of less than two years and only 4 a life of more than three years. The reasons given for closure corresponded closely to the reasons given by the NCB.

Questioned further about the closure, three-quarters of the miners thought it was inevitable and nothing could have been done to prevent it. Of the remainder four thought the NCB or Government policies were the cause, the implication being that these should be changed. Only seven thought the pit could have been kept open, four by selling the coal, two by opening up new workings. Thus it can be said that the miners' views of the situation of the pit and likelihood of closure did not diverge markedly from that of NCB officials, although there was considerable feeling about the closure itself. Seventeen men said they didn't care one way or the other when they heard the news; fourteen were disappointed and ten were pleased. Older miners tended to have firmer views one way or the other. Those in middle age tended to be less concerned. These were some reactions:

'Came as no surprise'.

'Foregone conclusion: rumours going about'.

'More or less expected and just took it that way'.

'Don't feel so bad, been expecting it at least two years'.

'Properly disappointed. Quite contented down there'.

'Depressed, very depressed. A load of coal is a big help'.

'Very disappointed. Thought I was there for life'.

'I'm disappointed. When you've been there for 24 years, it's part of your life.'

'Miss a way of life'.

'Happy, quite happy. I can hardly believe it now'.

'I was over the moon'.

'I was pleased, when you've been 50 years in the pit, you've had enough'.

Half of the sample had some regrets at the closing and many of these would have liked the pit to remain open:

'Been a good little pit. Happy pit. I've been very happy'.

'In a way, yes. If it had gone on 20 years, I would have been happy'.

'Wish it had kept open. Would have worked there as long as it went'.

'I would have liked to have kept on. Everybody was pleasant and sociable and near at hand. Not as far as pit work was concerned – 12, 14, 16 inches in the goaf area'.

(This last comment refers to distance between roof and floor in the mine, in the 'goaf' area immediately behind the coal face which has been cleared of coal.)

Moving on from the context of action to the means available to those affected, there is a tendency in economic models of labour markets to treat resistance to change as due merely to force of habit or ignorance about available alternatives. Such a view is clearly inadequate. In the present closure, the fact of closure signalled a change in the relationship between men and their employer. Evidence of cohesive work groups in mining also shows that there is a considerable degree of informality in the relationships between supervisors and men. The immediate supervisor, the Deputy, very often works alongside the men and may indeed have been promoted from among them. The overmen, under-manager and manager of the pit, though more remote, are known to all men in a small pit and on a first name basis in many cases. Moreover, they have regular dealings over a long period (for example, in disputes over piecework payment) and strong feelings are often expressed in the course of disagreement (only to be forgotten the next day). (Such face-to-face dealings can be characterised as affective and particularistic.)

The redeployment of men at closure, however, was not handled by the pit-management but by area staff from South Durham headquarters. The relationship was therefore at once more impersonal, since it was between relative strangers. It was conducted, moreover, in a relatively formal manner, through interviews explaining the openings which are available and then the sending of formal offers in writing. This formality was only partly offset by the visits of colliery managers and NUM branch secretaries from other collieries, hoping to persuade men to transfer to the colliery through interviewing them.

In such interviews, questions were naturally focussed upon problems such as wages and shift-working and on finding out about the future of the pit. They did not necessarily (and perhaps could not) deal with questions about local conditions underground (except in general terms), or the possibility of groups of men who worked together then, working together in the new pit. Thus, the affective, particularistic, diffuse, collectivity-orientation of the miner in his day-to-day work in his present pit was replaced by an affectively neutral, more universalistic relationship with people he did not know. Moreover, this was only partly overcome by actual visits to collieries. A significant change therefore took place in the quality of relations between miners and Coal Board officials during the closure, and one which put many miners at a significant disadvantage.

The effect of the Redundancy Payments Act, moreover, was to accentuate built-in conflict between employer and employee. This has been discussed in detail in the article already referred to.[16] The NCB wanted, in its own interests, to transfer as many miners as possible to other pits. The men wanted to be made redundant and qualify for lump-sum payments. Before closure the local NUM Secretary at Tudhoe was quite clear about his members' attitudes to redundancy. He said: 'The men want it if they can get it. They think they've been in mining long enough and want to get out and get their redundancy payment'.

The relationship between employer and employee, however, permitted of no such simple solution. The Act places an obligation upon the employer to provide alternative employment if it is available and in the South Durham Area of the NCB, at the time of the closure such vacancies *were* available.

To whom, in this situation, could the miner turn for advice?

Officials of the Department of Employment and Productivity, who interviewed the men before closure, merely gave advice on alternative employment opportunities and said nothing about redundancy. As far as the Redundancy Payments Act is concerned, the main direct function of the Ministry is to dispense the forms on which employees apply to the Tribunal. No advice was provided on the situation of offer and counter-offer to which the men were exposed.

The Union, which represents the men in industrial relations matters, did not see the redundancy situation raising special problems. At the mass meeting held in April, the NUM representative from Durham told the men that they had to accept the closure, and this advice was also given by the Lodge.

The expectations of fellow-miners seem, therefore, to have been one of the major influences upon the course of action followed by miners, particularly in the absence of any other guidance. The general view of the mining industry was a poor one. When asked what they would advise someone to do who was thinking of going into mining and asked their advice, only two out of 44 were at all in favour, with qualifications. The other 42 were all against in differing degrees. Twenty-two might be said to be firmly against (half the sample) – twenty against with qualifications (twelve in favour of coastal pits, four for the Midlands coalfield and four for someone going into a craft). Even then the criticism was sharp:

> 'You want your head knocking off; except for a trade'.
>
> 'Stop out now'.
>
> 'Conventional mining's no good at all'.
>
> 'Wouldn't advise anybody at the present time if they could get a job out of mining'.
>
> 'Dead industry now. Wouldn't have said it once. If somebody was interested, they'd have to go to the Midlands'.
>
> 'Stop out now. Nothing but bloody hard work in the pit. I've a cousin in the pit – I told him that'.
>
> 'Not if I could get another job. No matter how they glamorise it, they can't make it any different from what it is'.

The criticism did not seem to be concentrated among different groups – those of all ages doing all kinds of work expressed views like these. Nor did they vary according to what they were going to do after closure. Even those still working for the NCB after closure were pessimistic about the future prospects of the industry.

What, then was the outcome of the closure for the men involved? This can be considered in two stages. First there was the process of negotiation *before* closure between miners and NCB, summarised in Table 15.2. Secondly there is the position at closure and eleven months later, shown in Figure 15.1. Despite the existence of vacancies in coastal pits and of subsidised travel, few miners were prepared to travel there, or even to the nearer collieries of Fishburn or East Hetton. One reason why the proportion remaining in mining was so high was that shortly before the closure the NCB suddenly created 20 vacancies at Whitworth Park, having failed to persuade many men to transfer to collieries in the east. The three principal reasons for unwillingness to transfer to collieries further away were the travelling involved (in some cases an hour or more each way), working among strangers, and pessimism about the future of mining.

Travelling was mentioned by many miners when discussing the handling of the closure:

> 'Offered ment work far away. One hour, one and a half hours. Killed the goose that way'.
>
> 'More men could have been paid off. Men in their fifties are being made to travel'.
>
> 'As far as coastal pits, handled badly. There should have been a stipulated distance. They (NCB) say 26 miles is reasonable'.

One miner said:

> 'Travelling would have spoilt my social life. You're out of the house ten to eleven hours a day for seven and a quarter hours work'.

The more complex explanation of a refusal was as follows:

> In this area in the last three years, six biggish collieries have closed. Bowburn, Dean and Chapter, Doggy, Mainsforth, Chilton, Tudhoe Park. Cannot see how all these [miners] are going to be absorbed – and then they tell you in the papers that closures are going to be accelerated. They want all men to go to other pits but no man is secure in the pit for five years. [So I'm going to] make the break now.

In addition to lack of confidence in the future of the industry and resistance to travelling, the outcome shown on the left-hand side of figure 15.1 was partially due to attachment to the locality. This is very important, because one economically rational solution for the miner faced with closure would be to transfer to a coastal colliery and move house. Asked about this possibility, 16 said they would *not* move to another area to get work; one said he would move if several were going but wouldn't move on his own. Several gave their wife and her family as the reasons, but others were clearly attached to the locality regardless of other considerations:

> 'No, I've no fancy for moving house, I like living here'.
> 'No, bred and born here'.

Evidence of local attachment to place in Spennymoor is also strikingly shown in research conducted in 1973, reported by Townsend and Taylor,[17] which shows markedly stronger attachment to place in a sample in Spennymoor than in three other towns in the North-East which form parts of conurbations.

The outcome of the closure 11 months later is shown on the right-hand side of Figure 15.1. A detailed analysis of the different groups is contained in the article on the Redundancy Payments Act and the closure,[18] which will not be repeated here. Several points in relation to job search will, however, be made since they are significant for the theme of strong local and particularistic attachments.

Firstly, one section of the pit labour force was not looking for work. All men in the closure age 55 and over were made redundant (some after a period on salvage). At this time the special scheme to make up the pay of redundant mineworkers over 55 to nine-tenths of their former net earnings was in operation, and there was therefore little immediate incentive to look for work among this group (though the special scheme only operated for three years). This highlights the extent to which pit closure in County Durham has meant *de facto* early retirement for many miners. This is difficult to quantify exactly from unemployment statistics, but there are pointers. In January 1971, for example, out of 30,432 men registered as wholly unemployed in Durham County, 8,883 (or 29 per cent) were aged 55 or over. (Six months earlier, in summer, the proportion was 33 per cent.) In four local Employment Exchange areas where ex-miners were heaviiy represented among the unemployed, the proportions aged 55 and over were, in Crook: 43 per cent; Stanley, 58 per cent; Consett, 45 per cent; Durham (City), 41 per cent. In Crook and Durham, nearly 80 per cent of those aged 55 and over registered as unemployed had been so for over six months.[19]

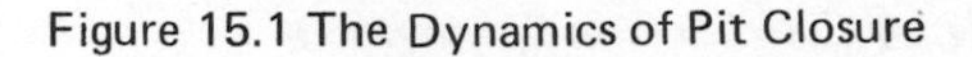

Figure 15.1 The Dynamics of Pit Closure

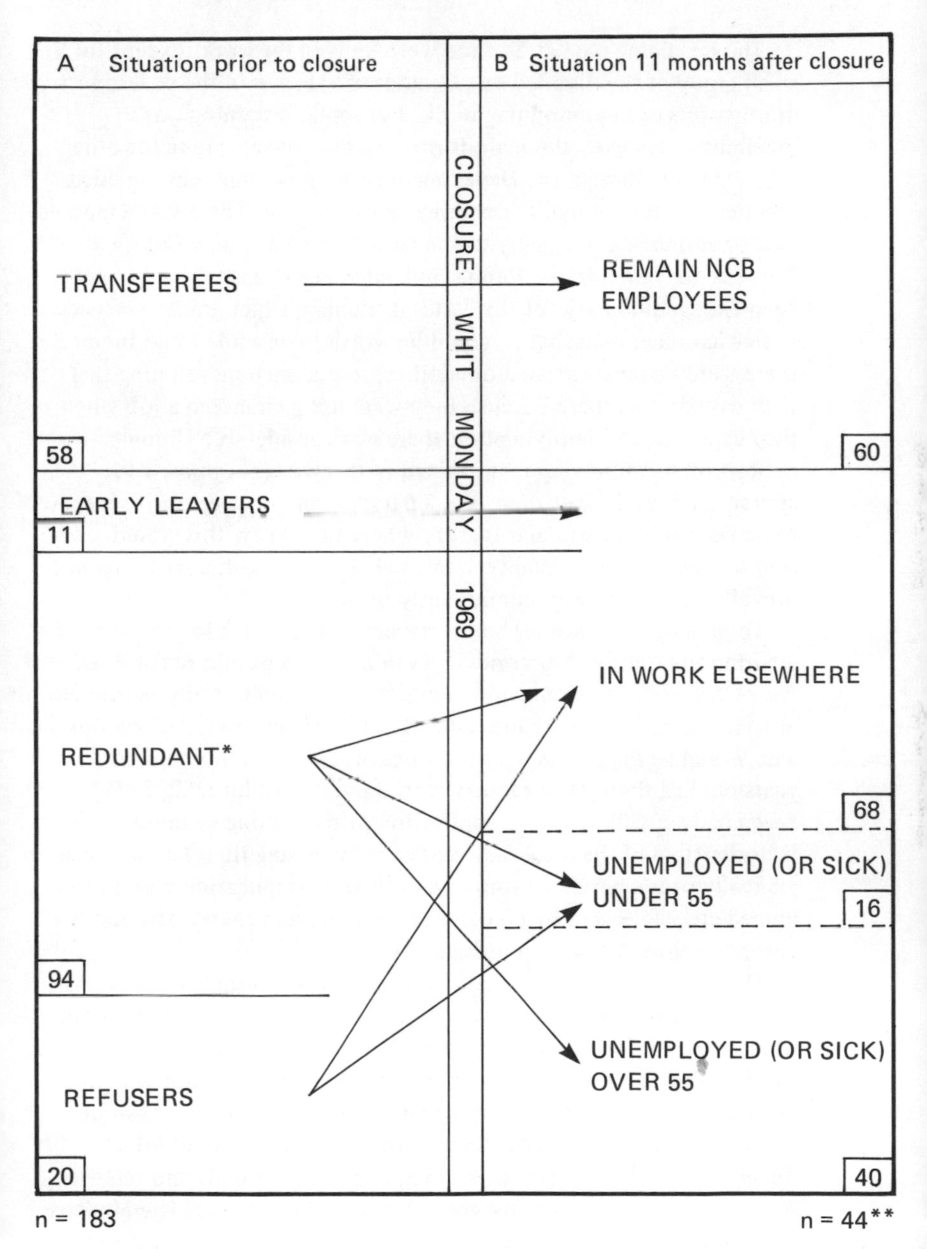

*Including 38 men retained on salvage work for several months and then made redundant.

** Figures are multiplied by 4 to produce estimate for population.

Source (A): NCB Employment Data

Source (B): Second Interviews

The remaining men at Tudhoe were looking for work (except for a small group of the disabled or sick under 55) either in the coal industry at other pits or in non-mining work. For some, retraining was a possibility. However, the main formal avenue for retraining for other jobs available through the Department of Employment was regarded sceptically, even though there was a centre nearby. There was a marked lack of enthusiasm for going to the Government Training Centre at Tursdale to learn a trade. Replies indicated partly that there has not been enough publicity for this kind of training, which might persuade somewhat older men that it would be worth their while to go there. But there were also institutional objections, several men mentioning that they wouldn't go there because they were not guaranteed a job when they came out and implying that there was considerable Union opposition to employing men trained in this way (as opposed to apprenticeship). In fact there was a paradox, miners were quite prepared to be trained in a particular factory where they knew this would lead to a job (see next chapter), but the approach to the government-provided facilities was predominantly negative.

There was, on the other hand, considerable interest in prospects of securing work at local factories. Eleven men at the colliery forfeited their claims to redundancy payments by leaving voluntarily before closure. Most did so to start work immediately at local factories. Among those who would be made redundant after closure, half of those under 55 years old had thought of factory work (and two of building work). Seven had actually filled up application forms for one or more factories (two of the local factories were increasing their labour force gradually over a period of some months, so an application was not immediately followed by an offer of work in most cases). The result a year after closure is shown in Figure 15.1.

The most striking evidence for the absence of formal and institutionalised means of action in the labour market was the way in which the men found their new jobs. It was already known from the work of Kahn and Wedderburn that informal means predominate for manual workers affected by redundancy. (Wedderburn, for example, found that one half of her railway workshop sample found jobs through being 'spoken for' or known, or through friends and relatives. A further quarter got jobs by going 'on spec' to factories. The Ministry of Labour was no more important than newspaper advertisements; one-eighth got jobs by each of these means.) In the present study the men were asked how they went about finding work. Of the four main means used, there were fourteen mentions of going to factories 'on spec' and filling in application forms; seven sought help from friends and relatives; three replied to newspaper advertisements and three had been sent to employers by the Labour Exchange.

Asked how they found their present job, over three-quarters had obtained work through a personal approach, either on their own or on their behalf. Formal means of replying to advertisements or being placed by the Employment Exchange were not important. The personal approach was epitomised by one respondent: 'I went over to the factory and they refused to see us. So I found out who was the shop foreman and went to see him and he set us on'. Thus, in a situation where one might expect universalistic criteria to operate, in fact a more particularistic approach was characteristic.

This case study inevitably raises more questions than it answers, and only includes some of the data originally collected. And yet the picture of strong diffuse and particularistic local ties showing long attachment to and familiarity with particular pits, is striking. The National Coal Board operates at area, regional and national level, but for many of its employees, the particular enterprise is the focus for loyalties and involvement.

The attachment of miners to the industry undoubtedly reflects their lack of experience of other work, and their integration into a settled stable pattern of work and leisure social relationships. The sign of attachment to the industry was very often free coals. But this was symbolic. What was valued was to work among people you knew in an industry you knew and there was great reluctance to make the break.

This was reflected in comments made both by men who remained in mining and men who took up factory work. For men still working in mining, an attempt was made in the second interviews to elucidate differencies between Tudhoe and the new pit. Some found it easy to make the change; others commented on different working conditions and social relationships:

> 'Very low. You're on your shoulders, on your side all day. Tudhoe was 2′2″ to 2′4″. This is seventeen inches. The men up there are terrible as well. They called us "strangers" '.
>
> 'Bit strange at first. Hadn't seen these plough and trepanner faces – all power supports. In a week or a fornight I got used to it'.
>
> 'If you don't come from B—— [a local village], that's it. More or less in the know. Union men, overmen, all come from B——'.
>
> 'Prefer Tudhoe. Got to know men better at a small pit. Meet a lot of different men in a large pit. Little pit easier'.

'Knew no-one before I went. Thirteen on the bus, four of us from Tudhoe. As far as working, the majority of men are pretty genuine; the odd one is biased. But you're still a stranger. They say: "he's one of the strangers" '.

'The men [are different] . Down Tudhoe more sociable. At ——, I reckon you've got to work up there a lot of years before you're in the know'.

'The men. At Tudhoe, all went to school together, left school together, knew each other intimately. Here, the mechanical side is divorced from the others. So different, trying to adapt yourself to being regimented, like you are at ——'.

To leave the industry, on the other hand, was to cut oneself off from known and tried ways and it is a difficult step to take; more difficult in mining than in other industries. Three comments provide a conclusion: the comparison between pit and factory work is pursued in the next chapter.

'No doubt about it. It was a happy little pit, small number working there, everybody knew everybody, very happy community'.

'Wished I left the mines thirty years since. The work (in the factory) is a long way easier and pleasanter. No bed of roses going down the mine but I've always been used to it. If Tudhoe had still been going, I'd still be there'.

'Had the pits still been going, I'd be content to work in them. But now it has closed, I wish they had closed thirty years ago'.

Appendix: Research Methodology

The aim of the research was to follow the course and effects of this particular colliery closure, which was announced only two and a half months before it took place. At the time the writer was engaged upon field research in Spennymoor, and the closure provided a readymade opportunity to make a case-study of local industrial change.

A strategic decision had to be made six weeks before the closure as to when to carry out interviewing. The difficulties of deciding when to carry out research in redundancy have been noted by Wedderburn:

> The research worker has to reconcile various objectives; of obtaining data about immediate reactions and experience without over-great reliance upon memory and also of obtaining data about some new 'equilibrium' position (which it is almost impossible to define) when

> the immediate effects have worn off. At the very beginning of the enquiry, therefore, we had decided to use two interviews, the first within a few weeks of the closure of the workshop and the second perhaps six months to a year after the closure.[20]

The solution adopted here was rather different from the above. In order to study the *course* of the redundancy, it was decided to interview a sample of the miners involved *before* closure, in order to illuminate their view of the situation before they became unemployed, moved to a new employer or moved to a different pit. This was followed up by a second interview with the same men approximately eleven months after the closure, in order to guage the *effects* of the closure and in an attempt to study the new 'equilibrium' position. Clearly any choice of this kind is open to objections. The advantage of carrying out interviews before closure was that the men's views of prospects were less likely to be clouded by subsequent experience after closure. On the other hand, the second interview was carried out after a sufficient interval for the men to be established in a new job, where this was relevant.

The quantitative data in this chapter derive from two sources. The NCB Area Industrial Relations Department provided a list of all the men working at the colliery before closure, including data on age, employment status, length of employment continuously in mining, and destination after closure. (This is referred to as *NCB Employment data.)* Table 15.3 is from this set of data.

Table 15.3 Age and length of Continuous Employment in Mining (n = 183)

	Length of Service (in years)								
Age	Under 10	10-14	15-19	20-24	25-29	30-35	36-41	42-46	47+
15-24	11								
25-29		7							
30-34		1	10						
35-39		4	4	12	2				
40-44		4	1	7	13	2			
45-49	1	4	2	4	2	26	1		
50-54		2		1		4	17	1	
55-59		1		2			12	10	
60-65		1		1			2	10	1

Source: *NCB Employment Data*

From the first source, the list of 183 names of men working at the colliery before closure, every fourth name was selected and 44 out of these 46 miners were interviewed as described above. (This is referred to as *First Interviews.)* Two refused. Eleven months later, 42 out of the original 44 interviewees were re-interviewed. Two could not be contacted. (This is referred to as *Second Interviews.)* In addition to data such as Table 15.4 below, these interviews are also the sources of most of the verbatim quotations in the text.

Table 15.4 Age and Length of Employment at Tudhoe Park (n = 44)

	Length of Employment (in years)					
Age	Under 2	2-5	5-10	11-20	Over 20	Total
15-29	1	1	2	1		5
30-39	1		1	4	1	7
40-44	1		2	3	1	7
45-49		4	2	2		8
50-54	2	2		1		5
55-59		1	4	1	2	8
60+			2	1	1	4
TOTAL	5	8	13	13	5	44

Source: *First Interviews*

Interviews were also carried out with the principal officials involved in the closure: staff of the NCB Industrial Relations Department in Spennymoor, the Colliery Manager, the local NUM officials, and staff of the Spennymoor Employment Exchange. Certain additional observational data were also obtained in the course of interviews about redeployment.

All data, including the two sets of interviews, were gathered by the writer himself. The interview schedules used in the first and second interviews are not reproduced here for reasons of space but are available in the longer report referred to on page 235.

The limitations of the data presented should also be borne in mind. Verbal responses to open-ended interview questions by a strange university research worker, in two interviews twelve months apart, can provide only a partial view of experiences and interpretations of their situation by the miners affected. The voices of those interviewed are fragmented and brief. No strong claims for the data are made in this respect; they seemed, nevertheless, of sufficient interest to be worth reproducing.

The representativeness of the interview sample compared to all Tudhoe miners is examined in Table 15.5 based on comparisons between First Interviews and NCB Employment Data. It will be seen that, while the sample is representative in terms of age-distribution and continuous service in mining, it over-represented datal and surface workers and under-represented pieceworkers underground. This should be borne in mind in interpreting the results.

How far were the miners at Tudhoe representative of miners elsewhere in the county and in the work-force at large? Some comparative data is provided in Table 15.6. This shows that the Tudhoe miner was on average older than the labour force in general. He was also older than Durham miners as a group, due principally to more miners being in the 30 to 49 age group and fewer in the 15 to 29 age group. How different was the Tudhoe miner from the Durham miner in work experience? Many of the Tudhoe miners had worked at other pits. This reflected the fact that following the closure of other pits in the area, men had been transferred to Tudhoe Park, just as the NCB was transferring men from Tudhoe Park to Whitworth Park and Metal Bridge. In this respect, Tudhoe Park typified the movement of miners which had gone on between west Durham pits in recent years. Table 15.7 shows the large number of the men who had worked at other pits before being transferred to Tudhoe. Moreover, of the 36 who had worked at other pits, 25 had worked at another pit for more than ten years. Not all of these men, of course, had transferred to Tudhoe recently.

To what extent were the Tudhoe miners a self-selected group in the sense of being men in an industrial backwater, whose more adventurous colleagues had either moved to coastal pits or left the industry altogether? Certainly there was some evidence in the sample that those who looked further ahead tended to be more inclined to leave the industry. There is no simple answer but again it limits the extent to which one can generalise from the case-study. Tudhoe is not representative of mining in the county as a whole but it is probably representative of mining in the Spennymoor area and to that extent of the *decline* of mining in that part of south-west Durham. The type of colliery, location of nearby pits and alternative employment opportunities differed from those typical of either the Ryhope area in 1967[21] or the Houghton-le-Spring area in the middle 1960s.[22]

Table 15.5 The Representativeness of the Sample: A comparison of the sample with all Tudhoe miners

A: Age Distribution

Age	In Sample	Expected from Data on All Miners*
15-29	5	4
30-39	7	8
40-44	7	8
45-49	8	10
50-54	5	6
55-59	8	6
60+	4	4
No response	2	

Mean age of sample = 45.6 years
Mean age of all Tudhoe miners = 45.5 years

B: Continuous Service

	In Sample	Expected from Data on All Miners*
Less than 5 years	2	2
6-9 years	2	1
10-19 years	9	10
20-29 years	9	11
30-39 years	14	13
More than 40 years	8	9
No response	2	

Mean length of continuous service in mining — sample = 27.9 years.
Mean length of continuous service in mining — all Tudhoe miners = 28.1 years

C: Breakdown by Type of Work

	In Sample	Expected from Data on All Miners*
Under-Official	6	5
Craftsman	3	4
Surface	6	4
Datal	13	10
Piecework	16	23
No response	2	

* Expected number = distribution of data relating to all Tudhoe miners, divided by four and rounded to nearest whole number.
Sources: *NCB Employment Data,* and *First Interviews.*

Table 15.6 Comparison of the Ages of Tudhoe Miners with Other Sections of the Labour Force

	Age Distribution (%)						
Occupational Group	15-20	21-29	30-39	40-49	50-59	60+	Total
Tudhoe Miners, 1969 (n = 183)	3.2	6.4	18.0	36.6	27.6	8.2	100
Durham Miners, 1967	8.1	11.1	16.7	26.3	28.3	9.7	100
Miners (GB), 1967	7.2	11.8	17.2	26.1	26.9	10.8	100
Male Employees, 1967 (GB)	12.1	18.4	19.2	20.2	19.0	11.1	100

Mean Ages:		
	Tudhoe Miners, 1969	45.5 years
	Durham Miners, 1967	42.9 years
	Miners (GB)	40.7 years
	Males Employees 1967	
	Northern Region	40.6 years
	Great Britain	40.1 years

Sources: Tudhoe miners, *NCB Employment Data.* For the remainder, the author is indebted to Mr R.W. Grainger and Mr. J. Hurst, then of the Department of Economics, University of Durham, for comparative data on the ages of the male labour force (as at June 1967).

Table 15.7 Experience of Working at Other Pits (n = 44)

Worked in all mining life at Tudhoe	8
Worked at one other pit	11
Worked at two other pits	13
Worked at three other pits	9
Worked at four other pits	1
Worked at five other pits	2
	n = 44

Source: *First Interviews.*

Notes

1. N. Dennis, F. Henriques and C. Slaughter, *Coal in Our Life,* London, Eyre and Spottiswoode, 1956.
2. J.W. House and E.M. Knight, *Pit Closure and the Community,* Newcastle University, 1967.
3. *Ryhope: a pit closes: a study in redeployment,* London, HMSO, 1970.
4. R.C. Taylor, *The Implications of Migration from the Durham Coalfield: an anthropological study,* unpublished Ph.D., Durham University, 1966; R.C. Taylor, 'Migration and Motivation', in J.A. Jackson (ed.), *Migration,* Cambridge University Press, 1969, pp. 99-132. See also R.H. Wignall, 'The Migrant Miners', *New Society,* 29 July 1965.
5. E.M. Knight, *Men Leaving Mining: West Cumberland, 1966-67,* Geography Department, Newcastle University, 1967.
6. T.J. Farmer, *A Study of Redundancy, Redeployment and Re-training of Personnel resulting from colliery closures in South Wales,* Llantwit, Glamorgan Polytechnic, mimeo, 1967.
7. J. Sewel, *Colliery Closure and Social Change: a study of a South Wales Mining Valley,* University of Wales, Social Science Monograph, Cardiff, University of Wales Press, 1975.
8. S.W. Town, *After the Mines: Changing Employment Opportunities in a South Wales Valley,* University of Wales, Social Science Monograph, Cardiff, University of Wales Press, 1977.
9. M.I.A. Bulmer, 'Mining Redundancy: a case-study of the workings of the Redundancy Payments Act, 1965, in the Durham Coalfield', *Industrial Relations Journal,* Vol.2, No.4, December 1971, pp.3-21.
10. See M.I.A. Bulmer, *Collectivities in Change,* ms. deposited in Durham University Library, and more briefly, Appendix B below.
11. It is, therefore, not legitimate to use neologisms such as 'voluntary redundancy', for redundancy is by definition involuntary on the part of the employee, as it was in the Tudhoe closure. There are several studies of redundancy available, three of which are particularly relevant. These are the study of large-scale dismissals by the British Motor Corporation in 1956 by Hilda Kahn, *Repercussions of Redundancy,* London, Allen and Unwin, 1964; the run-down of white-collar staffs in English Electric factories at Luton and Stevenage (following the cancellation of a missile contract) by Dorothy Wedderburn, *White Collar Redundancy,* Cambridge University Press, 1964; and her study of the closure of two railway workshops at Gorton, Manchester and Faverdale, Darlington, *Redundancy and the Railwaymen,* Cambridge University Press, 1965. All three focus primarily on the *effects,* rather than the cause of redundancy. See also: Acton Society Trust, *Redundancy: three studies of redundant workers,* London 1959; and A. Fox, *The Milton Plan,* IPM, London 1965, for shorter studies of particular redundancies. R. Martin and R. Fryer, *Redundancy and Paternalist Capitalism,* Allen and Unwin, 1973 is an important later study.
12. Wedderburn, *Redundancy and the Railwaymen,* p.186.
13. *Ryhope: A pit closes.*
14. E. Trist, *et. al.*, *Organisational Choice,* London, Tavistock, 1963.
15. S. Chaplin, *The Thin Seam,* Oxford, Pergamon, 1968, (first published 1950).
16. Bulmer, 'Mining Redundancy'.
17. A Townsend and C.C. Taylor, 'Regional culture and identity in industrialised societies: the case of North-East England', *Regional Studies,* 9, 1975, pp.379-393. C.C. Taylor and A. Townsend, 'The Local sense of place as evidenced in North East England', *Urban Studies,* 13, 1976, pp.133-146. More generally see Royal

Commission of Local Government in England, *Research Studies 9: Community Attitude Survey,* England, London, HMSO, 1969.
18. Bulmer, 'Mining Redundancy'.
19. Source of data: answers to Parliamentary Questions put down by Mr Ernest Armonstrong, MP, 29 January and 8 April 1971, *Hansard,* Vol.810, 1970/71, Written answers, cols. 209-11, and Vol.815, Written answers, cols. 256-7.
20. Wedderburn, *Redundancy and the Railwaymen,* p.211.
21. *Ryhope: A Pit Closes.*
22. House and Knight, *Pit Closure.*

16 THE GROWTH OF FACTORY INDUSTRY: MINERS BECOME TEXTILE OPERATIVES

Martin Bulmer

Parallel to the decline of traditional heavy industries in County Durham has been the rise of factory industry. This began in the inter-war period. As described in chapters 10 and 12, efforts to bring industry to the county intensified after the war and have continued up to the present. New towns such as Newton Aycliffe and Peterlee were one focus for development. Another characteristic pattern, however, has been the establishment of industrial estates in existing settlements, particularly those categorised as 'growth points' by the County Development Plan. Spennymoor is one such centre.

Factory employment in the town first developed on a large scale after the war, when a former Royal Ordnance Factory was taken over by an expanding electrical manufacturing company. This had grown further, particularly in the 1960s, so that by 1970, with further expansion planned, the group of factories owned by Thorn Electrical Industries on the Merrington Lane Industrial Estate employed about five thousand people, half men and half women producing electric cookers, refrigerators and lighting equipment. The County Council and Spennymoor Urban District Council had also promoted jointly a new industrial estate at Green Lane, on the A 1, and this was to be the centre for the main expansion of employment in the area. After a chequered start and well-publicised withdrawal of the one firm, a number of companies were attracted to Spennymoor by the late 1960s to set up expanding factories on this site. At the time of research reported on here, in 1969/70, two large enterprises dominated the estate, and indeed provided the main prospects for employment growth in the town. Black and Decker Ltd. had come there in 1965, and by 1970 employed 1,600 people, half men and half women. Further major expansion was underway and it was expected that the labour-force would increase to three thousand by the end of 1971. Courtaulds' Worsted Spinning Division factory was of more recent origin. Construction of Phase 1 of their factory, alongside the A 1 at High Butcher Race Farm, had begun in May 1968. Recruitment of operatives began in January 1969 and the factory began round-the-clock operation in May 1969. At the end of that year about eight hundred people were employed, all men with the exception of about forty office staff. Further major building expansion was under way, and a new extension opened in October 1970. The number employed was expected to double to 1,600 by the end of 1971 and production was projected to rise from 200,000 pounds of yarn a week in the factory at the time of research to 450,000 pounds a week in the whole when fully operational. Further expansion beyond that was projected for the early 1970s.

The decision of Courtaulds to locate a factory in the North-East was taken in the light of the availability of male labour accustomed to shift working, the Development and Special Development Area status of the town at the time (which resulted in a high level of Government financial help to the firm by various means), and the favourable geographical position of Spennymoor near the A 1. In addition, a Training School was to be run as part of the factory, which would receive substantial financial support from the Wool Industry Training Board.

The growth of the textile industry in the North-East is not a new phenomenon. The main development in the post-war period was the opening of Paton and Baldwin's factory at Darlington in 1947 (manufacturing woollen and acrylic yarn) and in 1970 it employed about four thousand people. It also had subsidiary factories at Crook, Jarrow, Billingham and Peterlee. Other small concerns in the region included weaving at Team Valley and woollens also in Darlington. The most striking development, however has taken place within four or five years, in the late 1960s, for there were by 1970 eight firms in the Crook-Bishop Auckland-Shildon-Aycliffe area starting up or established to produce man-made fibres of various kinds (much of it nylon). Several of these factories were quite small but two or three were sizable, employing between five hundred and one thousand people. Thus, although Patons were already established, this growth of textile factories in the area in the late 1960s was a significant development. Indeed, an impression may even be created that textiles may have replaced mining as the characteristic industry of south-west Durham, though in terms of the proportion of jobs in textiles in the area, this is far from being the case. Courtaulds was the largest development proposed, doubly significant because it was backed by one of the dominant groups in the industry.

The present chapter describes a study which was made of the opening of this new factory and of the experience of ex-miners working in the textile industry for the first time. The choice of Coutaulds out of the three large enterprises to study in Spennymoor was made for two reasons. Firstly, unlike the other two concerns it was a new factory, where one could study the dynamics of change at first hand, as the factory opened up. Secondly, it was known that the firm intended to recruit male labour for all except office jobs. Following the closure of Mainsforth Colliery in Ferryhill, a larger number of miners were out of work in the area than before and it was known that the factory intended to recruit ex-miners to meet their labour requirements. This suggested that a study of the factory would be a particularly good opportunity to look at the short-term effects of industrial change and at the experience of ex-miners working in new manufacturing industry. It would also provide a counterpart to the study of the Tudhoe Park closure.

The interviewing was carried out in the autumn of 1969 at a time when the recruitment of the first 800 operatives was nearly complete. The data here are derived from interviews with 74 respondents, 25 in supervising and training grades and 49 operatives. Details of the sample are given in the appendix to this chapter.

It should be emphasised that this is a study of short-term change and short-term adaptation. It should ideally be followed up by studies of the longer-term effects of the change from mining to factory work. Nevertheless, there was strong arguments for carrying out the study as the factory was being opened. The new experience of the factory was most readily 'caught' by a study carried out within a short time of opening. If it had been postponed for two or three years, the immediate experience of new employment would then be overlaid by subsequent experience, and possible contrasts between former and present employment might have become less sharp.

The part of the Spennymoor factory opened in 1969 manufactured 'Courtelle' yarn, a process intermediate between the manufacture of the artificial fibre itself at Courtaulds' Grimsby works and the subsequent manufacture of fabrics from the yarn produced at Spennymoor. The production of man-made fibres is the fastest-growing part of the textile industry and the establishment of a factory in the North-East by Courtaulds was indicative of the breakdown of the traditional pattern of textile production – cottons in Lancashire and woollens in Yorkshire. Moreover, Courtaulds' group structure is vertically integrated, embracing fibre production, yarn production, and fabric production, so that much of the output of the Spennymoor factory (though not all) goes to other firms in the Courtaulds group. Thus close proximity to customers was unlikely to have been an important factor influencing the location of this plant.

In its passage through the factory, the raw fibre goes through a number of processes, including dyeing, to produce finished yarn. These processes are carried out on modern textile machinery (imported from Germany, Switzerland or France) which requires overlooking by semi-skilled operatives to regulate and watch their working and ensure a steady flow of material on and off each machine in the process. In addition, unskilled workers are employed on general labouring on the shop-floor and in the warehouses. Fitters and craftsmen maintain the textile and other machinery in the factory, including the extensive air-conditioning. Above the level of operative, there are a number of supervisory grades (assistant foremen, foremen, supervisor) and, alongside these, the trainers. Above this level there are managerial staff and in addition a sizable office staff.

The picture of the labour-force at the factory is of one attached to a particular locality but for whom it is relatively easy to travel to work in Spennymoor and for whom this seems to raise few problems. (The data which follow are derived from interviews with 49 operatives, a sample of 1 in 7 of shop-floor workers in the factory at the time of the study. For further details see the Appendix to this chapter.) Of the sample, half lived in Spennymoor or Ferryhill, the remainder were scattered over a wide area of south-west Durham. The labour-force of the factory was by no means drawn from its immediate locality – Spennymoor and Ferryhill – but from places further away. At least a third of the sample travelled daily eight to twelve miles in each direction. This points out the company's policy of recruiting almost all of its staff, with the exception of three or four senior managers, either within the immediate locality or within the southern part of the county. Only 2 out of 49 men interviewed walked or bicycled to work. Two-thirds travelled by car, one-third by bus. This was encouraged by the company, which put buses in certain routes where many of their operatives lived, and arranged for people with cars to give lifts to others without a car. The latter step, indeed, was a way of men who lived in the same place and worked on the same shift getting to know each other. A new employee starting might straightaway have a lift to work and this would reduce the strangeness of the changeover to the new factory.

There was a strong mining background among those interviewed. Sixty per cent of the men in the sample had been miners most of their working lives. Of the remainder, a further ten per cent had had some experience of mining (mostly soon after leaving school), even though they had worked predominantly in other industries. In the sample, therefore, about two-thirds of the men had had experience of mining and slightly less than that were ex-miners. Of the men who had worked predominantly in mining, 23 were on skilled piecework immediately before leaving and a further 4 were craftsmen. In the sample, therefore, there was a preponderance of the more highly-paid ex-mineworkers. For most of the ex-miners, the war or national service had not interrupted their experience of pit-work: 24 out of the 29 ex-miners had never been in the Forces.

Among the sample as a whole there was, not surprisingly for the area, a family history of mining. The fathers of 35 had been miners and (of those who could remember) the grandfathers of 26 out of 37 had been miners. This proportion of seven out of ten men being miners in earlier generations corresponds to the proportion of the occupied male population and mining traditionally found in homogeneous mining communities.

The experience of work and unemployment immediately prior to being taken on at the factory was very variable. Although there was a high unemployment rate in Spennymoor at the time and there had been a number of serious pit closures in the previous three years, in fact only 21 of the sample were unemployed immediately prior to starting at the factory. Eighteen of the twenty-one were previously employed in mining and had left as a result of pit closure. (Eight had been unemployed for more than six months, the rest for less.) The more striking point, however, is that 28 of the sample had joined Courtaulds direct from another job and 10 of these were miners. One had joined directly following being made redundant, the remaining nine from a pit to the east which was still working.

This throws an interesting light on the workings of local labour markets in areas of industrial transition such as County Durham. It is not necessarily the case that new factories opened in areas of high unemployment directly 'mop up' workers currently unemployed. Only two-fifths of the men interviewed fell into this category, despite the high unemployment rate in the area and large-scale recent closures.

What is more striking is the attraction of new factory employment. The operation of the local labour market is not necessarily such that new industry employs immediately ex-miners who have been made redundant by pit closure. It may also attract labour from other enterprises in the area. In this sample, 18 had come direct from employment in another, non-mining job. Although this would require much more detailed investigation, the process by which new factory employment replaces pit-work seems to be considerably more complex than just a new factory opening its doors and taking on unemployed miners sent by the Employment Exchange. The effects of new industrial location, indeed, are more than simply replacing jobs in coal-mining which have disappeared. The effects of new industrial development seems to be the more diffuse and indirect – though extremely important – one of increasing the availability of new jobs in the local labour market *as a whole.* Men for example, move out of *existing* factory employment to the new factory, thus creating a vacancy which might be filled by an unemployed worker. The overall level of employment in the area is raised, but in the process there is a certain amount of movement around between employers.

This is particularly likely to be the case where the employment opportunities at the new factory are no more unattractive than those at other firms in the area. This was certainly the case in the factory studied. The 'market power' of Courtaulds was strong as an employer, compared particularly to the coal industry. A factory such as Courtaulds could compete strongly for labour even in comparison with the most modern pit. At the time of the study (late 1969) the pay for a 42-hour week for a machine operative at Courtaulds was a few shillings over £25 per week, and that for a 37.5-hour week for Durham pitmen under the National Power Loading Agreement was a few shillings less than £25 per week. Thus, the traditional financial attraction of skilled pit-work was absent in the case studied, and there was possibly an incentive to leave mining for such factory work, taking other factors like working conditions into account.

The further attraction of work in such a factory was that it provided prospects of secure work in the future and prospects of promotion for those with ambitions in this direction. Coal-mining could not compete in either respect, for with decline and contraction, the certainty of any one man's job continuing was not great (depending on the pit) and the prospects of promotion were not good, since supervisory and managerial staff release by pit closure could not easily be accommodated in the remaining pits in the county (although some were). The pool of labour from which Courtaulds selected its recruits was therefore quite large and this is reflected in the wide area from which they were drawn.

Two other features of work at the factory should be noted. The company pursued a policy of recruiting relatives of existing operatives: just under half of those interviewed (23) had relatives working there. The firm thus seemed to be exploiting a feature of the informal workings of the local labour markets, that of relatives 'speaking for' someone to be taken on.

All applicants for jobs were also warned of the four-shift system which all except senior management and office staff worked. Courtaulds factory was planned to work 24 hours a day, 7 days a week, using the 'continental' shift system shown in Figure 16.1. The labour force was divided into four shifts of equal size (A to D), and in any period of 4 weeks a man worked 14 twelve-hour shifts; two weeks on days and two weeks on nights; two weeks mid-week and two weeks over weekends. In effect each man worked seven days out of fourteen, knowing ten to twelve months in advance which days he was working. The cycle shown in Figure 16.1 was the same for each, except that at one point in time, each shift is at a different point in it.

The remainder of this chapter reports the views of the sample about aspects of work in the factory after a few months' experience. It focuses particularly on the comparison with mining; physical differences between pit and factory; training and adaptation to the new type of work; and social relations outside of work.

The actual situation locally in mining was described in the previous chapter. But it is how men subjectively interpret and act in the situations *as they define it* which is of greatest significance. Views of the prospects of the coal industry in Durham were uniformly pessimistic. Men were asked if they had considered going into minding and if they had applied for a job in mining when seeking work at Courtaulds. There had been in 1969 and 1970, vacancies in mining at all levels (except surface work) within the south Durham area of the NCB. Not one man had looked for a job in mining and only one man out of 49 said that he had even considered it. The respondents were then asked what they would advise somebody to do who was thinking of going into mining and came to them for advice. Thirty-four were emphatically against, without any qualification:

'Get yer head examined'.

'Don't go in. It's nae life at all, I'd seen two lads killed and that's enough.'

'Never go down the mine. Forget about it. Dangerous, dirty, hazardous job. Wet, dusty – it's a lucky man who gets out without scars. Not much danger in the factory in comparison.'

'There's no need. Reason pits have been so full, there's no other work. Don't know why young lads go into the pit. They say the money's good – not worried about the future.'

'Don't be such a bloody fool.'

'Don't. Too dangerous. No prospects either anyway. My dad had one or two close shaves – lost a finger, just missed by rocks falling.'

'Would say not to. From experience within family, always considered rough and dangerous. Talking to ex-miners, if they'd known what it was like there they would have left years ago.'

Figure 16.1 The Continental Shift System

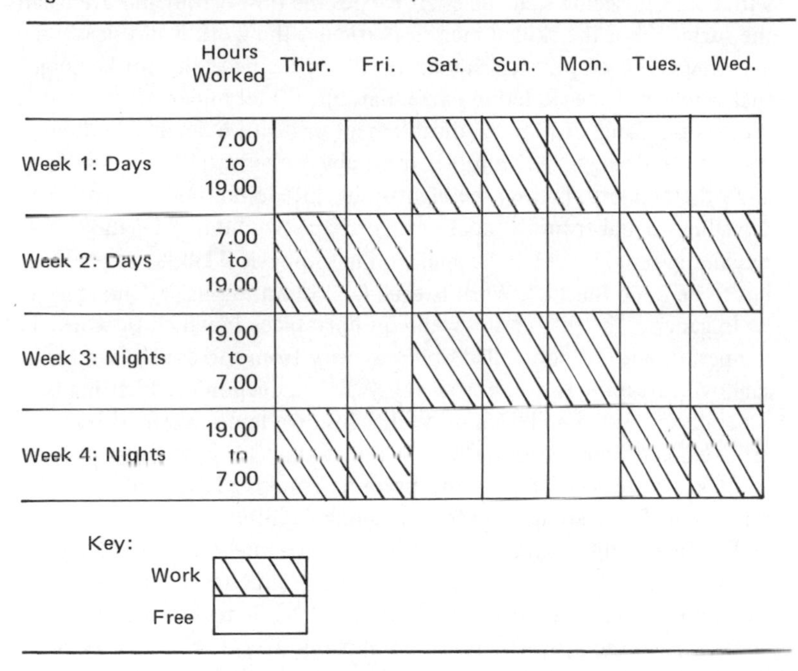

Four others made qualifications for craftsmen or technical staff and another four for long-life coastal collieries or for the industry in the Midlands. Only three were favourably inclined toward coal mining:

> 'They say there's years of work in the pits. Pit-work is a good job. Only evil – pneumoconiosis. Top men get good wages. Wouldn't try and put them off. NCB treated me pretty decent.'
>
> 'I would go back to my old job. More privileges – coals, rent, good holiday pay.'
>
> 'When I was down, I found it alright. A lot complain though.'

Pursuing the comparison with mining, the physical condition of pit and factory were and are very different. The pit underground is dirty, cramped, dark and damp. Although there is provision for air-circulation, this is a difficult matter to regulate satisfactorily. Miners do a variety of work, but in the conventional mine the skilled men work at the face cutting and filling, on stonework in the 'goaf' area and so on. Other skilled men work cutting new road-ways to open up new coal measures, less-skilled men are concerned with watching the belt, filling the tubs with coal and seeing that the coal reaches the pit-bottom and eventually the surface. For the skilled men in particular the work is physically most exacting – indeed physical stamina is the prime necessity for keeping such a job. For the skilled in particular, but for all miners underground, there is the danger of injury, disablement or death in an accident, and in addition to doing his job a miner must always be watchful for his own and others' safety. During the eight-hour shift some time is spent travelling to and from the coal face (perhaps two hours). Of the remaining time, most will be spent on hard physical labour to get what has to be done finished. Work is thus fairly continuous and energetic.

In general, the pit is not a well-equipped place in which to work. The temperature is not controlled and may vary from too cold in winter in a shallow drift mine to too hot all the year in a deep mine. Lighting is generally not good and each miner has his own lamp. No food is provided and there is no canteen. A miner takes his own bait and flask and takes a break when his work permits. Smoking is absolutely forbidden. There are no toilets or washing facilities underground.

In contrast the Courtaulds factory was extremely modern. There is full air-conditioning and air filtering to maintain constant temperatures and humidity levels in different sections of the factory, which is necessary for the processes involved in manufacture. The factory is lit entirely by artificial lighting and there are no windows. It is thus not possible to know when it is day or night, except when one goes to the canteen. A subsidised meal was available during each of the two breaks during the twelve-hour shift. Tea or coffee were obtainable in addition between meal breaks and men were allowed seven minutes in every hour off for refreshment. Smoking was allowed off the factory floor during these seven-minute breaks. There are toilets.

Operatives work twelve-hour shifts looking after machines, with two half-hour meal breaks during that time. While at work they are not tied to the machine constantly (in the way that, for instance, an assembler in a car factory is tied to the assembly line) but can walk around and talk to others who work in the same section. There is relatively little danger of accidents occuring, especially if care is exercised with the machines. The proportion of time spent actually working on the machines varies, but is by no means continuous. On spinning, for instance, the main work involves replacing full bobbins with empty ones every few hours. In between these periods of intense activity, however, the main task is to watch the machine for breaks or snags which only involves activity when something goes wrong.

The physical environment of the factory compared to mining

work was, not surprisingly, very favourably evaluated by the 29 ex-miners among the 49 operatives. They were asked how they found the factory compared, as a place to work, with the pit; and how they felt about the surroundings when they first started working at Courtaulds. The replies were very much in favour of factory work, 17 out of 29 being very favourable and 11 favourable:

> 'Canna compare. Impossible! If I had my life over again, the pit would never see me and the pits are far advanced to what they were when I started.'
>
> 'No comparison. It's as different again. Better in every respect. Good, clean, healthy life. Cannot compare it to pit.'
>
> 'Heaven. Never dreamed there were things like this. Should have come forty years ago.'
>
> 'I like the job, the people, the factory; the atmosphere's good. But strange – I didn't know if I would pick the job up.'
>
> 'Strange to start with, once settled it's much nicer. Don't keep glancing up at the roof to see what's going to drop on you.'
>
> 'Lot better in all ways. Good, clean, healthy life. Cannot compare it to pit. Shift-system gives you a lot of time off. No comparison with pit-work, it's wet and uncomfortable. You go on Monday and wish it was Friday already. Factory work, you don't notice.'
>
> 'I like it. You don't mind it. In the pit you're waiting for the end of the shift. Here, I'm working after the others have gone to dinner and you don't notice the time.'
>
> 'Lot pleasanter. 100% pleasanter.'
>
> 'No comparison. Like a palace – clean, well-lit, modern facilities good meals and washing facilities. Lacking two or three showers.'
>
> 'Green pastures. No matter where you go in the pit, you worked in bad conditions – polution, water and so on. At Courtaulds, it's air conditioned, warm, clean. You can ask for nothing more.'

This compared with somewhat less enthusiastic replies from non-miners in the sample. Out of twenty men, eleven thought the factory compared favourably with the previous employment, three thought it compared unfavourably and six thought it was the same. This compared to virtual unanimity among the miners that factory work was a change for the better. However, when asked how they thought miners found factory compared to the pit, 18 out of 20 non-miners said that it seemed to compare favourably or very favourably.

> 'They're over the moon. One man said he wouldn't go back (to the pit) if they offered him £90 a week.'
>
> 'Majority think it's grand.'
>
> 'Wish they'd known there were jobs like that sooner.'
>
> 'Comment about how they should have been out of the pits years ago. Heard this on several occasions.'

This favourable view of factory work by ex-miners was confirmed by trainers and supervisors.

The importance of the physical surroundings in the factory which emerged from this is striking. An imperfect attempt was made to assess the importance of this change, as compared to other possible considerations, by asking two sets of open-ended questions at different points in the interview. The first was: 'If you had to say what were the three main attractions of a job at Courtaulds, what would they be?' The answers were grouped as shown in Table 16.1. The most noteworthy point is that three areas account for more than half the answers – good working conditions, good pay and the good shift-system and the time off.

The second open-ended question was: 'What do you like most about working at Courtaulds?' The answers in this case stressed working conditions to a slightly greater extent, as Table 16.2 shows, and the money much less.

A particular focus of the research was the experience of retraining ex-miners as textile operatives. Courtaulds had at that time an eight-week training programme paid for largely by the Wool, Jute and Flax Industry Training Board with the proceeds from a levy on all employers in their industry, organised under the Industrial Retraining Act. In addition, some direct financial assistance was provided by the Department of Employment and Productivity. The in-firm training, with a guaranteed job available at the end of it, was quite distinct from training for skilled trades available at that time in Government Training Centres. It was organised in a Training School located within the factory. The background of the instructors in the factory were various. A number had been former operatives from neighbouring textile factories who had taken the opportunity of a new factory opening to achieve promotion. Others had come from mining backgrounds, or other industries.

The aim of training was to teach all men one operation, and eventually to teach operatives second and third operations, so that they could become more versatile and work on other machines when fluctuations in production prevented them working on the one for which they were first trained. The 38 operatives in the sample interviewed were trained for the following operations: 11 on spinning, 7 on twisting, 5 on the 'turbos', 4 on reeling, 3 on roving and pindrafting, 3 on hank to cone back-winding, 5 on other specialised operations, including dyeing. Training was continuous over an eight-week period, although more attention was given by the instructor in the initial two-week period.

Table 16.1 Attractions of a Job at Courtaulds

	Mentioned		
	First	Second	Third
Clean factory, good working conditions	14	12	6
Good pay	6	12	8
Good shift-system, time off	8	8	6
Secure job	5	1	1
Chances of promotion	2	2	1
People you know, friendly	1	2	1
Interesting work	–	1	5
Other	9	6	7
No answer	4	5	14
Total	49	49	49

(n = 49)

Table 16.2 Like Most About Working at Courtaulds

Clean, good surroundings	17
Good shift system	8
Interesting work	4
People you know, friendly	3
Money	1
Promotion	1
Secure job	1
Other	7
No answer	7
	n = 49

The remaining time was spent in familiarisation with the work, practice, and particularly increasing the speed of working up to the normal pace of factory working. At the end of the eight-week training period, men were than allocated to a shift and started normal working in the factory.

How successful was this policy of retraining ex-miners? Several pieces of evidence are available. One is the evaluation of the management. Another is the evidence gathered in interviews with trainers, men who dealt all the time with trainees and most of whom had had experience at another textile factory in the area. A third comes from the replies of operatives themselves who were asked of their experience of training. The main conclusion to draw from this evidence is that the policy is a very successful one and that miners of all ages are adaptable to work in a textile factory. This view was also confirmed by a brief article about the factory, published in a specialist journal.[1]

At Courtaulds, evidence was provided by the then Training Manager from his experience training ex-miners at another textile factory in the area, which pursued a policy similar to Courtaulds on a smaller scale. He commented: 'the much talked about problems of re-training did not materialise to any great extent, in fact, in some ways it had the opposite effect. The men were very co-operative, learned readily and eagerly and were extremely conscientious in producing quality work, more so the trainers found than female operatives'.[2] He attributed the success of this policy of training ex-miners to (i) their working in a team as they did in the collieries; (ii) a maintenance of the community feeling typical of mining areas; (iii) being already used to a shift system.

This favourable experience was repeated at Courtaulds, where ex-miners had proved most capable and adaptable as machine operatives. Moreover, an important feature of the firm's policy was to take on older men. Over a quarter of the operatives interviewed were over 40, an age at which some firms are reluctant to recruit. Though taking on few operatives over 50, Courtaulds showed that men between 40 and 50 could be successfully retrained.

One in five of trainers were also interviewed (see appendix to this chapter) and their replies to questions about the adaptability of men in training supported this picture. They were pleased – and even surprised – at the adaptability of the miner:

> 'Majority find it easy to make the change. Odd one not – more nervous than anything.'
>
> 'I'm surprised. Man who's worked with a pick and shovel. On machines where he has to use his fingers – its amazing.'

> 'Bit nervous when they come in. After an hour or two, they find they can do it. Takes a week or two to get their hands smoothed down.'
>
> 'Quite easy. At first very rough with the material, takes a day or two.'
>
> 'Bit rough first day or two. Been working with picks and shovels. Takes a day or two to get the feel of it.'
>
> '(Picked up work) very easily. Would say the majority are trained in less than the allotted time.'
>
> 'Some find it easy. Them that's a bit nervous take a bit longer.'
>
> 'Pick it up very easily. Get different training to what we got. Haven't a man standing behind you all the time.'

None of the trainers thought the eight-week training period should be extended and some thought it could be shortened. Indeed most remarked that the men had learnt the skills involved in the first one or two weeks and the remainder of the period of training was only necessary for them to speed up their work to that of the factory as a whole. This is all the more remarkable in that the men are doing work which in the textile industry is traditionally regarded as women's work. One or two trainers commented on difficulties experienced in hand knotting.

> 'Hand knotting, weaver's knot. Take a while to get used to that.'
>
> 'Miners and bricklayers – tying weaver's knot – lot of difficulty there.'

However, this intricate work is only needed for a few operations and the company seems to employ younger men on these operations to meet this. Moreover, supervisors, who might be expected to notice difficulties which men got into, were emphatic that ex-miners did not have particular difficulties in adapting to textile work:

> 'On the whole, adapted very well.'
>
> 'No, every operation I've seen them on, they can do it. Time element – but the others do eventually grasp what you are after.'
>
> 'Different materials and so on. Soon pick it up – learn very easily. One or two that've worked for me made instructors already.'
>
> 'Considering vast difference in type of work, they've adapted remarkably well.'
>
> 'Let's face it, miners are good workers and that's what you want.'

Nor did the men themselves report any difficulties in picking up the work, to which they seemed to adapt quickly.

To the extent that contrary views of the unadaptability of miners have any substance, they may derive from one or two factors. Firstly, it is quite clear that for a miner to leave mining is a big break and one that is not easily made. A number of ex-miners in the sample came from a pit to the east which was still working and they commented on the reluctance of fellow-miners to leave, even when told of the advantages of factory work. They said that fellow-miners attached more importance to their issue of free coals than to the likelihood of the pit closing and the securer prospects in the factory. Such a view would seem to be symptomatic of long attachment to the industry and lack of experience of other industries.

There is paradoxical evidence of the reluctance of men to leave mining, coupled with their favourable evaluation of factory work once they were in the new situation. One of the most striking features of the mining industry is the miner's extreme reluctance to leave it and the view formed of the new industry only follows a wrench away from an old job to which one is very attached. As one man succintly put it after commenting on the new job very favourably: 'I am much more happy to have left the mines now, than I was sorry to leave them when I did leave.' There is no inconsistency between a reluctance to leave mining work and a much more favourable view of the new industry when once in the new situation.

The second shred of support for the view that miners are not adaptable to other work is their sense of strangeness in the new work situation. Clearly, settling down in the new work took some time:

> 'Felt strange. Time seemed to go slow – thought it was a dead loss – always keyed up trying to learn. Didn't settle down right away. Things were different. Picked up after a week or two.'
>
> 'Bit strange. Didn't know if I would pick the job up. Not used to working in such a big place.'
>
> 'Funny sensation. I'd never been into a factory. Adapt yourself easy in a week. Very strange at first.'

This initial uncertainty was also reported by supervisors and trainers, who were asked if they thought miners found it easy to make the change from pit to factory work:

> 'They have a little bit of fear in their minds. They've been in the pits that long, they think there isn't any other kind of job. When they

> get there [the factory] they find they're wrong when they're pleased about it.'
>
> 'First day or so, they're frightened they are not going to fit in. Thing to do is to assure them that they will.'
>
> 'All adapted well. Turn round after a few weeks and say they thought when the pit closed it was the end of the world but everything has turned out alright.'

After the initial unfamiliarity had worn off, the ex-miners settled down well in their new work, and usually within one or two weeks.

This concludes the review of the evidence of the adaptability of miners to work in the textile industry. It was confirmed by conversations in the area with factory managers, union secretaries and DEP officials. In the course of these it was suggested, and is consistent with the present findings, that firms were more satisfied with ex-miners whom they have recruited where they take positive steps to retrain them, then where they merely put them to work without any training. A small survey of employers reported in the study of the Ryhope closure showed that 'employers were, in general very content with their ex-miner employees. They had settled in well, shown no particular problems in absorbing their training and with the occasional exception had been exemplary workers.'[3]

Going beyond the present study, a comparison is needed of factory and pit-work more generally, in relation to shift-work, supervision, industrial relations, and the social relations of work. Such a preliminary analysis has been attempted,[4] but the results were inconclusive. Further research is required. So too is work needed on unionism in mining and new manufactury industry. Negotiating rights for non-craft grades at Courtaulds had been given to the National Union of Dyers, Bleachers and Textile Workers, a relatively new union in the North-East, though long-established in the traditional textile areas. Although union membership was not a condition of employment, all the operatives in the sample were members. Other unions were also recruiting in the factory, for example among the craftsmen.

After this research ended, a serious industrial dispute occurred at Courtaulds. ASTMS had rapidly recruited a majority of supervisory staff in the spring of 1971; the dismissal of the union's acting Group Secretary at the plant in April 1971 precipitated a strike by 170 supervisory staff which dragged on for six months. (The NUDBTW, representing operatives and labourers, was not directly involved and these grades were not on strike at any stage.) Professor L.C. Hunter's official inquiry into the dispute[5] found fault on both sides, the dispute being intensified by the firm declaring all 173 strikers redundant within a month of the strike starting.[6] The complexities of the conflict are not our concern here. Its escalation seems to be due to a series of precipitate actions, commented on by Professor Hunter. How far the course of the dispute was influenced by the mining background of the work-force, how much by the character of the particular management and union concerned, cannot be determined. This industrial conflict does, however, provide testimony of the effectiveness of the retraining programme.

Paradoxically, the intensity of the dispute owed something to the success of the policy of retraining ex-miners. The firm claimed that it was making redundant supervisory staff because its retraining policy had been exceptionally successful:

> The Spennymoor area is essentially a mining one and, prior to the opening of the Company's factory, had no textile history. Accordingly the recruitment of operatives was mainly from former miners. In the Company's experience it was necessary in such cases, in the early years of the operation of a factory, to employ rather more supervisory staff in relation to operatives than would be employed in new factories in textile areas . . . [By 1971] the new labour which had been recruited at Spennymoor was showing much greater aptitude at textile work than had originally been thought likely . . . Labour recruited some 2½ years before, without textile background, was already fully able to assume much more responsibility . . . A major reduction in supervision would be possible over the next few months.[7]

This discussion of what E.P. Thompson once called 'life in the tunnel'[8] has focussed specifically upon the experience of ex-miners working in the textile industry, with reference to retraining. Such retraining of ex-miners at Courtaulds presented few difficulties. Indeed, the general view was that it was positively advantageous. In terms of industrial retraining, the work done at Courtaulds had far more impact quantitatively upon the problem of redundancy of miners, than the small-scale provision for skilled training in GTCs. The failure of Government Training Centres to make much impact in the North-East upon the problem of retraining miners up to 1970 was indeed striking. While the number of jobs lost in mining in the region from 1965 to 1969 was 40,000, provision of places at GTCs had only risen from three centres with 720 places in 1966, to five centres with 1,150 places in 1968 and 7 centres with 2,000 places in 1970. Yet even out of these very small totals, miners only formed a small proportion of traineees.

Lack of interest in Government Training Centres among Tudhoe miners was quoted earlier. More systematic evidence is available. B.A. Taylor, in an unpublished study of successful and unsuccessful GTC applicants in the North-East in the middle 1960s, showed that only 7.2 per cent of trainees had previously worked in mining and quarrying, compared to those industries' 15.7 per cent share of male employees in the Northern Region at the time.[9] In other words, miners were actually seriously *under*-represented in GTCs, compared to their share of the workforce. 'Contrary to popular supposition in the north-east [he wrote] the GTCs do not primarily retrain redundant mine-workers for other jobs. Fewer mine-workers than might be expected apply for and undergo training at GTCs'.

T. Rees, in a study in 1966-7 of trade union attitudes to GTCs, found evidence that the Durham area of the National Union of Mine-workers was much more interest in the role of Industrial Rehabilitation Units, which deal with men who are less than 100 per cent fit.[10] These have a vital role, given the high level of disability among ex-miners. They do not, however, strike at the root of the problem of retraining the large numbers of fit ex miners.

For this task, the experience of Courtaulds provides an interesting case-study. In contrast to a scheme without a guaranteed job at the end of it, this case provides evidence of the value of an integrated training programme with guaranteed employment at the end; one, moreover, in which a belief in the retraining potential and adaptability of ex-miners was fully justified.

Appendix: Research Methodology

At the time the sample for interview was drawn (October 1969) there were approximately 540 people working at the factory. Recruitment of operatives was begun in January 1969 and the aim was to build up the labour-force from nil to eight hundred in approximately twelve months. Thus the sample was drawn at a time when recruitment was still in progress. Table 16.3 lists the approximate number of people employed by the October, the number in the sample drawn and the sampling fraction.

The sample was drawn (from the personnel files at the factory) by taking every seventh, or fifth, name and address from the records for each category in alphabetical order. The aim of the particular sampling fraction chosen was to ensure a sample sufficient to give a reliable picture of work on the factory-floor from the point of view of all grades of labour involves. The sampling fraction was increased slightly in the case of craftsmen, trainers and supervisors, in order to ensure a slightly higher proportion in each group in the sample.

Table 16.3 The Sample

	Total	Sample	Sampling Fraction
Operatives	302	43	1 in 7
General Labour	49	7	1 in 7
Warehousemen	35	5	1 in 7
Fitters and Craftsmen	40	8	1 in 5
Trainers	29	6	1 in 5
Supervisors	51	10	1 in 5
Total	506	79	

(No sample was drawn from an additional 35 managerial and office staff.)

The data analysed in this chapter relate principally to operatives, general labourers and warehousemen. Of the 55 men in this group, completed interviews were obtained from 50 men (a response rate of 91 per cent). Of the remaining five, four refused an interview and one could not be contacted at the address given. Of the 50 respondents, one had been promoted to Trainer and was therefore excluded from the sample. The analysis here therefore relates to 49 men working on the shop-floor. Of these 33 had worked at the factory for more than three months, 9 had worked there for eight to twelve weeks, five had worked there for four to seven weeks and two had left.

The age distribution of this sample of 49 was as follows:

Age:	20-29	10
	30-39	17
	40-49	10
	50-59	12

The average of 40.1 years compared with an average of 40.6 years for the male labour-force of the Northern Region in June 1967 and an average age of 43.7 years for Durham miners at the same date.

The geographical distribution of the sample by place of residence was:

Spennymoor	10
Ferryhill	11
Ferryhill Station	2
Thornley, Wheatley Hill	9
Chilton, Cornforth, etc.	6
Leeholme, Binchester	2
Bishop Auckland	3
North of Durham City	3
Newton Aycliffe, Darlington	3

Despite the scatter of the sample over south-west Durham, this created few problems of travelling to work:

2 walked or bicycled to work
17 travelled by bus
18 in their own car
12 in somebody else's car

Forty-two out of forty-nine travelled from home to work in less than 20 minutes and no-one in more than half an hour. Thirty-one did so at a cost of less than 10s per week and a further thirteen at a cost of less than £1 per week.

The employment history of the sample was as follows: twenty-nine of the men had worked most of their working lives in mining, all but two for more than ten years and 21 all their working lives. Four had worked in the building and construction industries, two had worked in other factories, twelve in other manual occupations. Two had had non-manual jobs.

Completed interviews were obtained from 74 respondents in all, including 24 craftsmen, trainers and supervisors. Half the interviews were carried out by the writer, the other half by Mr David Southeard, at the time a sandwich-course student visiting Durham from Bath University. The interview schedule used differed slightly between shop-floor workers, trainers and supervisors. The interview schedule used for shop-floor workers is not reproduced here for reasons of space; very minor variations occurred in that used for trainers or supervisors. Copies may be consulted in the longer research report (p.235).

The evidence, from open-ended questions in a fairly standardised interview, was gathered systematically. It would be pretentious, however, to claim that this evidence is wholly satisfactory. In the present study, most respondents were interested in the questions asked because they related to experiences they had recently been through. The majority were most ready to co-operate and a number answered at great length, so that the interview became more of an extended conversation than a formal interview. Almost all answered questions frankly and straightforwardly, so that although 'deeper meanings' were not probed, the evidence gathered has an air of authenticity about it. This is not to deny that respondents fail to recall the courses of action they took in the past, or their reasons for doing so accurately, nor that there is a tendency to present a 'public' face to the interviewer. If, however, the data is treated as having a degree of plausibility, it can provide a useful basis for analysis and a pointer to future research.

Notes

1. E.M. Hargreaves, 'Still Young at Forty', *Work Study and Management Services* 14, No.5, May 1970, pp.394-5.
2. J.J. Stephens, 'Retraining of Male Labour,' unpublished paper.
3. DEP, *Ryhope: a pit closes,* HMSO, London, 1970, pp.79-83.
4. M.I.A. Bulmer, *Collectivities in Change,* ms. in Durham University Library, Ch.5.
5. *Report by Professor L.C. Hunter of an Inquiry into a difference between members of the Association of Scientific, Technical and Managerial Staffs and Courtaulds Ltd. over the termination of employment at Spennymoor of certain members of the Association,* Department of Employment, Conciliation Act, 1896, London, HMSO, September 1971.
6. Ibid., pp.8-10, 16-18, 25-29.
7. Ibid., pp.16-17.
8. E.P. Thompson, 'The Peculiarities of the English', in J. Saville (ed.), *The Socialist Register 1965,* London, Merlin 1965, pp.358-9.
9. B.A. Taylor, *Government Training Centres: Withdrawals and Terminations,* unpublished research, Durham University Business Research Unit, *circa* 1965.
10. T. Rees, *Trade Unions and Government Training Centres,* unpublished research, Durham University Business Research Unit, 1967.

APPENDIX A: GUIDE TO FURTHER READING ON COUNTY DURHAM

Martin Bulmer

The reader who has come this far may be inclined to follow up some topics further. The bibliography which follows is intended to help in this, though it is selective and not comprehensive. It is in two parts, first general background about the area, secondly, social aspects of coal-mining in County Durham.

Particularly useful sources are preceded by an asterisk (*). The place of publication is London except where stated.

A Background Material

General

On the area in general the main works available are geographical. Three standard texts are * K. Warren, *North-East England* (1973), * J.W. House *Industrial Britain: The North-East* (Newton Abbott, 1969), and A.E. Smailes, *North England* (1968). On Durham County in particular * J.C. Dewdney (ed.), *Durham County and City with Teesside* (Durham, 1970) is a useful source, particularly on geographical and economic subjects. An older survey is still of value, * G.H.J. Daysh, J.S. Symonds *et. al., West Durham* (Oxford, 1953).

There is no adequate general historical survey of Durham covering the period since the Industrial Revolution. The following may be consulted as sources. F. Whellan, *History, Topography and Directory of the County Palatine of Durham* (1894). W. Page, *Durham: Victoria History of the Counties of England* (3 vols., 1905-28). N. Pevsner, *The Buildings of England: County Durham* (1953). General literary descriptions of the region, which include material on the country, are S. Chaplin, *The Lakes to Tyneside* (About Britain, No.10, 1951) and G. Turner, *The North Country* (1967). More specific is P. White, *Portrait of County Durham* (1971).

Geographical and Social Characteristics

The characteristics of the area may be better understood if they are placed in comparative perspective, both intra-regional and inter-regionally. On the former see * G. Wilson, *Social and Economic Statistics of*

North-East England: sub-regional and local authority statistics on population, housing and employment (Durham, Rowntree Research Unit, 1966). Inter-regional comparisons are more plentiful. * E. Hammond *An Analysis of Regional Economic and Social Statistics* (Durham, Rowntree Research Unit, 1968) and *Regional Statistics* (HMSO, annual) are basic sources. More analytic studies are * B. Coates and E. Rawstrom, *Regional Variations in Britain* (1971); C.A. Moser and W. Scott, *British Towns* (Edinburgh, 1961); D.C. Marsh, *The Changing Social Structure of England and Wales 1871-1971,* (1977), Ch.4. On health see * R. Titmuss, *Poverty and Population* (1938), and Resource Allocation Working Party, *Sharing Resources for Health in England,* (HMSO, 1976). On education see, G. Taylor and N. Ayres, *Born and Bred Unequal,* (1970) and * D. Byrne, W. Williamson and B. Fletcher, *The Poverty of Education* (1975). For general analyses see * B.E. Coates *et al., Geography and Inequality* (1977), * M. Rutter and N. Madge, *Cycles of Disadvantage* (1976), and * I. Reid, *Social Class Differences in Britain* (1977).

Economic Policy

* G. McCrone, *Regional Policy in Britain* (1969) is a useful general survey. On the North-East, see Board of Trade, *An Industrial Survey of the North-East Coast Area* (HMSO, 1931); * Ministry of Labour, *Reports of investigations into industrial conditions in certain depressed areas* (HMSO, Cmd. 4728, 1934); E. Allen, P. Bowden and A.J. Odber, *Development Area Policy in the North-East of England* (Newcastle, 1957); P. Bowden and A.A. Gibb, *Economic Growth in North-East England* (Durham University Business School, mimeo, 1967); C.E. Storer *et al., The North in the 1960s: a survey of regional policy* (Newcastle, NEDC, 1971).

Planning Documents

Official planning documents about the North-East provide further material. They include the Hailsham White Paper, *The North-East: a programme for regional development and growth* (HMSO, Cmnd 2206, 1963); *Challenge of the Changing North* (Newcastle, Northern Economic Planning Council, 1966); *Outline Strategy for the North* (Newcastle, NEPC, 1969); National Parks Commission, *The Coast of North East England* (HMSO, 1968); and * Northern Region Strategy Team, *Strategic Plan for the Northern Region* (HMSO, 5 vols., 1977) the most comprehensive official survey to date.

On County Durham see particularly * G. Pepler and F.W. MacFarlane

North-East Area Development Plan (Ministry of Town and Country Planning, 1949, interim report); * Durham County Council, *County Development Plan: Draft Written Analysis* (Durham, 1951); and * Durham County Council, *County Development Plan Amendments* (Durham, 1964 and 1971). For a sociological study of regional planning, based on interviews with local notables and an analysis of planning documents, see * J.M. Cousins, R.L. Davis, M. Paddon and A. Waton, 'Aspects of contradiction in regional policy: the case of North-East England', *Regional Studies,* 8, 1974, pp.133-44.

Migration and Mobility

There is a considerable geographical literature on population settlement and movement. In addition to general sources already cited, see: North-East Development Association, *Migration* (Newcastle, 1950); Northern Regional Planning Committee, *Mobility and the North* (Newcastle, 3 vols, 1967); and * the series of studies directed by J.W. House (Newcastle University, Department of Geography, 1961-7) including No.2, House and E.M. Knight, *Migrants of N.E. England, 1951-61;* No.3 House and E.M. Knight, *People on the Move;* No.4, House and K.G. Willis, *Northern Region and Nation: a short migration atlas, 1960-61;* No.7, House *et al., Where did the School-leavers go?;* No.8, House *et al., Mobility and the Northern Business Manager;* No.9, House *et al., Northern Graduates of 1964: Braindrain or Brainbank?*

A recent study of inward migration is E. Hammond, *London to Durham; a study of the transfer of the Post Office Savings Certificate Division* (Durham, Rowntree Research Unit, 1968).

B Coal-Mining in County Durham

The number of books about coal-mining is vast. The most useful introductory guide, dealing with Britain as a whole, is the pamphlet, *Books on Coal,* available on request from the Librarian, NCB Central Reference Library, Hobart House, Grosvenor Place, London SW1X 7AE, which covers history, geology, industrial relations, and literature. The biblography which follows is much more narrowly focussed, in several ways: it is almost exclusively about mining or former mining areas in *County Durham;* it is limited almost exclusively to the *present century* it does not go back much before 1900; and it is concerned with *social structure and social policy,* rather than the purely historical, geographical or economic literature.

Population in the coalfield

The movement of population into the Durham coalfield in the nineteenth century may be traced in * J.W. House, *North-East England, Population Movements and Landscape since the early nineteenth century* (Newcastle, 1957); A.E. Smailes, 'The Development of the Northumberland and Durham coalfield', *Scottish Geographical Magazine,* 51, 1935, pp.201-14; A.E. Smailes, 'Population changes in the colliery districts of Northumberland and Durham', *Geographical Journal,* 91, 1938, pp. 220-32; I. Leister, *The Sea Coal Mine and the Durham Miner* (Durham University Geography Dept., 1975); P.A. Grant, *The Coalmines of Durham City* (Durham Geography Dept., 1973).

The Geography of Coal-Mining

This is summarised usefully in * Durham Geography Curriculum Study Group, *Coal in County Durham* (Durham, 1972) and * W.A. Moyes, *Contracting Coalfield* (Newcastle, 1973). On travel to work patterns, J.C. Dewdney, 'The daily journey to work in County Durham', *Town Planning Review,* 31, 1960.

Local Histories

There are a number of local histories of mining settlements of which the following are examples: * W.A. Moyes, *Mostly Mining* (Easington) (Newcastle, 1969); J. McCutcheon, *Troubled Seams: the story of a pit and its people* (Seaham, J. Greenwood, 1955) and *A Wearside Mining Story: Wearmouth Colliery* (Seaham, 1961); J.J. Dodd, *The History of the Urban District of Spennymoor* (Spennymoor, 1897); *Langley Park Colliery Centenary 1875-1975* (privately printed, 1975); and *The Pit on the Downs: a history of Eppleton Colliery 1825-1975,* by J.H. Griffiths and F. Rundle (privately mimeoed, 1975).

Mining Trade Unionism and Politics

The economic and social history of Durham mining can best be told through the history of the Durham Miners' Association. The main sources are: R. Fynes, *The Miners of Northumberland and Durham* (Sunderland, 1873); J. Wilson, *A History of the Durham Miners' Association 1870-1904* (Durham, Veitch, 1907); S. Webb, *The Story of the Durham Miners* (1921); * E. Welbourne, *The Miners' Unions of Northumberland and Durham* (Cambridge, 1923); and * W.R. Garside, *The Durham Miners, 1919-60* (1971), which is the most important source for understanding the history of the industry and union up to 1957. Other material is in E. Allen, *A History of the Durham Miners'*

Association 1869-1969 (Durham, 1969) and G. Metcalfe, *A History of the DMA, 1869-1915* (unpublished ms., NUM (Durham Area) Library). See also: W.S. Hall, *A Historical Survey of the Durham Colliery Mechanics' Association* (Durham, Veitch, 1929). An interesting interpretation of the rank and file in mining is * D. Douglass, *Pit Life in County Durham* (1971), republished in R. Samuel (ed.), *Miners, Quarrymen and Saltworkers* (1977), pp.205-96. See also D. Douglass, *The Miners of N. Durham*, Socialist Union Pamphlet No.3, mimeo, 1974.

The political history of Durham miners may be followed in * R. Gregory, *The Miners and British Politics 1906-14* (Oxford, 1968); * H. Pelling, *The Social Geography of British Elections* (1967); A. Mason, *The General Strike in the North East* (Hull, 1971); * M. Gibb and M. Callcott, 'The Labour Party in the North-East between the Wars', *Bulletin of the North-East Group for the study of Labour History,* 8, 1974, pp.9-19; M. Callcott, *Parliamentary Elections in County Durham 1929-35* (unpublished M.Litt. thesis, University of Newcastle, 1973); and through individual entries in the volumes of * *The Dictionary of Labour Biography,* ed. J. Bellamy and J. Saville (1972 onwards, three volumes to 1977).

The recent and contemporary political complexion of the NUM (Durham Area) has been little studied. One useful source is J.D. Edelstein and M. Warner, *Comparative Union Democracy* (1975), ch.8 on the NUM. The political speakers invited to address Annual Galas since 1871 may be traced in the DMA *Souvenir Brochure* published at each Gala.

Other areas of trade union, political and organisational activity are largely unresearched. E. Lloyd, *The Story of 50 years of Crook Co-operative Society* (CWS Printing Works, Pelaw-on-Tyne, 1916) is a rare exception. For the influence of miners in local politics, one has to rely on * Jack Lawson's biography, *Peter Lee* (1932).

Only the links between Methodism and local trade unionism and politics is an adequate study available: * R.S. Moore, *Pitmen, Preachers and Politics* (Cambridge, 1974), examines sociologically the effects of Methodism on political and trade union activity in four west Durham villages. It is an important monograph. See also a review * by E.P. Thompson, 'Of history, sociology and historical relevance', *British Journal of Sociology,* 27, 1976, pp.387-402.

Those wishing to pursue studies in this area may also consult three *general* biblographies on labour history with reference to mining. They are: J.E. Williams, 'Labour in the Coalfields: a critical bibliography', *Bulletin of the Society for the Study of Labour History,* 4, 1962, pp.24-32; R.G. Neville and J. Benson, 'Labour in the Coalfields II', *Bulletin of the Society for the Study of Labour History,* 31, 1975, pp.45-59; and R. Turner, 'The contribution of oral evidence to labour history', *Oral History,* Vol.4, No.1, 1976, pp.23-40.

Mining Work

All other aspects of mining in County Durham are much less well covered than labour history. In relation to mining work for example, the reader is referred to two Yorkshire studies, * N. Dennis *et al. Coal is Our Life* (1956), and * J.H. Goldthorpe, 'Technical organisation as a factor in supervisor-work conflict', *British Journal of Sociology,* 10 1959, pp.213-30. Specifically on Durham, Douglass (cited in previous section) discusses methods of working, and research in north-west Durham is reported in E.L. Trist and K. Bamforth, 'Some social and psychological consequences of the longwall method of coal-getting', *Human Relations,* 4, 1951, pp.3-38, and * E.L. Trist *et al, Organisational Choice* (1963). L.J. Handy 'Absenteeism and attendance in the British coal-mining industry', *British Journal of Industrial Relations,* 6, 1968, pp.27-50 is a national study. One important contributory factor is disability and ill-health. The former is described in * R.W. Grainger and J.W. Hurst, *A Report on the Incidence of Disability among Durham Miners* (Durham University, Department of Economics, mimeo, 1969), the latter in * 'The Miners: a special case?', *The Lancet,* 19 January 1974, pp.81-2. A detailed health study is R.C. Browne *et al, A Study of Coalminers' Nystagmus in Durham County* (Durham, 1949).

Pit disasters symbolise the danger of mining work most graphically. A popular history is H. and B. Duckham, *Great Pit Disasters: Great Britain 1700 to the Present Day* (Newton Abbott, 1973). On Durham disasters, E. Forster *The Death Pit* (Newcastle, 1970) is the story of the West Stanley Colliery Explosion if 1909. A more official tone is taken in Ministry of Fuel and Power *Report of the Explosion at Easington Colliery, 29 May 1951,* by H.C.W. Roberts (HMSO, 1952).

Mining Talk

There are several sources on the distinctive local usage of words in mining. On language in the area generally see, J.T. Brockett, *A Glossary of North Country Words* (Newcastle, 1846) and O. Heslop, *Northumberland Words: a glossary* (1892); H. Orton, S. Sanderson and J. Widdowson (eds.), *The Linguistic Atlas of England* (1977) and E. Kolb, *Phonological Atlas of the Northern Region* (Berne, 1966) are general. H. Orton, *The Phonology of a South Durham Dialect* (1933) was carried out in the

Byers Green area. On mining, see G.C. Greenwell, *A Glossary of Terms used in the Coal Trade of Northumberland and Durham* (1888; reprinted Newcastle, 1970); E.L. Trist, *Organisational Choice* (1963), Appendix A; and * D. Douglass, *Pit Talk in County Durham* (1972), republished in R. Samuel (ed.), *Miners, Quarrymen and Saltworkers* (1977), pp.297-348.

Social Conditions

Studies of social conditions were pioneered in the North-East. * Lady Bell's study of Middlesborough, *At the Works* (1907) remains a classic. A.L. Bowley and A.R. Burnett-Hurst, *Livelihood and Poverty* (1915) and A.L. Bowley and M. Hogg, *Has Poverty Diminished?* (1925) included Stanley in their sample. Other sources on housing in mining areas include J.Y.E. Seeley, *Coal Mining Villages of Northumberland and Durham: a study of sanitary conditions and social facilities, 1870-80* (unpublished M.A., Social Studies, Newcastle University, 1974); * P.H. White 'Some aspects of urban development by colliery companies, 1919-39', *Manchester School,* 23, 1955, pp.269-80; and D. Lloyd George, *Coal and Power* (1925), pp.128-32.

A personal account of the area in the depression is provided in J.B. Priestley's *English Journey* (1934), including visits to several Settlements. The history of one is found in the Spennymoor Settlement's *Twenty-first Anniversary Souvenir Booklet* (1951). The effects of unemployment in the 1930s are considered more systematically in * J. Newsom, *Out of the Pit* (1936), * The Pilgrim Trust, *Men Without Work* (1938) and E. Wilkinson, *The Town that was Murdered* (1939). R. Titmuss, *Poverty and Population* (1938) compares the North-East to more prosperous areas such as the Home Counties.

The Decline of Mining Employment

Ministry of Fuel and Power, *Regional Survey of the Coalfields: Durham* (HMSO, 1945/6) is a study of economic and social conditions in mining just before nationalisation in 1947. In the post-war period, there have been fewer studies of social problems specifically with reference to mining and more attention has been paid to manpower rundown and redundancy. * J.W. House and E.M. Knight, *Pit Closure and the Community* (Newcastle, 1967) is an important sociographic study, as is * *Ryhope: a pit closes: a study in redeployment* (HMSO, for DEP, 1970). M.I.A. Bulmer, 'Mining redundancy' *Industrial Relations Journal,* Vol.2, No.4, 1971, pp.3-21, is a case-study of the course of one pit closure and of the effects of the Redundancy Payments Act, 1965.

Coal's decline nationally may be followed in * M.P. Jackson, *The Price of Coal* (1973); M.V. Posner, *Fuel Policy* (1973) and I. Berkovitch, *Coal on the Switchback: the coal industry since nationalisation* (1977). Two committed viewpoints are given in * Alfred Robens, *Ten Year Stint* (1972) and * J. Hughes, *A Special Case? Social Justice and the Miners* (1972)

Migration of Miners

The principal study of the migration of miners is * R.C. Taylor, *The Implications of Migration from the Durham Coalfield* (unpublished Ph.D., Durham University, 1966); see also * R.C. Taylor, 'Migration and Motivation' in J. Jackson (ed.), *Migration* (Cambridge, 1969) pp.99-133; and E.H. Wignall, 'The Migrant Miners', *New Society*, 29 July 1965.

Leisure and Culture in Mining Communities

Distinctive patterns of leisure activity are to be found in mining communities. As yet they are sparsely documented. The club movement is commemorated in * Ted Elkins, Jr., *So they brewed their own beer: a history of the Northern Clubs Federation Brewery* (Sunderland, 1970), and its national history is described in * John Taylor, *From Self-Help to Flamour* (Ruskin College History Workshop, Oxford, 1972). Leek growing as a characteristic of local culture is discussed in G. Payne and W. Williamson, 'Communal Leeks', *New Society*, 18 Sept. 1969, p.445; pigeon fancying in * J. Mott, 'Miners, Weavers and Pigeon-racing', in M. Smith *et al* (eds.), *Leisure and Society in Britain (1973)*, pp.86-96. Juvenile jazz bands on Tyneside are discussed by E. Bird, 'Jazz Bands of North-East England: the evolution of a working class cultural activity', *Oral History* 4, No.2, 1976, pp.79-88.

Unfortunately a more enduring feature of mining music, the colliery band, awaits its historian. Its importance is recalled only by association with the banners of the Lodges of the Durham Miners' Association. * W.A. Moyes, *The Banner Book* (1974) is a splendid memorial to the banners of Durham pits. See also his earlier *Banner Parade* (1973). J. Gorman, *Banner Bright* (1973) surveys mining and other trade union banners throughout the country.

Songs of the coalfield are presented in A.L. Lloyd * *Come All Ye Bold Miners* (1952) and his *Folk Songs in England* (1967). A recent valuable study is * R. Colls, *The Colliers' Rant* (1971). Long-playing records such as * *The Bonnie Pit Laddie: A Miner's Life in Music and Song* (TOPIC 12TS271-2) *The Collier Lad* (TOPIC 12TS270), *Tommy Armstrong of Tyneside* (TOPIC 12T122), *Along the Coaly Tyne* (TOPIC 12T189) and others recreate them, though there is dispute about their typicality as working class culture – see D. Harker, 'The Professional Geordie', *New Edinburgh Review,* 32, March 1976, pp.34-5 (issue on *Miners and the Coal Culture).*

Beliefs of miners are recorded *in vitro* in M. Ringwood, 'Some customs and beliefs of Durham miners', *Folklore,* 67-8, 1957, pp.423-5, and by D. McKelvie, 'Aspects of Oral Tradition and Beliefs in an industrial region', *Folk Life,* 1, 1963, pp.77-94. R.C. Taylor's Ph.D. (above, under 'Migration') also has evidence on customs.

Three general sources on mining life in the area are the essays in S. Chaplin, *The Smell of Sunday Dinner* (Newcastle, 1971), and * *A Tree with Rosy Apples* (Newcastle, 1972); and * A. Plater, S. Chaplin and A. Glasgow, *Close the Coalhouse Door* (1969).

On the place of religion in mining areas, analytic studies are sparse, the main one being * R.S. Moore, *Pitmen, Preachers and Politics* (1974) on the effects of Methodism. Hensley Henson, *Retrospect on an Unimportant Life* (1942), by a former Bishop of Durham is a memoir from a Church of England point of view.

Mining Localities as Communities

There are comparatively few integrated accounts of Durham mining localities as communities. Research using oral history techniques has as yet had little impact in the region. The case for it has been argued by * C. Storm-Clark in 'The Miners 1870-1970: a test case for oral history', *Victorian Studies,* 15, 1971, pp.49-74 and his 'The Miners: the relevance of oral evidence', *Oral History,* No.4, 1972, pp.72-92. Their potential is shown by a Yorkshire study, J. MacFarlane, 'Denaby Main: a South Yorkshire Mining Village', in J. Benson and R.G. Neville (eds.), *Studies in the Yorkshire Coal Industry* (Manchester, 1976), pp.109-44.

A different more theoretical, approach has been adopted in recent research into the growth of mining communities in South East Northumberland: * R.L. Davis and J.M. Cousins, 'The "New Working Class" and the Old', in M. Bulmer (ed.), *Working Class Images of Society* (1975), pp.192-205, and * J.M. Cousins and R.L. Davis, 'Working Class Incorporation – a historical approach with reference to the mining communities of S.E. Northumberland, 1840-1890', in F. Parkin (ed.), *The Social Analaysis of Class Structure* (1974), pp.275-97.

For Durham in the first half of the twentieth century, the best account remains * Mark Benney's *Charity Main* (1946), which covers several aspects of mining community life including the role of the Lodge and Miner's Welfare. There is no parallel in Durham to N. Dennis *et al., Coal is Our Life* (1956), which is the classic British community study of a mining locality (in West Yorkshire).

Though differing in focus, the nearest to it in Durham are * R.C. Taylor's Ph.D. on migrant miners (see under 'Migration' above), and * R.S. Moore's study of Methodism (1974). Both are extremely valuable community studies, Taylor's of five west Durham villages, Moore's of four. Taylor's focus on villages of origin and attachment to the locality demonstrates the social influences upon mobility and immobility. Moore highlights the social and geographical mobility of Methodists, though he has been criticised for paying insufficient attention to non-Methodists as a whole in his localities. Unpublished studies by E. Thorpe on 'Coalport', *Coalport: an interpretation of community in a mining town* (1970) and *The Miner and the Locality* (1976) are available in Durham University Library, as is M. Bulmer, *Collectivities in Change* (1970), a study of the decline of mining in Spennymoor with reference to industrial change.

Two recent articles provide further evidence of social networks and community sentiment in a former mining area, Spennymoor. They are: * A.R. Townsend and C.C. Taylor, 'Regional Culture and Identity in Industrialised Societies: the case of North-East England', *Regional Studies* 9, 1975, pp.379-93, and * C.C. Taylor and A.R. Townsend, 'The local "Sense of Place" as evidenced in North-East England', *Urban Studies,* 13, 1976, pp.133-46.

There are as yet few comparative studies between mining areas analysing their common social structural features. Attempts in this direction include H.M. Watkins, *Coal and Men: an economic and social study of American and British coalfields* (1934), * J.H.M. Laslett, 'Some determinants of radicalism among British and American coalminers', *Bulletin of the Society for the Study of Labour History,* 28, 1974, pp.6-7 and * M. Bulmer, 'Sociological Models of the Mining Community', *The Sociological Review,* 23, 1975, pp.61-92.

Personal Documents about Mining

There are a few personal documents about County Durham which help to fill out the social science literature. They include memoirs by those in managerial and elite positions, labour leaders and less prominent miners, as well as novelists. * R.A.S. Redmayne, *Men, Miners and Memories* (1942) provides a picture of the coal industry from the point of view of an engineer. Bishop Henson's *Retrospect of an Unimportant Life* (1942) puts an ecclesiastical point of view, Sir Timoth Eden's *Durham* (1952) laments the decline of the gentry.

More immediate contact with mining is found in * John Wilson, *Memories of a Labour Leader* (1910), * Jack Lawson, *Peter Lee* (1932), Jack Lawson 'Our Village' in *Who Goes Home: Broadcasts and Sketches* (1945), * Jack Lawson, *A Man's Life* (1951) and * Alderman Ned Cowen, *Of Mining Life and aal its ways* (Durham County Hall, privately circulated, 1973). All three authors were active in a union or political party (though differing from liberal to radical socialist). All may therefore be somewhat circumspect in their accounts.

Less socially elevated authors may be more open. * G. Parkinson, *True Stores of Durham Pit Life* (1912) remains a rare fragment from the nineteenth century. G. Hitchin, *Pit Yacker*(1962) and Bob Jefferey, *The View from No.10* (Ramsden William Publications Ltd., Consett, 1975) are more recent.

Among novelists, Sid Chaplin's * *The Thin Seam* and *The Leaping Lad* (both 1950) are outstanding. A.J. Cronin, *The Stars Look Down* (1935) is of historical interest. D. Bean, *The Big Meeting* (1967) pictures the Durham Gala in decline, and does not adequately convey its full impact in its heyday.

A Case Study of Social Change: Village Categoriation

T. Sharp, 'A Derelict Area: a study of the S.W. Durham Coalfield' (Hogarth Press pamphlet, 1935) and A. Temple, 'The Derelict Villages of S.W. Durham', (unpublished M.Litt. thesis, Durham University, 1940) provide descriptions of one district 40 years ago. *Farewell Squalor* (Easington, 1947) and 'The Peterlee Social Survey: New Town for Old', *Bureau of Current Affairs Pamphlet,* No.75, March 5th 1949, 20 pp., deal with a different part of the county 30 years ago.

The case for village categorisation is made in the Pepler-Macfarlane Plan of 1949, and the County Development Plan and its Amendments of 1951, 1964 and 1971 (see references in Section A). A further justification is contained in D. Senior 'Growth Points for Durham', an undated 16-page pamphlet published in the 1960s by Durham County Council.

There is an analysis of the policy with reference to the Ferryhill area in A. Blowers, *The Declining Villages of County Durham,* Unit 12 of Course D 281, *New Trends in Geography* (The Open University, 1972, pp.143-57). Nathaniel Lichfield and Associates, *Gurney Valley Villages Study* (1971, from the partnership) included the results of a local social survey. J. Barr, 'Durham's murdered villages', *New Society,* 3 April 1969, pp.523-5, puts both sides of the argument and comes down in favour of the County Council. Norman Nicholson's 'Letters from Cumberland', *The Listener,* 91, No.2349, 4 April 1974, pp.427-31 are not about County Durham but the town of Millom. Nevertheless, they convey well some of the more intagible aspects of community in the face of economic decline.

APPENDIX B: THE STUDY OF COAL-MINING SETTLEMENTS AND THEORIES OF 'COMMUNITY'

Martin Bulmer

Since this book is both more than and less than a sociological monograph, theoretical issues in the sociology of community do not receive central attention. Indeed, the theoretical input is implicit rather than explicit, and this is designedly so. Despite a brilliant text-book treatment by Bell and Newby,[1] community studies in Britain have come under attack in recent years, and are distinctly unfashionable. Margaret Stacey argued in 1969 that 'it is doubtful whether the concept "community" refers to a useful abstraction.'[2] More recently ambitious macro-theories, particularly those of Harvey and Castells, have come to dominate urban sociology in Britain and eclipse locality studies. The evidence presented in this work may be regarded as a reassertion of the *empirical* relevance of 'community' to an understanding of local social relations, and a demonstration (in one area) of the continuing importance of *the locality* in the lives of a majority of the population.

Nevertheless, the limitations of the concept 'community' must be readily admitted. In addition to its normative overtones, discussed in chapter 2, at least three different scientific elements in the concept of 'community' as it has been used by sociologists may be distinguished. It may refer to a quality that people have in common (whether material objects, civic rights, or character). It may, secondly, refer to a body of people, who are said to form a collectivity. And thirdly, it may refer to people with a common land or territory. There is no general agreement on which of these interpretations is correct and indeed G.A. Hillery has pointed out that sociologists have employed no less than 16 concepts in formulating 94 different definitions of 'community'; no author uses all 16 concepts.[3] Two elements recur fairly frequently in sociological definitions, first that a community is a social group inhabiting a common territory and, secondly, that it is in addition characterised by certain social ties. Yet even here, there is no basis for agreement, for different emphases are given to the two elements by different writers. Hillery has summed up the sociologist's dilemma well:

> What does community mean then? Having something in common, a group of people, a piece of land? A group of people having land in

> common? or perhaps something else. The term as it exists in the general as well as the technical sense, has too many meanings to be understood. One may *believe* that his audience understands him when he says 'community' but in fact his audience will supply its own interpretation and chances are that the interpretations will differ. Consequently, even if a precise meaning were arbitrarily assigned, it would be misunderstood, because others would still be using their own definitions.[4]

It does follow, however, that the *study* of communities is, therefore, not worth pursuing.

The approach embodied in chapters 7, 12, 15 and 16 is derived from a sociological frame of reference, applied in empirical research, rather than from purely conceptual discussion which is ultimately self-defeating. Influenced by related work being carried out in industrial sociology at the time (particularly the *Affluent Worker* study and Durham ship-building research of R.K. Brown and others), both Mr Thorpe and the writer attempted to develop an action frame of reference to use in their research.[5]

This had the particular advantage that it tried to make explicit the relationship between social and geographical phenomena: whether there is any place in a definition of 'community' for a spatial or geographical component. Unlike the geographer, the sociologist using this approach does not accord primacy to spatial factors. As Talcott Parsons has indicated:

> while the phenomena of [social] action are inherently temporal, that is, involve processes in time, they are not in the same sense spatial. That is to say, *relations in space* are not as such relevant to systems of action analytically considered. For the analytic purposes of this theory, acts are not primarily but only secondarily located in space. Or to put it somewhat differently, spatial relations constitute only conditions and so far as they are controllable, means of action.[6]

In the case of community studies, it has been noted by several writers that *place* is of limited usefulness in explanation: 'Ways of life do not coincide with settlement patterns' (Gans);[7] 'Any attempt to tie particular patterns of social relations to a specific geographical milieu is a singularly fruitless exercise' (Pahl).[8] An action approach treats geographical factors as constraints, or 'conditions of action', but not of themselves as determinants of social behaviour. People who live in mining communities do not act as they do *because of* the shape, size and location of the community, but they are influenced by it. Geography restricts choice and freedom of action. Thus, over a whole range of social phenomena, the choices open to a man living, for instance, in a south-west Durham mining village are significantly different from those open to a man living in central Newcastle – in terms of employment opportunities, availability and price of housing, range of leisure facilities available, quality of education available for his children, social composition of the population and, therefore, the range of social contacts open to him; and so on.

Secondly, analytical primacy is given to social actors' own definitions of their situation, of how they see the world. The social structure of mining settlements, the social relations of work in mining, the responses of those affected by the rundown of the mining industry, are all constructed from the meanings which people attach to their social attachments and social situation. As W.I. Thomas put it, 'if men define situations as real, they are real in their consequences'. Hence the emphasis in chapters 15 and 16 on how miners and ex-miners describe their situation, and the use of quotation. If men are the product of their society and circumstances they also retain the capacity to act in ways which falsify deterministic predictions about their behaviour.[9]

This emphasis accords with recent trends in community studies. Bell and Newby have done something to rescue community studies from the critical attacks to which they have been subject in recent years. Suttles's sensitive theoretical discussion of the social relations of urban man in America stresses the capacity of social actors to construct their own social worlds.[10] And Gusfield's recent discussion of the concept, although it disavows much too firmly any interest in the traditional, geographical, connotations of 'community', does place the emphasis squarely on shared inter-subjectivity as defining the phenomenon. 'Community' is not an object, a 'thing in itself': 'When we look for the sources of communal affilation, our concern is that of process and situation. When do people define themselves as having important characteristics in common, and when do these become bases for communal identity and action?'[11]

Two aspects in particular of the community situation of coal-miners deserve further attention. Social processes at work in mining settlements may fruitfully be interpreted as being mediated by 'occupational communities' of miners, based on common work experience and the overlapping of work and non-work ties, but continuing in existence as a basis for social relations even after the disappearance of mining as an industry. Originally proposed by S.M. Lipset and others,[12] then developed by R. Blauner,[13] the concept has recently received renewed attention for its relevance to the study of class imagery.[14]

Secondly, the historical dimension of community life remains of great importance. As well as a chronicle and an objective analysis, history is also the past seen through the eyes of the present. What Gusfield calls the 'social construction of traditions'[15] is particularly evident in County Durham, but has a wider relevance. Recent work by Marc Field on Boston integrates in a remarkable way contemporary survey data on urban social structure with an acute historical analysis of the position of the urban working class.[16] The present work, despite far less adequate data and a much more local focus, attempts a similar sort of analysis for twentieth century coal-mining communities in County Durham, without the same degree of theoretical explicitness or elegance of research design.

The further refinement of sociological models for the study of the mining community[17] is part of a continuing broader comparative study of the social structure of mining localities. Such an emphasis, however, is distinctively different from the more empirical approach adopted in the present work.

Notes

1. C. Bell and H. Newby, *Community Studies,* London, Allen & Unwin, 1971.
2. M. Stacey, 'The Myth of Community Studies', *British Journal of Sociology,* 20, 1969, p.134.
3. G.A. Hillery, 'Definitions of Community: areas of agreement', *Rural Sociology,* 20, 1955, pp.111-23.
4. G.A. Hillery, *Communal Organisations: a study of local societies,* Chicago, 1968, p.4..
5. E. Thorpe, *Coalport: an interpretation of 'community' in a mining town,* University of Durham, mimeo, 1970, Introduction and Ch.1; M.I.A. Bulmer, *Collectivities in Change: some sociological reflections on the decline of mining in the Durham coalfield,* University of Durham, mimeo, 1970, Ch.2 and 'An action frame of reference in community studies', unpublished paper, University of Durham, 1972.
6. T. Parsons, *The Structure of Social Action,* New York, Free Press, 1949, p.45, n.1.
7. H. Gans, 'Urbanism and suburbanism as ways of life', in A.M. Rose (ed.), *Human Behaviour and Social Processes,* London, Routledge, 1962, p.641.
8. R.E. Pahl, 'The rural-urban continuum', *Sociologia Ruralis,* 6, 1966, p.322.
9. Cf . the discussion of deterministic theories of the character of mining communities in M.I.A. Bulmer, 'Sociological Models of the Mining Community', *The Sociological Review,* 23, 1975, pp.61-92.

10. G. Suttles, *The Social Construction of Communities,* Universities of Chicago Press, 1972.
11. J. Gusfield, *Community,* Oxford, Basil Blackwell, 1976, p.30.
12. S.M. Lipset *et al, Union Democracy,* New York, Free Press, 1956.
13. R. Blauner, 'Work satisfaction and industrial trends in modern society', in W. Galenson and S.M. Lipset (eds.), *Labor and Trade Unionism,* New York, Wiley, 1960, pp.339-60.
14. M. Bulmer (ed.), *Working Class Images of Society,* London, Routledge, 1975, esp. chs. 2, 4, 8, 9, 11, 12 and 13.
15. Gusfield, p.38.
16. M. Field *et al, The World of the Urban Working Class,* Harvard University Press, 1973.
17. M. Bulmer, 'Sociological Models'.

APPENDIX C: PERSONAL DOCUMENTS AS SOCIOLOGICAL DATA

Martin Bulmer

> 'Have you ever thought of that?' said an old man to me one day, 'that life is a journey?' Audibly 'Aye, Billy'. Thinking: the old bore. Then, the surprising old devil. 'Or that every day is a little journey?' 'Aye.' 'Or that as we journey forward we also journey back, and that as one journey draws to an end the other begins?'
> 'No!'
> 'Memory, lad. That's what Ah mean. So we journey forwards backwards. Ye canna rest nor stop. Fix a minute and it's gone. Slipped through your fingers like a minnum. We only command when the event's over. Daydreaming. A stop and start journey'.
>
> from *The Thin Seam* by Sid Chaplin.

Chapters 3, 4 and 5 contain personal interpretations of aspects of north-east life, two (by Mark Benney and Sid Chaplin) dealing with the general characteristics of mining communities, one (by Bill Williamson) discussing a particular feature of north-east culture, the leek. All write on the basis of personal experience. Chaplin and Williamson grew up in and have lived much of their lives in the North-East, Benney was a southerner who during 1944-45 worked in the Ministry of Fuel and Power based on Newcastle, but spent most of his time in the Durham coalfield. All have their stylistic variants. Benney's narrative is a thinly-veiled fictionalised account of his own experiences, written in the third person. Chaplin's paper is based on a talk he gave to the Durham Sociology Department staff-graduate seminar. Williamson's chapter was originally a talk on BBC Radio Three.

What are accounts of this kind doing in a work of social science? The sociological study of coal-mining communities in the Northumberland and Durham coalfield has, as noted in the first two chapters, been slow in developing, and there is a certain irony in the fact that they have been studied most intensively in the period when the industry to which most of these settlements owe their existence has been very rapidly contracting. The major monographic studies are those by Moore on Methodism[1] and R.C. Taylor on migration.[2] Apart from these works and two very thorough sociographic studies of the immediate social effects of pit closures,[3] there is a paucity of available sociological material on Durham mining communities, itself illustrating a more general paradox about the literature on mining communities throughout Britain. For while there are few *sociological* studies of mining communities, the general literature on the object is abundant and ought *a fortiori* to be of social-scientific interest. A good reason for their inclusion is therefore that they provide data and a perspective on phenomena of interest, which are not available from other sources. This also applies to chapters 6 and 8 by Lawson and Turner on aspects of Durham politics; they are included in the absence of more substantial research.

To say, however, that autobiography and reminiscence (as well, possibly, as more impressionistic accounts) are of sociological interest requires some justification. Much effort in the onward movement of sociology as an academic discipline has been devoted to increasing the precision and rigour of the methods used, whether these be based on social surveys, participant observation, content analysis, laboratory experiments or official statistics. What advantages are there in turning, in the absence of other data, to the possibly fallible and certainly subjective accounts of those who have lived in mining villages and have experienced life there on the inside? And what are the possible pitfalls?

One important and influential tradition or cluster of doctrines in sociology – variously described as the 'voluntaristic theory of action', 'understanding', or *verstehen* – regards such first-person accounts of social actors' own experiences as being of primary value as sociological data. Whether formulated in terms of Max Weber's 'interpretative understanding of social action,'[4] W.I. Thomas's emphasis on the actors' 'definition of the situation',[5] or G.H. Mead's 'generalized other'[6] this approach requires than an attempt be made (however difficult in practice it may be to carry out) to obtain a picture of the subject's own view in any particular social situation. Man is not only (or even) the object of the scientific study of social action; he is first and foremost the subject of social action, and his subjective experience must be understood (however imperfectly) if adequate understanding is to be achieved. In pursuing this aim, first-person reminiscence and autobiography is clearly of particular importance.

Even if the more extreme tendencies in this tradition or approach are resisted, it surely directs attention to the sociological importance of accounts of *lived experience.* Most, if not all, sociological research abstracts from the ongoing flow of events and processes partial and particular aspects, in line with the particular problem and interest of the researcher. The answer to the question on the interview schedule, the observation made in the laboratory, the set of figures taken from the census, are all in different ways slices of social reality of a more or less artificial kind. On the whole sociologists have not directed attention, except when using historical materials, to the totality of experience, to social actors' own interpretations of the past, to the understanding of processes of action in time.[7] The value of personal documents such as Sid Chaplin's lies partly in enabling us, however partially and provisionally, to attempt such a reconstruction of life in Durham mining villages.

And it has the further advantage, from the point of view of sociology as a humanistic discipline, that it provides an interpretation of life as lived in a setting very different from that of a university (and indeed very different from that within the experience of (too) many people within universities). The American sociologist Robert E. Park, who did so much to establish empirical social research in the United States, once wrote of why he himself places such emphasis on the point of view of the subject of social experience:

> While I was at Harvard, William James read to us one day his essay on 'A Certain Blindness in Human Beings'. I was greatly impressed at the time and, as I have reflected upon it since, the ideas suggested there have assumed a steadily increasing significance. The 'blindness' of which James spoke is the blindness each of us is likely to have for the meaning of other people's lives. At any rate what sociologists most need to know is what goes on behind the faces of men, what it is that makes life for each of us full or thrilling . . . Otherwise we do not know the world in which we actually live.[8]

The methodological value of personal accounts of experience does not, however, exempt them from being scrutinised for the reliability and validity of their evidence and interpretation, or from questions being asked about how precisely sociologists can make use of them in their research. Indeed scepticism about the kinds of answers which can be given to these two sets of questions probably explains why personal documents have been so little used in recent years as a source of data in sociological research, and why studies based on their use have been severely criticised as lacking in rigour and precision.

Data from personal accounts such as chapter 3 to 5, or indeed from other sources such as Lambert and Beales's *Memoirs of the Unemployed*, need to be treated with particular scepticism. Some readers will undoubtedly feel that Chaplin or Benney's portrayal of the mining community is unsatisfactory or exaggerated. When Chaplin's account was first circulated as a Departmental Working Paper, a local Durham educationalist wrote to say: 'I was at first irritated and then saddened that this curious collection of statements and opinions should be presented as in any sense an accurate account of mining life in this century.' Some would perhaps stress much more the limitations of mining settlements, their closed nature, limited social horizons and opportunities, social deprivation and incidence of poor sanitation, bad housing and health problems. Yet people lived in such places, and died there, and built a social life in that setting, and whatever else they do, Chaplin's and to a lesser extent Benney's accounts give some impression of the strengths, as well as the weaknesses, of such communities.

This does not, however, reduce the need for a sceptical reading of them. The use of such personal material in sociology has a long history, and there are a number of general sources to look to in evaluating the different types of personal document – autobiographies, diaries, series of letters, specially collected life histories, less structured kinds of reminiscence, and so on. The criticisms of this approach may be examined in the light of four criteria, suggested by Herbert Blumer in 1939,[9] to apply to documentary material which does not meet the rigid canons of scientific measurement. These are:

(a) the adequacy of the data
(b) the reliability of the data
(c) the representativeness of the data
(d) the validity of the interpretation of the data

The value of autobiographical accounts of life in mining villages may be evaluated in terms of these criteria by comparing such accounts with more impressionistic journalistic accounts. Several sources are available. As autobiographies (to pick out three), Jack Lawson's *A Man's Life,*[10] B.L. Coombes's *These Poor Hands*[11] and N. Harrison's *Once a Miner*[12] provide first-hand accounts of life and work in parts of the Durham, South Wales and Kent coalfields respectively. As journalistic accounts (to pick out three), J.B. Priestley's *English Journey,*[13] F. Zweig's *Men in the Pits*[14] and C. Sigal's *Weekend in Dinlock*[15] provide general or particular views of life in certain mining villages. How do they compare in terms of Blumer's four criteria?

Adequacy. In the case of autobiographies, data is derived from the author's own experience over a number of years in a mining community.

In the case of the journalistic account this safeguard is absent, and the adequacy of the data depends entirely on the skill of the writer: the presumption must be that the account is not based on adequate data, unless the contrary is demonstrated.

Reliability. In neither case is the reliability of the data easily open to check. In the case of the autobiography or reminiscence, the fallibility of memory is a prime cause of the scepticism with which such accounts are treated by sociologists. This is justified to the extent that recollections are mistakenly treated as entirely reliable and correct, and so far as possible they must be cross-checked and set against other sources on the same subject. Moreover, the selectivity of remembering means that any such account is likely to be structured in terms of the actor's normative model of the past, and this needs to be taken into account in judging their reliability. But there seems little warrant for the total scepticism with which this type of account is sometimes regarded, since there is some evidence that people do recall fairly clearly the main events *in which they themselves were personally involved,* and which are part of their own biography. This is not to say that memory is infallible or that the past is not reinterpreted in terms of the present, but that to ignore such sources entirely is quite unwarranted. In the particular case of mining autobiographies, the length of experience of the writer in one place or one type of community is some safeguard. The impressionistic account by a journalist is more insidious from the point of view of reliability because it usually pretends to knowledge which has in fact a slight basis in personal experience. In Priestley's book this is apparent from the narrow range of people talked to in mining villages; in Zweig's account there is the familiar broad pastiche but very slight evidence of sustained involvement in the ongoing life of mining communities. This reservation particularly applies to Turner's account of Durham politics in chapter 8, which is presumably based on information given to him by local people who knew the political structure, as well as on personal interviews with political notables.

Representativeness. This is unlikely to be satisfied in any single personal document, and the best safeguard is the comparison of several documents from different points of view on the same problem. The lack of representativeness is apparent in the autobiographies cited: Lawson became an eminent Labour politician, Coombes was a miner who was also a writer, and Harrison was a 'Bevin-Boy' from a middle-class background who later went into mine management. In the case of the journalists the problem is not only their background and experience prior to writing about mining villages, but also the small number of people that they are able to meet in the course of a short visit. Sigal's artistic miner, like the politically ambitious Lawson, is probably untypical of the community as a whole. And the problem of selectivity on a short visit is much more salient than for someone resident in the settlement for a long period of time. As John Dollard has observed:

> We should remark how the bizarre is likely to stand out in experience and how selective our perception is, how we tend to see what makes us comfortable or wards off painful feelings. Odd people and those under pressure do and say the conspicuous things and we must beware of judging the whole situation by them. Comfortable people talk less and come forward less readily to the newcomer.[16]

This is a pitfall to which the journalistic approach is particularly prone, and into which the autobiographer is perhaps somewhat less likely to stumble.

Validity of Interpretation. This is the most difficult criterion of all to satisfy, and in general cannot be met in the case of personal documents. In their nature the interpretations offered are purely personal, generally in terms of the writers' own experiences, and cannot be definitive in the way more rigorous sociological methods attempt to be. One of the important uses of personal documents is indeed to suggest new ideas which can then be developed and investigated in other ways. One might argue, however, that in some respects the autobiographer is closer to the sociologist than to the journalist. Though 'journalistic' is an epithet sometimes perjoratively and indiscriminately applied to much non-quantitative sociology, in fact there are fairly clear distinctions to be made between most sociology and journalism, in terms of the emphasis upon immediacy, upon data, upon interpretation, and upon theory. In particular, as Jacobs says:

> public interest and novelty justify journalism, but sound theory justifies sociology . . . An essential difference between journalism and sociology is that journalists write from the top down, in triangle fashion, and sociologists do the opposite. The most important and sensational items of a journalist are put in in the lead, with less newsworth items at the end. The sociologist puts his data first and the conclusions at the end. A reader of science must read the full article for complete information. Only the publication's

reputation is the newsman's validation.[17]

These cautions should be particular borne in mind in reading chapter 8.

The best check upon the validity of interpretation provided in a personal document is either to compare it with similar accounts from others in the same situation or writing about the same problem, or to supplement it with data gathered from other sources such as the written record, the observation of behaviour, or the social survey. Ideally one should combine several types of data. This is attempted in a fragmentary way in this collection, but the separate pieces are not as well-integrated as is desirable. Such an approach to sociological evidence – known as 'triangulation': using more than one method to gain different perspectives on the same phenomenon[18] – is one which has not been fully developed, but is more promising than blanket scepticism about particular types of data.

Personal documents are *interpretations* of phenomena. Their use or non-use has too often turned on wholesale acceptance or total rejection. The record of lived experience deserves a more central place among the methods available than it has had of late, but such data is most satisfactory when juxtaposed to other more systematically collected evidence. Howard Becker's image of the mosaic is useful: 'Each piece added to a mosaic adds a little to our understanding of the total picture. When many pieces have been placed we can see, more or less clearly, the objects and the people in the picture and their relation to one another. Different pieces contribute different things to our understanding'.[19]

The sociological usefulness of autobiographical and other personal documentary accounts is thus not negligible, even when their limitations are admitted. Indeed they are something more than merely an 'interesting' slice of life, or a 'good read' for sixth-formers, first-year undergraduates and the general public. Robert Angell's six-fold scheme, put foward in 1945, still appears useful as a way of formally stating the purposes which personal documents can fulfil in sociology.[20] They may:

(i) Serve as a means of securing conceptual 'hunches'.

(ii) Suggest new hypotheses to an investigator who is thinking in terms of an established conceptual scheme.

(iii) Serve as a source from which to select data which seem important in terms of common sense, and to formulate rough hypotheses from these facts.

(iv) Serve in the verification of hypotheses.

(v) Secure greater historical understanding of how a particular social unit has developed.

(vi) Serve as a means of exposition in the communication of sociological findings.

The autobiographical recollection, as a personal document over the collection of which (unlike the life history) the sociologist has no control, does not serve all these purposes but would seem to be of value in relation to the first three and the fifth. If this is doubted in relation to Durham mining villages, examples can be cited from other areas of sociology than community studies where autobiographical accounts of high social documentary content and considerable sociological interest provide fascinating source material both in their own right and as a basis for re-analysis and fresh theoretical interpretation. In industrial sociology,[21] in the sociology of education,[22] in the sociology of race relations,[23] and in the sociology of culture,[24] works of this kind are of considerable value.

In other ways than in the use of autobiographical reminiscence, personal documentary methods are enjoying something of a renaissance in sociology. The rediscovery and reinterpretation[25] of the studies of crime and social deviance carried out by the Chicago School between the two world wars is one source of this. In particular, the deliberate collection of life histories – on the model of Clifford Shaw's *The Jack Roller*[26] – seems likely to become more important as a means by which the sociologist tries, in a more structured way than relying on mere recollection, to gather an account of social actors' own biographies and lived experience.[27]

Other stimuli come from the neighbouring disciplines of history and social anthropology. In particular the growth of oral history in recent years has encouraged an analytic approach to mining work and mining communities in earlier periods. Christopher Storm-Clark has examined mining in west Yorkshire and George Ewart Evans, the doyen of British oral historians, mining in South Wales.[28] An appreciation of anthropological studies of oral tradition[29] also sensitises sociologists to the possible value in their own discipline of people's recollections of their past experiences.

Personal documents such as those presented earlier are indeed, despite the methodological problems which their collection and interpretation involve, a rich treasure-house, and a fruitful source of sociological insights.

Notes

1. R.S. Moore, *Pitmen, Preachers and Politics,* Cambridge University Press, 1974.
2. R.C. Taylor, 'The Implications of Migration from the Durham Coalfield; an anthropological study', unpublished thesis presented for the degree of Ph.D., University of Durham, 1966. See also, R.C. Taylor, 'Migration and Motivation', in J.A. Jackson (ed.), *Migration,* Cambridge University Press, 1969, pp.99-133.
3. J.W. House and E.M. Knight, *Pit Closure and the Community,* Newcastle, 1967, and *Ryhope: A Pit Closes: a study in redemployment*, HMSO, London, 1970.
4. M. Weber, *The Theory of Social and Economic Organisation,* New York, Free Press, 1947, (first published 1922 as *Wirtschaft und Gesellschaft),* Ch.1.
5. W.I. Thomas and F. Znaniecki, *The Polish Peasant in Europe and America,* Chicago and Boston 1918-20; W.I. Thomas, *The Unadjusted Girl,* Boston, 1923; W.I. and D.S. Thomas, *The Child in America,* New York, 1928.
6. G.H. Mead, *Mind Self and Society,* University of Chicago Press, 1934.
7. Cf. P. Abrams, *Being and Becoming in Sociology,* Inaugural lecture, published by the University of Durham, 1972.
8. R.E. Park, *Race and Culture,* Glencoe, Free Press, 1950, pp.vi-viii.
9. H. Blumer, *Critiques of Research in the Social Sciences I: An Apparaisal of Thomas and Znaniecki's 'The Polish Peasant in Europe and America',* New York, SSRC, 1939.
10. London, Hodder and Stoughton, 1932.
11. London, Gollancz, 1939.
12. Oxford University Press, 1954.
13. London, Heineman, 1934.
14. London, Gollancz, 1948.
15. Harmondsworth, Penguin, 1962.
16. J. Dollard, *Caste and Class in a Southern Town,* Yale University Press, 1937.
17. Cf. R.H. Jacobs, 'The Journalistic and Sociological Enterprises as Ideal Types', *The American Sociologist,* 5, 1970, pp.348-350. Jacobs was herself a journalist before becoming a sociologist.
18. Cf. E.J. Webb *et al, Unobtrusive Measures,* Chicago, Rand McNally, 1966; and N. Denzin, *The Research Act,* London, Butterworths, 1970.
19. H.S. Becker, 'Introduction', to C. Shaw, *The Jack Roller,* University of Chicago Press, 1966 edition, p. viii.
20. R. Angell, 'A Critical Review of the Personal Document Method in Sociology 1920-1940', in L. Gottschalk *et al, The Use of Personal Documents in History, Anthropology and Sociology,* New York, SSRC, 1945. See also: J. Dollard, *Criteria for the Life History,* Yale University Press, 1935, and G. Allport, *The Use of Personal Documents in Psychological Science, New York, SSRC, 1942.*
21. See P. Berger (ed.), *The Human Shape of Work,* New York, Macmillan, 1964, R. Fraser (ed.), *Work: twenty personal accounts,* Harmondsworth, Penguin, 1968, and R. Fraser (ed.), *Work 2: twenty personal accounts,* Harmondsworth, Penguin, 1969.
22. See the relevant parts of B. Jackson and D. Marsden, *Education and the Working Class,* London, Routledge, 1962.
23. See, for example, on black ghetto life in the United States: *The Autobiography of Malcolm X,* London, Penguin, 1966; C. Brown, *Manchild in the Promised Land,* London, Penguin, 1966; E. Cleaver, *Soul on Ice,* London, Cape, 1967.
24. On working-class culture in Britain compare: R. Hoggart, *The Uses of*

Literacy, London, Chatto, 1957, Part One 'An "Older" Order'; and R. Roberts, *The Classic Slum: Salford Life in the first quarter of the twentieth century,* Manchester University Press, 1971.

25. Cf. D. Matza, *Becoming Deviant,* Englewood Cliffs, N.J., Prentice-Hall, 1969.
26. C. Shaw, *The Jack Roller: a delinquent boy's own story,* Chicago, 1930 (republished 1966). Cf. also, C. Conwell and E.H. Sutherland, *The Professional Thief,* Chicago, 1937. More recently: H. Williamson, *Hustler,* edited by R.L. Keiser, New York, Doubleday, 1965, and J.D. Douglas, *The Social Meanings of Suicide,* Princeton University Press, 1967, Ch.17.
27. Discussion of personal documentary methods are contained in: H. Becker, *The Jack Roller* (1966 ed) pp. v-xviii; reprinted in H. Becker, *Sociological Work,* London, Allen Lane, 1971, Ch. 4, and N. Denzin,*The Research Act: a theoretical introduction to sociological methods,* London, Butterworths, 1970, Ch.10.
28. C. Storm-Clark, 'The Miners: a test case for oral history', *Victorian Studies,* 10, 1972, pp.358-74 on West Yorkshire; George Ewart Evans, *From Mouths of Men,* London, Faber, 1976, Chs. 8 to 12, on South Wales. See also C. Storm-Clark, 'The Miners: the relevance of oral history', *Oral History,* Vol.1, No.4, 1973, pp.72-92; J. MacFarlane, 'Denaby Main: a south Yorkshire mining village', *Bulletin of the Society for the Study of Labour History,* 25, 1972, pp.82-100; and more generally on the potential of this approach to labour history, Robert Turner, 'The Contribution of oral evidence to labour history', *Oral History,* 4, 1, 1976, pp.23-40, which includes a useful bibliography of more than 100 items. On oral history generally G.E. Evans, *Ask the Fellows Who Cut the Hay,* London, Faber, 1956; G.E. Evans, *The Days that we have seen,* London, Faber, 1975; R. Blythe, *Akenfield, a portrait of an English Village,* London, Allen Lane, 1969; P. Thompson, 'Memory and History', *SSRC Newsletter 6,* June 1969, pp.16-18. And the issues of *Oral History,* Vol.1, 1971, to date, available from Dr P. Thompson, Department of Sociology, University of Essex, which contain lists of British scholars working in the field of oral history and articles of methodological and substantive interest. For the United States, cf. Studs Terkel, *Hard Times: an oral history of the Great Depression,* London, Allen Lane, 1970.
29. J. Vansina, *Oral Tradition: a study in historical methodology,* London, Routledge, 1965, (first published 1961); J. Vansina, 'History in the Field', in D. Jongmans and P.C.W. Gutkind (eds.), *Anthropologists in the Field,* Assen, Van Gorcum, 1967, pp.102-115; P.D. Curtin, 'Field Techniques for Collecting and Processing Oral Data', *Journal of African History,* 9, 1968, pp.367-385; R. Finnegan, 'A Note on Oral Tradition and Historical Evidence', *History and Theory,* 9, 1970, pp.195-201. Cf. also: L.L. Langeness, *The Life History in Anthropological Science,* New York, Holt, 1965. For a recent anthropological example of the use of life-history material see: D.L. Barnett and K. Njama, *Mau-Mau from Within: Autobiography and Analysis of Kenya's Peasant Revolt,* New York, Monthly Review Press, 1970.

ACKNOWLEDGEMENTS

Permission to use previously published material is gratefully acknowledged from:

Dr J.C. Dewdney for chapter 2 by the editor, originally published in a slightly different form in *Durham County and City with Teesside,* J.C. Dewdney (ed.), British Association, 1970.

Mrs Sophia Benney of Chicago for chapter 3, originally published in Mark Benney, *Charity Main: a coalfield chronicle,* Allen and Unwin, 1946, pp.161-73. © Mrs Sophia Benney.

The Methodist Publishing House for chapter 6, originally published in Jack Lawson, *Peter Lee,* The Epworth Press, 1949. © Methodist Publishing House.

Mr Graham Turner and Eyre and Spottiswoode (Publishers) Ltd for chapter 8, originally published in Graham Turner, *The North Country,* Eyre and Spottiswoode, 1967. © 1967 Graham Turner.

Professor G.H.J. Daysh and Basil Blackwell, Publisher, for chapter 10, originally published in G.H.J. Daysh, J.S. Symonds *et al., West Durham,* Blackwell, 1953. © 1953 Basil Blackwell.

Dr J.M.J. Rogister, Editor of the *Durham University Journal,* for chapter 12 by the editor, which first appeared in a slightly different form in the *Journal,* Vol.LXV, No.3, 1973, pp.284-306. © 1973 University of Durham.

This book is both a memorial to a way of life and an epitaph upon a research programme in the late 1960s. The former is to be found throughout the preceding pages, but in conclusion a word must be said about the latter up to 1970.

The Joseph Rowntree Memorial Trust has, since 1962, supported economic and social research with a local focus at the University of Durham. It is solely due to the enlightened and beneficent support of the Rowntree Trustees that research reported here was carried out and is now published. Between 1966 and 1970 Dr Bowden, Mr Patton, Mr Thorpe and the editor all worked at various periods as research staff within the Rowntree Research Unit in the Department of Economics and the Department of Social Theory and Institutions. During the same period Mr E Hammond published *An Analysis of Regional Economic and Social Statitistics* (University of Durham,

Rowntree Research Unit, 1968) and *London to Durham: a study of the transfer of the Post Office Savings Certificate Division,* University of Durham, Rowntree Research Unit, 1968, and Miss G. Wilson *Social and Economic Statistics of North-East England,* University of Durham, Rowntree Research Unit, 1966.

In those years the Rowntree research was overseen by an Advisory Committee which met half-yearly, and whose members from their different backgrounds provided valuable guidance. They included Mr R. Wood, Regional Director of the (then) Ministry of Technology, Mr G.C. Booth of the Department of the Environment, and Mr H.O. Mateer of the Northern Economic Planning Board; until his death in 1967, Mr S. Watson of the National Union of Mineworkers, Durham Area; Mr F. Longman of the Rowntree Trust; and Professor E. Allen, Mr R. K. Brown, Professor W. Elkan, Mr R. Grainger, Mr R. Morley and Professor J. Rex of the University of Durham. This Committee was wound up in 1970, and the task of securing the publication of the outstanding projects fell to others.

The Trust and its Director, Mr L.E. Waddilove, have endured patiently and with fortitude the long road since 1970 to the appearance of this publication. Their continuing support is gratefully acknowledged. That this road was so long and hard was largely due to the vicissitudes of research direction and administration. The Trust's programme of research at Durham had, in a space of ten years, four principal investigators in succession. The first moved on to another university after a short while; the second retired after a brief though productive tenure; the third left for greener pastures after a lively period of leadership; while after an interregnum the fourth gave the programme a different direction. Such changes of course are not generally productive of cumulative research or of continuity in subject-matter or personnel. The interested reader may consult Jennifer Platt's *Realities of Social Research: an empirical study of British sociologists* (London, Chatto and Windus for Sussex University Press, 1976), which provides an account in general terms of some of the problems of conducting sociological research in Britain at this period. For those of us directly involved, 51 Old Elvet will long retain associations with the '*Gemeinschaft* of place' of social research in Durham in those years.

In addition, the editor wishes to mention many people who have been associated in one way or another with the research and the appearance of this book. Of the original advisory committee, he personally would like to thank particularly Richard Brown, Walter Elkan and John Rex for encouragement at various points. At a later stage, Philip Abrams helped in a number of ways toward the completion of this work.

The immediate intellectual roots of this book go back to a group which met in Durham in 1968-69 to discuss urban sociology and community studies. Discussions with Mike Featherstone, Ken Patton, Geoff Payne, John Rex and Ellis Thorpe about the work of Hillery, Stacey, Pahl, and Castells may have generated more scepticism than optimism concerning the future of locality studies, but in that we were not alone. The attempt to ground an analysis of diffuse, affective, particularistic local social relationships in the classical theories of Toennies, Max Weber and Talcott Parsons failed to develop further due in large measure to the institutional difficulties mentioned but some of these concerns find expression either in this book or in the longer research reports by Mr Thorpe and the editor referred to The subsequent development in British urban sociology of a preference for over-determinist macro-theory in no way undermines the validity of the analyses which we were then attempting within an action frame of reference.

More generally, both before and after 1970 colleagues in the (then) Department of Social Theory and Institutions and (now) Department of Sociology and Social Administration provided intellectual stimulation in many different ways, among them Philip Abrams, Jim Beckford, Peter Brannen, Richard Brown, David Byrne, David Chaney, Stanley Cohen, Paul Corrigan, Philip Corrigan, Jim Cousins, Bob Davis, Peter Kaim-Caudle, Peter Lassman, Robert Moore, Michael Paddon, Ken Patton, Ian Procter, John Rex, Michael Samphier, Michael Stant, Ellis Thorpe, Irving Velody, Alan Waton, Robin Williams and Bill Williamson.

Secretarial help in Durham was originally provided by Susan Hodges. After 1971 June Wallis, her successor as Rowntree Research Unit secretary, was a model research secretary. Both to her and to Gay Grant and Bridget Atkinson at LSE, who helped materially with the completion of the manuscript, grateful thanks for careful and meticulous work.

Miss A.M. McAulay and the staff of Durham University Library provided excellent service over a number of years, and displayed a willingness to obtain out-of-the-way material. Help was also received from the staff of the Durham City Reference Library in South Street, and from the National Coal Board Central Reference Library in London.

More variously, the editor would like to thank the following for exchange of ideas and advice at different stages: Bob Blackburn, Sid Chaplin, Ronald Dore, Tom Ellison, Mike Featherstone, Ronald Frankenberg, John H. Goldthorpe, Bill Brainger, June Hines, Jeremy Hurst, Vic Jupp, John H.M. Laslett, Helen M. Lewis, Norman Long, Rex A. Lucas, Bruce Taylor, Clive C. Taylor and Rex C. Taylor.

Specific research assistance was provided by several people. Philip Corrigan collected the electoral data in Chapter 9 as part of an undergraduate research project class. David Southeard conducted half the interviews on which chapter 16 is based while on an undergraduate research placement from Bath University. The Area Statistician of the National Coal Board provided data on colliery manpower for Table 15.1.

For facilities to study the closure of Tudhoe Park Colliery (chapter 15) I am grateful to the National Union of Mineworkers Durham Area, the National Coal Board and the Department of Employment; and particularly to Mr W. Dowding of the Durham Miners and Mr G.L. Atkinson, NCB Area Industrial Relations Officer for the South Durham area, and his staff for facilities granted which made the research possible.

The study of ex-miners working in the textile industry (chapter 16) was made possible through the good officers of the National Union of Dyers Bleachers and Textile Workers and of Courtaulds' Worsted Spinning Division at Spennymoor. In particular I should like to thank Mr. J. Rooney of the NUDBTW and Mr J.J. Stephens, then of Courtaulds, for their assistance in getting the research under way while the factory was opening.

To those who consented to be interviewed while working at Tudhoe Park Colliery and Courtaulds factory, a particular word of thanks is due. The older among them have lived through the changes described in these pages. A Tudhoe miner approaching retiring age in 1969 when the pit closed was first going to work in 1919 when Britain was drawing breath after the First World War and Peter Lee had just taken control of Durham County Council. There is continuity as well as change over the intervening 60 years, but in the space of two generations Durham County has become a very different place. The past is indeed another country.

INDEX